Pro SharePoint 2010 Administration

Robert Garrett

Apress®

Pro SharePoint 2010 Administration

ISBN-13 (pbk): 978-1-4302-3792-1

ISBN-13 (electronic): 978-1-4302-3793-8

President and Publisher: Paul Manning
Lead Editor: Jonathan Hassell
Development Editor: Tom Welsh
Technical Reviewer: Daniel Cohen-Dumani
Editorial Board: Steve Anglin, Mark Beckner, Ewan Buckingham, Gary Cornell, Morgan Ertel,
    Jonathan Gennick, Jonathan Hassell, Robert Hutchinson, Michelle Lowman, James Markham,
    Matthew Moodie, Jeff Olson, Jeffrey Pepper, Douglas Pundick, Ben Renow-Clarke, Dominic
    Shakeshaft, Gwenan Spearing, Matt Wade, Tom Welsh
Coordinating Editor: Adam Heath
Copy Editor: James Compton
Compositor: Bytheway Publishing Services
Indexer: SPI Global
Artist: SPI Global
Cover Designer: Anna Ishchenko

Distributed to the book trade worldwide by Springer Science+Business Media New York, 233 Spring Street, 6th Floor, New York, NY 10013. Phone 1-800-SPRINGER, fax (201) 348-4505, e-mail orders-ny@springer-sbm.com, or visit www.springeronline.com.

For information on translations, please e-mail rights@apress.com, or visit www.apress.com.

Apress and friends of ED books may be purchased in bulk for academic, corporate, or promotional use. eBook versions and licenses are also available for most titles. For more information, reference our Special Bulk Sales–eBook Licensing web page at www.apress.com/bulk-sales.

I dedicate this manuscript to my sweetheart, Jessica, without whose support and encouragement for writing, this book would never have become a reality.

Contents at a Glance

Contents

xiii

Foreword

Thank you for taking the time to read my book. Whether you are interested in dipping into this book to find answers to a question, or you intend to read it from cover to cover, I am pleased that you've chosen this book to quench your thirst for SharePoint 2010 Administration knowledge.

If SharePoint 2010 were an automobile, this book would provide knowledge primarily to those who expect to get oily hands—SharePoint 2010 administrators. This is not to say that it is the wrong choice if you want an end-user SharePoint 2010 manual. In fact, I provide plenty of useful information about the new SharePoint 2010 platform, the changes since SharePoint 2007, and expert information for non-administrators.

SharePoint, like any other web-server-based product, requires a certain amount of care and feeding to keep it operational, and so the underlying theme of this book is about ensuring that both end users and administrators gain valuable insight into making sure SharePoint 2010 runs at its finest, according to Microsoft and SharePoint industry best practices.

My aim is to provide you with consistent and reliable knowledge of the SharePoint 2010 platform, so that you have an arsenal of information to install SharePoint 2010, configure it, and look after the care and feeding of your SharePoint 2010 infrastructure for your organization and the users of your SharePoint infrastructure.

Within this book's ten chapters I cover a variety of topics: the installation and securing of a SharePoint 2010 farm, management of content, documents, metadata, new social networking features (akin to that of Facebook), business intelligence, integration of Microsoft Office 2010, and how to minimize downtime and preserve data integrity with disaster recovery.

Why should you buy this book? Reading it will give you an all-round understanding of SharePoint 2010 administration and the features of the new platform. This book is not pitched as a quick read, nor yet as a huge reference text book for the occasional glance, but a nice comfortable read for anyone seriously interested in SharePoint 2010.

I sincerely hope that you enjoy reading this book as much as I enjoyed writing it, and that no matter what type of SharePoint reader you are, you find valuable insight in the content of these pages.

Robert Garrett

About the Author

Robert Garrett has worked in the field of SharePoint since prior to Microsoft Office SharePoint Server 2007. Rob graduated from a London university with a Computer Science degree in 1996 and entered the professional world of software development, which turned out to be a fun decade of software development in languages such as C++, Visual Basic, C#, and even Java.

In the fall of 2006, Rob decided that the days of home-brew and custom software development were becoming a thing of the past, and so he looked to implementing software within SharePoint. As Microsoft readied to launch SharePoint 2007, Rob took a technical development position with Portal Solutions LLC—an established consulting firm in Rockville, MD, USA—and accelerated his career in SharePoint 2007 development on what was then the Beta 2 version of the product.

Since 2007, Rob has grown with SharePoint, and has designed, developed, and deployed various high-profile customer web sites, as well as intranet and extranet solutions on the SharePoint 2007 and SharePoint 2010 platform.

These days Rob works exclusively as a SharePoint 2010 Architect (when not writing or reviewing books), and continues to design and build custom SharePoint solutions with Portal Solutions. As Microsoft continues to invest in the SharePoint product, Rob plans to continue staying ahead of the SharePoint technology curve and to disseminate new and interesting information to anyone who cares to read his words.

When not working, Rob enjoys spending time with his family and enjoying all the fun activities that the DC metro area has to offer.

About the Technical Reviewer

 **Daniel Cohen-Dumani** is founder and CEO of Portal Solutions, a successful practice focusing on Microsoft SharePoint solutions. Daniel has more than 20 years experience in the computer science field. Prior to founding Portal Solutions, Mr. Cohen-Dumani was Chief Technology Officer for On Campus Marketing, a leading firm for the college fund-raising marketplace. Mr. Cohen-Dumani was CIO for Execustay by Marriott from 1997 to 2000 where he successfully built a technology organization to support the company mission and growth strategy. Mr. Cohen-Dumani earned a Master Degree in Computer Science from the Swiss Federal Institute of Technology in Lausanne, Switzerland.

Acknowledgments

I would like to take this opportunity to thank the following people for their support and encouragement in my writing of this book:

Graham John Garrett—my father, who introduced me to computer programming on his first Commodore 64 8-bit home computer. Had he not done so, perhaps I would never have ended up in the computer business.

Jessica Kaplan—my sweetheart, who tirelessly encouraged me to write this book, fed and watered me during some of the long chapters, and provided me with endless emotional support when I became fatigued.

Daniel Cohen-Dumani—my boss and esteemed colleague at Portal Solutions, who is both the technical reviewer of this book and my inspiration in the field of SharePoint.

All my colleagues at Portal Solutions, many of whom suffered no embarrassment in asking for a plug in my book—this is for you—and for their shared knowledge of SharePoint.

My children, Simon and Bella—for being you and for loving Daddy unconditionally.

Introduction

Hello, and welcome to *Pro SharePoint 2010 Administration*. My name is Rob, and together we are about to spend 10 chapters discovering administration of the latest version of SharePoint.

SharePoint administration can be intimidating to anyone looking at the platform for the first time, and so I have written this book to cover all the major areas and demonstrate configuration in a step-by-step fashion. Chapter 1 kicks off with an overview of the new SharePoint 2010 platform, its changes from the previous product version, and what you can expect of the new features.

In this book you and I will walk through the installation of a SharePoint Server 2010 on a new Windows server. I'll highlight the prerequisites for the installation and the minimum hardware and operating system software requirements. If you're a seasoned SharePoint administrator and have performed many installations of SharePoint before, you might gain additional insight in what I have written; if you are not, Chapter 2 serves as a great instruction set for anyone looking to install SharePoint 2010 for the first time.

With SharePoint installed, we embark on the journey through the various areas of SharePoint 2010 throughout Chapters 3-10, which include detail on these topics: Security and Policy; Users and User Profiles; Social Networking; Documents, Records, and Metadata; Business Intelligence; Microsoft Office Integration; and Health and Disaster Recovery.

You may be asking "Why no chapter on Search?" I considered it, but the search capabilities in SharePoint 2010 are vast, and with the new FAST Enterprise Search Platform included as an option in SharePoint 2010 Enterprise, I decided that search was best left to a dedicated book on the subject.

Thank you for your interest in my book. I hope you have as much fun reading it as I did writing it. I am always interested in reader feedback, so feel free to visit my blog at http://blog.robgarrett.com or write me an email at feedback@robgarrett.com. Enjoy.

A word about the Target Audience

The title gives it away—this book is focused on SharePoint administrators (or budding administrators), but that is not to say that this book has no value for business experts or developer audiences. I've tried to write this book to appeal to anyone with an interest in SharePoint 2010— installing it, configuring it, and using many of the best features the platform has to offer.

If you're new to SharePoint—congratulations on joining a large community of like-minded SharePoint enthusiasts—you'll gain a wealth of information about greenfield installation, configuration, and administration of SharePoint 2010 from my book. For those audience members familiar with SharePoint 2010, this book serves as great reference material and best-practice for what you may already know. For the casual reader in the bookstore, this book should hopefully whet your palette for what SharePoint 2010 has to offer and provide you an overview if you're curious about what SharePoint is, or if you're interested in finding out how the platform has changed since the previous 2007 version.

CHAPTER 1

SharePoint 2010 Overview

Hello and welcome to SharePoint 2010. Microsoft SharePoint has journeyed a long way since the early days of 2001 and SharePoint Portal Server 2003. SharePoint administrators and developers jumped for joy in 2007 when Microsoft launched Microsoft Office SharePoint Server 2007 (MOSS), because that version shipped with many more features and enhancements that meant SharePoint had truly become a "platform" of substance. Now, I am pleased to write about the latest version of the SharePoint platform—SharePoint Server 2010.

You might be an experienced SharePoint administrator or developer, or SharePoint might be a new project that your organization is undertaking and you are reading this book to gain more knowledge and insight into the product. Whether you are looking to SharePoint 2010 as your new platform for Intranet, Extranet, public Web Site, or Business Intelligence infrastructure, implementing a new installation, or upgrading from MOSS 2007, this book is for you. As the title indicates, this book targets SharePoint Administration but I am confident that anyone interested in SharePoint in any way will glean some useful information from the text in these pages. At the very least, this book will show you how to install the product—the right way—in Chapter 2.

What Is SharePoint?

What exactly is SharePoint? Ask anyone in the know and you will likely get a different flavor of answer to this question—it is kind of like asking "What do potatoes taste like?" It all depends on whom you ask and how you cook them. The following quote is from the Microsoft SharePoint web site (http://sharepoint.microsoft.com):

> *Microsoft SharePoint 2010 makes it easier for people to work together. Using SharePoint 2010, your people can set up Web sites to share information with others, manage documents from start to finish, and publish reports to help everyone make better decisions*

That statement is somewhat vague, so I shall try to distill the answer to our question. The very core of SharePoint is a web-based collaborative platform that allows users to share documents and lists of information, render reports and data dashboards, and present web pages of information in the enterprise that is your organization. Figure 1-1 shows the major capability areas that make up the SharePoint 2010 platform; we'll examine all of them in this chapter.

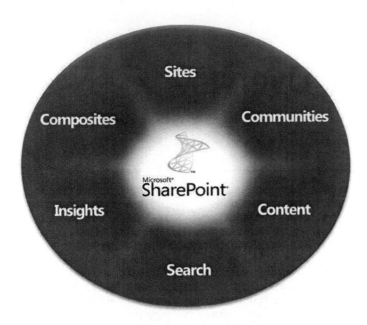

Figure 1-1. Major capability areas of the SharePoint 2010 platform

SharePoint Foundation versus SharePoint Server

Before going any further, let me compare "SharePoint Foundation" with what you pay for when you buy "SharePoint 2010 Server."

Once upon a time, SharePoint collaboration and Content Management System were two distinct products. Microsoft then decided to merge the two and build the content management system (CMS) atop a free collaboration platform, called Windows SharePoint Services (WSS). SharePoint Portal Server 2003 existed as a purchasable server product with Client Access Licenses (CALs) and operated atop of WSS 2.0, which shipped free with Windows Server 2003. When Microsoft released SharePoint 2007, they renamed the server portion as Microsoft Office SharePoint Server 2007, which built on version 3 of WSS—again, free with a Windows Server license. MOSS introduced a number of functional components for organizations to build enterprise solutions, with the appropriate licensing, and the whole platform leveraged the core collaboration model that was WSS at the core.

With the introduction of SharePoint 2010, Microsoft has relabeled its platform product. What was originally WSS Microsoft now calls SharePoint Foundation 2010. Microsoft aptly named the server portion of the platform "SharePoint 2010 Server." (Generally, I'll use the broad term "SharePoint 2010" to refer to the full server product and the term "Foundation" when explicitly talking about the free collaboration offering. However, you might see me reference the term SharePoint 2010 when the context applies to one or the other.)

Only some of the component areas, mentioned in Figure 1-1, exist in the SharePoint 2010 Server product, and Microsoft enables various features of these areas depending on the license version—Standard or Enterprise. The following subsections explain the wedges of the SharePoint donut in Figure 1-1 in more detail.

Sites

At the core of the collaboration and foundation model are "sites." SharePoint manages site hierarchies as "site collections" where each site within a site collection exists as a container for lists, document libraries, pages, metadata (content types), and other elements. A SharePoint site provides collaboration access to users in the enterprise to collaborate on documents, work with data, and review displays such as data dashboards. Each site represents a single node in the site collection structure. Sites may (and often do) contain sub-sites, with the site collection comprising the hierarchy of an Intranet/Extranet/web site, and so on.

A site collection exists as the main content container for related sites in a hierarchy. Site collections occupy a single content database in the SharePoint farm, and any content database may host multiple site collections. Site collections typically house explicit security permissions at the highest level, which then trickle down to the sites through inheritance. I shall say more about SharePoint Security in a later chapter. In SharePoint 2007, the site collection was the highest-level container at which content owners could define metadata content types. By default, the same holds true for SharePoint 2010, although SharePoint 2010 now permits sharing of content types via a designated content type "hub," covered later in this book.

Communities

Communities are all about the "people" aspects of SharePoint, and the new version has plenty of new features that engage end users and immerse them in an experience that promotes ownership in the platform.

MOSS 2007 provided My Site technology so users of an Intranet/Extranet could have their own little island of content to share and disseminate throughout the organizations. Some companies embraced this technology and let their staff members create some interesting information personal sites, while other companies disabled the feature for fear of loss of control over the type of information staff members might share. In the day of Twitter and Facebook, and a growing public infrastructure that is the social network, Microsoft has embraced information sharing in the social space and added features to My Sites to promote further content sharing and collaboration.

In SharePoint 2010, the My Profile and My Site technology now includes status updates and a log of user events. Users may "like" and "tag" content and have this information show up alongside their profile, similar to the way Facebook works. SharePoint 2010 includes a dedicated Metadata Taxonomy Service to handle hierarchical tagging (taxonomy) and user-created tagging ("folksonomy"). I cover taxonomy and folksonomy in Chapter 5, as part of social networking.

SharePoint 2010 boasts enhancements to the blogs and wiki site definitions, and now both features include Records Management technology in page libraries—something that in MOSS 2007 required a records repository site. This means that site owners of blogs and wikis may now impose policy on their content.

Composites

Composites are what Microsoft refers to as the building blocks for connected and collaborative business solutions. The idea is for SharePoint to allow site owners and users to create content based on real-time data, from various sources. Composite functionality allows content editing via standard user interfaces, similar to Microsoft Office. Composites brings the SharePoint 2010 platform closer to its true calling as an Office Suite Product, with features such as Access and Excel Services, Business Connectivity Services, SharePoint Designer, and the new Ribbon user interface.

I am sure all administrators groan at the mere mention of Access databases (I know I do); but the simple fact is that Access provides convenience and portability with database files; and although it is not as secure or robust as SQL Server, Access does allow end users to quickly evolve a relational database to share data with peers. Access Services enables users to host Access database files in SharePoint, to avoid the problem of multiple file copies and user locks on shared database files.

Excel Services are as powerful as the previous version in MOSS 2007, and allow end users to host Excel workbooks and sheets in SharePoint for display, without requiring end users to have Microsoft Excel installed on client machines. In a related vein—InfoPath Services (also present in the MOSS 2007) provide hosting and rendering capabilities for custom InfoPath forms. Unlike the previous version of InfoPath Services, Microsoft has baked InfoPath Services into the platform, so custom list forms (forms with different styling or conditional formatting) leverage the power of InfoPath under the surface. Custom forms integrate well into existing SharePoint pages, instead of opening a new window and showing an ugly InfoPath Services UI to host the form, as in MOSS 2007.

Business Connectivity Services (BCS) replace the Business Data Catalog service from MOSS 2007, and BCS provides site owners and users real integration of external line of business data. BDC required the use of complicated connection files; and even then, users could only display BDC data via dedicated BDC web parts. BCS includes the concept of *external content types*, so site owners may render external data as if they were like any other SharePoint list, and users may also update and delete data from BCS lists as they would any other SharePoint list. Furthermore, developers can target lists of external data via the API without ever giving the list special treatment.

MOSS introduced SharePoint Designer—a tool for developers and designers to edit SharePoint site collection content within a Smart Client environment. SharePoint Designer 2010 goes further than its predecessor, in that the tool integrates more into the platform. Users of SPD 2010 experience a more context-oriented tool and can access all relevant information about a site collection from a single page. SPD 2010 also embraces the Ribbon, now common to all new Microsoft Office products.

The web user interface in SharePoint 2010 now provides users with the Ribbon; Figure 1-2 shows an example of the Ribbon in action. The Ribbon, similar to the way it operates in all Microsoft Office applications, provides the user with operations, via eye-appealing icons, that are relevant to the current context. For example, if the user is editing list items within a SharePoint list, then the Ribbon shows icons for commands relating to list and list item operations.

Figure 1-2. The Ribbon

Insights

Insights are about providing business intelligence in SharePoint 2010, which includes the ability to work with Office data without the need for fat Office clients installed. Visio Services is a good example of what Insights has to offer. Now site owners can host Visio diagrams in their site to appear in the web page and user's browser. Furthermore, workspace ties into Visio Services so that creators of custom workflows may leverage Visio to define their workflow graphically.

The whole Business Intelligence (BI) platform in SharePoint 2010 underwent enhancement. For example, Performance Point Server is now built into the SharePoint Server 2010 platform (Performance Point used to exist as a separate server application). Users may leverage Performance Point Services to build rich dashboards, rendering real time data correlated from OLAP cubes, line-of-business data sources, SharePoint lists, BCS (Business Connectivity Services), and so on. With the Performance Point client, site designers may generate these reports and dashboards and seamlessly publish them to SharePoint 2010, where end users may seek immediate benefit. Data experts may publish interactive reports, which allow users to drill down to data with filtering, all with the power of Performance Point

Services. Organizations that decide not to use PPS can still benefit from rudimentary chart web parts and KPI lists, to show real-time data from BCS and SharePoint list sources.

Content

The *content* wedge covers what MOSS called Enterprise Content Management. ECM aims to drive user adoption through content transparency and increased content value, provide records management policy for content, and reduce organizational costs by decreasing storage requirements for content. So what does this mean?

Records management—policy, auditing, retention, and so on—is now woven into all document libraries in the SharePoint 2010 platform. MOSS 2007 introduced basic records management as a feature, enabled in the records center site definition. Records management and policy are pertinent to all content in SharePoint, so Microsoft has ensured availability. Definition of policy is not just limited to the SharePoint context—Office documents that flow in and out of SharePoint retain policy compliance, so that even if users pass a document around via email, outside SharePoint, the original policy intended by the document creator remains preserved.

Decreasing storage costs and reducing content clutter was always a difficult process. Using SharePoint 2010 ECM and multi-stage retention policies (see Figure 1-3), administrators may now decide how much content remains online and what content meets policy for archival.

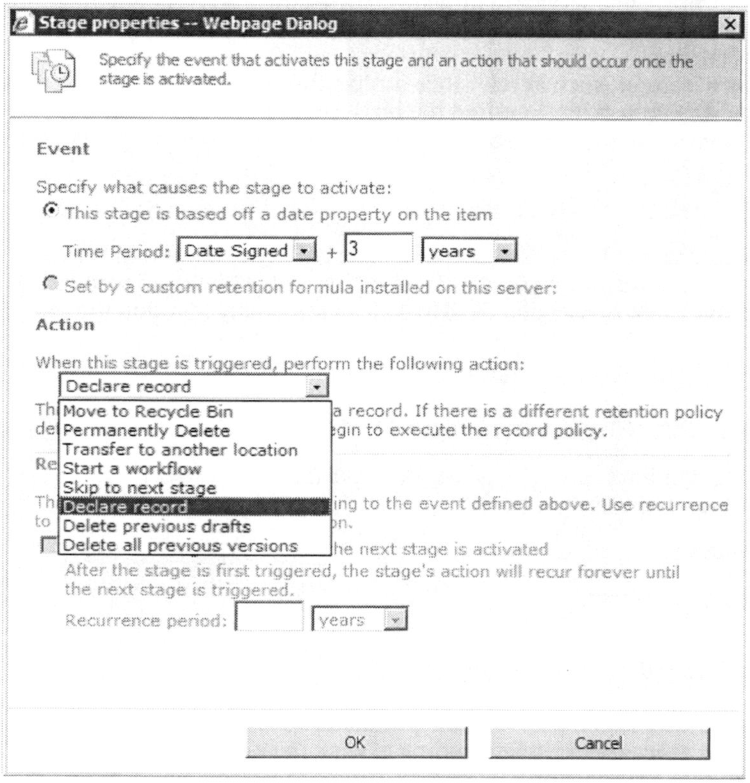

Figure 1-3. Policy options

Search

Search has always existed as a cornerstone of SharePoint. Beginning in MOSS 2007, Search came into its own by providing federation of third-party content as well as indexing of internal SharePoint data to allow users to find information rapidly.

Search is no miracle worker, and it relies on the diligence of content owners to classify content correctly—using content types, context, and so on, to assist the search crawler and query engines in SharePoint to index and retrieve content on demand. SharePoint 2010 now enhances the search offering in the platform and provides two choices for SharePoint architects—Enterprise SharePoint Search or FAST Search. SharePoint Enterprise Search works much like MOSS 2007, but with more bells and whistles. FAST, on the other hand, is an Enterprise Search Platform in entirety, and because of the high cost premium, Microsoft aims FAST at large -scale organizations with large amounts of data and heavy search demands, akin to dedicated Google Search Appliance for their site.

Whether you choose Enterprise SharePoint Search or FAST, SharePoint 2010 Search aims to help your users find their content quicker, provide drill-down and refinement capabilities, and assist connection to others (social networking) by search. Refinements are new to SharePoint 2010 and provide facet filtering of content—a common feature in any enterprise search application. The Managed Metadata Service, which provides tagging capabilities, integrates nicely with search, so that users may seek information based on tag search or restriction. Since tag taxonomies already provide a hierarchy of vocabulary terms, site designers may leverage this service to provide browse and search capabilities similar to those of product companies and retail web sites, which offer narrow-down search based on product categories and, brands, and features.

The FAST ESP provides many more features, such as relevance tuning, thumbnail previous in search results, better scaling, and ability to add custom extensions into the platform to tailor searching and search results.

SharePoint 2010 System Requirements

I shall not spend much time here, since Chapter 2 is dedicated to the installation of SharePoint Server 2010, and covers system requirements. However, since you may be glancing at this book and wondering if that old MOSS hardware will suffice for a new SharePoint 2010 install, let me briefly mention the requirements, as follows:

- All servers must be 64-bit, including SQL Server.

- SQL Server minimum version of 2005 with SP3, or 2008 SP1, or 2008 R2.

- SharePoint Servers running Windows 2008 SP2, or Windows 2008 R2 (Windows 7 and/or Vista supported for development purpose).

- At least 4GB of RAM on each server.

- .NET 3.5 with SP1 installed on all servers.

Overview of New Functionality and Changes

If you have never used SharePoint nor had an experience with the product, you can skip this section of the chapter, aimed at those who want to gain a quick understanding of what the new SharePoint 2010 version offers over the previous SharePoint 2007 version.

Nevertheless, I recommend taking note of the new functionality and changes mentioned in this section, as it gives a useful high-level overview of some of the cool features that SharePoint 2010 provides. New functionality in SharePoint 2010 is a vast topic, as Microsoft has included many new features and capabilities in the new platform. However, I try to include most of the significant changes in this section.

Do not worry if some of the features and terminology mentioned in this section are new to you. Following this section, I'll take a grass roots approach to SharePoint and walk you through the SharePoint user interface and baseline functionality, creation of sites, lists, use of web parts, and so on.

The Central Administration Web Site

For those experienced with SharePoint, perhaps coming from a MOSS 2007 background, the Central Administration Web Site comes as no surprise, but you should know that the presentation and layout is very different from that of MOSS 2007 Central Admin. Those new to SharePoint 2010 will see that like almost everything in SharePoint, the administration user interface of SharePoint 2010 is web-based and the Central Admin web site is the main user interface for making configuration changes.

■ **Note** Not all configuration uses the Central Admin Web Site; see Chapter 2 for details about the use of PowerShell and the STSADM command-line tool.

Figure 1-4 shows a screenshot from the Central Admin site in SharePoint 2010.

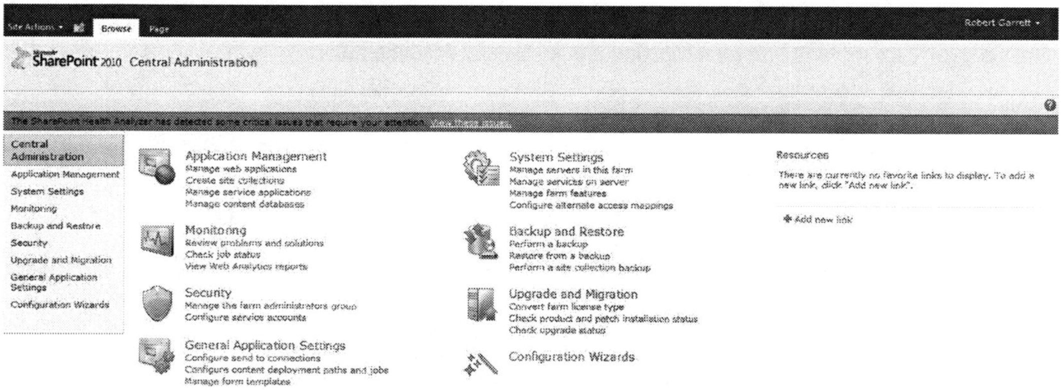

Figure 1-4. SharePoint 2010 Central Administration web site

I'll delve into the ins and outs of the Central Administration web site (Central Admin for short) in Chapter 2. For the benefit of those coming from MOSS 2007, the following are some noteworthy changes:

- Microsoft has dropped the Operations tab, and the Application Management tab is now a section on the home page of Central Admin.

- Central Admin displays links to common operations under each of 8 main section headings. Clicking the section title takes the administrator to a dedicated page for the section and more link operations.

- There is no Shared Service Provider list or SSP Administration Web site. Shared Services now exist as Managed Service Applications under the Manage Applications section.

- Like all SharePoint 2010 sites, Central Admin relies on the Ribbon to display icons for common contextual operations.

- Figure 1-4 shows a red bar indicating that SharePoint needs some attention; this was generated by the Health Analyzer Service (more on this in Chapter 10).

- Some of the operations in SharePoint 2010 cause a dialog to display. Dialogs display over the current context page and do not use bowser popups or new windows.

Microsoft has clearly tried to simplify the administration UI in SharePoint 2010. I remember opening up MOSS 2007 Central Administration site and being overwhelmed with the number of links and areas I could dive into. SharePoint 2010 Central Admin might still overwhelm the newest SharePoint administrator, but I am glad to see that Microsoft has attempted to limit confusion and link overload with common operations on the home pages; less page navigation for similar operations; and use of the Ribbon and dialogs to keep the user focused.

■ **Note** See Chapter 2 for more details on navigating around Central Administration.

User Interface Changes

The whole user interface is now cross-browser compatible, out of the box. Microsoft has released SharePoint 2010 from the shackles of Microsoft Internet Explorer and now supports other browsers, such as Safari and Firefox on different platforms (Mac, Linux, and so on). The SharePoint 2010 web user interface uses compliant CSS, JavaScript, and XHTML markup, making for better cross-browser compatibility. SharePoint 2010 also provides for a range of mobile browser formats without extensive customization of the user interface. Developers and designers can still customize the branding of SharePoint, as they did with MOSS 2007, and the publishing infrastructure provides the same rich set of web content management functions to allow custom branding in the case of public web sites.

SharePoint 2010 lists also benefit from user interface improvements; they now support in-line editing. Users must turn on this feature (via web interface or SharePoint Designer) for list instances, and this feature makes for compelling data input for lists without making the user leaving the list view page.

The Ribbon

SharePoint 2010 brings a number of user interface changes, the most obvious being that of the new Ribbon (see Figure 1-2 earlier). The Ribbon is Microsoft's new approach to simplifying navigation and functionality in Office applications, by giving the user a ribbon of icons for operations based on the current context. Just look at Microsoft Word XP (pre Ribbon) and see the large number of menu options available to the user, many for functions that did not make sense in a given context. For example, if a user is inserting a table into a Word document, then it is a fair assumption that the user wants to see functions concerning table formatting and configuration. Now with SharePoint 2010, users can expect the same user experience with the Ribbon as that of other Office applications.

SharePoint Designer

I cannot discuss the user interface of SharePoint 2010 without mentioning the integration of SharePoint Designer 2010. SharePoint Designer (SPD) has always allowed UI designers and developers access to more SharePoint back-end functions and the ability to make changes to the branding (look and feel) of a SharePoint site collection. However, SPD is much more than a design tool for changing look and feel—developers may interact with SharePoint lists and configure properties that a user is unable to control through the web interface. SPD also allows manipulation of the sophisticated metadata model—content types, and so on—and with the introduction of Business Connectivity Services (BCS), SPD allows developers to create external content types and associated workflow with external data—all without writing any custom code.

SPD is no longer a silent application that only developers and designers know about. The web interface consists of functional references to launch SPD on the fly to configure aspects of the site or list in context. Figure 1-5 shows the Site Actions menu in a typical SharePoint 2010 publishing site, with the ability for site owners to edit the contextual site in SPD.

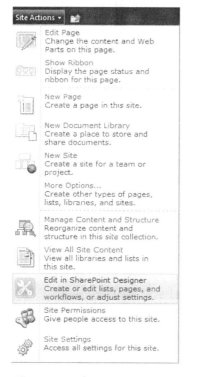

Figure 1-5. *The Site Actions menu and the existence of SharePoint Designer functions*

I mentioned earlier that Microsoft has re-engineered InfoPath forms integration in SharePoint 2010. Now site owners and designers can customize list views and forms with custom styling and conditional formatting, using SharePoint Designer. Under the hood, SharePoint uses InfoPath forms to provide the functionality. Developers may continue to create their own InfoPath forms using the smart client and deploy forms for use in SharePoint, and SharePoint 2010 provides a seamless integration into the platform, so InfoPath forms no longer look like an afterthought.

Multilingual User Interface

SharePoint 2010 has made enhancements to the Multilingual User Interface (MUI), shown in Figure 1-6, to support users of the platform who read and write in different languages. Users can change language on the fly and see all text in the chrome of their site change to the language of preference. Similar to MOSS 2007, SharePoint 2010 provides a fully functional language translation workflow, so site owners may translate their content from English to another language via a process, governed by SharePoint.

Figure 1-6. The multilingual user interface

Microsoft Office Web Applications

New to SharePoint 2010 are Microsoft Office Web Applications. SharePoint has always provided a centralized storage for documents, and beginning with MOSS 2007, embraced document management with specialized document tracking and management functions. Until now, users of SharePoint were required to have the rich Office applications installed on their client machines to view and edit documents stored in SharePoint. Office Web Applications removes this requirement by providing users with a lightweight version of Word, Excel, Visio, OneNote, and PowerPoint, so that users may make basic changes to Office documents within the SharePoint 2010 web environment.

Office Web Applications remove the need to install Office smart clients, of which many versions exist. Users without the latest 2010 version of Office can still edit Office documents in the new document XML format (.docx, .xlsx, .pptx) within the web browser.

My Sites, User Profiles, and Social Media

Microsoft has embraced the concept of the social network and added social networking features into SharePoint 2010, which fit nicely with the My Sites and User Profiles features that have always provided users of SharePoint with a space of ownership in any SharePoint portal.

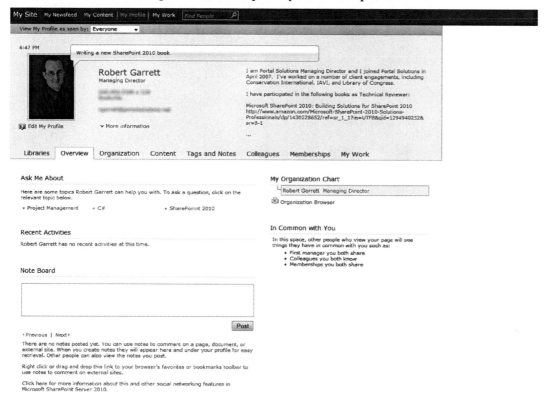

Figure 1-7. A User Profile page

Like sites, such as Facebook and Twitter, that provide a social space for users to provide status update of their work and social happenings, SharePoint 2010 also provides a history log of status updates. Figure 1-7 shows an image of my profile page on my company Intranet, which includes my present status (near my profile picture), recent activities, and notes I make. In the Ribbon of most SharePoint 2010 pages exist Like and Tag icons (bookmarks) so that users may tag the page with a specific enterprise keyword tag of their choice, or simply say, "I like this page." Any status update, tag, or "like" appears in the Recent Activities section of a user's profile page or the Newsfeed page. Users may also bookmark pages that live outside of SharePoint with Like and Tag.

SharePoint 2010 includes *active monitoring* capabilities, and users may select events they wish to track in their profile (Figure 1-8). As events occur in a SharePoint community, the newsfeed of a user's site reflects changes—again, similar to the way Facebook provides a running newsfeed of current events from friends.

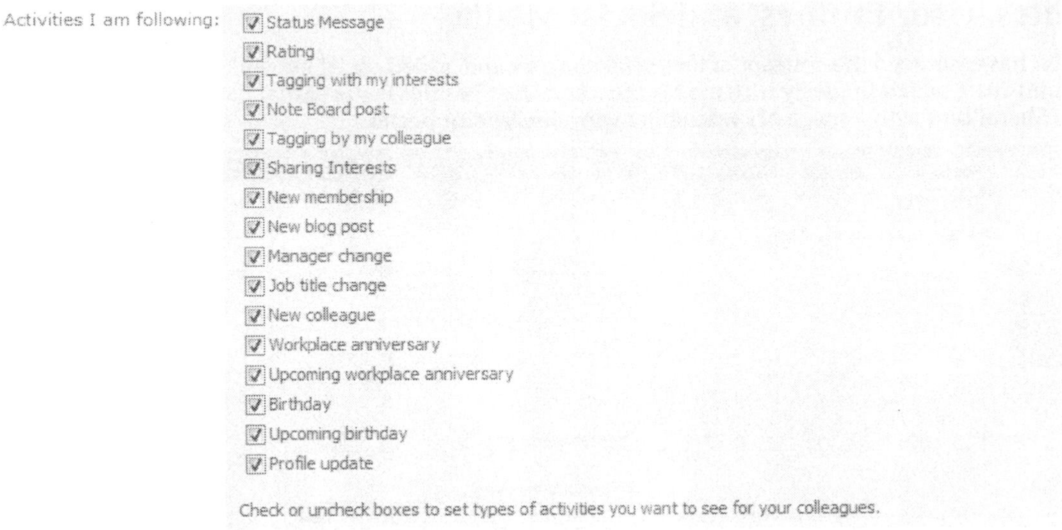

Activities I am following:
- ☑ Status Message
- ☑ Rating
- ☑ Tagging with my interests
- ☑ Note Board post
- ☑ Tagging by my colleague
- ☑ Sharing Interests
- ☑ New membership
- ☑ New blog post
- ☑ Manager change
- ☑ Job title change
- ☑ New colleague
- ☑ Workplace anniversary
- ☑ Upcoming workplace anniversary
- ☑ Birthday
- ☑ Upcoming birthday
- ☑ Profile update

Check or uncheck boxes to set types of activities you want to see for your colleagues.

Figure 1-8. Active monitoring of events in a user's profile

Site and list owners can turn on *ratings* for list items, which include publishing pages, so that other users may rate content within a SharePoint list. The publishing infrastructure includes a specific site field control to display rating for a given page, and page designers can place the rating control in the flow of the page to promote user rating.

The user interface for My Sites flows much better than that of the previous version. At the top of all profile and My Site pages you see quick links to My Newsfeed, My Content, and My Profile.

The *My Profile* page is similar to that in MOSS, but with additional web parts for social network interaction, and the layout determined by the farm administrator and owner of the My Site host application. Notice the new tabs that provide access to various sections to the user's profile to avoid clutter in one large page.

The *My Content* link navigates users to the familiar home page of their My Site, and those users who created a My Site collection may tweak this page and any other in their My Site collection to host their own content (pages, libraries, and sub sites).

The *My Newsfeed* link navigates the user to the default page of the My Site host application that displays the current social happenings for the current user—a snapshot of current news that includes recent bookmarks, active events of colleagues followed, and any external newsfeeds that the organization elects to include.

Wiki Pages

By default, all new SharePoint 2010 team sites use wiki pages for display of content (Publishing sites use page layouts). This change enhances the capabilities for site owners, compared to the legacy approach in MOSS 2007 using web part pages. Wiki pages allow fluid and dynamic layout, and inclusion of web parts and lists in any part of the page. Wiki pages provide site owners with much more control over the presentation of their site, similar to of the control available to content owners using the Publishing features of SharePoint.

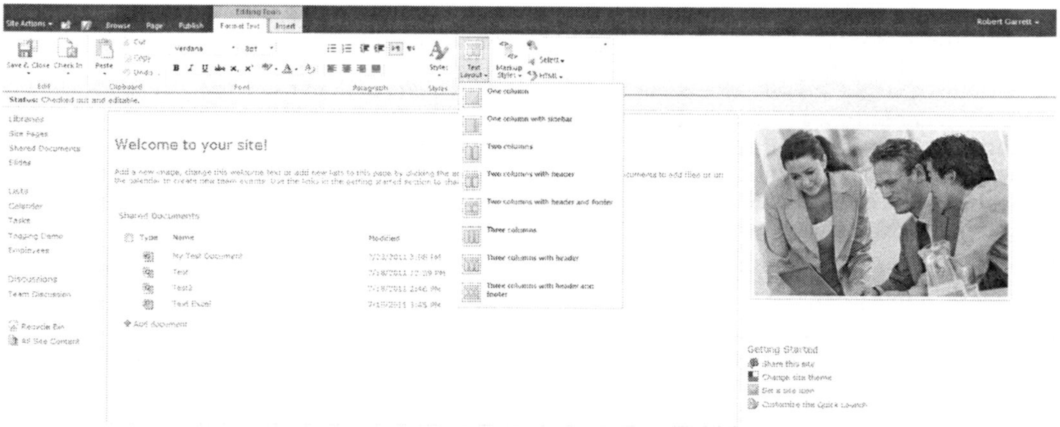

Figure 1-9. Wiki pages default in team sites

Figure 1-9 shows a typical team site page in edit mode with the ability to change the page layout, because this page is a wiki page.

Enterprise Content Management

Enterprise Content Management (ECM) umbrellas traditional content management (web and document) with social computing and search to provide users of SharePoint with a platform to manage, store, and retrieve their content. Microsoft designed the ECM platform as easy to use and single location, within SharePoint, for storage and management of documents, records, web content, and media.

Document Management

At its core, SharePoint provides document storage in document libraries, but document management in SharePoint is much more than the storage of documents. Document management includes the management of document lifecycle (retention), categorization (metadata tagging), accessibility (document IDs), and relationships (document sets). SharePoint 2010 now bakes these major document management principles into the platform, and users may access these features from any document library in any site collection. SharePoint 2010 provides the following new features as part of the document management capability:

- **Document IDs** are SharePoint's "permalink" for documents. In previous versions of SharePoint, when a user uploaded a document to a document library, the URL of the document included the location context (path to the file). Users like to email links to documents around and bury links into content web pages, but doing that makes trouble if a user then wishes to reorganize structure and move a document to new library or folder, or change its filename. Document IDs are unique IDs that SharePoint assigns to documents as users upload them to document libraries (the site administrator must enable this feature; SharePoint does not turn on this feature by default). As long as a document (or file) remains within SharePoint (that is, the user does not delete the file and then reload it somewhere else), SharePoint can track the document movements, and the permalink will always get the user to the document in the new location.

- **Document Sets** allow users to collect related documents together as a single entity. A document set is a special content type that defines the metadata for all documents in the set, and users may move, copy, and perform certain actions on a document set as they would a single document. One good example of the use of a document set is for proposal work—proposals typically consist of several documents (each with a lifecycle and creation process of its own), and a proposal can only exist in entirety with all the relevant document pieces together. With document sets, different users may work on different areas of the proposal, as individual files in the set, and when all is complete, the set represents the completed proposal.

- **Metadata and Tagging** are covered in Chapter 6 of this book. Tagging of documents and content in SharePoint 2010 helps users retrieve documents and content more easily, as this mechanism of categorization assists the SharePoint search engine to pinpoint desired documents. As you'll see, the Managed Metadata Taxonomy service provides structured and hierarchical tagging (term sets and terms), from which users can choose tags based on administration configuration, or users may invent their own tags by way of *enterprise keywords*.

SharePoint 2010 also provides for other categorization mechanisms, such as the use of content types, and the rich inheritance model that content types provide. With the adoption of social computing, Microsoft has included rating control into lists and document libraries, and users may also "like" document and list content, and tag this content for view on their newsfeed of their My Site.

Records Management

SharePoint 2010 opens up the feature of records management to all site collections (not just the Records Center), so users can choose to enact policy on documents, as records, throughout their SharePoint content infrastructure. The SharePoint Records Center site definition still exists for those organizations who want a centralized repository for storage of documents as records, but users may now take advantage of records retention anywhere documents reside. Microsoft terms this functionality *in-place records management*.

While viewing a document library with in-place records management enabled, users may manually declare a document as a record, and SharePoint will lock the document for edit and delete (according to policy settings); SharePoint denotes a document record with a padlock icon. Site owners may also automate the delegation of documents to records with workflow.

Media Integration

ECM provides media management via *asset libraries*. The asset library template defines a special type of document library to contain media files (music, video, and photos) and metadata columns, automatically populated from the media properties, such as EXIF or MP3 tags. Figure 1-10 shows a typical Media Asset Library.

Figure 1-10. A media asset library

The asset library also allows users to configure automatic population of default metadata based on placement within a folder. For example, if the list owner arranges images by year taken, then each folder representing the year maybe set up to associate logic to apply a year value to the images contained.

SharePoint 2010 brings the Media Player Web Part—a Silverlight media control, wrapped in a web part, so that site/page owners may display streaming video. This web part removes the headache of ensuring visitors to the SharePoint site have the correct media player plugin installed in their browser. As long as every user has Silverlight installed (it's easy to download and install via the web part), users can view streaming media without complexity.

Web Content Management

Web Content Management (WCM) is a vast topic, and this small section in this overview chapter cannot do justice to the features that WCM provides. Microsoft introduced the *publishing* feature in MOSS 2007, which embraced WCM and allowed owners of public-facing web sites to host their sites in SharePoint. WCM at the basic level provides:

- **WYSIWYG authoring**—And the Ribbon harmonizes with the rich in-place page editing that content owner expect when editing public facing web pages.

- **Approval workflow**—Maintaining web site integrity by ensuring an approval process before publishing to the public.

- **Versioning and Check-out**—These allow rollback to a previous edited or published version and checkout to ensure that there is no collision when two content owners require edit of a single piece of content.

- **Page layout**—The separation of content (metadata) from presentation by the use of page layouts (templates), which define presentation through content field controls (placeholders for real content). SharePoint also integrates the approval workflow process with page layouts so that page designers may also ensures site integrity with presentation change, just as content owners do with content.

SharePoint 2010 provides the same reliable publishing model for public web sites but now makes the process of editing pages, submitting for approval, viewing changes, and publishing much easier via the Ribbon user interface.

SharePoint 2010 introduces Web Analytics, so owners of public-facing web sites may track user visits to their site and create custom reports. Web Analytics allows site owners to analyze web traffic from the web application level down to an individual site in the hierarchy.

Goodbye, Shared Services Provider

MOSS 2007 relied on the Shared Service Provider (SSP) to maintain all shared services in the farm. The SSP consisted of a dedicated SSP database, SSP Administration content database, SSP Administration web site, Search database, SSP Web Application, and My Site Host web application. Under the hood, MOSS also maintained various timer service jobs to manage SSP configuration with the rest of the farm.

As the title of this section suggests, the Shared Service Provider is no more in SharePoint Server 2010. The replacement to Shared Service Provider is *managed service applications.*

To understand the rationale behind Microsoft's decision to redesign the shared services infrastructure in SharePoint is to understand the limitations of the SSP. The SSP was and still is a single point of failure and performance bottleneck in a SharePoint farm. The SSP application and site collection maintain the configuration for ALL shared services in the farm, along with the SSP database. Search, user profiles, and Business Data Catalog tightly couple with the SSP configuration, so if the SSP dies, then the administrator is looking at several days to reconfigure search, user profiles, BDC, and so on in the farm. What happens if the SharePoint farm design team wishes to host search on one server, and user profile services on another? The short answer—they cannot with MOSS (they can create several query and index servers, but search configuration remains at the SSP).

It's as if Microsoft took a large hammer and cracked open the SSP and pulled out all the services into their own applications. While piecing the parts together, Microsoft also created a host of new service applications. Essentially, a managed service application is an application that performs a dedicated task and has a service interface (Service Oriented Architecture). SharePoint communicates with the service application via a client, called a proxy. Each service application leverages one or several content databases (as opposed to a shared database used by the legacy SSP) and maintains autonomy from the farm in which the service application resides. This is very important, because managed service applications may reside on any SharePoint 2010 Server farm, and another farm may access the service via proxy across a network boundary.

Managed service applications reduce the attack surface that was a problem with the legacy SSP. SharePoint infrastructure designers may stand up multiple farms and pick and choose a la carte, which service to host in which farm, thus maintaining load and providing redundancy options.

SharePoint Basics

If you are new to SharePoint, then you probably skipped to this section or glossed over the previous section, which talked about some of the changes since SharePoint 2007. Readers already familiar with SharePoint get their chance to save some reading in this section, in which I walk you through the basics of creating sites and lists, placing web parts, and so on.

Creating a new Web Application and Site Collection

Chances are that a new web application and site collection already exist in your SharePoint farm, ready for you to add content. Since this book is all about administration, I am going to assume that's not the case yet, and at the beginning of this back-to-basics section, I shall walk you through the creation of both.

Before creating a new site collection, we must create a new web application, if one does not exist. As far as SharePoint is concerned, a web application is the physical application instance that registers inside Internet Information Server (IIS) and consists of files that live on the servers in the default location of `c:\inetpub\wwwroot\wss\VirtualDirectories`.

Administrators of the farm may create new web applications via PowerShell, or quickly via the Central Administration web site, from the Application Management section, as follows:

1. Click the Manage Web Applications link from Central Admin in Application Management.

2. From the Ribbon, click the New icon.

3. A new dialog appears. Complete the form details as follows:

    • The Authentication section provides two options—classic mode and claims-based authentication. This choice tells SharePoint how you would like to authenticate users visiting site collections in your web application. For now, choose classic (I cover CBA in Chapter 3).

    • Give the new application a name (or choose an existing application in IIS from the drop-down). In the IIS Web Site section, also provide a port number (typically 80), host header (blank if not required) and location on the server (the default typically works). The name you provide appears in the list of IIS sites when you open the Internet Information Server Management Console, so choose an apt name.

    • Select the desired security settings in the Security Configuration section. I usually recommend at least creating an application using NTLM authentication, with anonymous access turned off, and no secure sockets. When extending an application (at a later time) to allow alternate access to sites on different zones and domain names, then you can provide different security configuration. For now, the default settings demonstrate creating a new web application.

- Review and do not change anything in the Public URL section, which defaults to the name of the server with the port number appended.

- Provide a suitable database name in the Database Name and Authentication section. Check with your DBA on best-practice naming standards for database names in your organization, but WSS_Content_AppName is typical. If you have set up your farm correctly (see Chapter 2) and are hosting the content database on the same server as the farm, then you can leave the database authentication settings blank.

- Leave the Failover Server section blank, unless you have a failover database server configured in your farm.

- In the Service Application Connections section, choose the service applications you wish to associate with your new web application, or leave blank to choose the default set of applications on the farm.

- Last, you can choose to opt into the Customer Experience Program, I typically leave this as "no."

4. Click OK and SharePoint will take a moment to create a new SharePoint Web Application.

■ **Note** Chapter 2 also includes steps to create a site collection as part of an overall SharePoint 2010 installation.

I briefly touched on site collections earlier, but I'll elaborate here for consistency. As the name suggests, a site collection consists of a collection of sites, where each site is a node (level) in a web site hierarchy. For simplicity, think of a site collection as "the web site." A typical SharePoint site collection has the following characteristics:

- It consumes at most one content database.

- It is associated with an IIS web application (maintained via Central Admin).

- It maintains its own security groups and permissions, starting at the root of the site collection.

- It maintains its own metadata (content types), shared and inherited through the collection.

- It consists of at least one root site and potentially other sibling sites and sub sites of the top-level sites.

- Site collections come in two flavors: root site collection and non-root site collections. Only one root site collection exists per IIS web application (at path "/").

- The location of non-root site collections is governed by managed paths, defined in Central Admin (for example, /sites/ SiteCollection).

- Some features are scoped at the site collection level; others are scoped to a site, web application, or the whole farm.

- The site collection definition defines the default features installed and activated in the site collection. For example, the Enterprise Publishing site collection site definition enables Publishing Features in the collection.

You can create a new site collection, based on a site collection definition, in one of two ways—via PowerShell (or STSADM), or via Central Admin and creating a site collection for a given web application. Following on from the instructions to create a new web application, the steps below detail creating a new site collection:

5. Click on the Create Site Collections link, from the Application Management section of Central Admin.

6. SharePoint shows you a form to complete for new site collection details, as follows:

    - Select the correct web application in the yellow combo box in the Web Application section. Give the new site collection a name and description in the section the follows.

    - With the Web Site Address section, SharePoint provides a space to complete the URL for the new site collection. If this is the first site collection for the web application, then SharePoint provides the option to host the site collection at the root of the web application address, typically `http://servername/`. Give the site collection a URL name under one of the other managed paths, if it is not a root site collection.

    - The Template section allows you to choose the desired site template for your site collection. Deciding on the right site template is an important step, as each of the available SharePoint site collection templates includes a different set of features, such as Enterprise Content Management or Publishing features. For this demonstration, choose the Team Site template.

░ **Note** In this context, a site template is a site definition. Do not confuse this with site template STP/WSP files, which are snapshot templates of individual sites in a collection.

    - Provide the primary and secondary Site Collection Administrator Usernames in the relevant section (I recommend providing the username of the current logged Windows user, at least). You may add additional site collection administrators later from the new site collection that SharePoint provides, and the username in this section depends on the authentication and security settings established at the creation of the web application, discussed earlier. If your farm has quota restrictions enabled, you may choose the quota template; otherwise, leaving this default to No Quota ensures unrestricted quotas.

7. Click OK and SharePoint will create a new site collection at the URL you chose.

If everything went according to plan, you should be able to point your browser at the default URL of the new Team Site collection, authenticate (if your browser is not set up to login automatically with current Windows credentials), and see a page similar to that in Figure 1-11.

Figure 1-11. *The SharePoint Team Site*

The Team Site template is similar to that of the team site in SharePoint 2007, consisting of collections of sites that contain default document libraries, pages, image libraries, calendar lists, task lists,, and so on. The horizontal navigation remains below the main site title, and the left navigation behaves as it always has, with links to lists at the current site level and any sub-sites. The default Team Site Template has only one root sub site in the collection (called "Home"), so the image in Figure 1-11 may look a little bland.

The Site Actions Menu

The Site Actions menu on the top left (it used to be on the top right in SharePoint 2007) is the main access point to administrative functions. Figure 1-12 shows the Site Actions menu in the Team Site— different site templates use different features, which may add or remove items from the Site Actions menu.

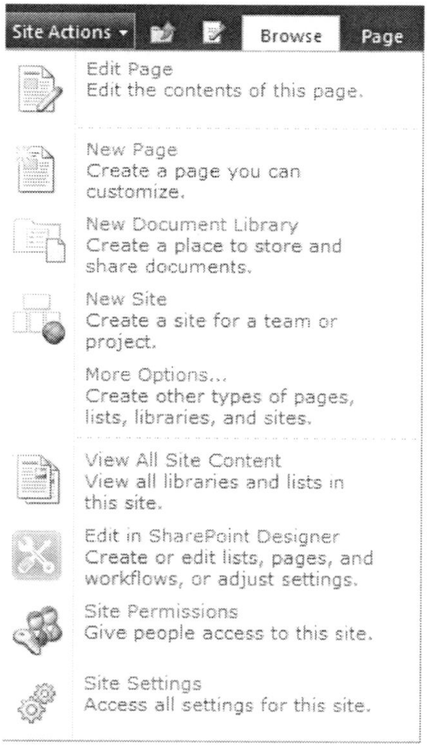

Figure 1-12. The Site Actions menu on a team site

The following list provides an overview of the functions of each item in the Site Actions menu:

- **Edit Page**—Allows a user to edit the current viewing page in WYSIWYG mode.

- **New Page**—Allows a user to create a new page at the current site, with WYSIWYG editing.

- **New Document Library**—Allows a user to create a new document library, a list for storing and managing documents uploaded to the site collection.

- **New Site**—Allows a user to create a new sub-site at the current site in the hierarchy.

- **More Options**—Opens a dialog (built on Silverlight) to create Libraries, Lists, Pages, and Sites, as shown in Figure 1-13.

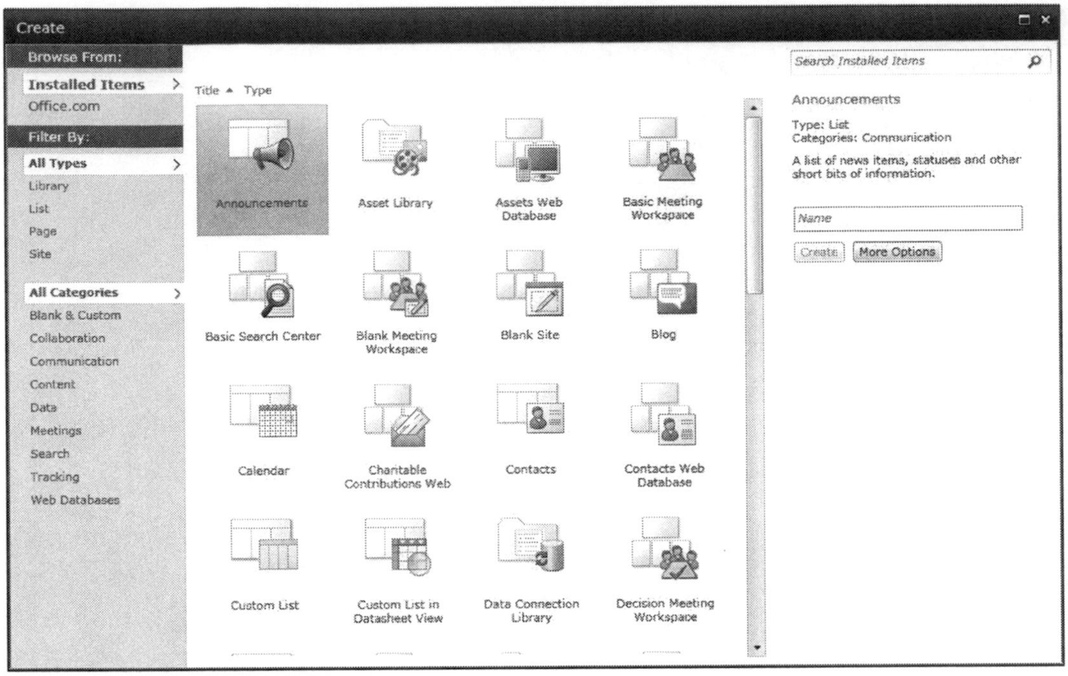

Figure 1-13. More Options to create

- **View All Site Content**—Provides a summary of all content at the current site, sectioned by document library, lists, sub sites, and so on.

- **Edit in SharePoint Designer**—Launches SPD so site designers may directly edit the current site, without having to open SPD first and then navigate to this site using the URL.

- **Site Permissions**—Allows administrators and owners of the current site to secure the site and sub-sites with user permissions.

- **Site Settings**—Provides entry to the main settings for the site (and site collection if at the root site).

The Ribbon

New to SharePoint 2010 is the Ribbon. Notice the Browse and Page tabs, and the two icons next to the Site Actions menu (shown earlier, in Figure 1-12). The leftmost icon provides a way to navigate up the site hierarchy, and the rightmost icon puts the current page in edit mode, which in-turn activates the Ribbon (see Figure 1-14).

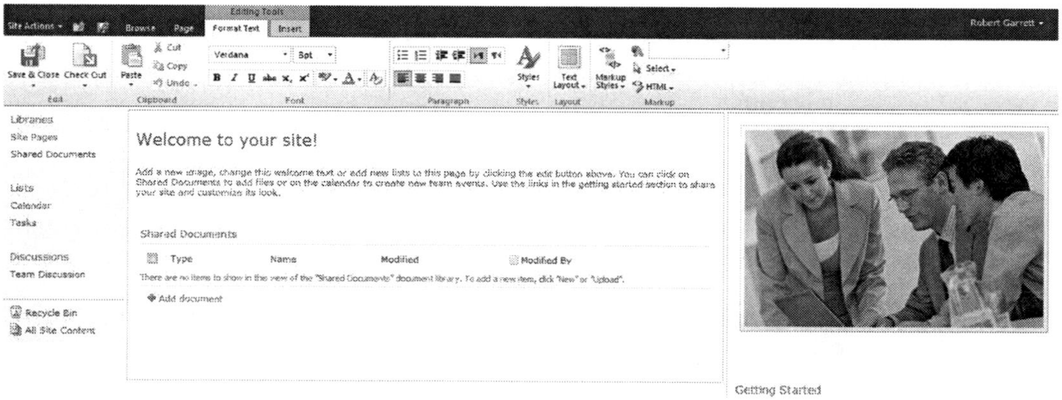

Figure 1-14. *Edit Page mode and the Ribbon*

The Ribbon provides users with contextual control of functions in SharePoint. In the illustrated case, the Ribbon shows a number of rich-text editing controls because Figure 1-14 shows a default Team Site page in edit mode. All team site pages in SharePoint are wiki pages; therefore the Ribbon shows functions for editing text in real time on the page, in any of the two main placement areas shown.

The leftmost icons in the Ribbon are significant because they allow the user to check out the page, save the page, and check it back in. By default, pages reside in the `SitePages` document library and the library has content approval workflow enabled (users must check out to edit, check in to share, and publish to show to non-approver users).

The Ribbon makes use of tabs to group related functions in the current context—similar to the behavior of the Ribbon in other Microsoft Office products. In Figure 1-14, the Format Text tab shows all functions relating to formatting of rich text. Clicking the Insert tab displays an array of functions specific to inserting content into the page, including web parts, pictures, list views, and the like.

As you explore in this book more of the delights that SharePoint 2010 has to offer, we will see more of the Ribbon and discuss various functions in relevant contexts.

Lists

SharePoint uses lists as content containers at the very core of the platform. Users of Foundation have access to basic list types and the ability to create custom lists, and users of the SharePoint server have additional list types available to them.

Lists behave like tables, or records in a database. A SharePoint list in its raw form consists of a collection of rows and columns. The columns—sometimes Microsoft refers to them as *fields*—vary in type and define a metadata element. For example, one column type in SharePoint is Single Line of Text, which is a fancy name for a String. Any list item (row) that contains a column of single line of text may contain text data up to 255 characters in length.

A list item—a row in the list—typically consists of a collection of column values associated with each column defined for the list. See Table 1-1 for the standard Site Column types, which users may include in custom lists. Site columns provide the same kind of storage definition capability as column types in a SQL table.

Table 1-1: Site Column Types

Column Type	Description
Single Line of Text	Users may enter a series of characters up to a maximum of 255.
Multiple Lines of Text	User may enter multiple lines of text; this column provides additional options to support rich text editing.
Choice	Users may choose from a predetermined list of choices, defined in the column definition. Options include default value and presentation as either a drop down list control or radio button controls.
Number	Users may enter numeric values only. Options include percentage values, min and max limits, and decimal places.
Currency	Works like the number column type but geared to currency values and currency types.
Date and Time	Users may enter a date, or date and time. This column displays using a date picker for easy date selection. Options include date only, or date and time entry, and default to today's date.
Lookup	Users may select a value for the column in the list from another lookup list. For example, a list may exist with country names, and a lookup column in a different list provides users with single or multiple-choice lookup of country from the countries list. Lookup columns provide more flexibility than choice fields because their choice values are stored in another list and are not baked into the site column definition as in choice columns.
Yes/No (check box)	A Boolean value—users may check (yes) or uncheck (no) the value in the column. Checked values give back 1 and unchecked values give back 0 in a query.
Person or Group	Users may enter a username or group name, known to SharePoint. Users may query SharePoint for a specific user or group using the people picker control—presented on list edit forms. Options include people only, group only, or both type, and single or multiple user/group values.
Hyperlink or Picture	Users may enter a URL to another SharePoint page or file, or an external page. Options include rendering of the URL as a hyperlink or image (if the URL points to an image location).
Calculated	Users may calculate the values in columns of this type using formula, similar to that of Excel, and provide input from other columns in the list.

External Data	This is a new column type in SharePoint 2010. If it is enabled by the administrator, users may enter data into columns of this type that SharePoint will link to external data sources, such as a SQL table.
Managed Metadata	Also new to SharePoint 2010, this column type allows users to tag the list item with data stored in the managed metadata service. Options include the ability to link the field to a particular taxonomy node in a hierarchy and to enable self-user tagging as folksonomy.

By default, SharePoint provides a series of custom list definitions (read on for the defaults in our Team Site), which are lists with predefined sets of site columns. All site columns defined and used in a list definition exist in the Site Columns gallery, found in the Site Settings page at the top level of the site collection. When creating a custom list definition for yourself, you may create new columns in your custom list or use existing columns from the Site Columns gallery.

Before moving on with a discussion of lists, I shall briefly mention *content types*. I cover content types in depth in chapter 6 on metadata, but they are worth mentioning here as an important capability within list management. Content types are synonymous with table schemas in SQL. Just as list owners may create a list with a defined set of columns, site owners may create content types that include a series of columns and represent an entity in the metadata model. For example, let us take a scenario of a list that contains information about cars. Each list item in the list represents a car in a car dealership. Each list item has certain attributes—the columns, which define the name, make, color, retail price, purchase status, and invoice price, and so on. There is nothing preventing the site owner from creating a custom list with a series of columns that represent the cars in the dealership. However, what happens if the site owner wants to use the same definition of car in another list that itemizes cars on back order from the manufacturer? Rather than define another list with the same set of columns, the site owner may create a content type (called Car) that contains the column definitions, and then apply that content type to both lists. If, later, the site owner wishes to add a new column to the content type, he or she may do so without having to visit the various lists that use the content type.

Content types are powerful entities in SharePoint, which provide rich metadata modeling via inheritance and mapping to external sources. Lists have the capability to allow for multiple content types, so when adding list items to a list, users can define different metadata values based on the chosen content type. This paradigm comes into great use when incorporated into document libraries when users may wish to upload different document types with different metadata values to a single project documents list—more on this later.

Now that you understand the importance of metadata, site columns, and content types, we can resume exploring the various lists included by default in our Team Site.

From the home page of the team site, see the left navigation bar. Left navigation provides links to the various lists and libraries, as well as sub-sites of the current site—in this case the home site. By default, the team site includes the following lists and library types, as shown in the navigation:

- **Site Pages**—Document library new in SharePoint 2010 to contain pages for the current site.

- **Shared Documents**—Office documents shared with users accessing the site.

- **Calendar**—List of calendar events .

- **Tasks**—List of tasks, with workflow to delegate tasks to other users.

- **Team Discussions**—Rudimentary discussion forums list.

Click the All Site Content link, and SharePoint shows a page (Figure 1-15) with additional lists and libraries, not included in the left navigation:

- **Customized Reports**—Document library containing Web Analytic reports.

- **Form Templates**—Document library containing XML InfoPath forms (Administrator approved).

- **Site Assets**—Asset library to contain media assets for use in pages, such as Wiki pages.

- **Style Library**—Document library that contains custom cascading style sheets (CSS) files.

- **Links**—List of links to external sites (or internal).

- **Announcements**—List of announcements with expiration dates.

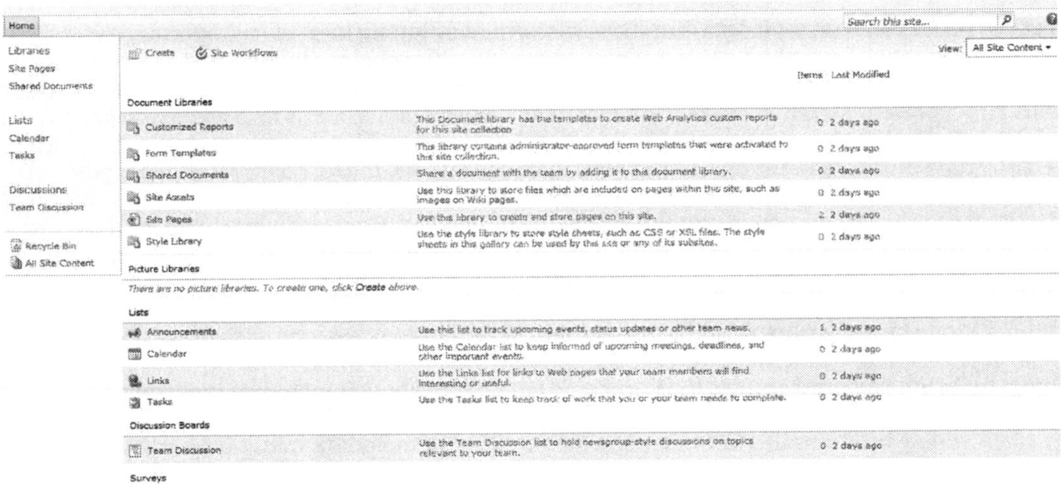

Figure 1-15. The All Site Content page

■ **Note** Site owners may create site workflows (new to SharePoint 2010) from the page in Figure 1-15.

Clicking the Create link in the page shown in Figure 1-15, or the More Options link from the Site Actions menu, displays the dialog shown in Figure 1-13 earlier. Users may filter the options shown via the left navigation of the dialog to drill down to a desired list template or sub-site template. Click the List link in the filters, and the dialog shows various list options, some of which I highlighted in the previous section of this chapter.

From the page in Figure 1-15, click the Announcements link to see a view of the announcement list. The team site template created a single list item announcement. Click the title Get Started with Microsoft SharePoint Foundation to see its list item details (Figure 1-16).

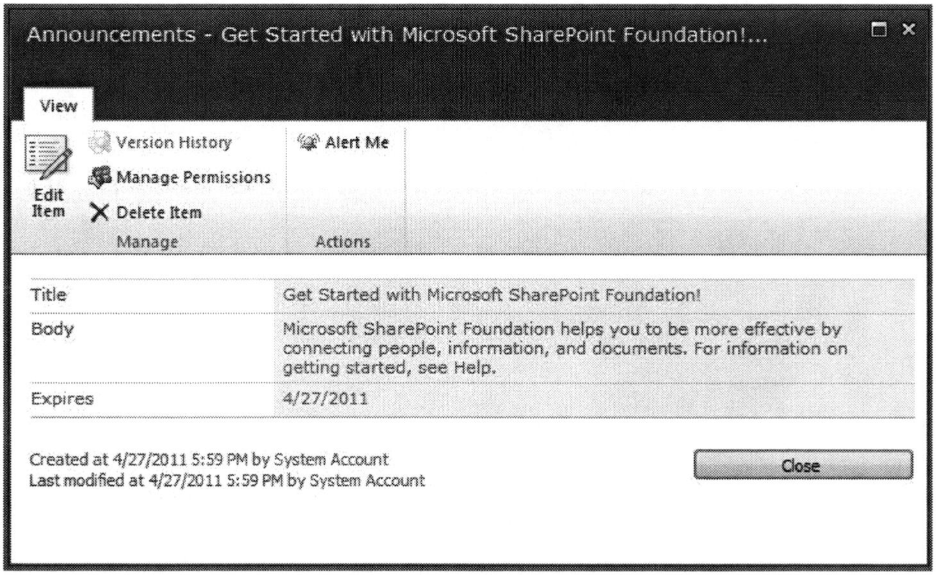

Figure 1-16. *List Details, showing an announcement*

The List Details dialog shows the content for the various fields (site columns) defined for an announcement. Notice the small Ribbon navigation present in the dialog.

Close the List Items dialog and go back to the Lists View page, and we shall explore the various components of this page. Click the Items tab of the Ribbon, and the list item on the page (not the title, which brings up the list item details dialog). The Ribbon then enables icons for management of the list item selected. Functions to note include:

- **New Item**—Create a new list item, and SharePoint shows a new item form.

- **View Item**—Shows the list item details dialog.

- **Edit Item**—Opens a dialog displaying a form with content to edit.

- **Attach file**—Uploads a file and attaches it to the list item.

Click the List tab of the Ribbon to see many more icon options for the list in scope. Taking each section in turn, from left to right, the following is an overview of list functions:

- **Standard and Datasheet view**—Datasheet allows editing of the list data in an Excel-like view.

- **Datasheet**—Functions available in datasheet mode.

- **Management of views**—Read on for more details about views.

- **Email a link to a list link and view the list as an RSS feed.**

- **Connect and Export**—Export the list content as Excel or export to an Outlook list, and so on.

- **Customize the list**—Using InfoPath and SharePoint Designer to apply styling and conditional styling.

- **List Settings, Permissions, and Workflow**—Worth noting is the List Settings option, which shows a page to configure all aspects of the list, including use of content types (metadata), creation and inclusion of site columns, and so on.

Click the List Settings icon from the List tab in the Ribbon. You should see a page like Figure 1-17.

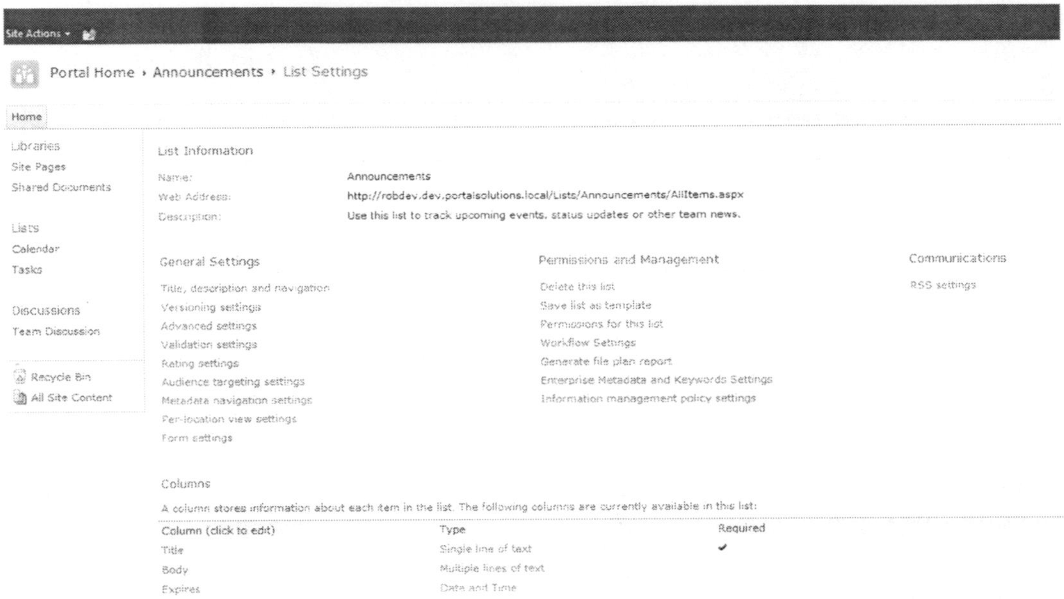

Figure 1-17. The List Settings page

At the top of this page, SharePoint displays information including the name, URL, and a description of the list. Following are the General Settings, Permission and Management Settings, and Communications settings. Most of your configuration will probably take place in the General Settings area, detailed here:

- **Title, description, and navigation**—This does pretty much what it says on the can! Site and list owners may change the title, description and navigation settings (presence in the left navigation for example).

- **Versioning settings**—Provides configuration of versioning, such as the requirement for major/minor, just major, or no version numbers, enforcement of check-in, and checkout.

- **Advanced settings**—Provides many options to influence list behavior, such as the use of content types for metadata, use of folders, datasheet settings, and more.

- **Validation settings**—Provides rules for validation formulas for submitted column data.

- **Column default value settings**—A list of columns that a site owner or list owner may set default values for the given list.

- **Rating settings**—These enable/disable list item ratings so users may provide a star rating to list content.

- **Audience targeting settings**—These enable/disable audience targeting so web parts, such as the Content Query Web Part, may display certain data according to audience group inclusion for the current user.

- **Metadata navigation settings**—These configure metadata navigation hierarchies and key filter controls (more in Chapter 6 on metadata).

- **Per-view location settings**—These control the inheritance of list views.

- **Form settings**—These configure the settings for the list forms and use of InfoPath for customization.

The Permissions and Management section contains the following configuration links:

- **Delete this list**—Does exactly what the title suggests.

- **Save list as template**—Allows list and site owners to customize a list (with views) and then save that list as a custom template. Site owners may then create new list instances using the saved template for similar configured list behavior and presentation.

- **Permissions for this list**—Sets explicit user permissions and inherited user permissions from the site for the list (more on this in Chapter 3, on security).

- **Workflow settings**—Allows the application of stock and custom deployed workflows to the list. users cannot create workflows from here, just apply them to the list.

- **Generate file plan report**—Allows you to create a report of list content and policies and save the report in a document library.

- **Enterprise Metadata and Keywords settings**— Allows you to enable/disable keywords and metadata sharing for the list.

- **Information Management Policy settings**—Sets retention and auditing policy on items contained in the list.

Last in the Settings sections, the RSS settings allow list owners to expose the list data as RSS and provide configuration options to control the RSS output.

Moving further down the List Settings page is a section showing the metadata columns for the list (site columns). If the list enables content types, then a section shows content types applied to the list/library—again, you'll learn more about metadata and content type use in Chapter 6.

The last section at the bottom of the List Settings page shows the various list views available for the list, and is the topic of the next section in this chapter.

List Views

SharePoint allows users to store their data in any tabular form, using lists. Users may tailor how they present and arrange their list data, using views. A *list view* is a metaphorical perspective of list data, and list and site owners may construct many views over the same list data. Think of views as looking out of different windows of a house—the landscaping around the house is always the same at any one moment, but the perception of the landscaping changes depending on what window the person in the house looks out.

To see how views work, go back to the Team Site of our previous section in this chapter, click the All Site Content link, and then click the Announcements list. With the Announcements default list page open, take a quick peek at the breadcrumb navigation (just below the blue Ribbon bar), as shown in Figure 1-18.

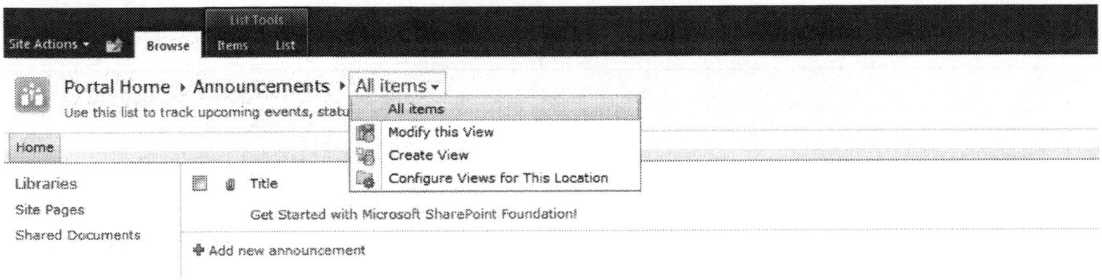

Figure 1-18. *Breadcrumb and view for list*

■ **Note** The breadcrumb provides navigation history to the current location.

SharePoint 2010 now embeds the ability to change the current list view from the breadcrumb. The Announcements list happens to have just one list view—the default list view, called All Items. If you navigate to the List Settings page (see the previous section), you will also see the list views listed. The default list view typically shows all list items in the list and all site columns of the list.

From the page breadcrumb, shown in Figure 1-18, click on Modify this View to explore the various list view options available. The list view edit page has numerous options and far too many to show a screenshot, so be sure you are following along at home. It has the following options:

- **Name**—Users may change the list view name and the file extension name in the URL. SharePoint provides a helpful RSS icon should you want to publish the RSS feed for the current list view in context.

- **Columns**—This section enables the user to select, deselect, and change the order of site columns (fields) presented in the view. Changing the numeric Position from Left value for any column changes the numeric value of the other selected columns.

- **Sort**—Sorts the list items by one or two columns, either ascending or descending in series. The Sort Only by Specified Criteria option ensures that folders sort by the sort criteria provided. When this option is unchecked, SharePoint places folders above list items.

- **Filter**—The filter section provides capability to add multiple column filters to the data displayed in the view. This capability is similar to multiple column filters in Excel in that SharePoint will present a filtered view of list items based on the union of all column filters. Users may apply the dynamic value [Today] to date/time column filters and [Me] for the current user in people-picker column filters.

- **Inline Editing**—This is a new option in SharePoint 2010 that enables AJAX inline editing on the view. With inline editing, users may provide values for new list items or edit existing list items in place in the view page, without opening another dialog or page.

- **Tabular View**—Enabling this option instructs SharePoint to apply check boxes next to list items in the view. Users may apply batch operations to multiple list items in the view when it is checked.

- **Group By**—Users may select one or two columns to group list items in the view. Grouping of list items allows users to expand and collapse groups for easier navigation of list views with large numbers of items. Using two group-by columns instructs SharePoint to present two levels of grouping in tree-view style.

- **Totals**—The list view owner may configure the view to show sum, average, count, and similar totals at the bottom of the list view for designated columns.

- **Style**—This section enables users to change the style of the list view. The default list view displays a vanilla tabular list of list items with selected columns, other styles add boxing, shading, and similar effects around list items.

- **Folders**—Provides the option to display all list items, regardless of containment in folders, or list items inside open folders.

- **Item Limit**—Provides restriction of items shown in batches or total. By default, list views show a defined number of list items per list view page.

- **Mobile**—Provides configuration options for the mobile phone view of the list view.

Going back to the breadcrumb in Figure 1-18, users may create their own views of an existing list. Clicking the Create View link provides you with a page like Figure 1-19:

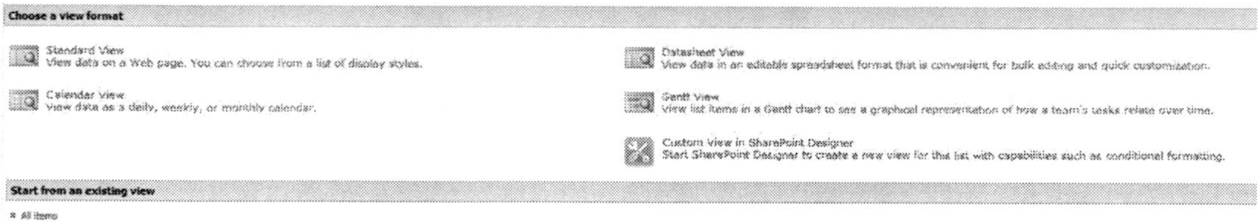

Figure 1-19. The Create View page

Standard Views are default tabular views, similar to that which we edited for the announcement list default view above. Calendar View displays a traditional month view calendar for calendar lists, Datasheet shows an Excel-like view, and Gantt View shows a task list breakdown with Gantt bars. After choosing a create view template, the user sees a screen similar to that for modifying a list view but with configuration based on the chosen template. Within the Name section of the Create List View page is a check box to allow the view as public for other users. Users that do not have list editing permissions may only create their own list views, they may not share them with other users of the site.

The Configure Views for This Location function, shown in Figure 1-18 earlier, enables users to configure whether views of a given list inherit from the parent site, or list view definitions are specific to the location. List owners may also configure certain list views to show or hide, based on preference.

Document Libraries

Document libraries in SharePoint are no more than a special type of list. Basic list types allow for file attachments, but document libraries go steps further in providing the user with an interface that embraces the storage of documents similar to a network file share, classified by type and associated with metadata.

The first thing to note, after you create a new document library, or open an existing one in our Team Site, is that the Ribbon changes. Most of the icons and associated functions that exist in the document library Ribbon are similar to those in the Ribbon of a basic list. Additional capabilities exist in document libraries, such as the ability to upload and download documents, check in and check out documents for edit, and so on. SharePoint also relabels many of the functions common to list functionality in document libraries. For example, the List tab now shows Document Library, and the Items tab is replaced with Documents. This change in labeling assists in making the user aware of the different list type and environment without them ever really knowing that under the hood SharePoint sees a document library as another list.

In my career working with SharePoint, a common issue I run into with new clients, looking to embrace SharePoint to sort out their document repository nightmares, is the lack of categorization of their existing documents. The old thinking was to store organizational documents on a shared drive on the network because this enabled nightly backup and promoted sharing of documents, as multiple users had access to the same shared-space. The problem is that shared drives seldom work. They typically turn into a conglomerate of scattered files with categorization limited to location context, and often collections of versions of the same document. This is where SharePoint document libraries come to the rescue.

In the earlier section about lists, I briefly discussed the use of site columns and content types as metadata. Metadata associated with documents in a document library provides powerful categorization of document content. Documents stored in SharePoint document libraries with metadata applied now have more context. No matter where a document is stored in SharePoint, if the document has metadata associated, users may gain an understanding of the document's content based on the metadata descriptive columns. Of course, this assumes that users apply metadata to documents uploaded to SharePoint document libraries.

Return for a moment to the discussion of content types, which provide the perfect capability for tagging documents. For example, assume that a document library contains multiple types of project documents—Contracts, Project Plans, Presentations, Specification documents, and so on… Now assume that each of these document types has specific metadata, and each type is different; for example, contracts have metadata about the client, project plans have metadata about project metrics, and so on. SharePoint allows site owners to define content types for each document type, apply multiple content types to a single document library, and to use the same content types in different lists (if, for example, the site has a document library for archived proposals). This metadata is not just associated with the document in SharePoint; when a user opens an Office document in one of the Office applications, the user may edit the metadata within the Office application when editing the document—how neat!

How does one upload a document to a SharePoint document library? The simplest way is to click the Upload Document icon from the Ribbon for the document library. After uploading, SharePoint will provide a dialog box, asking for metadata, when uploading a new document that has none.

■ **Note** Users with Office installed on their client computers, and using IE, may upload documents to a document library in batch, using the Upload Multiple Documents functionality.

Document libraries provide much more than the capability of storing documents and associating documents with metadata. They also enable us to manage versions and check-in and check-out to retain integrity. SharePoint 2010 brings document ID referencing, so users can move documents around in the farm without worry about broken URLs, and many other functional features. The list below summarizes some of the more common features specific to document libraries:

- Version control—major/minor version numbers of major only

- Draft/Pending/Publish approval status—workflow for approval

- Check-in/checkout capability

- Portability of metadata to Office Applications

- Policy and information rights, which also carry into Office applications

- Viewing document libraries as Explorer view, using WebDAV

- Multiple related documents per document library list item, using document collection content types (new feature of SharePoint 2010—covered later)

- Retention policy and expiration of documents using records management

Use of Folders

I left this topic to the end of the section about lists and document libraries so that I may leave you with an impression. Folders are both a good and a bad thing as far as content organization is concerned. Users tend to cling to folders like their last cup of water on a hot day, and this is mainly because historically, that's how to organize content.

Before the days of SharePoint and other more expensive content and document management systems, organizations pretty much relied on the use of file systems. The IT department drilled into us that we should store all working documents on the shared network drive, because IT backs up network drives onto tape each night. Furthermore, as a group of people working on a single proposal document, we can collaborate on the same version out on the file share. Users can make use of folders to organize content in a logical fashion, so other users may access the content. The principle sounds solid, but in practice, this approach has many issues.

The first major issue with central file share storage and folder hierarchies is that this paradigm assumes due diligence of the users to organize the folder hierarchy well. In large organizations where people are not working in the same room, department, or office, there is a lack of communication about where certain documents reside. I have seen some well-organized groups that apply rudimentary governance in the form of a table of contents, or documents that outlines guidelines for file naming scheme and location, but the system still consists of much hunting and pecking through folders to find recent documents for work. File shares also lack any form of categorization and tagging, and the folder structure and location in the file system is too weak to categorize a document.

Along comes SharePoint to make life easier. SharePoint sites and document libraries provide a central location of documents to collaborate. The check-in and check-out process ensures that no two people are editing the same document at the same time, versioning control allows rollback of edits if a mistake is encountered, and so on. So why would Microsoft then allow folders in lists and document libraries? The short answer is because it keeps old-school folks, who cannot leave the life of folders behind, to transition their world from the file share to SharePoint.

Folders provide a nice way to separate content in libraries and secure their contents with different permissions. Enable folder functionality in your document libraries (it is disabled by default), but govern the use of folders judiciously. If you are using folders to categorize and separate like content, consider categorization of documents with metadata (content types), incorporate the new SharePoint 2010 Managed Metadata tagging system so users may tag documents, and help the SharePoint Enterprise Search Engine find documents of relevance based on tagging, ratings, and use of metadata. If you have concerns about document libraries listing too many documents and users suffering from information overload, then leverage list views to provide users with specific views of documents.

Finally, to put to rest a common excuse for the misuse of folders—SharePoint 2010 now incorporates large list support. SharePoint 2007 suffered from performance degradation as the number of list items reached and exceeded 2,000 items, and the use of folders circumvented the problem by partitioning list data. Microsoft has since addressed this issue with support for large lists in SharePoint 2010, with health indicators that warn users (and developers) when a list has too many items for query, and capability to perform expensive queries on large lists in off hours.

Pages

SharePoint *pages* play an important role in the infrastructure of the platform; they render content, stored in SharePoint, to the user in a given presentation format. When SharePoint renders a page, what the user sees is the result of the completed process of collecting various content components and merging them with layout and styling.

Unlike the days when web developers integrated content with presentation on a web site using HTML (Hypertext Markup Language), today SharePoint automates this process. SharePoint abstracts content from presentation markup, so that content owners may deal with just raw content data, and web designers may work on separate style and design without needing the content in the first place. When both parties complete their changes, SharePoint provides the glue to render the content in the presentation style. How exactly does SharePoint do this? I am glad you asked.

With the release of ASP.NET 2.0 (Active Server Pages), Microsoft introduced the paradigm of *master pages*. ASP.NET master pages enable web developers to code up common page areas, and define placeholders where content changes from page to page in the site. Look at any contemporary web sites and you will notice that its pages have a common theme about them. Themes typically consist of distinct coloring, text fonts, consistent navigation, logos, and common graphical areas. For example, the banner of most pages on a typical web site is usually the same—except perhaps for the site home page. Master pages enable web developers to develop the common theme markup of a web site once, and then reuse the master page across all pages on the site. Since SharePoint 2007, SharePoint has been built on top of ASP.NET, and it uses master pages extensively. If you peek at the site settings for our Team Site, you will see a link to the Master Page Gallery, which exists as a special document library, containing… you guessed it—master pages.

Master pages are only half of the technology behind rendered pages in SharePoint. SharePoint uses *page layouts* to define page templates, which describe the flow and layout of content in pages. Layouts themselves inherit common branding from a single master page, so page layouts typically only concern themselves with organization of content for particular page types. For example, a SharePoint site may have several page layouts to define page templates for News Articles, People Biographies, Events, Journal Content, Project-Space, Blog, and so on. Each of these page types may render content differently; for example, News Articles may consist of a three-column newspaper layout, whereas a Blog page may render as a single column of continues text content. The master page for each of these page layouts (traditionally the same master page for all page layouts in a given site collection) still provides the common branding elements that is on each page, regardless of layout type.

MOSS 2007 introduced page layouts as part of the publishing features of the platform, but more on that in moment. Team Sites, and SharePoint site templates not using the publishing features of SharePoint, use *text layouts*. Text layouts are the new name that SharePoint 2010 gives to pages that define varying row and column layout capabilities. Figure 1-20 shows a glimpse of the various layout types available.

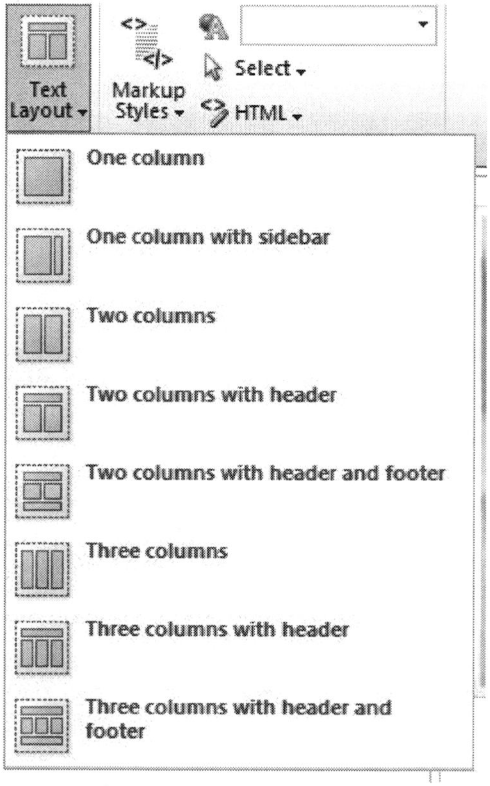

Figure 1-20. *Text layouts*

In the previous version of SharePoint, owners of non-publishing sites could create Web Part Pages, which consisted of various placeholder zones in which page editors and content owners could drop web parts (more on web parts in the following section of this chapter). To add text and image content to pages, SharePoint 2007 provided a Content Editor Web Part that allowed for rich text and HTML editing within the space the web part provided on the page. SharePoint 2010 now makes life even easier for page owners and contributors; text layouts exist as wiki pages in the site collection (stored in the Site Pages document library of the site). Wiki pages/text layouts still provide the same Web Part zones, allowing insertion of web parts, but page editors may now edit text in place, similar to the way they would edit text in Microsoft Word. Of course, the Ribbon integrates well into the page editing features of SharePoint, so users start to get that same consistent feel that they associate with other Microsoft Office applications.

The other type of page layout technology in SharePoint is *publishing page layouts*. These layouts, which also reside in the Master Page Gallery, bind presentation with metadata content of page instances. If that last sentence sounds like a mouthful, that is because it is. Explaining Master Pages, Publishing Page Layouts, and Page Instances to new users of SharePoint is sometimes difficult. Allow me to break down the components:

- **Master Pages**—Discussed above, they consist of common branding and styling markup and include placeholders, where inheriting page layouts will provide concrete markup for the areas of a page that change from page to page.

- **Publishing Page Layouts**—They inherit from a single master page to provide common site branding. Publishing page layouts and text layouts satisfy the placeholder areas of their master page with real markup. A publishing page layout defines additional Field Content placeholders that map to metadata content of a page instance.

- **Page Instances**—A page instance is no more than a list item in the Pages document library of a site that has publishing features enabled. Just like any other list item, page instances consist of a collection of column values for the given row in the list, and the site columns define the type and shape of content values permitted. Page document libraries allow content types, check-in/checkout,, and so on—all the features of a regular document library. What makes page instances special is in the actual document file that SharePoint stores in the pages library. If you attempt to download a page instance from SharePoint to your local computer and then open the file with Notepad, you'll find very little markup—just XML that marries the page instance with a publishing page layout in the Master Page Gallery (plus some other relevant XML markup information).

How does SharePoint combine the components just listed to render a finished page? SharePoint combines the metadata of the page instance with the markup defined in the Page Layout, which inherits common styling and branding markup from the master page. With both content (metadata) and presentation markup mashed together, SharePoint is able to send combined HTML down the wire to the client browser for page rendering. Of course, this brief description trivializes the page rendering lifecycle of SharePoint (and ASP.NET)—there much more to it—but it should provide you with the basic premise.

Page Editing

With the home page of our Team Site open in browse mode (non-edit mode), click on the Page tab, and then the Browse tab in the Ribbon. You should see a page similar to Figure 1-21.

Figure 1-21. *Page editing in a team site*

The Ribbon in Figure 1-21 shows a different set of icons than we saw when playing with lists earlier in this chapter. First, note the Edit icon on the far left—the most convenient place for it to be. Go ahead and click this icon to put the page in edit mode.

Once in edit mode, the page shown in Figure 1-21 does not change much. SharePoint shows the web part zone outlines and you may click on any of the zone areas to edit text. For example, select the Welcome To Your Site title and then type something else to change the text. In edit mode the Ribbon also changes—notice two new tabs (Format Text and Insert) in the Editing Tools group. The Format Text tab contains a number of formatting options, like that of Microsoft Office applications, where you can format selected text without having to know HTML markup syntax. If you decide you would like to edit the HTML of the page, the Markup section the Ribbon provides for HTML editing.

Other interesting areas of the Ribbon to note in edit mode are the Styles and Layout sections. SharePoint defines a set of default styles for the site template so that content owners may format text to align with the overall presentation theme of the site. The Layouts section allows users to change the page layout, as discussed in the previous section, and shown in Figure 1-20.

Click the Insert tab on the Ribbon to see options available for inserting pictures, links, tables, and web parts into the page. Clicking on the icon to insert a picture (image) in the page provides the user with a dialog to select a picture from the Site Assets Media Library. Users may store image files in any document library or other Media Asset library on the site for inclusion in the page, or link to an external image via URL. Users may also upload images from their local computer, to include in the page, and SharePoint assists by asking the user where they would like to upload the file (Site Assets Library by default).

Click back to the Page tab on the Ribbon. While in edit mode, SharePoint replaces the Edit Page icon with a Save & Close icon. Clicking the Save & Close icon commits any page changes. It's worth noting that if you attempt to navigate away from the page in edit mode and you have pending changes, SharePoint will inform you that you have unsaved changes and give you the opportunity to save the change or cancel. SharePoint also attempts to force save changes if you change the URL in the browser address bar, thus leaving the SharePoint environment, using JavaScript.

Conflict Resolution and Checkin/Checkout

By default, the Site Pages document library does not enforce content approval or checkout prior to editing. Without enforced checkout, multiple users may edit the same page at the same time. Fortunately, SharePoint provides conflict resolution to deal with changes that may have occurred from another user while you have the page in edit mode. When SharePoint detects a conflict, at the time you save the page, SharePoint will display a dialog with the following options:

- **Continue Editing**—instructs SharePoint to leave the page in edit mode.

- **Merge Changes**—SharePoint opens another browser window with the latest version of the page in edit mode, so you may apply your new changes to the most recent page.

- **Discard Your Changes**—Instructs SharePoint to throw away your changes and return the page to browse mode with the latest page presented.

- **Overwrite the Page**—Instructs SharePoint to replace the latest page version with your current edits.

Ordinarily, I recommend merging in changes to avoid loss of changes. To avoid conflict in the first place, enable the option to enforce checkout from the Version Settings link in the Site Pages list settings page.

■ **Note** Users can avoid conflict by checking out the page before edit, even if enforced checkout is not enabled, by clicking the Checkout icon on the Ribbon before entering edit mode. Ensure that you check out the page *before* editing to avoid loss of current changes.

Turning on the option to enforce checkout prior to edit instructs SharePoint to prompt the user to check out the page before editing. When you check out a page in edit mode, SharePoint shows a helpful yellow status bar on the page, as shown in Figure 1-22.

Figure 1-22. *Page checked out and in edit mode*

While the page is checked out, other users will not have the capability to edit the page. Even if the user who checked out the page saves their changes, the page is not available for edit by other users until the user checks in the page.

Content Approval and Publishing

Site page document libraries do not default to enable content approval. *Content approval* enables the built-in SharePoint parallel approval workflow. Enable this option in the Version settings for the Pages Document Library (within the library settings page).

With content approval enabled, those users not in the Approvers SharePoint group, and not the person who edited the page last, will only see the last published version of the page. SharePoint refers to page publishing as the process of approving page edits and making the page edits live for all users to see.

With content approval enabled, enter edit mode for the page in Figure 1-22. Make some changes to the page, then save and check in the page. The yellow status bar then shows the status: Waiting for Approval. The page is now in pending approval mode. Users in the SharePoint Approvers group have permissions to approve pending pages, and receive email notification to review changes before publishing. Click on the Publish tab in the Ribbon (assuming you have approval permissions) and see Figure 1-23 for the Publish options.

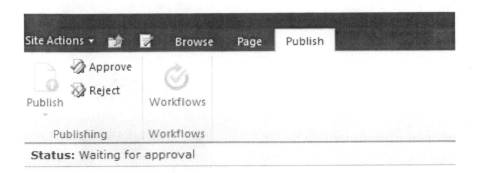

Figure 1-23. Publish options

After clicking Approve (or Reject if you would like to send the page back to the editor for revision), the page is ready for publish. The page is now in the state Approved and now published to for all users to view.

■ **Note** No Approvers Security Group exists in Team Sites. Instead, users in the Owners group have the explicit permission to approve list items.

Web Parts

A SharePoint *Web Part* is a contained unit of functionality that renders output in a dedicated segment of a SharePoint page. Users with page editing permission (or customized personal view of pages) may add and remove web parts from the SharePoint Web Part Gallery to customize the content on the page. At the basic level, a Web Part is an ASP.NET user control on steroids, which integrates with the SharePoint platform and UI to enable custom functionality integration. Third parties often develop web parts and package them into solutions so organizations may deploy new and extensible capabilities.

Web Parts have existed in SharePoint for some time, but became mainstream development entities with ASP.NET 2.0. SharePoint 2003 supported the use of web parts built from SharePoint proprietary APIs. When ASP.NET 2.0 introduced .NET web parts, Microsoft supported the new ASP.NET web parts in the SharePoint platform since SharePoint 2007 builds atop of ASP.NET 2.0. Today, most web parts supported by SharePoint inherit from a base ASP.NET Web Part control.

Web Parts extend the capabilities of SharePoint and allow users to add more than just static content to their pages. For example, SharePoint includes a number of web parts in the gallery, which include rendering of list content, displaying RSS feeds, showing media content, rendering content aggregated from external sources, rich text content, and so on. In this section, we see how to add a web part to an existing page in our Team Site.

From the home page of the Team site, click the Page tab and then the Edit Page icon, to put the page in edit mode. Click the Insert tab of under the Editing Tools group in the Ribbon. The Ribbon should look as shown in Figure 1-24.

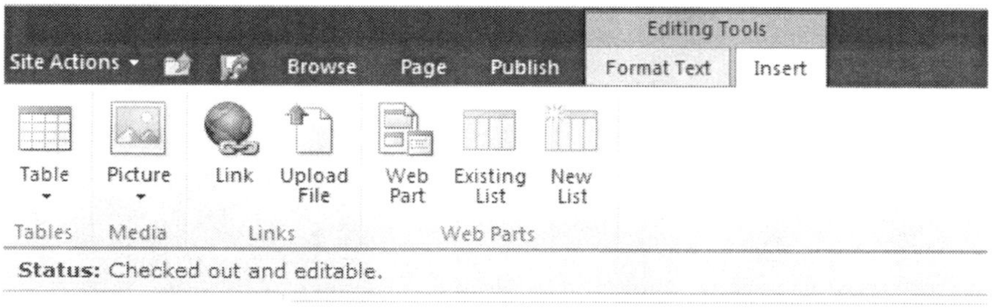

Figure 1-24. The Ribbon state for adding a web part

Click the Web Part icon, shown in the Web Parts section of the Ribbon. SharePoint displays the Web Part selection tool to select from the web parts in the gallery (Figure 1-25).

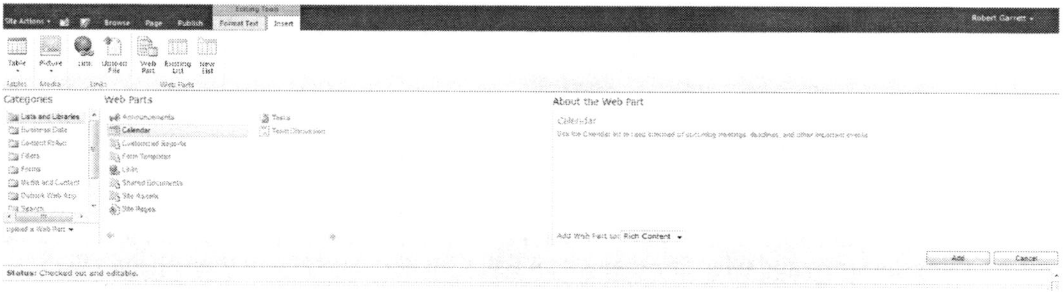

Figure 1-25. The Web Part Selection tool

The selection tool shows web parts in the various categories; choose a web part (I choose the calendar) and then select the zone in the panel on the right (the Team Site home page has no zones, just the rich text area of the page). Click Add to add the web part. Figure 1-26 shows my page with the added calendar web part.

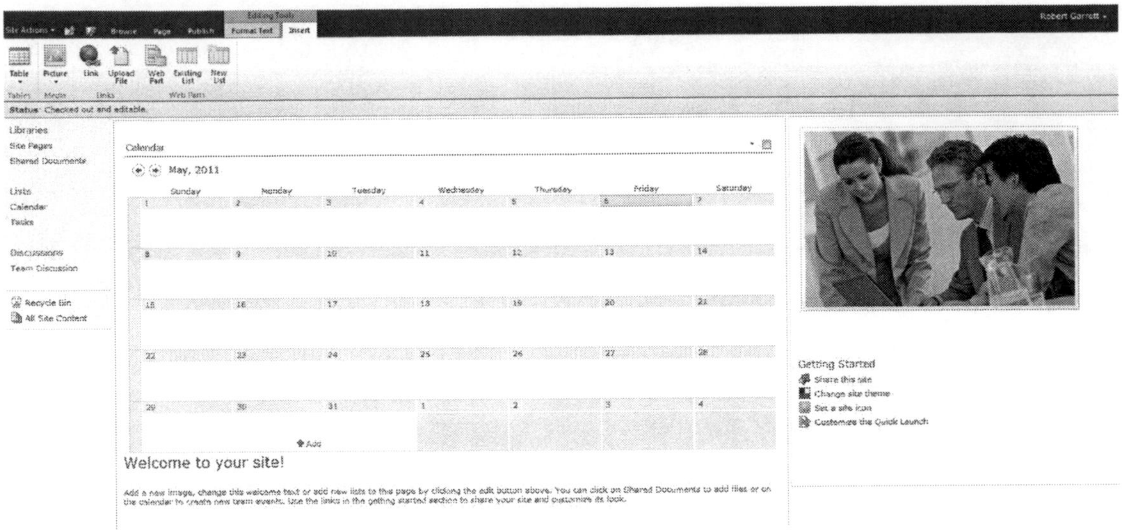

Figure 1-26. Team Site home page with Calendar web part added.

Web Parts maintain their own set of properties for presentation, functionality, and general configuration. The top-right corner of the Web Part (see Figure 1-26) shows a check box and down-arrow (in edit mode). Click the arrow and select the menu item Edit Web Part. SharePoint then opens a Web Part configuration panel on the right side of the page with various options (see Figure 1-27).

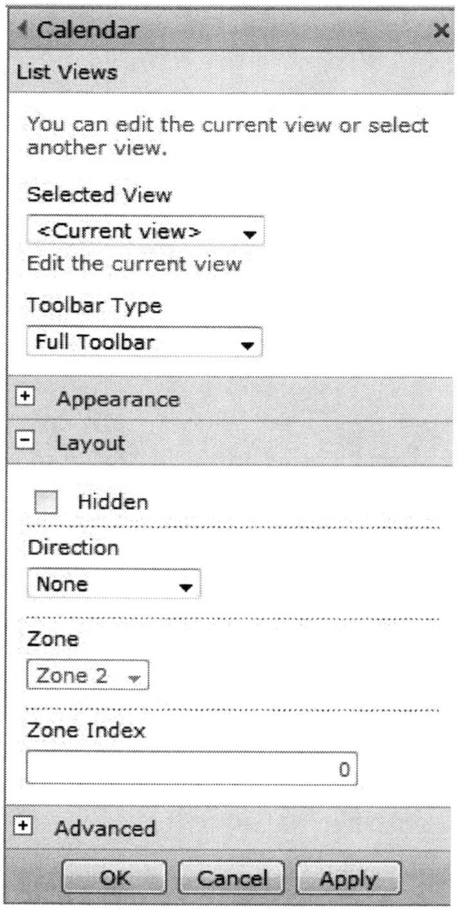

◀ Calendar ✕

List Views

You can edit the current view or select another view.

Selected View

<Current view> ▾

Edit the current view

Toolbar Type

Full Toolbar ▾

⊞ Appearance

⊟ Layout

☐ Hidden

Direction

None ▾

Zone

Zone 2 ▾

Zone Index

0

⊞ Advanced

OK   Cancel   Apply

Figure 1-27. Web Part options

Summary

In this chapter, I provided an overview of the new features in SharePoint 2010 compared to the previous SharePoint 2007 version. We visited the various functional areas that Microsoft details in the SharePoint donut diagram. For those users unfamiliar with SharePoint, the chapter provided the basic information for creating new web applications, and a site collection. Then, as part of building a new Team Site, we learned the fundamentals of lists, document libraries, list views, site pages, and web parts. After reading this chapter, you should have a basic understanding of the SharePoint 2010 platform. Chapter 2 introduces the technical aspects of installing a new SharePoint 2010 farm, either as a new installation or upgrade from Microsoft Office SharePoint Server 2007.

Installing and Configuring SharePoint 2010

In this chapter, you will install and configure SharePoint 2010. SharePoint 2010 ships in various flavors—Standard Edition, Enterprise, and the free Windows SharePoint Foundation (to name a few—but the installation steps I give here work for all editions of SharePoint 2010 unless I say otherwise. I'll guide you through the installation of SharePoint 2010 binaries on a new Windows Server; upgrade options for installing SharePoint 2010 after Microsoft Office Server 2007; the prerequisites for the new platform; and configuration options via the Central Administration web site.

This chapter will also visit the Visual Upgrade process for upgrade of SharePoint branding. So without further ado let us get started on our SharePoint 2010 install.

Infrastructure Requirements

Since its previous version, SharePoint 2007, Microsoft has built the SharePoint platform to scale to meet the demands of users accessing SharePoint—be it a public-facing web site, a client Intranet, extranet, or however you use it. SharePoint 2010 has a set of minimum hardware requirements that you must provide to run it on a single server farm for modest user traffic.

Note Microsoft SharePoint 2010 requires, at the very least, a server with four cores running at 2.5 GHz, 8GB of RAM, and 80GB of disk space.

In high-demand environments, a single server will not suffice for a reliable SharePoint site. The Microsoft document at the following link details capacity planning for SharePoint deployments:

http://technet.microsoft.com/en-us/library/cc261700.aspx

Microsoft made a decision in 2010 to move all server-based products to 64-bit architecture. Unlike SharePoint 2007, which ran on both 32-bit and 64-bit hardware, SharePoint 2010 now requires a 64-bit Windows operating system. SharePoint 2010 also requires one of following software environments:

- 64-bit edition of Windows 2008 Standard, Enterprise, Data Center, or Web Server with SP2

- 64-bit edition of Windows 2008 R2 Standard, Enterprise, Data Center, Web Server

SharePoint 2010 requires one of the following SQL Server environment configurations:

- 64-bit edition of Microsoft SQL Server 2008 R2

- 64-bit edition of Microsoft SQL Server 2008 with Service Pack 1 (SP1) and Cumulative Update Package 2 for SQL Server 2008 with Service Pack 1

- 64-bit edition of Microsoft SQL Server 2005 with Service Pack 3 (SP3) and Cumulative Update Package 3 for Service Pack 3

SQL Server configuration, on dedicated hardware for SharePoint (not shared with other services or products, and not on the same web server as SharePoint), typically requires a quad-core CPU and 8GB of RAM to provide a reasonable level of performance. For more demanding installations, consider 16GB of RAM and eight CPU cores. SQL Server requires 80GB of disk space and above for hosting a SharePoint 2010 Farm but space requirements vary depending on the number of documents, media items, and other content hosted within the farm.

SharePoint 2010 Prerequisites

SharePoint 2010 comes with a prerequisites installer application, which ensures that SharePoint has all the necessary software components to operate. Such components include various hot fixes, SQL Server Reporting and Analysis components, .NET 3.51 with SP1, Microsoft Sync Framework, and Windows Identity Framework to name a few.

The prerequisites installer is available in the root folder of the SharePoint 2010 installation media and named PrerequisiteInstaller.exe. Executing this application with no command-line argument parameters will present you with the dialog shown in Figure 2-1.

▓ **Note** If you have a single `OfficeServer.exe` installation file, you can extract the contents with `OfficeServer.exe /extract: c:\install` and then access the installation files in `c:\install`.

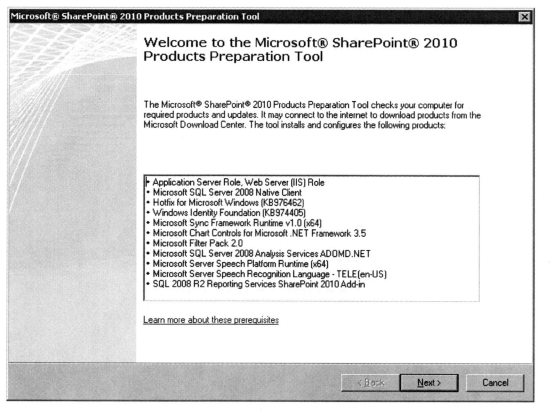

Figure 2-1. *The prerequisites installer opening dialog*

■ **Note** When executing any of the installation applications for SharePoint 2010, be sure to run as an elevated privilege administrator if Windows User Account Control is enabled. See the following link on Windows UAC: http://windows.microsoft.com/en-US/windows-vista/What-is-User-Account-Control.

As you can see in Figure 2-1, the prerequisites installer also configures the server with the Application Server and Web Server (IIS) roles, which SharePoint 2010 requires to operate.

The prerequisites installer does not require all the packages to be available on the server before installing them and will attempt to download any package before installing. Of course, in certain scenarios, automatic download of software may violate company policy in a secure environment, so the prerequisites installer allows the administrator to choose which packages to install using the command line, by providing the path to previously downloaded packages. Running the prerequisites installer from the command line with the '/?' option will display the dialog shown in Figure 2-2.

```
About                                                          ✕

***Command Line Options***
/continue - This is used to tell the installer that it is continuing from a restart
/unattended - No user interaction. Exit codes:
  0  - Success
  1  - Another instance of this application is already running
  2  - Invalid command line parameter(s)
  1001 - A pending restart blocks installation
  3010 - A restart is needed
  Other error codes - From the prerequisite installation that failed last
/? - Display this message

The installer installs from the file specified in the command line options below
where 'file' denotes the file to install from. If the option is not specified, it
downloads the file from the internet and installs. If the option is not
applicable to the current operating system, it ignores it.

/SQLNCli:file - Install Microsoft SQL Server 2008 Native Client from file

/ChartControl:file - Install Microsoft Chart Controls for Microsoft .NET
Framework 3.5 from file

/W2K8SP2:file - Install Windows Server 2008 SP2 from file

/NETFX35SP1:file - Install Microsoft .NET Framework 3.5 SP1 from file

/PowerShell:file - Install Windows PowerShell 2.0 from file

/KB976394:file - Install Hotfix for Microsoft Windows (KB976394) from file

/KB976462:file - Install Hotfix for Microsoft Windows (KB976462) from file

/IDFX:file - Install Windows Identity Foundation (KB974405) from file

/IDFXR2:file - Install Windows Identity Foundation (KB974405) for Windows
Server 2008 R2 from file

/Sync:file - Install Microsoft Sync Framework Runtime v1.0 (x64) from file

/FilterPack:file - Install Microsoft Filter Pack 2.0 from file

/ADOMD:file - Install Microsoft SQL Server 2008 Analysis Services
ADOMD.NET from file

/ReportingServices:file - Install SQL 2008 R2 Reporting Services SharePoint
2010 Add-in from file

/Speech:file - Install Microsoft Server Speech Platform Runtime from file

/SpeechLPKDEDE:file,/SpeechLPK:file,/SpeechLPKESES:file,/SpeechLPKFRFR:
file,/SpeechLPKITIT:file,/SpeechLPKKOKR:file,/SpeechLPKPTBR:file and
/SpeechLPKRURU:file - Install Microsoft Server Speech Recognition Language
- TELE from file for de-de, en-us, es-es, fr-fr, it-it, ko-kr, pt-br and ru-ru
locales respectively

                                              [      OK      ]
```

Figure 2-2. Prerequisites installer options

Choosing the Installation Type

Like its predecessor, SharePoint allows an administrator to install either a stand-alone or a server farm configuration. Running setup.exe from the installation media presents you with the dialog shown in Figure 2-3, at which point you must make a choice.

░ **Note** Setup.exe will determine if the system requires a reboot—the prerequisites installer is not always good at ensuring a reboot and leaves this determination to the individual packages it installs.

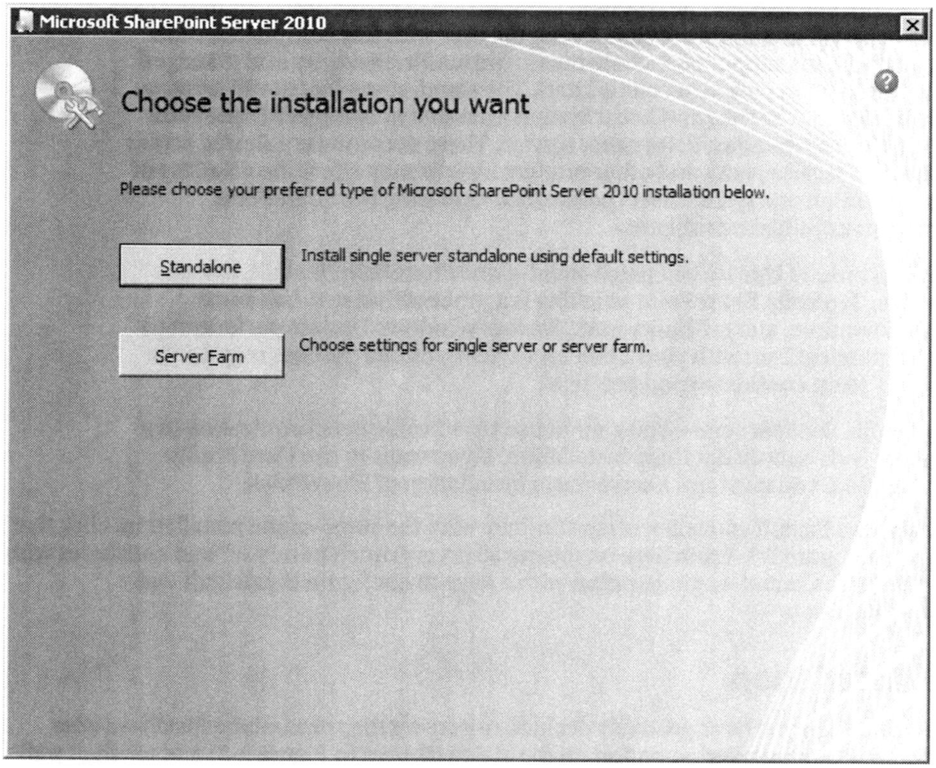

Figure 2-3. Choosing a SharePoint installation type

Stand-Alone Installation

First and most importantly, be sure that the stand-alone installation is right for you. Too often, SharePoint administrators install a stand-alone configuration of SharePoint to try out the product and then find they have to support it in production, because end users have quickly loaded SharePoint with working content (documents, and so on).

If that scenario does not scare you away, or does not apply, then consider the following list of limitations specific to the stand-alone installation:

- Installation of SQL Server Express 2008—Yes! The installer will install a shiny new instance of SQL Server 2008 express edition, regardless of whether you have an installation of full SQL Server 2005/2008 on the same server. Express has a limit of 4GB storage, causing a major headache for the IT team later when the stand-alone install of SharePoint generates increased user adoption.

- Inability to scale—The stand-alone installation does not allow the integration of additional web-front-end (WFE) servers or query/index servers to scale the farm. Essentially, a stand-alone installation tells SharePoint that the one single server is the farm in its entirety and that the administrator is fine with not scaling out later.

- Use of Network Service and Local System accounts—Microsoft designed the stand-alone install as a simple option, facing the user with few complications in setup. The decisions simplified include those surrounding security and managed accounts (more on managed accounts later). The stand-alone install will leverage the built-in Network Service and Local System accounts to configure SharePoint service—including the SharePoint timer service. These accounts are shared across the server, and service packs and other product installs may affect the volatility of their configuration and system-level passwords, rendering the SharePoint installation susceptible to problems.

- Patching—Windows Update will patch stand-alone SharePoint installs, but not farm installs. Typically, SharePoint patching is a process that requires some planning, downtime, and off-hours work. Having Windows Update performing a SharePoint patch at 2am with your other server and product patches may not be what your IT team considers good practice.

- No User Profile Services Sync—You cannot use User Profile Synchronization in a single server with built-in database installation. If you want to use User Profile Synchronization, you must use a server farm installation of SharePoint.

After considering these facts, if you still wish to continue with the stand-alone installation, click that option on the dialog as in Figure 2-3. From here on the install is very much hands-off and concludes with Internet Explorer opening to Central Administration with a page to configure the default web application and site collection.

Server Farm Installation

If you are reading this far, then you have probably decided to pass on the stand-alone install—a wise decision. Click the Server Farm installation option on the dialog (shown in Figure 2-3) and we shall walk through the steps.

■ **Note** Microsoft Office SharePoint Server 2007 provided a Web-Front-end Only install option, for adding additional WFE servers to an existing farm. This let you avoid the overhead of the full Server Farm install. Microsoft removed this option from the GUI because it was rarely used. SharePoint 2010 still provides for WFE Only install, but only via scripted installation.

After choosing the Server Farm installation option, the setup application shows you the dialog in Figure 2-4. You should notice the question about complete and stand-alone installation yet again. As the installer of SharePoint, you are probably wondering just how the stand-alone installation option in the Server Farm install dialog differs from the stand-alone installation we just avoided. The short answer to your question is "not at all," and it is unclear why Microsoft felt compelled to ask us twice, so click the

Complete option. If you feel so inclined, you can change the destination folder in which SharePoint installs by clicking over to the File Location tab; otherwise proceed by clicking the Install Now button.

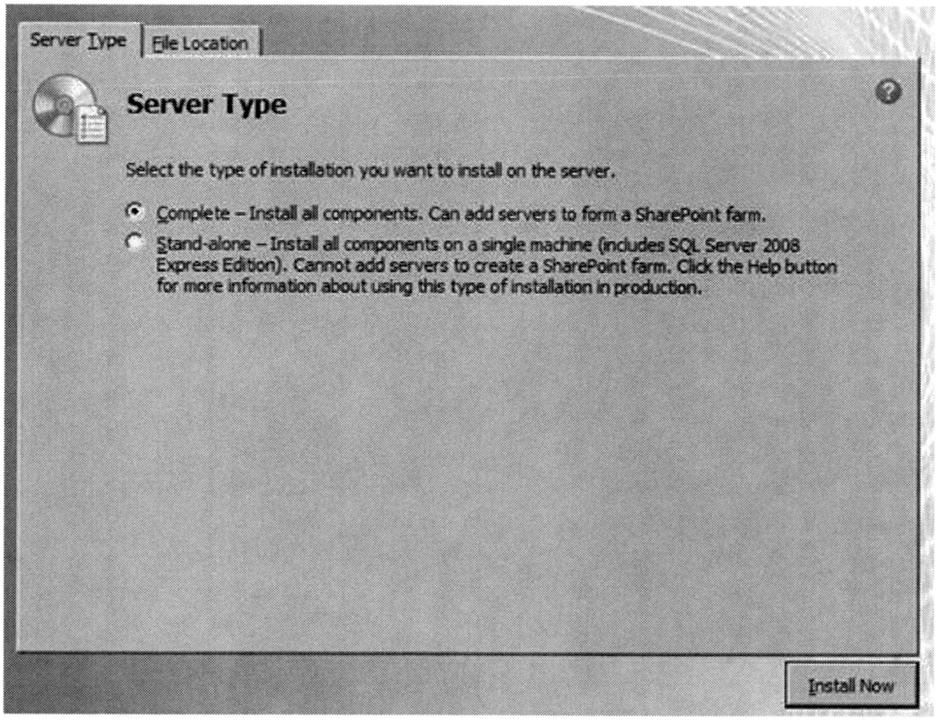

Figure 2-4. The Server Type dialog

After a brief break to refresh your cup of coffee, while the installer installs SharePoint 2010 (the binary installation) you should see the dialog shown in Figure 2-5 on your return. Leaving the check box checked and closing this dialog will launch the SharePoint Products Configuration Wizard to allow you to configure your new SharePoint Farm or join this server to an existing farm.

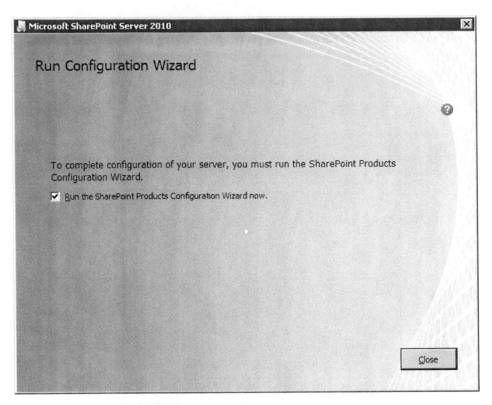

Figure 2-5. Conclusion of the binary Server Farm installation

A Quick Mention of AUTOSPINSTALLER

One of the annoying things about setting up a new SharePoint farm is that Microsoft chose to name configuration databases with Global Unique Identifier (GUID) extensions. This was not such a big deal when working with SharePoint 2007. However, SharePoint 2010 introduces *managed service applications*, to replace the previous Shared Services Provider infrastructure. Each managed service application creates one or more configuration databases in SQL Server with GUID extensions. If you hear your team database admins screaming from the other side of the office, it is because their shared database server with nicely named databases has a boatload of new databases with strange GUID extensions.

■ **Note** It is good practice to dedicate a SQL instance to a SharePoint 2010 farm, even if several instances exist on the same server—this allows isolation of SharePoint databases from different farms.

To get around this problem, the CodePlex product called AUTOSPINSTALLER, created by Brian Lalancette, provides a nice PowerShell script to configure SharePoint 2010 with nicely named databases and no GUID extensions. You can download AUTOSPINSTALLER at the following location:

`http://autospinstaller.codeplex.com/.`

SharePoint Products Configuration Wizard

From now on, I shall assume that you have decided to proceed with the Server Farm installation, have completed the installation of the SharePoint 2010 binaries, and are ready to proceed through the SharePoint Products Configuration Wizard—or Configuration Wizard for short. After a brief welcome message and a popup message about restarting some services, you will see a dialog like that of Figure 2-6.

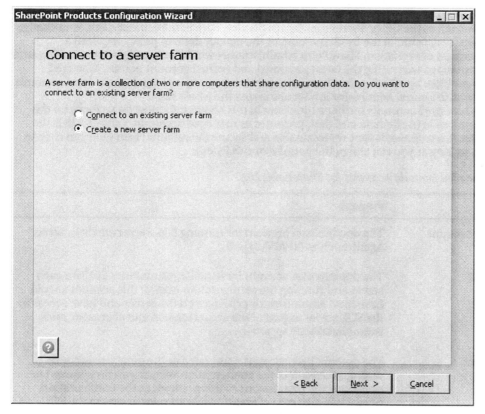

Figure 2-6. *The Connect to a Server Farm wizard page*

Assuming this is your first installation of SharePoint 2010 and you have no existing SharePoint farm to connect to, select Create a New Server Farm and then click Next.

The next dialog asks you to specify a SQL Server name and default configuration database name for SharePoint 2010. This server is the location of the main farm configuration and database for the Central Administration web site.

The dialog that follows is new in SharePoint 2010 and asks for the passphrase for the installation. SharePoint requires the passphrase later when adding additional servers to the farm or removing existing servers from the farm, so be sure to keep the passphrase safe. An administrator may change the passphrase with the PowerShell cmdlet SP-SetPassPhrase, but retrieving the passphrase is impossible. You may only reset it.

Managed Accounts

SharePoint makes use of various domain-level accounts to operate securely. Even if your SharePoint installation operates on a single server and is part of a workgroup, all accounts used in SharePoint 2010 require the full domain name syntax: DOMAIN\username. SharePoint 2007 had the same requirement.

One notable difference in SharePoint 2010 is the introduction of *managed accounts*. SharePoint 2007 required different domain accounts for different purposes, and the administrator was responsible for knowing the password of every account and specifying the account name when provisioning services or making changes—such as the Office SharePoint Search Service. If an administrator decides to change the password of a service account in use by SharePoint, or the default domain policy required a password change because of expiration, SharePoint administrators would have a nightmare making sure that SharePoint installations were using the latest password and correct account names. Managed accounts avoid this problem by allowing the SharePoint administrator to register domain-level accounts in a single location within Central Administration for use across the whole farm.

We will discuss Managed accounts further a little later in this chapter; for now let us focus on the various accounts required in the domain and their purposes as managed accounts. Table 2-1 lists the accounts that Microsoft recommends for a maintainable and secure SharePoint Farm (you can choose the account names, as long as you can assign the permissions as listed):

Table 2-1: Recommended Domain Accounts for SharePoint 2010

Account	Purpose
SQL Server Service Account	The domain user account for running SQL Server and SQL Server Agent, such as DOMAIN\sp_sql.
Setup User Account	The domain user account for installing SharePoint 2010 on each server and running the configuration wizard; this account should have local administrator privileges on the server and have access to the SQL server as part of the securityadmin and dbcreator roles. Example: DOMAIN\sp_admin
Server Farm Account	The domain user account nominated as the database account during execution of the configuration wizard; you do not need to apply specific permissions to this account, as the configuration wizard will take care of granting this account access to the SQL Server databases and configuring the SharePoint Timer Service, Code Host Service, and Central Administration site application pool. In addition, the farm account is a member of the following security groups on the local server: • IIS_IUSRS • WSS_ADMIN_WPG

Account	Purpose
	• WSS_WPG
	• WSS_RESTRICTED_WPG
	• Performance Log Users
	• Performance Monitor Users
	The farm account also has the following local security policy rights:
	• Adjust memory quotas for a process
	• Logon as a service
	• Replace a process level token
	Example: DOMAIN\sp_farm
Application Pool Account	The domain user to run all SharePoint we site applications in the farm; do not grant any explicit privileges—you may have several managed accounts (one for each web application) in the farm, but only need one domain user account. Example: DOMAIN\sp_app_pool
SharePoint Service Account	The domain user account with no explicit privileges to run SharePoint Service applications. Example: DOMAIN\sp_service
Search Crawl Account	The domain user account with no explicit privileges to crawl content for indexed search. Example: DOMAIN\sp_crawl
Business Intelligence Account	The domain user account and trusted account for Reporting Services and Performance Point when not using Kerberos; grant database access as appropriate to access external content. Example: DOMAIN\sp_bi

You only need the first three accounts in Table 2-1 to install SharePoint 2010, and in many test and development environments, you can live with just these three accounts for all aspects of the farm configuration. However, in the spirit of good practice and in preparation for the day when you have to stand up a production SharePoint 2010 farm, I recommend getting in the habit of creating all of these accounts for configuration.

■ **Note** To ensure smooth installation of the User Profile Synchronization Service (later), grant the farm account Replicating Directory Changes permission in the domain.

Continuing with the Configuration Wizard

We took a quick segue to discuss domain and managed accounts and are now back to where we paused from working with the SharePoint Products Configuration Wizard. We had just chosen the Server Farm installation type and can now continue with the configuration…

The next dialog, shown in Figure 2-7, allows you to enter the SQL Server name, database for farm configuration, username, and password. Be sure to use the SharePoint Farm account credentials discussed in the previous section.

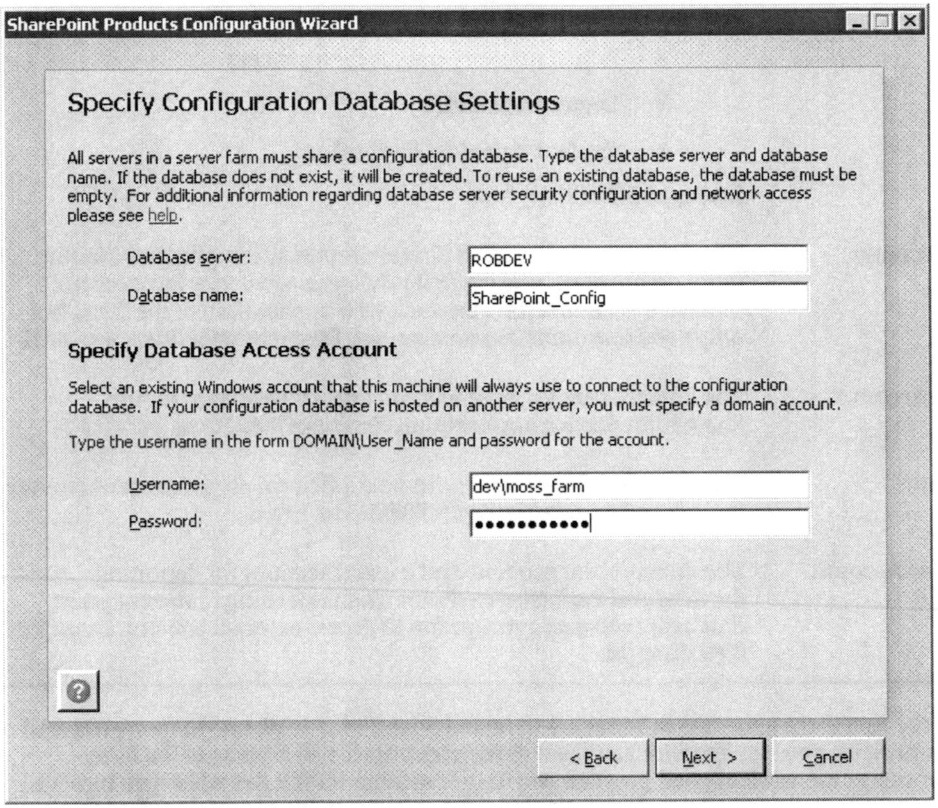

Figure 2-7. The configuration database dialog

Following the Configuration Database dialog is a dialog requesting the SharePoint Farm passphrase—make a note of the passphrase you enter, as you will likely need this later in the lifetime of your installation.

The final entry dialog of the configuration wizard requests details for the the Central Administration web site, as shown in Figure 2-8.

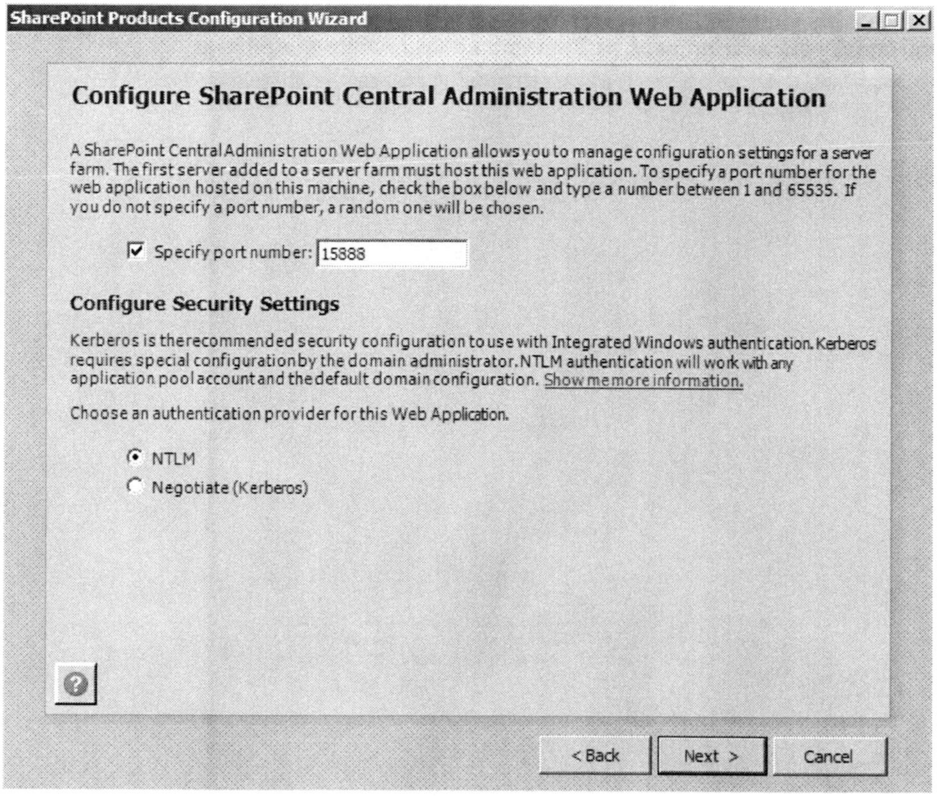

Figure 2-8. *The Central Administration web site settings dialog*

You can leave the port number as default or change it to a number that is more memorable. I like to change mine to 8000 or 8080, but any free TCP/IP port on the server will work. Typically, you will not want to expose your Central Admin web site to the Internet, but if you do need outside access to this site, then you must ensure that the port you choose for the Central Admin site is open on your firewall.

▪ **Note** Even if you change the port number in Figure 2-8, SharePoint will still create a directory for the Central Administration at %wwwroot%\wss\VirtualDirectories*port* where the port number is the default port specified by the wizard.

Leave the authentication as NTLM and click the Next button to see a summary dialog before proceeding with the configuration. If you are familiar with Kerberos, you may choose this option instead of NTLM, but if you have not configured Kerberos correctly, you will likely find that the Central Administration web site will not work or the wizard will fail the configuration.

Click Next on the summary dialog and then go grab yourself another coffee while the configuration wizard completes the install. If all is well, you should see a completion dialog like that in Figure 2-9. If you see an error message with a long URL to an error log file, it is time to Google the error, retrace your installation steps, and check your environment, as SharePoint does not like something.

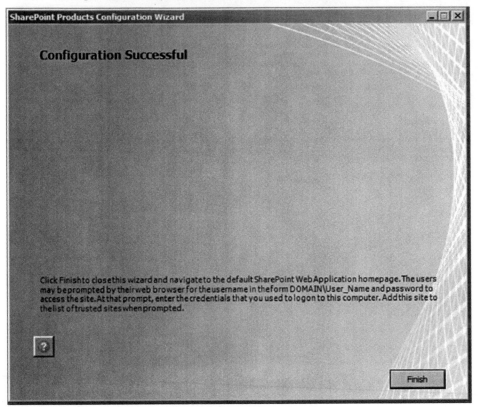

Figure 2-9. The Configuration Wizard success dialog

Congratulations. If you see the dialog in Figure 2-9. you have completed the configuration of your SharePoint Farm. Well, not quite—there's another wizard in the Central Administration web site, to configure your Managed Service Applications, which are key services required for the operation of your farm. Click the Finish button and your default browser should launch with the Central Administration web site, where you will be prompted to participate in a Customer Improvement Program, followed by a page called "How do you want to configure your SharePoint farm," which is the topic of our next section.

ADACM (SharePoint Foundation Only)

If you are installing SharePoint 2010 Foundation, the Advanced button on the summary dialog allows you to configure Active Directory Account Creation Mode (ADACM)—on any other installation but Foundation; you will see the advanced button as grayed out.

The ADACM feature allows SharePoint to create users in an Operating Unit (OU) of a given Active Directory domain when adding new users to SharePoint. Users may receive an email when SharePoint creates an account, existing users may invite users to the site, and SharePoint will manage Windows accounts on behalf of the user. The downside of this feature is that SharePoint Foundation will not allow administrators to add existing domain users to the farm, which may explain why this feature hasn't been widely adopted.

Configuring Your SharePoint Farm

The SharePoint Farm Configuration Wizard (sometimes called the "White Wizard" in some circles, as opposed to the "Gray Wizard" that is the Products Configuration Wizard) walks the administrator through configuration of the farm. In SharePoint 2007, Microsoft pretty much left the farm configuration up to administrators and guided them with a task list of items. SharePoint 2010 assists you— the administrator—further with the wizard. As with any wizard, SharePoint makes certain assumptions to guide you. If you are looking to avoid these assumptions with a more hands on-tailored configuration setup, then you will need to perform configuration manually. The wizard avoids most of the complications of manual configuration and thus is the chosen approach to configuring your farm.

■ **Note** If you skip the Farm Configuration wizard after completing the SharePoint Products Configuration Wizard, you may execute it at any time from the bottom-right link of the main Central Admin home page.

The first page of the farm configuration wizard asks if you want to participate in a Customer Experience Improvement Program—a worthwhile exercise if you have not done this before. Skipping this dialog takes you to the page with a wizard summary and the chance to cancel the wizard or begin the process, as shown in Figure 2-10.

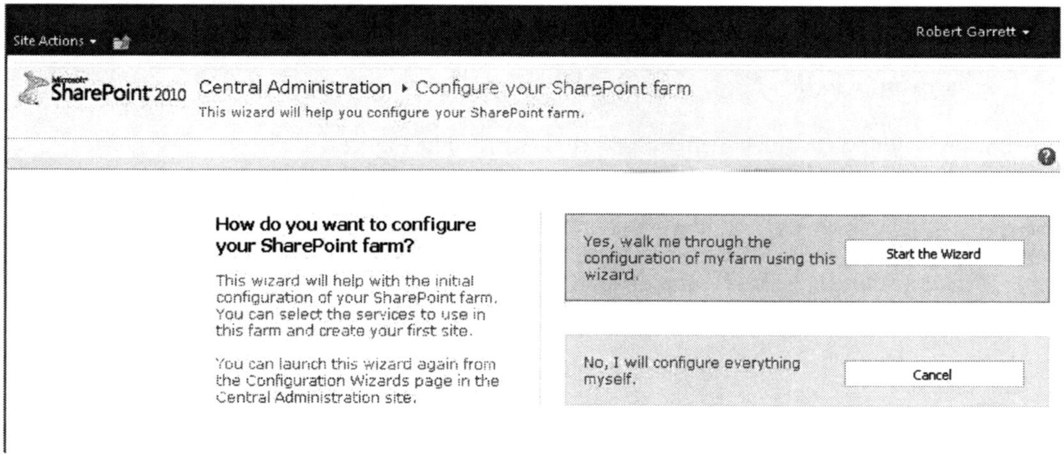

Figure 2-10. Summary page for the Farm Configuration Wizard

Click Start the Wizard to kick off the wizard, and you should see the page shown in Figure 2-11. The top section of the page allows you to specify the service account for all Managed Services, created by the wizard. Use the DOMAIN\sp_service account you read about earlier in this chapter. You may be tempted to use the SharePoint Farm account to run your services. Microsoft recommends supplying a dedicated service account, with lesser privileges than the farm account.

The remainder of the page, shown in Figure 2-11, allows you to configure the various Managed Services included in the default service group of the farm.

Figure 2-11. Service configuration

Right about now your SQL Server will probably look a little like Figure 2-12, not too pretty with various databases containing GUID extensions. The use of GUIDs in the database names is Microsoft's way of preventing collision of database names when hosting multiple SharePoint farms on the same SQL Server. Even so, with database names differing only by the GUID extension in the name, a DB admin will have a hard time matching farm to database, which is why Microsoft also recommends the use of a dedicated SQL instance for each SharePoint farm.

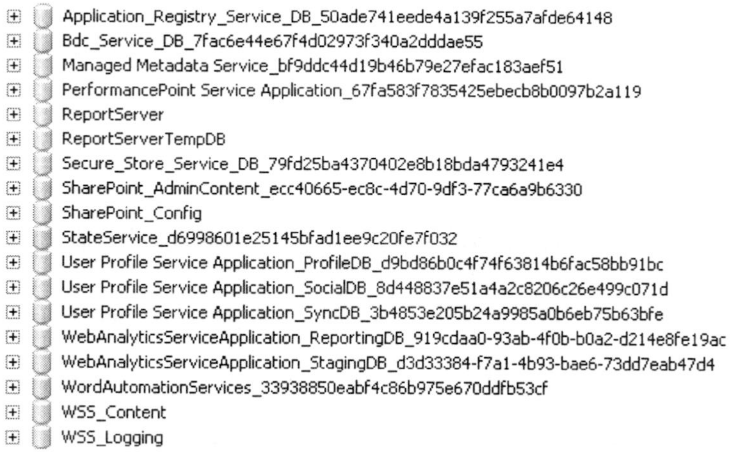
Application_Registry_Service_DB_50ade741eede4a139f255a7afde64148
Bdc_Service_DB_7fac6e44e67f4d02973f340a2dddae55
Managed Metadata Service_bf9ddc44d19b46b79e27efac183aef51
PerformancePoint Service Application_67fa583f7835425ebecb8b0097b2a119
ReportServer
ReportServerTempDB
Secure_Store_Service_DB_79fd25ba4370402e8b18bda4793241e4
SharePoint_AdminContent_ecc40665-ec8c-4d70-9df3-77ca6a9b6330
SharePoint_Config
StateService_d6998601e25145bfad1ee9c20fe7f032
User Profile Service Application_ProfileDB_d9bd86b0c4f74f63814b6fac58bb91bc
User Profile Service Application_SocialDB_8d448837e51a4a2c8206c26e499c071d
User Profile Service Application_SyncDB_3b4853e205b24a9985a0b6eb75b63bfe
WebAnalyticsServiceApplication_ReportingDB_919cdaa0-93ab-4f0b-b0a2-d214e8fe19ac
WebAnalyticsServiceApplication_StagingDB_d3d33384-f7a1-4b93-bae6-73dd7eab47d4
WordAutomationServices_33938850eabf4c86b975e670ddfb53cf
WSS_Content
WSS_Logging

***Figure 2-12.** Database listing for a typical configured farm*

After completing the configuration of farm services, the farm wizard prompts you to configure the top-level root site collection, as shown in Figure 2-13.

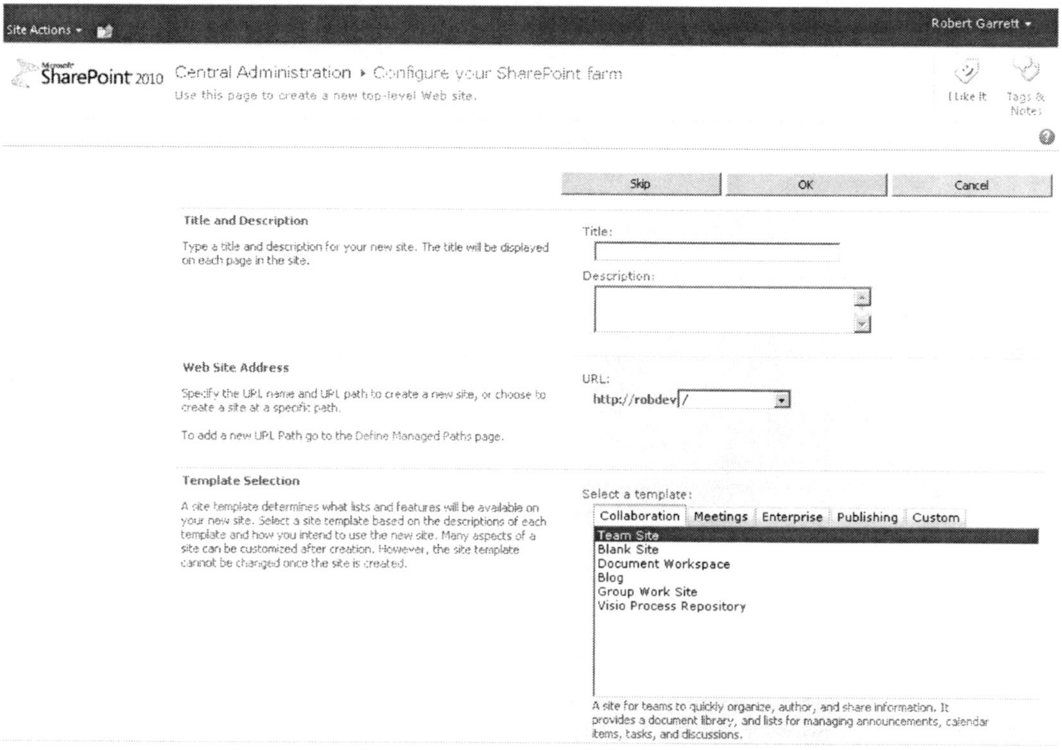
Site Actions
Robert Garrett
SharePoint 2010
Central Administration ▸ Configure your SharePoint farm
Use this page to create a new top-level Web site.
I Like It
Tags & Notes
Skip
OK
Cancel
Title and Description
Type a title and description for your new site. The title will be displayed on each page in the site.
Title:
Description:
Web Site Address
Specify the URL name and URL path to create a new site, or choose to create a site at a specific path.
To add a new URL Path go to the Define Managed Paths page.
URL:
http://robdev /
Template Selection
A site template determines what lists and features will be available on your new site. Select a site template based on the descriptions of each template and how you intend to use the new site. Many aspects of a site can be customized after creation. However, the site template cannot be changed once the site is created.
Select a template:
Collaboration
Meetings
Enterprise
Publishing
Custom
Team Site
Blank Site
Document Workspace
Blog
Group Work Site
Visio Process Repository
A site for teams to quickly organize, author, and share information. It provides a document library, and lists for managing announcements, calendar items, tasks, and discussions.

***Figure 2-13.** Configuring the-top level site collection*

At this stage, SharePoint has already provisioned a new IIS Web Application—called SharePoint 80—on the default HTTP port (80) and presented the page shown in Figure 2-13 so the user may choose the site definition (template) for the new site collection at the root of this new application. Administrators of SharePoint 2007 may already be familiar with creating new site collections and the above page is similar to that of the previous version.

▪ **Note** If you already have a working non-SharePoint IIS application/site on port 80, SharePoint will disable it in IIS to allow creation of the default application in SharePoint.

After creating the default site collection, the farm wizard should show a summary completion page, similar to Figure 2-14. The summary page lists the URL of the default site collection and the various service applications configured in the farm. If you wish to go back and change the default service applications, you may do so by running the farm wizard again from the home page of the Central Administration site. To change the default web application and site collection, visit the Application Management section in the Central Administration site.

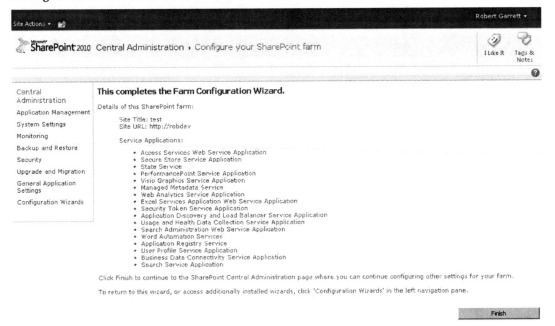

Figure 2-14. The farm wizard complete

We are almost finished configuring our new SharePoint farm—the wizard completed, but we have a few more manual steps to perform to complete what is a typical configuration.

If you have closed your browser, open it back up to the home Central Administration page (or click the Finish button if on the page in Figure 2-14). Click the main heading for the section System Settings, then click the Configure Outgoing E-Mail Settings link. Provide configuration for your outbound SMTP server and From and Reply, email address settings.

Click on Application Management, either from the left navigation section on the Central Admin site or from the Central Admin home page. Click Manage Service Applications to see a list of configured service applications and associated proxy instances in the farm. Find the Secure Store Service application and click it, then from the Ribbon click Generate New Key. Provide a new key passphrase and verification when prompted.

Navigate back to the Manage Service Applications page. Find and click the Enterprise Search Service Application. Underneath the Crawling group in the left navigation, click Content Sources. Hover over the Local SharePoint Sites content source and select Edit. From the content source edit page, create a schedule for crawling all local SharePoint site collections in this farm.

▪ **Note** Configuring SharePoint Search would take a chapter (or a whole book) of its own; the few sentences above merely allow the user to establish a schedule to an existing crawl content source.

Presto, you have just completed configuration of your SharePoint farm. Of course, there is much more to the care and feeding and continued configuration of a SharePoint farm, but the instructions so far in this chapter are enough to get even the newest SharePoint administrator off the ground. Most elements you'll want to configure are available through Central Administration, so proceed to the "Welcome to the Central Administration Web Site" section of this chapter.

Upgrading from Microsoft Office SharePoint 2007 (MOSS)

One of the major gripes about moving from SharePoint Portal Server 2003 to Microsoft Office SharePoint Server 2007 was that the upgrade was not a clean process. In defense of Microsoft, the difference in architecture between SPS 2003 and MOSS 2007 was significant, and one could only imagine the complexities involved in migrating data from an SPS 2003 database schema to that of MOSS 2007.

Microsoft heard our cries loud and clear, and because MOSS 2007 had been widely adopted, when they introduced SharePoint 2010 they made sure an upgrade strategy was in place.

In-Place or Database Attach Upgrade

SharePoint 2010 essentially provides two possible upgrade methods—*in-place* and *database attach*. Each method has pros and cons, which you will read about further in this chapter.

In-place upgrade does exactly what the name says—it upgrades an existing MOSS 2007 installation "in place" and takes care of upgrading the SharePoint infrastructure to the new SharePoint 2010 platform while preserving all user content, custom features, and branding. The in-place upgrade also upgrades existing Shared Services to the new Managed Services infrastructure without the headaches administrators have become accustomed to with past SharePoint version upgrades.

In-place upgrade is ideal for those small-to-medium-size SharePoint deployments where the administrator is looking for a quick upgrade with minimal fuss and problems, and the end-result is a working farm with same functionality as the legacy MOSS 2007 platform, but running on the new SharePoint 2010 platform with all the new features and functionality it provides. Of course, an in-place upgrade is not without its downside—for larger farms containing huge volumes of content, or farms with lots of customizations, an in-place upgrade is not necessary the best option because of the hands-off click-and-pray approach. Furthermore, an in-place upgrade consists of taking down the farm while the upgrade takes place, which is not a viable option in mission-critical production deployments. This is where the alternative method, database attach, comes into play.

Database attach provides administrators with the capability to apply existing content, user profile, and Microsoft Project databases to a new installation of SharePoint 2010 and have SharePoint upgrade the database schema to meet the new version. Database attach is a safer alternative to in-place because the original MOSS 2007 farm remains intact and operational while the DB Attach upgrade continues on separate hardware and isolated from the production service. Database attach also gives administrators more control over the legacy features installed because there's no requirement to host both MOSS 2007 and SharePoint 2010 binaries (hives) on the same servers. However, unlike in-place, database attach requires more from the administrator to stand up a new SharePoint 2010 environment and to migrate users over from the legacy MOSS 2007 farm to the new platform without loss of data, or the data in the new farm becoming stale because of delays in the cut-over. In addition, several components are not upgradable with a database attach upgrade. These include search settings, scope, and managed properties.

Considerations Before Performing an Upgrade

No matter which upgrade method sounds right for your situation, there are some other considerations to take into account before diving into the upgrade process.

■ **Note** As in any other upgrade process, always back up your SharePoint Farm before performing any upgrade—especially the in-place upgrade.

First, both upgrade paths require that the infrastructure running SharePoint 2010 installation meet the minimum requirements. Therefore, if you are considering an in-place upgrade, this may not even be possible if your MOSS 2007 infrastructure is not 64-bit and operating on the correct version and patched version of Windows and SQL Server.

Upgrade to SharePoint 2010 only permits upgrade from MOSS 2007 with Service Pack 2. If you were hoping to upgrade that aging SPS 2003 farm direct to SharePoint 2010 or decided to skip the various MOSS 2007 service packs and Cumulative Upgrades and assumed you could go easily to the latest and greatest version of SharePoint 2010, then I am afraid you are in for disappointment.

Often overlooked, SharePoint version is an important consideration before starting an upgrade—if you have a Standard edition of MOSS 2007, then you cannot upgrade to SharePoint Enterprise. Seems obvious, right? Table 2-2 documents the supported and unsupported upgrade paths for given starting SharePoint 2007 version and ending SharePoint 2010 version.

Table 2-2: Supported and Unsupported Upgrade Paths Based on SharePoint Edition

Starting Edition	Supported Ending Edition	Unsupported Ending Edition
Office SharePoint Server 2007 with SP2, Standard edition	SharePoint Server 2010, Standard edition	SharePoint Server 2010, Enterprise edition
SharePoint Server 2010,	SharePoint Server 2010,	

Starting Edition	Supported Ending Edition	Unsupported Ending Edition
Standard edition	Enterprise edition	
Office SharePoint Server 2007 with SP2, Enterprise Edition	SharePoint Server 2010, Enterprise edition	SharePoint Server 2010, Standard edition
Office SharePoint Server 2007 with SP2, Trial edition	SharePoint Server 2010, Trial edition	SharePoint Server 2010, full product
SharePoint Server 2010, Trial edition	SharePoint Server 2010, full product	

The Pre-Upgrade Check

After patching all servers in your existing MOSS 2007 farm to Service Pack 2, you can proceed to running the pre-upgrade check. Microsoft provided a new STSADM command option to check an existing MOSS 2007 farm for potential failures before starting with one of the upgrade methods. Figure 2-15 shows the display after executing the following command: STSADM -o preupgradecheck.

```
C:\>stsadm -o preupgradecheck

Processing configuration file: OssPreUpgradeCheck.xml
        SearchContentSourcesInfo... Information Only
        SearchInfo... Information Only
Processing configuration file: WssPreUpgradeCheck.xml
        ServerInfo... Information Only
        FarmInfo... Information Only
        UpgradeTypes... Information Only
        SiteDefinitionInfo... Information Only
        LanguagePackInfo... Information Only
        FeatureInfo... Information Only
        AamUrls... Information Only
        LargeList... Information Only
        CustomListViewInfo... Passed
        CustomFieldTypeInfo... Information Only
        CustomWorkflowActionsFileInfo... Passed
        ModifiedWebConfigWorkflowAuthorizedTypesInfo... Information Only
        ModifiedWorkflowActionsFileInfo... Passed
        DisabledWorkFlowsInfo... Passed
        OSPrerequisite... Passed
        WindowsInternalDatabaseMigration... Passed
        WindowsInternalDatabaseSite... Passed
        MissingWebConfig... Passed
        ReadOnlyDatabase... Passed
        InvalidDatabaseSchema... Passed
        ContentOrphan... Passed
        SiteOrphan... Passed
        PendingUpgrade... Passed
        InvalidServiceAccount... Passed
        InvalidHostName... Passed
        SPSearchInfo... Information Only

Operation completed successfully.

Please review the results at C:\Program Files\Common Files\Microsoft Shared\Web
```

Figure 2-15. Running a preupgrade check

What exactly does the pre-upgrade checker do? You can probably glean your answer from Figure 2-15, but for brevity's sake the following list is a summary of its output:

- All servers in the farm and whether they meet the upgrade requirements

- Alternate Access Mappings configured in the farm

- Site definitions, site templates, features, and language packs installed in the farm

- Any unsupported customizations to the database schema

- The existence of any database site orphans in the farm

- Any missing or invalid configuration items, such as Web.config, invalid host name accounts, or the like

At the conclusion of the pre-upgrade check, SharePoint opens a web browser and provides a lengthy report, containing details of the above items. Figure 2-16 shows a snippet of the report. Fortunately, the report highlights blocking issues so that you may deal with these before looking at any warnings or recommendations contained in the report.

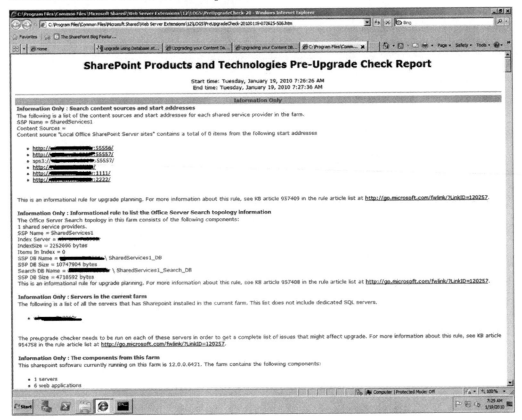

Figure 2-16. The pre-upgrade report

Performing an In-Place Upgrade

An in-place upgrade leverages the existing hardware, running the MOSS 2007 farm, and performs all the necessary steps to upgrade the MOSS 2007 farm to SharePoint 2010. After the upgrade completes, whether successfully or not, the legacy MOSS 2007 farm is no longer operational. If all has gone according to plan, you should end up with a working SharePoint 2010 farm with existing content, configuration, and supported customizations intact. One of the major benefits of the pre-upgrade check discussed in the previous section is that you can determine with some level of certainty whether an in-place upgrade will go smoothly, or cough at a misconfiguration or unsupported customization. Of course, life is not always plain sailing, so be sure to back up your MOSS 2007 farm and databases before starting your in-place upgrade.

▨ **Note** Be sure to backup ALL servers in the MOSS 2007 farm, especially the databases on the SQL server.

The following list details the various steps taken during an in-place upgrade in fixed order:

1. After completing the pre-upgrade check, run the SharePoint 2010 installation setup.exe file on the Central Admin server, the installer will detect the presence of WSS/MOSS and show a dialog asking the user if they wish to upgrade the existing farm—as in Figure 2-17.

2. Run the installation on other web front-end servers and application servers in the farm.

3. Run the SharePoint Products Configuration Wizard on the server that hosts Central Admin. SharePoint will upgrade the Central Admin server, configuration database, services, and content databases in sequential order.

4. SharePoint opens the Central Admin web site, after completing the previous step, and then schedules a timer service job to upgrade each of the site collections in the farm.

5. Run the SharePoint Products Configuration Wizard on all other servers in the farm (excluding the SQL Server, which has no SharePoint components installed).

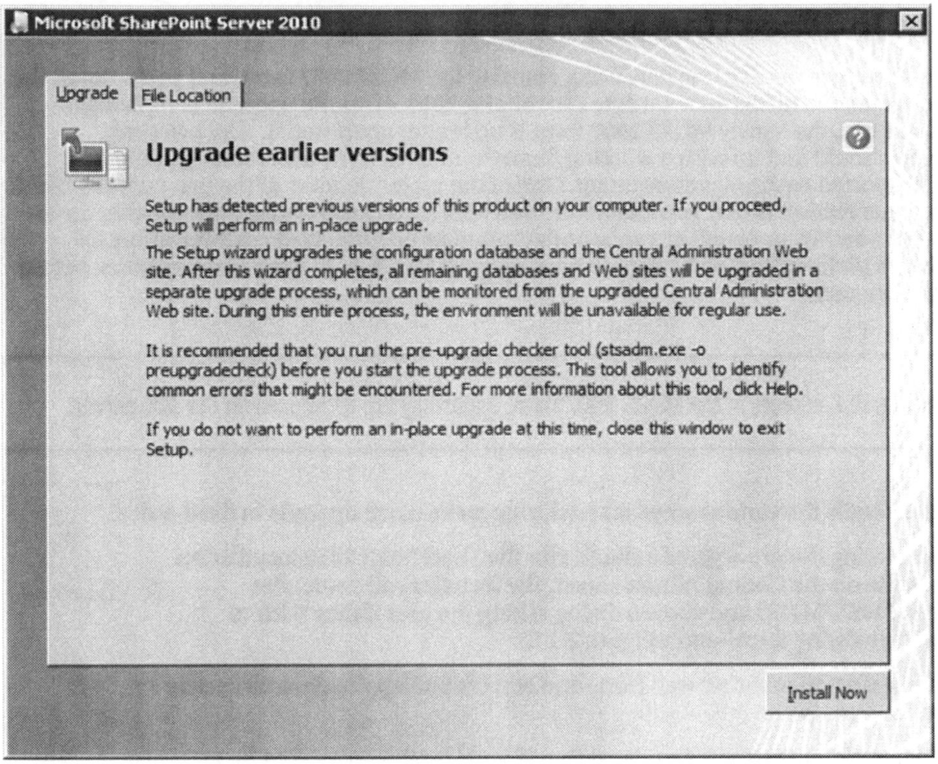

Figure 2-17. Upgrade an earlier version of SharePoint.

What Happens to the Shared Services?

During an in-place upgrade, SharePoint will convert existing Shared Services to the new SharePoint 2010 Managed Services infrastructure. Shared Services in MOSS 2007 resided together and shared a common SSP database and SSP administration web site. In SharePoint 2010, each service maintains its own separate database, service application, proxy, and managed settings (via Central Admin).

Assuming you named your SSP *SharedServices1*; SharePoint will name each new managed service as SharedService1_*ServiceName*, during the in-place upgrade. For example, SharedServices1_Search might be the name SharePoint gives your new Search managed service application. The in-place upgrade copies all service configuration data from the SSP to the respective managed service application database.

At the end of the in-place upgrade, an SSP administration web site remains with mostly legacy Business Data Catalog pages, and if it is not required for BDC administration, you may delete this site.

Performing a Database Attach Upgrade

A database attach upgrade involves detaching databases from the legacy MOSS 2007 farm and attaching them to a new installation of SQL Server hosting the SharePoint 2010 farm.

The database attach upgrade process is intended for upgrades where the SharePoint 2010 infrastructure is completely independent of the legacy MOSS 2007 farm, and thus reduces the risk of destroying the legacy farm during the upgrade process. Database attach also allows the administrator, while performing the upgrade, to copy the databases from a legacy 32-bit environment to the new 64-bit SharePoint 2010 environment.

Database attach is a favorable alternative to the in-place upgrade because it allows users to continue using the legacy farm while the administrator performs the upgrade in the new SharePoint 2010 environment. If something should go wrong, users can continue using the legacy farm with no apparent loss of data or availability of the system. Database attach also allows parallel upgrade of content databases, so the administrator may shorten the upgrade time by running simultaneous database mounts once all the legacy databases are attached to the new SQL Server hosting the SharePoint 2010 farm.

Database attach is not without its own downside. Since the upgrade is only concerned with upgrading content stored in databases, any customizations that rely on file changes in the hive (the SharePoint file system on the web servers) will not carry over to the new 2010 farm. In an ideal world of best practices, the administrator would simply deploy a handful of feature packages, containing the customizations and supporting the new platform, and all customizations and content would come together in the new SharePoint 2010 farm. However, it is often the case that developers have made changes to the hive files manually. Some customizations involve code development that may not be compatible with the SharePoint 2010 architecture. Customization may consist of branding (more on the Visual Upgrade later in this chapter), and other customizations may make assumptions about the SharePoint database schema (I shudder at the thought of this last one). All of a sudden, the in-place upgrade does not seem so bad, does it?

If database attach is the way to go for you, the following list details the various steps taken during this upgrade method:

1. Stand up a new SharePoint 2010 farm, according to the Microsoft requirements and best practices (see earlier in this chapter for installing SharePoint 2010 fresh).

2. Detach the content and SSP databases (or make backups) from the SQL Server hosting the legacy farm, and then attach these databases to the SQL Server hosting the SharePoint 2010 farm.

   a. In SQL Server 2005, use SQL Server Management Studio. Right-click the database and select Tasks and then Detach. Copy the MDF and LDF files to the SQL Server hosting SP2010. Right-click the detached database and select Tasks, and then Attach.

   b. In SQL Server 2008, use SQL Server Management Studio. Expand the server and databases node; right-click the database and select Tasks and then Detach. Copy the MDF and LDF files to the SQL Server hosting SP2010. Right-click the detached database and select Tasks and then Attach.

3. Add the new content databases to the SharePoint 2010 farm via PowerShell command or STSADM command-line, and SharePoint will upgrade them (read on for more details).

Read-only Databases

As an administrator of SharePoint, you will want to consider the time it takes to perform an upgrade of SharePoint 2007 to 2010 and the impact on the users, whether in-place or database attach is used. As discussed, in-place takes the legacy farm offline, and users will no longer be able to access the SharePoint system until the new version is up and running. The database attach approach allows users to continue accessing the legacy system while the upgrade takes place in the new SharePoint 2010 environment—but what about any changes that users make to the legacy farm while the upgrade is in process?

To avoid losing new changes made in the legacy system during a database attach upgrade, Microsoft recommends making databases read-only in the legacy farm. The following steps document the recommended approach to using read-only databases:

▪ **Note** SharePoint will not allow an upgrade on a read-only database, so when using the this approach, be sure to restore the database copy to SQL Server and then enable read-write mode before adding the database to the farm.

The following list details the steps involved in upgrading with the read-only database attach approach:

1. Set the source database to read-only mode, as follows:

    a. In SQL Server 2000, use SQL Server Enterprise Manager. Right-click the database, select Properties, and under the Options tab check the Read-Only check box under Access.

    b. In SQL Server 2005, use SQL Server Management Studio. Right-click the database, and select Properties and then Options, and under Other Options in the State section set Database Read-Only to true.

    c. In SQL Server 2008, use SQL Server Management Studio. Expand the server and databases node, right-click the database, and select Properties. Then select Options, and under Other Options in the State section set Database Read-only to true.

2. Back up the content and shared services databases, as follows:

    a. In SQL Server 2000, use SQL Server Enterprise Manager. Right-click the database, and select All Tasks and then Backup Database. Back up the Complete database and specify the destination as a location on disk.

    b. In SQL Server 2005, use SQL Server Management Studio. Right-click the database, and select Tasks and then Backup. Back up the Full database and specify the destination as a location on disk.

    c. In SQL Server 2008, use SQL Server Management Studio. Expand the server and databases node; right-click the database and select Tasks and then Backup. Back up the Full database and specify the destination as a location on disk.

3. Restore the content and shared services databases to the new SQL Server, hosting SharePoint 2010, as follows:

   a. In SQL Server 2005, use SQL Server Management Studio. Right-click Databases, and then select Restore Database. Select the most recent backup from your disk backup of the legacy database.

   b. In SQL Server 2008, use SQL Server Management Studio. Expand the server and databases node, right-click Databases, and then select Restore Database. Select the most recent backup from your disk backup of the legacy database.

4. See the next section for details about adding the new databases to the SharePoint 2010 farm.

Attaching a Content Database to a SharePoint 2010 Web Application

With the new SharePoint 2010 SQL Server Farm populated with a content database, it is now time to attach the content database to a web application, so that the content is usable within SharePoint. First, verify the database using the following PowerShell command:

▨ **Note** To run PowerShell commands, from the Start menu, choose All Programs, click Microsoft SharePoint 2010 Products, and then click SharePoint 2010 Management Shell.

```
Test-SPContentDatabase –Name <Database Name> -WebApplication <URL>
```

Database Name is the name of the database you wish to check and *URL* is the web application URL that we will eventually attach the content database.

Because a web application may leverage multiple content databases, which contain one or many site collections, be sure to attach the content database that has the root site collection *first*. Once you have attached the content database containing the root site collection, you may then attach other content databases.

To attach (and thus upgrade) a legacy content database to a SharePoint 2010 web application, use either the following PowerShell command or the equivalent STSADM command. Microsoft does not support attaching a legacy content database via Central Admin. Here's the PowerShell command:

```
Mount-SPContentDatabase -Name <DatabaseName> -DatabaseServer <ServerName> -WebApplication <URL> [-Updateuserexperience]
```

For more information about this PowerShell command, please see: http://technet.microsoft.com/en-us/library/ff607581.aspx. The STSADM command looks like this:

```
stsadm -o addcontentdb -url <URL> -databasename <DatabaseName>
```

For more information about the STSADM add content DB command, please see: http://technet.microsoft.com/en-us/library/cc263422%28office.12%29.aspx.

After completing the database attach to the web application, assuming you did not see any glaring errors, open Central Admin, and check the status of the upgrade:

1. In Central Admin, click Upgrade and Migration.

2. Click Check Upgrade Status.

If you run into issues, check the upgrade log file at the following location: %COMMONPROGRAMFILES%\Microsoft Shared\web server extensions\14\LOGS. SharePoint names the logs in the following format: Upgrade-YYYYMMDD-HHMMSS-SSS.log.

Attaching the Shared Services Database to SharePoint 2010

If your legacy SharePoint made little use of the Shared Services, then an upgrade of the SSP database is unnecessary and you can set up new instances of Managed Service Applications. However, in all likelihood, your site may have at least configured SharePoint Search, or perhaps the User Profile Import, Excel Services, or Business Data Catalog.

■ **Note** Be sure to attach and upgrade the SSP database before upgrading My Site site collections.

Before diving into the SSP upgrade, you must ensure that the Managed Metadata service is up and running and the User Profile Service configured. The Managed Metadata service is not complicated to set up, and you can ensure that it is running from Central Administration's Services tab on the server. The UPS requires a little more work, and thus is the topic of the next subsection. Shortly thereafter, we will visit the steps to upgrade My Sites.

Configuring the User Profile Service

Now I would like to take you on a whirlwind installation of the User Profile Service. The UPS can be fiddly to set up and get working correctly, and it is one of those services that will stall in a Starting mode before rudely informing you something is wrong after you have sat around waiting for a few minutes. UPS relies on the Forefront Identity Manager (FIM) application, which you may have observed installing during the install of the prerequisites, earlier in this chapter. Discussion of FIM is outside the scope of this book, but it is important to know that UPS requires it, and if anything goes wrong during the configuration of UPS, it is almost often because of misconfiguration in the SharePoint farm, lack of user permissions, or Active Directory related. The following steps should keep you on a straight road to installing UPS with minimal issues:

1. Create a new Application Pool for the User Profile Service with the following PowerShell command (see earlier in this chapter for details about recommended domain accounts):

New-SPServiceApplicationPool -Name <ApplicationPoolName> -Account <DOMAIN\username>

2. Verify that the Managed Metadata Service is started:

a. Visit Central Administration.

b. Click Application Management.

c. Click Manage Service Applications.

d. Check in the list for the Managed Metadata service and verify that it is started.

3. Create a new User Profile Service Application (delete an existing one from Central Admin, if it exists) with the following PowerShell command: \

```
New-SPProfileServiceApplication -applicationpool <ApplicationPoolName> -Name
<ServiceApplicationName> -Profiledbname <DatabaseName> [-Profiledbserver <ServerName>]
```

4. Where: `ApplicationPoolName` is the name of the application pool created earlier.
   `ServiceApplicationName` is the name of the new service application created.
   `DatabaseName` is the name of the database to contain user profile data
   `ServerName` is the name of the SQL Server hosting the user profile database
   Make sure to use the legacy SSP database, containing the user profile data in the `DatabaseName` parameter.

5. Check the upgrade status in Central Administration, in the Upgrade and Migration section.

6. Create a proxy for the new User Profile Service Application, with the following PowerShell command:
   ```
   New-SPProfileServiceApplicationProxy -ServiceApplication
   <ProfileServiceApplicationID> -Name <ProxyName> -DefaultProxyGroup
   ```
   Where:
   `ProfileServiceApplicationID` is the GUID of the profile service just created.
   `ProxyName` is the name of the new proxy.
   `DefaultProxyGroup` indicates proxy be added to the default service farm group

7. Ensure the farm account has full control of the User Profile Service, as follows:

   a. Visit Central Administration.

   b. Click Application Management.

   c. Click Manage Service Applications.

   d. Click on the User Profile Service application row (not the link), to highlight it.

   e. Click Administrators on the Ribbon.

   f. Add the farm account and account running the UPS service to the Administrators for the User Profile Service box.

8. Start the User Profile Service, as follows:

   g. Visit Central Administration.

   h. Click System Settings.

   i. Click Manage Service on Server.

   j. Click Start, next to the User Profile Service.

k. In the Select the User Profile Application dialog, select the new UPS application.

l. In the Service Account Name and Password section, type and confirm the UPS service account credentials, click OK.

9. Check for availability of user profiles. From the User Profile Service Application (created earlier), you'll find them under Application Management Manage Service Applications.

10. Under Manage Services on Server within Central Admin, start the User Profile Synchronization Service; then specify the UPS service application created earlier, and the UPS service account name and password.

USER PROFILE SERVICE BEST PRACTICES

The User Profile Service is one of the more problematic aspects of configuration to get right when setting up a new SharePoint 2010 or upgrading to a new SharePoint installation. This being the case, the following list includes some best practices to get UPS working:

- Never start the User Profile Service from the server services control panel, as this will corrupt the configuration– always start the service from Central Administration.

- The UPS service will show as Starting for some time, do not be disheartened, it will eventually change status to Started (or Stopped if something has gone wrong).

- Ensure the UPS service account has Replicating Directory Changes permissions in the Active Directory.

- Grant Replicating Directory Changes permissions on the Configuration Naming Context for the domain, ADSIEdit.msc, Connect to Configuration Partition, right-click the partition, choose Properties, and grant the permission from the Security tab.

- If the Active Directory is running on Windows 2003 or earlier, ensure that the UPS service account is a member of the Pre Windows 2000 Compatible access group.

- All SharePoint 2010 service accounts must have the AD permissions: Read and Allowed to Authenticate.

- Ensure the UPS service account is a local admin on each front-end web server.

- Ensure all SharePoint 2010 service accounts are a member of WSS_WPG and WSS_ADMIN_WPG on each front-end web server.

- SharePoint supports SQL named instances (ServerName\Instancename), but UPS does not. Either install June 2010 CU or configure an alias (http://www.harbar.net/articles/sp2010ups2.aspx#ups4)

Upgrading My Sites

Not every MOSS 2007 installation makes use of My Sites, but those organizations that provide My Site functionality probably understand and embrace the benefits of personalization capabilities in the SharePoint platform. Therefore, these same organizations will most likely want to upgrade their My Sites to the new SharePoint 2010 platform.

■ **Note** Ensure the User Profile Service and Managed Metadata Services are up and running before performing My Site upgrades. See the previous section in this chapter on UPS configuration.

Every user's My Site in SharePoint consists of a dedicated site collection, housed in a single My Site content database, which itself, may stand alone—hosting all My Site collections—or with siblings for distribution of data. Similar to the upgrading of content-based site collections, the process of mounting My Site databases in the new SharePoint 2010 farm and attaching the collections to a My Site host application is detailed in the following steps:

1. Create a new web application (this is going to be the My Sites host application), via Central Administration, under Application Management

2. Click Manage Content Databases, under Application Management on the home page of Central Admin, and then remove the new content database attached to the new web application you just created.

3. Run the following PowerShell command:
   `Test-SPContentDatabase –Name <Database Name> -WebApplication <URL>`
   Where:
   `Database Name` is the name of the legacy My Sites database.
   `URL` is the URL of the My Sites host application, just created.

4. Fix any errors indicated in the output of the previous command, especially any pertaining to missing features or missing files in the hive.

5. Add the My Site database to the SharePoint 2010 farm with the following STSADM command (or `Mount-SPContentDatabase` PowerShell command):
   `STSADM -o addcontentdb -url http://<mysitehostURL> -databasename <2007 MySite content database> [-databaseserver <the database server from above>]`

6. Check the upgrade status in Central Admin, under Upgrade and Migration.

7. Navigate to the User Profile Service application under Manage Service Applications

8. Click the Setup My Sites link, under the My Site Settings heading.

9. On the page presented, enter the My Site Host URL and the Personal Sites Location (for example, `/personal`).

10. You should now be ready to check out the presence of My Sites for those users who had a My Site in the legacy MOSS 2007 farm, and create new My Sites for those users who have yet to provision one.

What is the Hybrid Upgrade Approach?

Just when you were thinking to yourself that neither in-place nor database attach upgrade approaches were particularly attractive, there is another option available to you that consists of a hybrid of both in-place and database attach and may smooth over some of the wrinkles associated with in-place and database attach. Microsoft aptly names this—the *hybrid upgrade approach*, and we will explore this further in this section of this chapter.

The hybrid approach to upgrade takes the best of both in-place and database upgrade approaches and provides two flavors.

Hybrid Approach 1

In this scenario, we want to upgrade a production MOSS 2007 farm to SharePoint 2010. The farm has a number of customizations and some third-party software installed, so we wish to take advantage of the in-place capabilities for retaining features and configuration and, in parallel, utilize another SharePoint 2010 farm (staging) to perform the upgrade on the content databases separately.

1. Detach the content databases, My Sites, and SSP databases from the legacy MOSS 2007 farm and make a copy of each.

2. Ensure that the main farm configuration database remains attached, so that Central Administration functions in the legacy farm.

3. Perform an in-place upgrade on the MOSS 2007 farm, which should go quickly, since the only parts to upgrade are binary files, files in the hive, and the SharePoint farm configuration.

4. In parallel, attach the legacy content, My Sites, and SSP databases to a separate SharePoint 2010 farm, following the steps indicated in the prior section of this chapter.

5. You may upgrade the content databases in parallel to speed up the process in the prior step.

6. Finally, detach the new upgraded databases from the staging SharePoint 2010 farm and attach them to the production farm. Since the databases are now in SP2010 format, the attach process should not take very long.

The above approach assumes that the hardware running the legacy MOSS 2007 farm is sufficient and meets the requirements for hosting SharePoint 2010, but it does allow the administrator to upgrade on existing production equipment with no loss to installed customizations or third party components.

The process of separating the databases and performing an upgrade on another farm adds a layer of protection in retaining backups of the legacy data and rollback path if the administrator holds off on the in-place upgrade portion until the database upgrades complete.

Hybrid Approach 2

In this scenario, we plan to upgrade a production MOSS 2007 farm to SharePoint 2010. The farm has customizations and third party components installed. We do *not* have a spare SharePoint 2010 staging server to perform the database attach upgrades.

1. Detach the content databases, My Sites, and SSP databases from the legacy MOSS 2007 farm, and make a copy.

2. Ensure that the main farm configuration database remains attached, so that Central Administration functions in the legacy farm.

3. Perform an in-place upgrade on the MOSS 2007 farm, which should go quickly, since the only parts to upgrade are binary files, files in the hive, and the SharePoint farm configuration.

4. After confirming that the new SharePoint 2010 production farm is operational (Central Admin is running), attach the legacy MOSS 2007 content, My Site, and SSP databases to the new production farm.

This approach is ideal when hardware is sparse, but the hardware and configuration running MOSS 2007 meets the requirements for hosting SharePoint 2010. Detaching the databases before the in-place upgrade ensures that we retain the original content configuration, and may roll back if we are able to reinstall MOSS 2007. Unlike scenario 1, scenario 2 does not allow us to parallel track the upgrade process with the in-place, nor do we have the opportunity to try the database attach process before attempting the in-place for faster rollback. However, this scenario is better than a straight in-place upgrade in that it affords the administrator greater control of the content, My Sites, and SSP upgrade, without the risk to the content—typically, the most valuable part of any online service.

Using Alternate Access Mappings to Avoid Downtime

Upgrading a SharePoint 2007 farm is troublesome if the farm is critical to users, and administrators must avoid downtime. An in-place upgrade takes the server offline too long and has risk of failure, a database attach upgrade is too costly in hardware resources and time to rebuild customizations, and the hybrid approach requires time to perform the upgrade on databases. In short, upgrading SharePoint involves some downtime, but Microsoft has provided an additional feature to ease the pain for users of a critical system, using *Alternate Access Mappings*.

Alternate access mappings allow SharePoint 2010 to redirect URL requests at the site collection level to another farm when the site collection does not exist at the requested source URL. The following list explains the process for configuring AAM to route all new site requests to a new SharePoint 2010 farm and redirect to the legacy farm when a site does not exist in the new platform. The following steps assume the existence of a MOSS 2007 platform at the address portal.domain.com:

1. Configure a new SharePoint 2010 farm on the domain name *portal.domain*.com.

2. Configure the legacy MOSS 2007 farm on another domain, *oldportal.domain*.com.

3. Configure Alternate Access Mappings in the new farm from command-line to redirect the old farm in cases where the site collection does not exist, as follows:
   stsadm -o addzoneurl -url http://*portal.domain*.com -zonemappedurl

```
http://portal.domain.com -urlzone default -redirectionurl
http://oldportal.domain.com
```

This command instructs SharePoint 2010 to perform a redirect using HTTP 302 to the *oldportal.domain*.com address when the site collection does not exist.

Alternate access mapping redirection, in conjunction with a database attach upgrade, allows administrators to perform a gradual upgrade of the content on the legacy MOSS 2007 farm to SharePoint 2010 without disrupting the users. As soon as a database attach upgrade for a given site collection completes, and a new requested site collection is available in the new platform, SharePoint will cease redirection.

Of course, this AAM redirection and database upgrade still involves all the same considerations as that of a regular database attach upgrade; the administrator has to ensure carry-over of customizations in the new farm, and account for stale content in the new farm if changes are made in the legacy farm. However, with this approach the users should see no downtime as the migration to the new platform takes place.

■ **Note** Redirection is only at the site collection level, so if a user links a page that does not exist but the site collection does exist, then the user will experience an HTTP 404 error.

Visual Upgrade

Microsoft has adopted a no-break policy when it comes to the user interface and upgrading a MOSS 2007 farm to SharePoint 2010. By default, when upgrading the legacy farm to the new platform, the chosen configuration for a visual upgrade is to leave the UI in the legacy MOSS 2007 look and feel. This ensures that site owners and site users are not alarmed when switching over to the new SharePoint platform. Retaining the legacy look and feel is paramount when upgrading public-facing web sites, hosted in SharePoint, as Internet sites typically contain a large amount of custom branding, which should not break when upgrading the platform.

Before diving deeper into Visual Upgrade specifics, let us take a moment to review the inner workings of the SharePoint User Interface from a high-level view…

Every SharePoint site collection contains a hidden document library, called the Master Page Gallery. This gallery contains various master pages and page layouts in use or potential use within the site collection. If you are unsure of what I mean by master pages, then I recommend taking a quick visit to your nearest bookstore and picking up any good book on ASP.NET 2.0 or above, since master pages, and pages based on them, are a large part of ASP.NET development. Page layouts are born of the SharePoint publishing feature (as of MOSS 2007), and provide template capabilities to render page instance content as a web page. I shall leave discussion of the specifics of the SharePoint publishing features to another time, and for now you,—the reader,—can think of page layouts as templates containing presentation markup (HTML) and placeholders for page content (metadata).

All new sites created in a site collection (the root site included) contain pages that use the master page called default.master, for common branding elements shared across all pages in the site. This master page provides the common look and feel that users have grown to recognize in SharePoint. Alongside this master page is a cascading style sheet file, called core.css, which contains most of the branding and styling specifics for HTML elements contained in the master page and page layouts.

Public-facing Internet sites and sites based on the publishing site definition use a master page called custom.master. This master page differs from the traditional default.master file in that Microsoft expects web site designers to customize its elements to provide the common branding elements for pages of the Internet web site. One other master page file used a lot in SharePoint is the application.master file, which lives in the SharePoint hive and provides common branding for application pages (also in the hive). Application pages provide the core administration of the platform and allow site administrators to configure sites and sub sites, among other such operations.

Microsoft redesigned the SharePoint 2010 User Interface from scratch, incorporating new UI features, such as the Ribbon (see Figure 2-18). SharePoint 2010 introduces two new master pages, called v4.master and minimal.master, both of which provide the new common branding elements for SharePoint 2010 pages. The minimal master page lacks some of the chrome elements, such as the Site Actions menu, Top Navigation bar, Quick Launch, and Ribbon. SharePoint 2010 also retains the legacy default.master to support MOSS 2007 and WSS 3 look and feel.

Figure 2-18. *The new SharePoint 2010 Ribbon*

It's worth noting that application pages in SharePoint 2010 can now link to master pages in the site Master Page Gallery, and many of the site application pages link to v4.master to provide a consistent look and feel that is SharePoint 2010.

The v4.master and minimal.master files now include a DOCTYPE in the markup, which is a major change from that of MOSS 2007, which did not. The inclusion of the DOCTYPE tells the browser to use the new CSS rendering engine—without it, the browser defaults to quirks mode, which is an older compatibility mode for rendering pages.

■ **Note** SharePoint 2010 does not support quirks mode or IE6-style rendering, and much of the out-of-the-box UI does not render on IE6 or earlier as a result.

Switching from Legacy to SharePoint 2010 Branding

After upgrading an existing site collection to the new platform, SharePoint 2010 retains the legacy look and feel of the site collection. If the site collection is based on the publishing template, the custom.master remains intact; otherwise, the site leverages the backward-compatible default.master.

Individual site owners may elect to switch over to the new v4.master for their site, on a site-to-site basis, or the site collection administrator may choose to upgrade the entire site collection to the new skin. Figure 2-19 shows the option to perform a visual upgrade from the Site Actions menu for any site in a site collection that upgraded from SharePoint 2007 and has not yet undergone a visual upgrade.

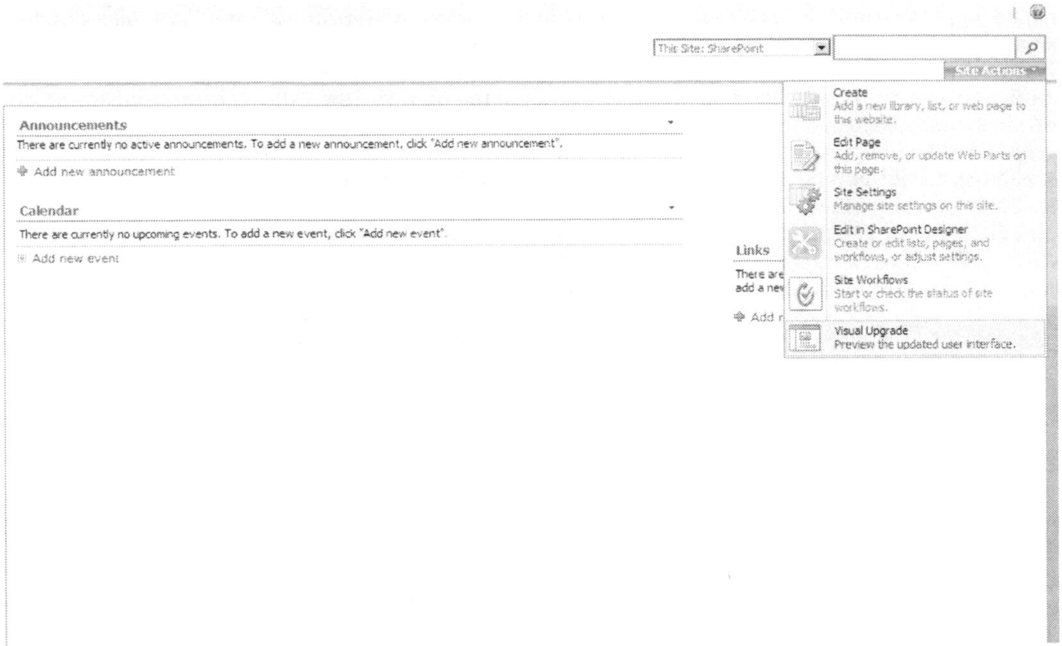

Figure 2-19. *Existence of the visual upgrade option in the Site Actions menu*

Site owners may choose to retain the legacy SharePoint 2007 look and feel, preview the new SharePoint 2010 skin, or adopt the new SharePoint 2010. Figure 2-20 shows the options available to a site owner when they click Visual Upgrade in the Site Actions menu.

Figure 2-20. *Visual Upgrade options*

Think of the middle option, Preview, as the site owner's chance to try out the new SharePoint 2010 without committing, and the last option, Update, as making the step to upgrade the branding. The middle option changes the Site Actions menu and allows the site owner to revert to the legacy look and feel, whereas the last option commits the visual upgrade and removes all trace of Visual Upgrade from the Site Actions menu.

Site collection administrators may upgrade the entire site collection to the new SharePoint 2010 skin by clicking the Visual Upgrade link, under Site Collection Administration, which brings them to the page shown in Figure 2-21, with the option Update All Sites.

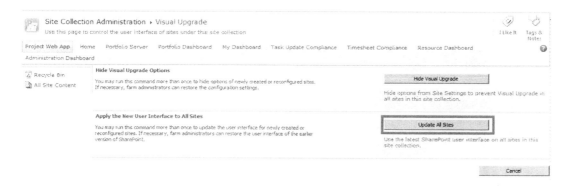

Figure 2-21. *Visual Upgrade for Site Collection Administrators*

Visual Upgrade PowerShell Commands

What happens if you upgrade the entire site collection to the new SharePoint 2010 skin, and then decide that certain sites should remain in the legacy skin? There is a PowerShell command for that:

```
Get-SPSite http://machinename/sites/V3UI | Get-SPWeb "webname" |
Foreach{$_.UIVersionConfigurationEnabled=1;$_.UIVersion=3;$_.Update();}
```

The following PowerShell command will revert to the legacy skin all sites in a site collection:

```
Get-SPSite http://machinename/sites/V3UI | Foreach{$_.
UIVersionConfigurationEnabled=1;$_.UIVersion=3;$_.Update();}
```

To upgrade a single sub-site to the new SharePoint 2010 skin, use the following snippet of PowerShell code:

```
$web = Get-SPWeb http://server/site
$web.UIVersion = 4
$web.UIVersionConfigurationEnabled = 0
$web.Update()
```

To upgrade a complete site collection to the new SharePoint 2010 skin, use the following:

```
$site = Get-SPSite http://server
$site.VisualUpgradeWebs()
```

This concludes the Visual Upgrade discussion in this chapter. Of course, there is much more information out there on the Internet, and one such article for designers to read is the article on converting custom branding from SharePoint 2007 to SharePoint 2010, to include the Ribbon: http://msdn.microsoft.com/en-us/library/ee539981.aspx.

Welcome to the Central Administration Web Site

If you have read this entire chapter so far, rather than jumping directly to this section, you will already have seen references to the SharePoint Central Administration web site, or Central Admin for short. In the earlier section I glossed over the use of Central Admin, so now I'll take you on a larger tour.

Simply put, the Central Administration web site is the user graphical user interface to management of the SharePoint 2010 platform and its configuration. Figure 2-22 shows the opening Central Admin home page, familiar to any administrator who has installed SharePoint 2010 and ready to use the platform for purpose.

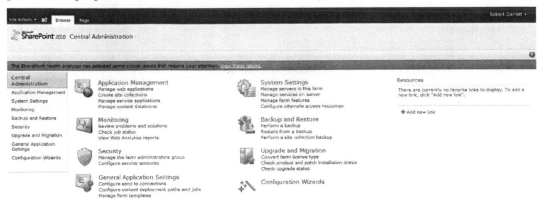

Figure 2-22. The Central Administration web site home page

The Central Admin interface is not the only means to administer SharePoint 2010. As in the previous version, SharePoint 2007, Microsoft provides a command-line tool, STSADM. In addition, SharePoint 2010 includes a collection of PowerShell commands. This part of the chapter focuses on Central Admin, which. is the most common interface used for configuration of the platform.

■ **Note** To launch Central Admin from the Start menu, choose Microsoft SharePoint 2010 Products ➤ SharePoint 2010 Central Administration.

No doubt, you have already realized that the Central Admin site runs atop of SharePoint itself and consists of the typical navigation elements and Ribbon that users of a SharePoint team site would expect. The center of the Central Admin home page provides a plethora of links to various functional areas for configuration and administration of the farm, and SharePoint groups these links by functional areas (also listed in the left navigation). Clicking on the heading name for any of these functional areas takes you to another sub-page with many more links to configure SharePoint in that functional category.

Application Management

Administrators coming from SharePoint 2007 are very familiar with the Application Management section. For those readers new to the SharePoint platform, Microsoft names all new IIS web sites in SharePoint as Web Applications. A web application consists of files on the IIS server, a connection to one or many content SQL server databases, and a web.config file. SharePoint keeps track of all web applications. Application Management provides administrators with the capability to create new web applications, administer existing web applications, and delete old web applications.

Every SharePoint web application hosts at least one site collection (the root site collection). A site collection consists of a hierarchy of sites and sub sites that constitute as the "web site" content and structure. SharePoint web applications may have multiple site collections associated, each site collection hosts in only one database (a database can have multiple site collections), and a web application may associate with multiple content database. Figure 2-23 shows the Application Management page.

Web Applications
Manage web applications | Configure alternate access mappings

Site Collections
Create site collections | Delete a site collection | Confirm site use and deletion | Specify quota templates | Configure quotas and locks | Change site collection administrators | View all site collections | Configure self-service site creation

Service Applications
Manage service applications | Configure service application associations | Manage services on server

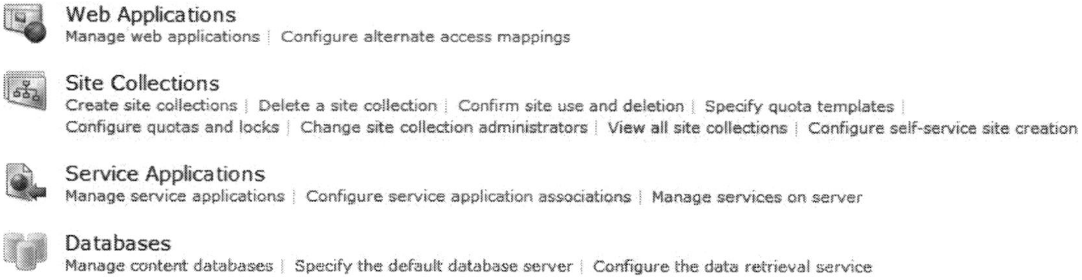

Databases
Manage content databases | Specify the default database server | Configure the data retrieval service

Figure 2-23. *Application Management*

Microsoft has attempted to disambiguate the various functions in Central Admin. Thus, many of the links shown in Figure 2-23, and other areas of Central Admin, consist of well-named titles—"Create site collections" or "View all site collections," for example.

Creating Your First Web Application

Typically, the first task of a SharePoint Administrator after installing SharePoint is to create a new web application, to host the organization's Intranet/Extranet/Public Web site. The following steps detail the process of creating a web application, adding a root site collection, and then configuring Alternate Access Mappings, so that the application is available to users on the network. All of the steps take place from the Application Management section of the Central Admin site.

1. Click on the Manage Web Applications link

2. The next page shows a list of already configured web applications, which includes Central Admin and the My Sites host application.

3. From the Ribbon, click the New icon.

4. Next, SharePoint shows a dialog with a form for you to enter details about the new web application, as in Figure 2-24. Here we see a new feature of SharePoint 2010—dialogs, reducing the amount of navigation between pages that users experienced in SharePoint 2007.

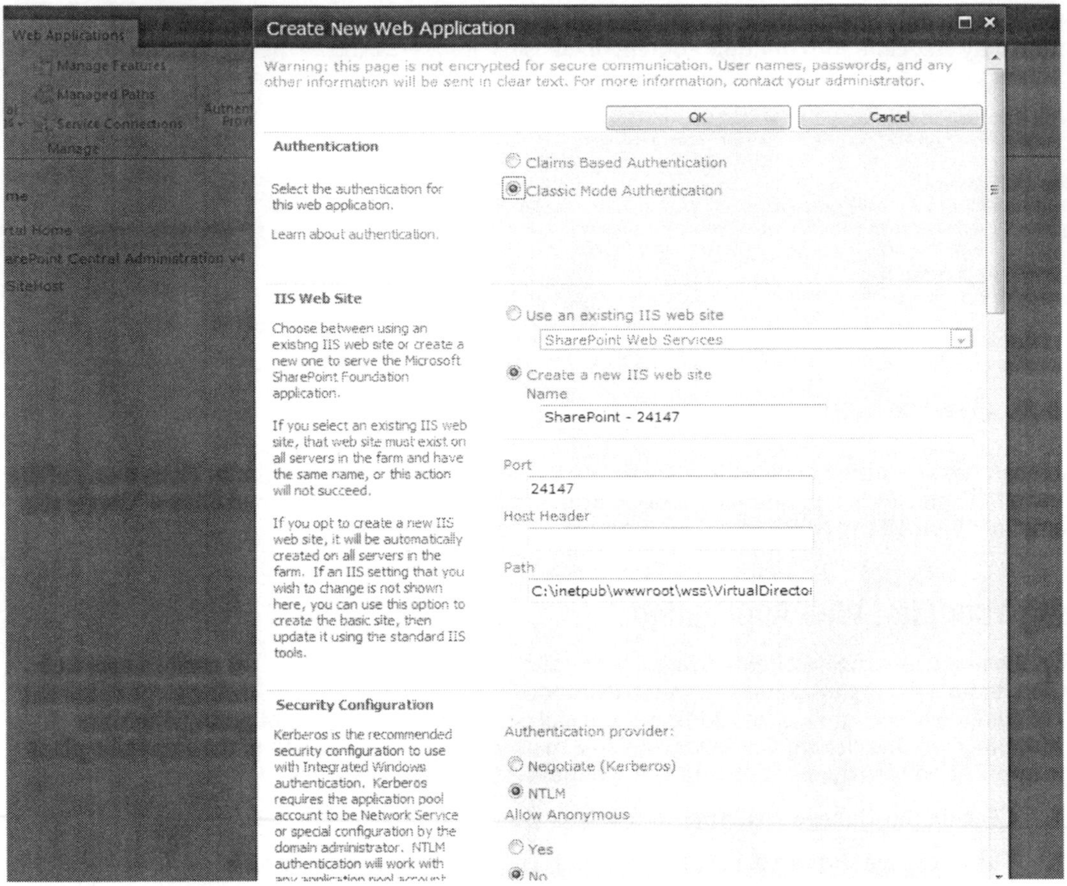

Figure 2-24. Create new web application dialog

Continue through the following steps, some of which I will explain as we go:

5. Leave Authentication set in Classic Mode. This configures the web application with standard NTLM or Kerberos authentication, as opposed to Claims-Based Authentication, which I will cover later.

6. Complete the details for IIS, the name of the web application, location on disk (I advise sticking with the default location), port number, and any host headers.

7. Configure security at NTLM, unless you have Kerberos enabled and know how to configure this with SharePoint.

8. Do not use secure sockets unless you have preconfigured a certificate for the web application and public domain.

9. If you plan to allow public access to your site, or parts of your site, click Yes to Allow Anonymous.

10. Leave the Public URL and Zone as default.

11. Create a new Application Pool, using an application pool manage account.

12. Provide the name of a new Content Database, and database authentication as Windows.

13. Leave Failover database as empty.

14. Leave the Service Applications group as default (more on Service Applications shortly).

15. Do *not* enable CEIP.

16. Click OK and wait a few seconds.

After SharePoint finishes creating the web application, you should see a dialog with a completion message, a link to create a site collection, and an OK button. Clicking OK, going back to the web applications list page, and then selecting the newly created web application will show more options on the Ribbon, as in Figure 2-25.

Figure 2-25. *Web Application options on the Ribbon*

Some of the icon options above might be self-explanatory; here is a quick summary:

- New—Create a new web application.

- Extend—Create a new web application that uses the same content as another web application, thus extending the capabilities of an existing web application.

- Delete—Delete the selected web application.

- Authentication Providers—Set up authentication for the selected web application.

- Self-Service Site Creation—Allow users to create their own site collections.

- Permissions—Available for web parts, blocked file types, and explicit user permissions for the web application selected.

- Policies for users, anonymous users, and configuration of permission levels—To make use of anonymous policy, ensure that the anonymous authentication option checked in the web application settings (under authentication providers for the zone).

Creating a Site Collection

With our web application created, it is now time to create a root site collection, so that we can host content and make use of our new web application as a SharePoint site. The following steps take you through the process of creating a new site collection on the web application created in the previous section.

1. Go back to the Application Management area of Central Admin.

2. Click the Create Site Collections link.

3. In the next page, select the correct web application in the drop-down box at the top left of the page.

4. Give the site collection a name and description.

5. Choose the desired template. Various template types (site definitions) exist, each with its own set of features enabled and default sub-sites and lists. Choose Team as an example of an Intranet collaboration work site.

6. Provide a *DOMAIN\name* username for the primary and secondary site collection administrators (you can add more later) using the site collection administrator settings on the site collection.

7. Leave the quota option default.

8. Click OK to create the site collection.

Assuming all is well, SharePoint should come back with a page containing the default link to the new site collection and a message indicating successful creation.

Alternate Access Mappings

Alternate access mappings allow mapping of multiple internal URLs, known to SharePoint, to a public URL, known to external users. Typical uses of AAM include the creation of multiple public URLs to map to a single SharePoint application so that the application is accessible from different zones, each with its own different authentication scheme. The topic of AAM can get quite involved, so I have attempted to explain the configuration of AAM, at a high-level, using the following scenarios.

Scenario 1: Extended Publishing Site with Forms-based Authentication

In this scenario, two web applications exist in SharePoint; the first is an internally based application on the URL http://intranet, which requires NTLM authentication for users on the internal network to access the company Intranet. The site collection attached to the web application is a publishing site. The extended web application uses forms-based authentication with a SQL database as the user store, and allows external users of the network to log into the company Intranet across the Internet using the URL http://intranet.company.com.

Figure 2-26 shows the Alternate Access Mappings for the Intranet application described in the scenario. Here we see two public URLs mapped to each internal URL. Depending on which URL a user connects to, the site will depict how this user sees absolute links to pages, documents, and other content, on the site: http://intranet/lists/mylist/blah.doc or http://intranet.company.com/list/mylist/blah.doc as an example.

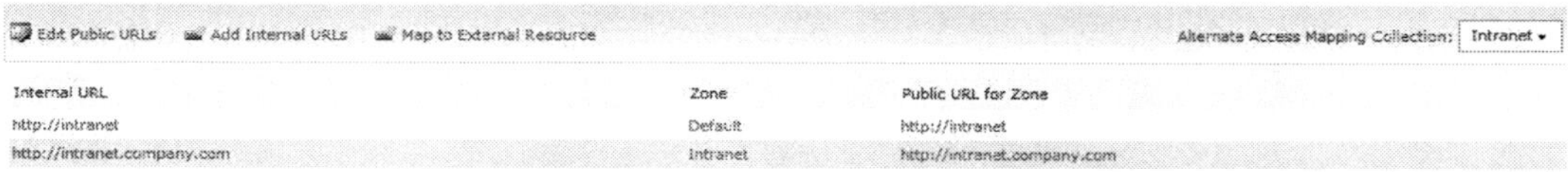

Internal URL	Zone	Public URL for Zone
http://intranet	Default	http://intranet
http://intranet.company.com	Intranet	http://intranet.company.com

Figure 2-26. Alternate Access Mappings for scenario 1

Click on Edit Public URLs to see the public URLs for a given application. Each public URL associated with a SharePoint application binds to one of five zones: Default, Intranet, Internet, Custom, or Extranet (shown in Figure 2-27). The names of these zones hold no functional meaning except to provide the administrator meaningful labels for each access public access point to the web application.

Alternate Access Mapping Collection: **Intranet ▾**

Default
> http://intranet

Intranet
> http://intranet.company.com

Internet
>

Custom
>

Extranet
>

Figure 2-27. Zones for public URLs

Scenario 2—Reverse Proxy and Load-Balanced Web Application

In this scenario, a reverse proxy server, like that built into ISA server (a firewall server application) sits between the users and the SharePoint application. The public URL of the SharePoint application is http://intranet.company.com, and the ISA server forwards requests to either http://intranet1.local or http://intranet2.local, depending on load.

Figure 2-28 shows the Alternate Access Mappings for scenario 2.

http://intranet.company.com	Intranet	http://intranet.company.com
http://intranet1.local	Intranet	http://intranet.company.com
http://intranet2.local	Intranet	http://intranet.company.com

Figure 2-28. Alternate Access Mappings for scenario 2

Users access the site using the public URL http://intranet.company.com and the ISA server performs reverse proxy to authenticate the users before forwarding the request to SharePoint. Regardless of which load-balanced server ISA redirects the user, all links on returned pages start with http://intranet.company.com. This ensures that there are no broken links and that the user does not see links to an internal server application. To add additional internal URLs, click the Add Internal URLs link and, in the resulting page, add the new internal URL and choose the zone to map to the public URL, in this case the Intranet zone.

Mapping to an External Resource

Clicking the Map to an External Resource link on the AAM page allows the administrator to map a URL not hosted in SharePoint to a web application. This feature is especially useful when configuring federated search to crawl an external resource. For example, let us assume that the administrator has configured search to crawl a separate HR site that is not in SharePoint—http://hrsite. This URL is not accessible to users coming into the SharePoint application on a public URL across the Internet, but is available on http://hrsite.company.com.

In Figure 2-29, I created a new external resource called http://hrsite, by clicking the Map to External Resource link. I then clicked Edit Public URLs and added the URL http://hrsite.company.com to the Intranet zone for the external resource I just created. SharePoint search will index the site http://hrsite but the links in the search results show http://hrsite.compamy.com if the user accessed the hosting SharePoint application from the Internet. This behavior is very much like that in scenario 1, but in this case, the resource is not a SharePoint application but an external HR site.

Edit Public URLs	Add Internal URLs	Map to External Resource		Alternate Access Mapping Collection: HR site ▾
Internal URL		**Zone**	**Public URL for Zone**	
http://hrsite		Default	http://hrsite	
http://hrsite.company.com		Intranet	http://hrsite.company.com	

Figure 2-29. External resource mapping

Service Applications

Service applications are the new approach taken by SharePoint 2010 to replace the legacy Shared Service Provider of MOSS 2007. The SSP centralized shared service architecture for use across a SharePoint farm, but suffered from a major flaw—the architecture did not allow sharing of services across multiple farms or dispersion of services on different servers in a farm. The new Service Application architecture addresses this flaw by separating the services as individual applications.

Clicking the Manage Service Applications link from the home page of Central Admin (or the link from the Application Management section) gives a page like that shown in Figure 2-30.

Name	Type	Status
Application Discovery and Load Balancer Service Application	Application Discovery and Load Balancer Service Application	Started
Application Discovery and Load Balancer Service Application Proxy_8fd781be-d448-4727-baa4-79a5af07bf99	Application Discovery and Load Balancer Service Application Proxy	Started
Enterprise Search Service Application	Search Service Application	Started
Enterprise Search Service Application Proxy	Search Service Application Proxy	Started
Metadata Service Application	Managed Metadata Service	Started
Metadata Service Application Proxy	Managed Metadata Service Connection	Started
Search Administration Web Service for Enterprise Search Service Application	Search Administration Web Service Application	Started
Security Token Service Application	Security Token Service Application	Started
WSS_UsageApplication	Usage and Health Data Collection Service Application	Started
WSS_UsageApplication	Usage and Health Data Collection Proxy	Stopped

Figure 2-30. Managed Applications list

Managed applications consist of a service and proxy. Service Orientated Architecture (SOA) allows administrators the flexibility to host service applications on any farm server and proxy on another to distribute functionality within and across SharePoint farms.

Earlier in this chapter we used the Farm Configuration wizard, which configures a number of the SharePoint Managed Service Applications, such as the Metadata Service, Excel Services, Enterprise Search, and WSS Usage Data application, to name a few. The SharePoint 2010 Service Application model allows developers to extend the capabilities of SharePoint by developing custom service for deployment in SharePoint farms.

Access to the configuration of each managed service is via the SharePoint Ribbon. Clicking on the managed service application in the list (not the proxy) enables its icons in the Ribbon. The Properties icon allows the administrator to change common application properties, such as the name of the service application, database, failover database, or other category. Clicking the Manage icon provides the administrator access to the specific configuration of the service application, which differs for each service application. For example, the Properties icon for the Managed Metadata store presents the administrator with a dialog to change the service application name, database, database authentication, application pool for the service, and so on. Clicking the Manage icon takes the administrator to the admin page for the term store for management of stores, term sets, terms, and related elements. (see Figure 2-31).

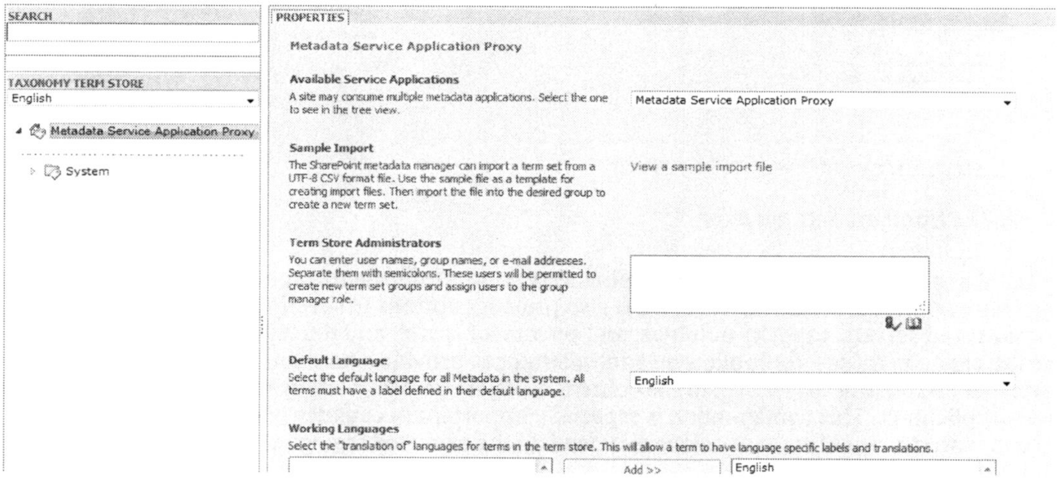

Figure 2-31. The Managed Metadata Store admin page

Configuration Databases

SharePoint stores all content for a given web application in one or many content databases. Each new site collection created and associated with a web application resides in at most *one* content database. A content database may house multiple site collections. This level of flexibility allows SharePoint Architects the ability to scale out their SharePoint farm.

Within Central Administration, under the Application Management section, click Manage content databases and SharePoint shows a page listing content databases for a selected web application. Clicking on the link for the database shows a page like Figure 2-32.

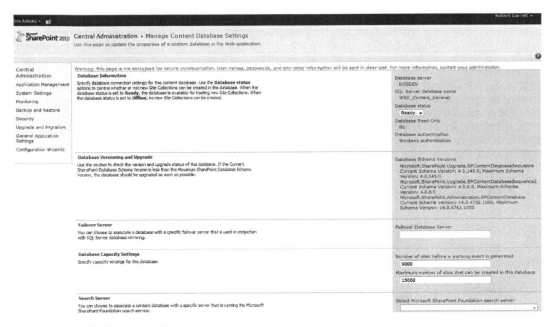

Figure 2-32. The Database Settings page

The Database Settings page shows the administrator status information about the content database, including Name, status, and schema versions. It also provides options to specify a failover database server for mirrored servers, capacity numbers, and servers for search and timer job operations.

Note the capacity fields—these allow an administrator to provide a hard limit on the number of site collections that SharePoint may assign to the content database before creating another content database for the web application. This configuration is especially important in capacity planning because the architect can plan the size of content databases based on the expected storage of each site collection created.

Going back to the content database list for the web applications, administrators can attach content databases not already associated with the web application (use the Remove Database check box in the database settings page to detach). Important to note is that administrators may not use this approach to upgrade a legacy SharePoint 2007 database and should use PowerShell or STSADM instead.

System Settings

A SharePoint farm constitutes as a collection of front-end web servers, index and query servers, application servers, and SQL server—tying everything together using a collection of configuration and content databases. The System Settings section of Central Admin provides configuration for the SharePoint farm major components—Servers, Services, E-mail, and general farm configuration.

In the previous SharePoint 2007 version, many of the settings in the System Settings section were available under the Operations tab. Microsoft did away with the Operations tab and separated the various configuration functions into the sections described in this chapter.

Servers

Within the Server subsection of System Settings, administrators may obtain a list of servers in the farm and manage the services running on any of the servers in the SharePoint farm. Clicking the Manage Servers in This Farm link displays a page similar to Figure 2-33, which lists the various servers and services running on each server. In the example shown, I have just one server running Central Administration, Web Applications, Search components, and a few managed service applications. In a real production scenario, I would expect to see more servers, and those services distributed among those servers for efficiency and service redundancy.

Figure 2-33. Servers in the farm

Using the Servers in This Farm page, you can remove servers from the farm, and assuming you are not trying to remove the only front-end facing web server or Central Admin server, the farm should continue to function. To add a new SharePoint server to an existing farm, choose the option to Join an Existing Farm when running the configuration wizard on a new installation of the SharePoint 2010 server.

Back at the System Settings page, clicking the Manage Services on Server link displays a list of services running (and some possibly stopped) on a given server. A drop-down box at the top right of the page allows an administrator to change the server in context to any other server in the farm. Some of the services in the list are those of the Managed Service Applications—established in the farm configuration and managed in application management. This makes sense, as each managed service application configuration consists of an actual service, an application to manage the service, and the proxy.

Email and Text Messages (SMS)

The E-mail and Text Message (SMS) subsection provides configuration location for the e-mail SMTP server, outgoing e-mail addresses, and the like, as well as the SMS web service, and SharePoint uses these configuration settings when notifying users and administrators of events occurring in the platform.

Farm Management

Notice under the Farm Management subsection the link to manage Alternate Access Mappings. This is just another link to the same configuration page covered in the "Application Management" section. I guess Microsoft just felt it made sense to provide a quick link to AAM configuration for administrators in the process of configuring the farm.

The other links in this subsection take the administrator to pages to configure farm features, solutions, privacy options (Customer Experience Program, Error Reporting, and Online Help settings), and cross-firewall zone settings (external PC and mobile URLs outside the firewall).

Solutions and Features

Farm solutions, features, and user solutions deserve a quick mention. *Features,* in SharePoint lingo, refer to custom or third party units of functionality (Microsoft uses them, too, as part of the platform) that deploy to farm, web application, site collection or sub-site scope. When developing custom components for SharePoint, the best-practice approach is to create a deployable feature that administrators may activate and deactivate at the designated scope (determined at development time). Pick up any good SharePoint 2007/2010 development book to learn about creating new features and deploying them. Features typically deploy via *solution packages*—also known as WSP files.

Clicking the Manage Farm Features link takes you to a list of features deployed at the farm scope. Some of these features show as Activated and some not. Farm features are those features that contain packaged functionality for use across the entire farm. Similar lists of features exist under site collection settings and site settings of a given SharePoint application, and in the manage application settings for a selected web application in Central Admin.

Clicking on Manage Farm Solutions will display a list of solution packages added to the farm (via STSADM or PowerShell). From this configuration screen, you may deploy a solution, retract a solution, or delete it from the farm. User solutions, configured from the Manage User Solutions link, are new to SharePoint 2010. User solutions scope to a specific site collection and do not deploy files or alter the hive—instead developers may create solutions that interact only within the world of the site collection from which the administrator deploys them.

Monitoring

Chapter 10 covers monitoring, so for now let us take a quick nickel tour of the features of SharePoint Monitoring configured via Central Admin. Figure 2-34 shows the Monitoring options in Central Admin.

Health Analyzer
Review problems and solutions | Review rule definitions

Timer Jobs
Review job definitions | Check job status

Reporting
View administrative reports | Configure diagnostic logging | Review Information Management Policy Usage Reports | View health reports |
Configure usage and health data collection | View Web Analytics reports

Figure 2-34. SharePoint Monitoring in Central Admin

New to SharePoint 2010 is the Health Analyzer, which consists of a service application to monitor various areas of the farm and report on problems via category. The default categories include Security, Performance, Configuration, and Availability. The Health Analyzer follows a defined set of rules to determine problems and report on them.

At the core of SharePoint is the timer service, which consists of a Windows service application running on each SharePoint server (except the database server). One of the many jobs of the timer service is to synchronize job activity in the farm. The timer service ensures that all front-end servers synchronize with the main central admin application server for configuration updates, solution deployments, manage health, collate search results, and so on. Out of the box, SharePoint has a large list of timer jobs, which you can display by clicking the Review Job Definitions link. Timer service jobs run on a particular schedule and perform a single or set of tasks. Administrators may enable/disable jobs, execute a job now, or change the schedule of a job from the central admin interface. Only developers may create and remove job definitions via feature activation and deactivation. The second link in this subsection—Check Job Status—enables administrators to check the status of a running job or job that completed, either because it succeeded or failed.

Reporting is another large topic in SharePoint 2010, as this capability has also grown since the release of SharePoint 2007. Within the reporting subsection of Central Admin, administrators may now configure SharePoint tracing—responsible for writing information, warning, and error status to the ULS logs on disk.

■ **Note** The Unified Logging Service (ULS) is very important to a SharePoint administrator. Logs typically live in the hive within the `logs` folder.

Whenever SharePoint 2010 fails to complete an operation, it will attempt to log all output to the most recent log file. Many log files exist in the `logs` directory of the hive (or wherever the administrator has changed the default logging location), typically, one for each day of logging. Clicking the Configure Diagnostic Logging link will allow you to set the verbosity of logging, from only critical errors to very verbose logging. You may also select which areas of SharePoint to log, so if a particular service is failing you may attempt to isolate the problem to the area.

■ **Note** To clear out the default logging directory on the application server, stop the SharePoint Tracing service in Windows first.

The reporting subsection of Monitoring allows administrators to create and review reports on Information Management Policy, Health, and Site Usage/Performance; and Central Admin devotes a whole page to viewing administrative reports.

ULS logs are an important tool to troubleshoot issues in a SharePoint environment. Unfortunately, ULS logs are hard to read and contains significant amount of information. To help make them usable, Microsoft makes available a new tool called SharePoint Diagnostic Studio 2010, which is available as part of the SharePoint Administrator Toolkit:

```
http://go.microsoft.com/fwlink/?LinkId=196866
```

Reporting is another large topic that really deserves more than a few paragraphs in the installation and configuration chapter of this book, so I shall revisit this topic within Chapter 10, on health, monitoring, and disaster recovery.

Backup and Restore

Similar to the Monitoring subsection of Central Admin, Backup and Restore requires more explanation than this brief section can provide, and I cover this topic in Chapter 10.

Since SharePoint 2007, SharePoint has allowed the administrator to back up all or sections of the farm content and configuration to disk. As with most of its automated tasks, SharePoint provides backup and restore operation via a timer service job. The interface in Central Admin allows you to localize the backup and restore to select web applications, managed service applications, and other categories, of the farm as a whole. Figure 2-35 shows the selection screen in the Backup section of Central Admin.

New to SharePoint 2010 is *granular backup*. Administrators could always perform granular backups in SharePoint 2007 via the STSADM command line, which offered a very convenient backup and restore for site collections. SharePoint 2010 now provides the same capability via the Central Admin interface. Likewise, you may also export a site or list via the Central Admin site, which required STSADM in the previous version. Similar to farm and farm component backup, granular backups utilize timer service jobs to accomplish automated backup/restore.

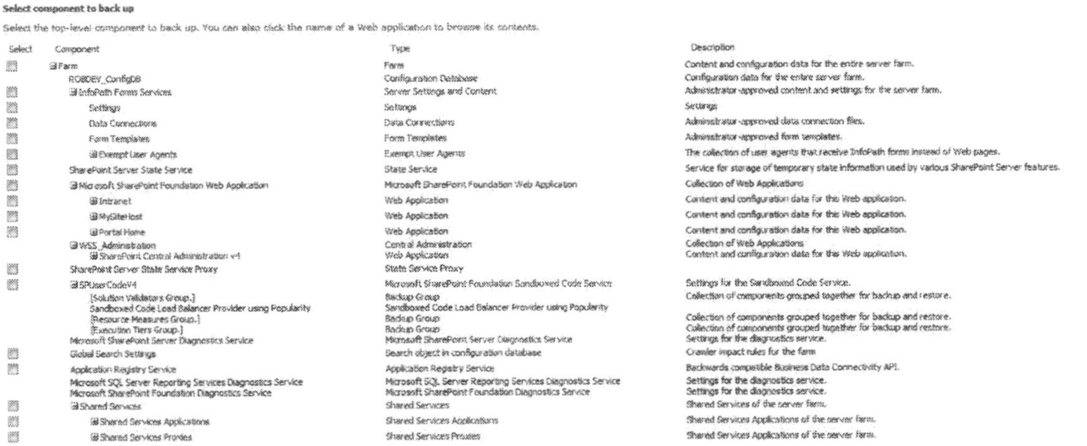

Figure 2-35. *Backup selection in Central Admin*

Security

Security has always existed as a core pillar of functionality in SharePoint, even in SPS 2003. Over time, the security infrastructure in the SharePoint platform has evolved—SharePoint 2007 introduced the concept of security trimming and baked the security fundamentals into the core of the product to provide end users with real-world view of the data they have access. SharePoint 2010 incorporates the same security principles and takes things a step further by introducing federated authentication and user identity with Claims-Based-Authentication.

I devote Chapter 3 to security in SharePoint 2010 and cover CBA in detail. Suffice to say for this section, Central Admin provides a section to manage farm administrators, configure authentication providers, manage trust, configure managed accounts (see earlier in this chapter), apply user policy management, manage antivirus settings, and control self-service site creation configuration. We will dive into security in detail in Chapter 3.

Upgrade and Migration

Earlier in this chapter, we visited the Upgrade and Migration section when checking on the status of content databases we upgraded from SharePoint 2007. Clicking on the Check Upgrade Status link shows a page of in-progress and completed (successfully or failed) upgrades. SharePoint 2010 allows parallel upgrade of content databases, and this page is a central location where an administrator may track the progress. The Review Database Status link provides a location to see all the databases in use in the farm and if SharePoint requires any action on them from the administrator.

The other links and subsections of this area concern the administrator with license and enterprise feature upgrade. With license key in hand, you may upgrade the farm from trial status to Standard or Enterprise or from Standard to Enterprise, and so on. If you configure the farm for Enterprise, then you may turn on Enterprise features on the farm and for all site collection in the farm from this subsection.

General Application Settings

The General Applications Settings section is, as its name indicates, a general configuration area for SharePoint 2010 general applications in the farm. Each subsection deserves a brief mention.

External Service Connections

External Service Connections allow administrators to configure "copy to" or "move to" locations within the farm for which users may copy/move documents of document libraries. Users of SharePoint might be familiar with the Edit Control Block (ECB)—the context menu shown when clicking a list or document item. Creating an external service connection instructs SharePoint to add a new entry to the ECB, under the "send to" menu, so users may send a document to another location in the farm. Think of this feature as taking document drop-off libraries (discussed in Chapter 7, on document management) a step further.

InfoPath Form Services

Microsoft introduced InfoPath Form Services for SharePoint in MOSS 2007. Organizations with a SharePoint Enterprise license could design custom forms in the Microsoft Office InfoPath smart client and then host them in SharePoint, allowing end users to post data to lists, email, or web services. Let us be honest, though, anyone who used InfoPath Form Services in MOSS 2007 would probably agree that the integration of the feature in the platform was a little clunky. Microsoft stepped things up with SharePoint 2010, and InfoPath Forms Service now fully integrates into the platform. Site designers, armed with SharePoint Designer, may customize standard list entry forms and as a result, the end user may never really know that SharePoint converted these forms to InfoPath forms under the surface.

I discuss InfoPath Form Services further in Chapter 9, on Microsoft Office Integration, so for now I will briefly cover the configuration subsection here in Central Admin. InfoPath Forms exist as template XSN files (essentially XML files with form markup) and administrators may upload and manage form templates for use across the farm using the Manage Form Templates and Upload Form Template links. InfoPath provides capability to connect to data sources so forms may contain live data (for multiple-choice selections, for example), and so users may submit form data to an end location, such as a Web Service, or a SharePoint list. Administrators may upload data connection files in this subsection to support forms of this nature.

Site Directory

The Site Directory feature in SharePoint 2007 consisted of a dedicated site template with embedded features enabled so that SharePoint could track the creation of new sites and register them with a category in the directory. Look at the Create Site Collection page in SharePoint 2010 and you will notice the absence of the Site Directory site template. How could this be? Because of incompatibility with upgrades from SharePoint 2007, Microsoft decided to hide this template, thus effectively dropping the functionality of the Site Directory. Administrators may re-enable the template as follows:

1. Browse to `C:\Program Files\Common Files\Microsoft Shared\Web Server Extensions\14\TEMPLATE\1033\XML`.

2. Open `webtempsps.xml`.

3. Find the section for Site Directory and change the Hidden value as shown here:
    ```
    <Template Name="SPSSITES" ID="34"><Configuration ID="0" Title="Site
    Directory" Type="0" Hidden="FALSE"
    ImageUrl="/_layouts/1033/images/template_site_dir.png" Description="A
    site for listing and categorizing important sites in your organization.
    It includes different views for categorized sites, top sites, and a
    site map." DisplayCategory="Enterprise"
    VisibilityFeatureDependency="5F3B0127-2F1D-4cfd-8DD2-85AD1FB00BFC">
    ```

4. Then open command prompt and browse to `C:\Program Files\Common Files\Microsoft Shared\Web Server Extensions\14\BIN`

5. Run following command:`stsadm.exe -o activatefeature -id 5F3B0127-2F1D-4cfd-8DD2-85AD1FB00BFC -url http://yoursite`

SharePoint Designer

Clicking the Configure SharePoint Designer Settings link provides a page to allow/disallow the following in a given web application:

-   Editing via SharePoint Designer 2010 (SPD)

-   Detachment of pages from site definitions using SPD

-   Customizing of master pages and page layouts using SPD

-   Administrators viewing site structure via SPD

If you are unfamiliar with SharePoint Designer, SPD is a development tool for customizing SharePoint for UI branding, List View web parts, external data connections (BCS), and similar design tasks. Skip this subsection if you have never used SPD—the default settings are to allow use of SPD at the web application level.

Search

SharePoint Search is another one of those iceberg topics to which authors have dedicated whole books. Anyone reading the table of contents of this book will notice the absence of a chapter on search, which is not a mistake. If you are looking for material on SharePoint search then I am afraid you are reading the wrong book—but stick around as this book has plenty of other interesting administrative topics to offer you on SharePoint 2010.

Organizations with the Enterprise license or those that purchased a separate license for FAST have a super powerful search "platform" available to them—the super charged GTX version of SharePoint Search. Everyone else can take advantage of standard SharePoint search offerings, and this subsection is a short cut into the world of SharePoint Search Configuration.

Like almost everything else in SharePoint 2010, SharePoint Search exists as a managed service application and consists of a crawler component, query component, index store, and interfaces to gain access to search results. Scanning down the Managed Service Application list in the Application

Management section of Central Admin, you will find the Enterprise Search service; click on Manage and you can begin configuring search (similar to the approach taken in MOSS 2007 via the SSP). However, you can also get to this search subsection under General Application Settings by clicking the Farm Search Administration link and then clicking the relevant Search Service Application in the list at the bottom of the resulting page.

Other options available to the administrator in this subsection include the ability to create crawler impact rules; you can adjust the load the search crawler applies to content sources, and choose to view the topology of the various search components for a given search service application.

Reporting Services

Microsoft created Reporting Services in SQL Server, some time ago, to provide its users with advanced reporting capabilities with OLAP cubes and related data sources. Reporting Services integrates with SharePoint 2010 so users of Reporting Services may view reports within the SharePoint environment. I dedicate Chapter 8 of this book to Business Intelligence, which includes integration of dashboards and reports via PerformancePoint, and I plan to revisit Reporting Services also.

Content Deployment

I saved the best for last (ignore the fact that this is also the last subsection listed on the page in Central Admin <wink>). What is Content Deployment?

I am certain that any administrator who has the role of looking after Development, QA, and Production SharePoint farms that host publishing sites (public web sites) has come across Content Deployment, or at least heard of it. In short, content deployment is a mechanism to automate deployment of publishing and list content from one farm to another.

Imagine a scenario where an organization has a team of staff working on a Development instance of SharePoint, busy making content changes using the full support of the Web Content Management features of the SharePoint platform. At a certain time on Friday night, the powers upstairs deem that a particular campaign must land on the production SharePoint farm so the public may see pages of the campaign that the content team worked on that week. Does this sound like a typical scenario? It should; I know of one such organization that I work with that works the way I describe.

In the early days of SharePoint 2007, content deployment had a number of issues, and I remember working with representatives from Microsoft on a client project to resolve these issues. The principle of content deployment is solid and simple—configure a connection from source farm to destination farm, configure the content to deploy, configure the schedule, and the let SharePoint do its thing. The problem was that Content Deployment assumed limited changes to the list structures and metadata model (content types and such), and it worked great when the only changes occurring were the actual content. To cut a long story short, as Microsoft rolled out Service Pack 1 and Service Pack 2, and the Cumulative Updates, content deployment issues became less and less significant, and assuming administrators stuck by the best practice rules, content deployment worked as documented. This is good news for anyone reading this book and looking to set up content deployment in SharePoint 2010. After this brief history lesson, let us dive in.

From the destination farm Central Admin, click the Configure Content Deployment link. SharePoint will show you a page much like Figure 2-36.

Figure 2-36. Configuring content deployment in Central Admin

Change the setting to allow this farm to allow incoming content deployment jobs. Ideally, a firewall should not hinder content deployment, if both development farm and production farm reside within the same network or any firewall between the environments allows for HTTP traffic on destination farm Central admin port.

Back on the source farm, click the Configure Content Deployment Paths and Jobs link. Click the New Path button and populate the resulting page with settings of the source web application, destination web application, destination authentication, and name for the path.

With the new path created, click the New Job button to establish a new content deployment job. Content deployment jobs come in two flavors—*full* and *incremental*. Full content deployment instructs SharePoint to copy over *all* content, regardless of change, from the source to the destination. This was a problem area in MOSS 2007 as creation of a new full deployment job to a server that had an existing site collection matching that of the source (partial content especially) would result in an error during the import part of the deployment job. Incremental deployment, as you would expect, only copies over changed lists and publishing changes.

In the New Job page, give the job a name, choose full content deployment, and leave the schedule as unchecked (for now). You may select the entire site collection to copy in the deployment, or select subsites a la carte.

■ **Note** When establishing a full content deployment job the first time, create a blank site collection at the destination web application. Content deployment will overwrite this site with source content, including master pages, page layouts, and page instances.

Go back to the main Configure Content Deployment Path and Jobs page and then manually run the new job you just created. SharePoint will utilize the timer job in both farms to export the content to disk, copy the content files across the network, and then import the content into the destination farm. In the page listing the job, you should see the status change from Preparing to Running once the export part of the process starts. Click the Running link to see a summary page of the content deployment process. If the content deployment job fails along the way, SharePoint will update the job status to Failed, and you may click this link to see a summary of the error at the bottom of the page.

If everything went according to plan and the content deployment job succeeded, you may go back and edit the job (via ECB), and apply a schedule to the job—such as Friday at midnight, for example.

A feature of SharePoint worth noting is the Quick Deployment capability. If you establish an incremental content deployment job content owners in the Quick Deploy Users group may have the option to quick deploy single pages, documents, or list items of content on demand. This is very useful if you cannot wait for a full or incremental deployment to happen outside business hours.

Configuration Wizards

There is very little to say about this section in Central Admin, because we have already covered executing of the Farm Configuration Wizard, early in this chapter. The Farm Configuration Wizard is the only wizard available in the RTM release of SharePoint 2010. My assumption is that Microsoft has provided this section in Central Admin to accommodate future wizard operations and so developers and third party vendors have a place to deploy custom wizards in the farm.

Summary

This chapter covered installation of SharePoint 2010 from scratch on a new server infrastructure. We visited the infrastructure requirements, had a look at the SharePoint 2010 prerequisites installer, and walked-though a server farm installation. I detailed Managed Accounts and which Active Directory Domain accounts Microsoft recommends for a best-practice setup of a SharePoint 2010 farm.

This chapter covered both the SharePoint Productions Configuration Wizard, detailing the process of establishing a new SharePoint farm with SQL Server 2008, and the SharePoint Farm Configuration Wizard in Central Admin, and we visited the various areas of the Central Administration web site.

This chapter is by no means exhaustive and I could write many, many, more pages on the topic of installation and configuration alone. However, I wanted to provide you with a blend of useful insight on the installation and configuration process with the right amount of technical detail to enable you to stand up a typical SharePoint 2010 farm for Development, QA, or Production purposes.

CHAPTER 3

Security and Policy

Asking users to upload important documents and information content to SharePoint without providing a level of security to protect their data is like driving without a seatbelt. Users like to know that their data is secure when asked to move it from their work machines to shared servers and collaborative platforms, like SharePoint. Therefore, Microsoft has ensured that SharePoint, since the early days, has had security measures baked into the platform. The security model in SharePoint 2010 itself has not changed a lot since the previous version, SharePoint 2007, which benefits users of the legacy version, since they do not have to learn a new model for securing user content.

Security in SharePoint has similarities to typical file system security—as in Windows' New Technology File System (NTFS), for example. The implementation of security in SharePoint is very different from that of file system security, but the model and security configuration are similar. The model consists of things to secure—sites, lists, files, and folders—permissions to perform actions on the secured objects, and users or groups with collections of permissions for the secured objects.

At the heart of any good security model is a set of permissions, allowing users of the model to perform certain actions in a specific context. The context might pertain to a location in a hierarchical structure and the set of permissions established for sets of users to a particular securable object. For example, in SharePoint terminology, the security model grants users, or groups of users, access to secured objects—such as sites, lists, and list items. This chapter walks you through the various concepts that constitute the security model in SharePoint 2010.

Security Administration

The IT department typically played a large role in web site security administration in days of old. For its SharePoint collaboration tool, Microsoft wanted to break this dependency on IT and empower end users—content owners—to have control of the content they create and disseminate to their audience. However, Microsoft also recognized that no large enterprise content management system operates completely without involvement from IT. So it structured the security model in hierarchical fashion so that IT can manage high-level access and overall control, while allowing content owners to manage their own content islands with SharePoint sites and site collections.

In Chapter 2, we visited the Central Administration web site, which allows the IT folks and SharePoint administrators to configure SharePoint 2010—and security configuration is no exception. From Central Admin, administrators may configure Web Application permission policies; grant users site collection rights to new and existing site collections, and configure the farm with farm administration rights.

You should have noticed by now that I throw around the term "SharePoint administrator" loosely. In fact, a well-organized SharePoint farm consists of various different types of administrator for different configuration areas. So before getting knee-deep in security terminology, we will visit the different types of SharePoint administrators.

SharePoint Administrators

Have you seen a SharePoint farm configured where the farm administrator account has rights to perform every SharePoint task under the sun? I am willing to bet that the farm administrator account has local server administration rights on the web front-end servers and database cluster, too. Convenient as this scenario is, it leaves a large attack surface open for hackers; once a hacker gains access to the farm account, they have access to the entire farm configuration. The alternative SharePoint provides is to assign administrators specific roles. Read on through this section for the various administration roles in SharePoint 2010.

- Local Server Administrator—Contrary to common belief, the main SharePoint Farm account does not have to be a local server admin—Microsoft recommends quite the opposite. One exception is when installing SharePoint 2010 (see Chapter 2), where making the farm account user a local admin ensures access to configure IIS, access to SQL, and installation of SharePoint binaries. After installation, ensure the farm account is not a SharePoint administrator by accessing the Administrators security group under Server Management in Windows.

■ **Note** All members of the local server administrators group are automatically SharePoint farm administrators.

- SharePoint Farm Administrators—These have full control of the entire SharePoint farm. Ensure that the main SharePoint Farm account is a member of this group (the default post-installation) for SharePoint 2010 to function correctly. Members of the Local Server Administrators group already have farm access. An existing farm administrator may add another user, not part of the local server administrators group, via Central Administration, as follows:

1. Select Site Settings   People and Groups.

2. Click the Manage Farm Administrators Group link.

3. SharePoint shows you the list of users already in the farm administrators group.

4. From the horizontal sub-menu, click the New button and select Add Users from the drop-down box.

5. A people picker dialog should appear and allow you to select users from any of the user credential stores (the default is typically Active Directory).

6. To remove one or more users from the farm administrators group, click the Actions menu after selecting existing users from the list (check the check box next to each user to delete) and then Remove Selected Users from Group.

- Service Administrators—Service administrators control specific service applications and cannot administer other service application but those granted access by farm administrators. For example, a farm administrator may delegate administration of the Managed Metadata Service Application to one set of administrators and the Search Service Application to another set. To grant administration access to a service application, visit Central Admin • Application Management • Manage Service Applications • Highlight the service application item, and then click the Administrators icon on the Ribbon for the selected managed service application.

- Feature Administrators—These administrators manage administration of particular features as part of existing managed service applications. Not all managed service applications permit such granular control with permissions, but for those that do—such as the User Profile Service application—you can highlight the managed service application item in Central Admin (see the previous bullet), and then click the Permissions icon in the Ribbon to access the settings.

- Site Collection Administrators –Site collection administrators have rights to configure and change settings across a particular site collection. Farm administrators by default do not belong to all Site Collection Administration groups, but they do have the power to add themselves to any Site Collection Administration group via Central Administration.
  Regardless of how users secure content within a site, list, or at the list item, site collection administrators have exclusive full control access to all content in the site collection. Thus, assign users to the site collection administrators group with care.
  A farm administrator may add a user as a site collection administrator from Central Admin as follows:

7. Click Application Management.

8. Under Site Collection, click Change Site Collection Administrators.

9. You should see a page like Figure 3-1.

10. Ensure the correct site collection in the drop-down.

11. Central Admin enables assignment of one primary and one secondary site collection administrator; use the people picker boxes on this page to assign them.

- Existing site collection administrators may add other users to the Site Collection Administrators group from the site collection, using the following steps:

12. Click the Site Actions menu.

13. Click Site Permissions from the menu.

14. Click Site Collection Administrators from the Manage tab in the Ribbon.

15. Add users in the dialog shown in Figure 3-2.

16. You should see existing site collection administrators, already assigned by a farm administrator—SharePoint will not allow you to remove all site administrators.

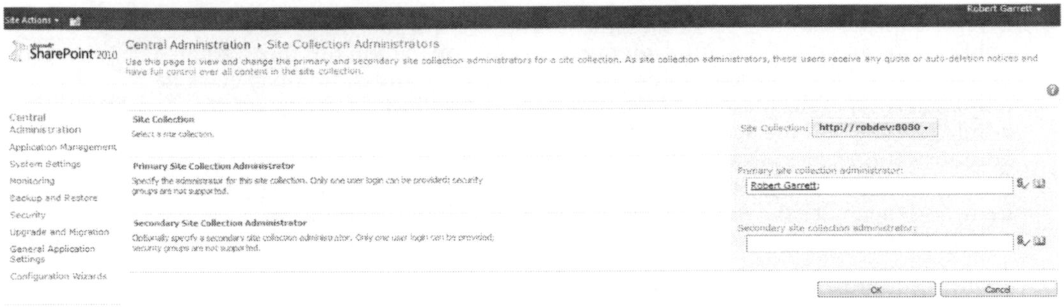

Figure 3-1. Assigning site collection administrators from Central Administration

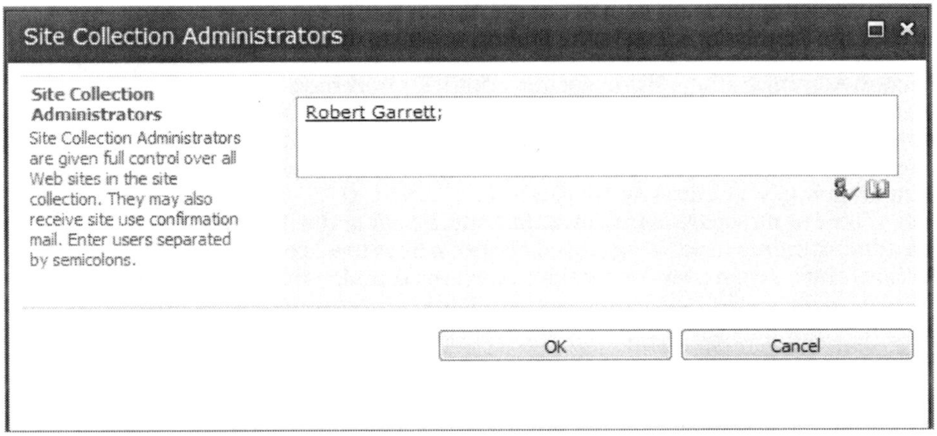

Figure 3-2. Assigning site collection administrators from Site Settings

Permissions and Permission Levels

A single permission in SharePoint is a specific action that a user may take on a securable object. For example—reading the value of a SharePoint list item is a specific permission, often granted to groups of users who need to read lists and their contained items. SharePoint 2010 maintains many permissions in the platform, and the different permissions available to users depend on what an administrator (or owner of content) wishes to secure. Documents in document libraries offer a different set of permissions to those of a site in a site collection. Table 3-1 shows a sample set of permissions available for lists, other permissions exist for sites and personalization.

Table 3-1: List Permissions in SharePoint 2010

Permission	Description
Add Items	Add new items to lists and add new documents to document libraries.
Edit Items	Edit items in lists and edit documents in document libraries.

Permission	Description
Delete Items	Delete items from lists, documents from document libraries.
View Items	View items in lists and documents in document libraries.
Open Items	View the content within documents of a document library, not just the metadata of the associated list item.
View Versions	View previous versions of a list of document library.
Delete Versions	Delete previous versions of a list of document library.
Create Alerts	Create email alerts for lists whenever something changes (configured when the user creates the alert).
View Application Pages	View forms, views, and application pages. The view lockdown feature turns off this permission on pages and document libraries in publishing sites so anonymous users may not view back end list content.
Approve Items	Approve a minor version of a list item in a list or document n a document library.
Override Check Out	Override checkout by another user on a list item in a list or document in a document library.
Manage Lists	Create and delete lists; add and remove columns in a list; and add and remove public views of the list.

With the vast number of permissions available in the SharePoint platform, managing them and assigning the correct permissions to users or groups of users is no trivial task, which is where *permission levels* come in. A permission level is analogous to a permission set—a set of permissions that group together, and when applied to a securable object provide the user or user group with related operations on the securable object. For example, the Read permission level consists of various read permissions for most read like operations of a securable object, and the Contribute permission level provides a number of write permissions to securable objects.

Microsoft labels permission levels with role-like titles, which new users sometimes confuse with those of SharePoint Security Groups. If you think about it, using role names makes sense as a set of permissions often defines the role of the user or groups of users applied. Table 3-2 defines the standard set of permission levels available in SharePoint 2010.

Table 3-2: Standard Permission Levels

Permission Level	Description
Full Control	Users with this permission level have full access to all operations on the secured object, including that of administrative operations. This is not the same as the distinct set of permissions granted to site collection administrators, who have a greater set of administration capabilities.
Design	Users at this permission level have contributor rights and certain permissions to effect change of a securable object, but not administrative rights. Designers typically have permission to change the content in containers (lists and sites) and configure containers, whereas contributors can only write and delete content within containers. Users with design permission level may also approve content in lists with content approval enabled.
Contribute	This is a standard permission level to grant users or groups of users add, edit, and delete rights to lists and list items. Typically, users asked to join a SharePoint site to collaborate on content have Contribute rights to make edits to existing content, add new content, or delete old content.
Read	Users with the Read permission level can access all content in containers in read-only mode. Readers may download documents in document libraries and view lists and list items, but not change anything.
Limited Access	This permission level is special in that SharePoint grants it to users or groups of users for a specific secured object that has custom permissions. For example, if the owner of a list applies specific permissions, not as part of a specific permission set, then SharePoint shows the permission set as Limited Access. Limited Access permissions typically apply only to one item at a time in the container, not to all other items.
View Only	Users or groups of users with View Only permissions cannot download content. This level has similar permissions to the Read permission level but does not allow users to download documents from document libraries.
Restricted Read	This permission level is similar to the Read permission level but has only four of the eleven permissions that Read contains. This permission is only available in publishing sites. It provides users with this permission level access to read content without the ability to create alerts, browse user information, or use client integration (interact with Microsoft Office).

Permission Level	Description
Approve	This permission level is available in publishing sites only and grants users or groups with the capability to edit list items and documents as well as approve items in lists with content approval enabled.
Manage Hierarchy	This permission level is available in publishing sites only and is similar to the Design permission level. It enables users or groups of users to create sites and edit list items and documents. The major difference between the Design permission level and the Manage Hierarchy level is that this permission level does not grant approval rights on list items or documents in lists that have content approval enabled.

Figure 3-3 shows an example list of permission levels applied to a site. To get to this page, either select Site Permissions from the Site Actions menu or select Site Permissions under the Users and Permissions section within Site Settings, and then click Permission Levels on the Ribbon.

Figure 3-3. *Site permission levels*

Creating Custom Permission Levels

SharePoint allows site administrators to create their own unique permission levels. For example, perhaps the content owner would like to allow contributor access to items in a list, but prevent deletion of any list item. The standard permission levels only provide Contributor or Read levels, but not a mix of the two, so a custom permission level can solve this requirement.

The easiest method for creating a permission level in SharePoint 2010 is to create the new level based on an existing permission level—in our case let us use the Contribute permission level. Permission levels reside at the site level and inherit through sub-sites in the hierarchy. Choosing to add a new site permission level at the top of the site collection enables use of the permission level across the entire site collection.

▪ **Note** Permission levels reside within sites.

---

1. Access the Site Permissions page from Site Actions   Site Permissions (or Site Actions   Site Settings   Users and Permissions   Site Permissions).

2. Click the Permission Levels icon in the Ribbon.

3. Click the link for the permission level you want to copy; in this case, the Contribute permission level. SharePoint will show you a page of the permissions contained in the selected permission level.

4. Scroll to the bottom of the page and click the Copy Permission Level button.

5. Provide a name and description for the new permission level and change the contained permissions. In this case, find the Delete Items permission and uncheck the checkbox.

6. Scroll to the bottom of the page and click the Create button. SharePoint will navigate you back to the site Permission Levels page with the new permission level shown along with the default permission levels (see Figure 3-4).

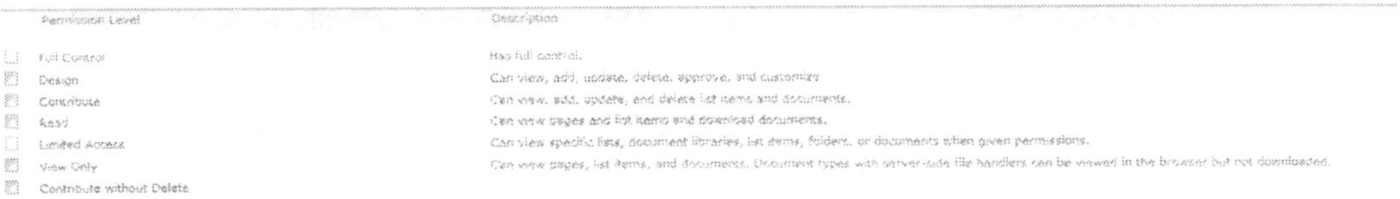

Figure 3-4. New permission level created

How do you create a new permission level without starting from an existing one?

7. Follow steps 1 and 2 in the previous procedure.

8. Click the Add a Permission Level button at the top of the list in the Permission Levels page.

9. Provide a name and description and select the desired permissions in the permission level.

■ **Note** Some permission items depend on others, so you may see SharePoint automatically select permissions based on the permissions you choose to include in the permission level.

10. Click the Create button to create the new permission level.

Editing an existing permission is also an easy process, although *not recommended*. Microsoft best practices stipulate that it is better to create a new permission level based on an existing one. Seasoned users of SharePoint expect that the stock permission levels behave as installed, and changing these permission levels may affect the stability of user permissions in the site hierarchy. If you wish to proceed, follow these steps:

11. Follow steps 1 and 2 of the first procedure in this section.

12. Click the permission level name to edit. SharePoint will show the name, description, and contained permissions in the permission level.

13. Edit the permission level and then click the Submit button at the bottom of the page.

Deleting permission levels is also an easy process:

14. Follow steps 1 and 2 at the beginning of this chapter section.

15. Check the checkbox next to the permission levels you desire to delete.

16. Click the Delete Selected Permission Levels button at the top of the page.

17. SharePoint will display a confirmation dialog, like that in Figure 3-5; click OK to proceed with the delete or Cancel to revert.

■ **Note** Deletion of a permission level that is in use by a user or group for a particular context (site, list, or whatever level) causes SharePoint to lose the permissions for the deleted level. Take care in deleting permission levels, especially the standard permission levels, which Microsoft does *not recommend*.

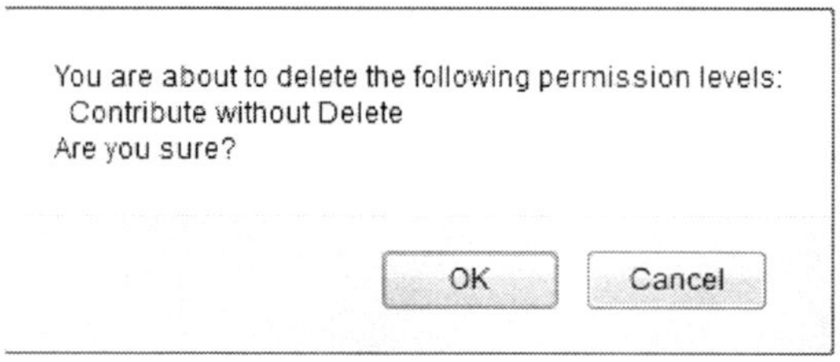

You are about to delete the following permission levels:
  Contribute without Delete
Are you sure?

OK   Cancel

Figure 3-5. Confirmation dialog to delete permission levels

SharePoint Users

Most security models assume the existence of users and groups of users. Different users require different sets of permissions to perform their work, depending on the level of access to data in the system. In a previous section of this chapter, we visited the topic of SharePoint administrators—an administrator is a specific type of user with elevated permissions within the SharePoint farm or site collection.

At the basic level, a user of SharePoint is an "identity." User identity typically consists of various attributes that describe the user with access to the SharePoint site collection. SharePoint 2010 retains minimal information about a user to distinguish one user from another, which typically involves the username, password, and display name, from the credential store that the user authenticates (Active Directory). SharePoint 2007 classified users using either the Active Directory username DOMAIN\username or a username with membership provider prefix (more on membership providers later in this chapter). SharePoint 2010 works in similar way, but also introduces Claims-Based-Authentication (CBA), which tracks user identity via abstract token (more on CBA later in this chapter).

■ **Note** With the exception of administrators, SharePoint maintains topmost user security at the site collection level. Farm administrators must grant relevant access to users for each site collection in a web application.

Most users of SharePoint identify other users by the friendly display name, and by default, Active Directory uses the first name and last name. Any object that I modify or own in SharePoint shows my name as "Rob Garrett," but under the hood, SharePoint uses the username or unique token (CBA) to identify my user identity.

Users have more than just username, password, and display name attributes in SharePoint 2010. In the next chapter, I discuss user profiles, which consist of collections of attributes for each user known to SharePoint. Each user profile associates with a user identity by the unique user identity token or username.

SharePoint tracks each user added to a site collection in a hidden list at the root of the site collection. To view this list, type the following URL into your browser (replacing the domain name of the server, as appropriate): `http://domain_name/_catalogs/users/`. Figure 3-6 shows the users list from within my environment.

Figure 3-6. All users in a site collection

SharePoint Security Groups

SharePoint Security Groups are groups of users, defined within a site collection, and assigned permissions to secured objects. Security groups work to make administration of security easier by collecting users in groups according to their access role. For example, the default Visitors, Members, and Owners groups of a site collection establish separation of users that have permissions to view-only secured objects (viewers), write and change secured objects (members), and have full access to secured objects (owners). Follow the steps below to view the current groups in the site collection:

1. Click the Site Actions menu from the home page of the site collection.

2. Click Site Settings from the menu.

3. Under Users and Permissions, click People and Groups.

4. By default, SharePoint will open a page of the Members group.

5. From the quick launch left navigation, click the Groups heading.

6. You should see a page like Figure 3-7.

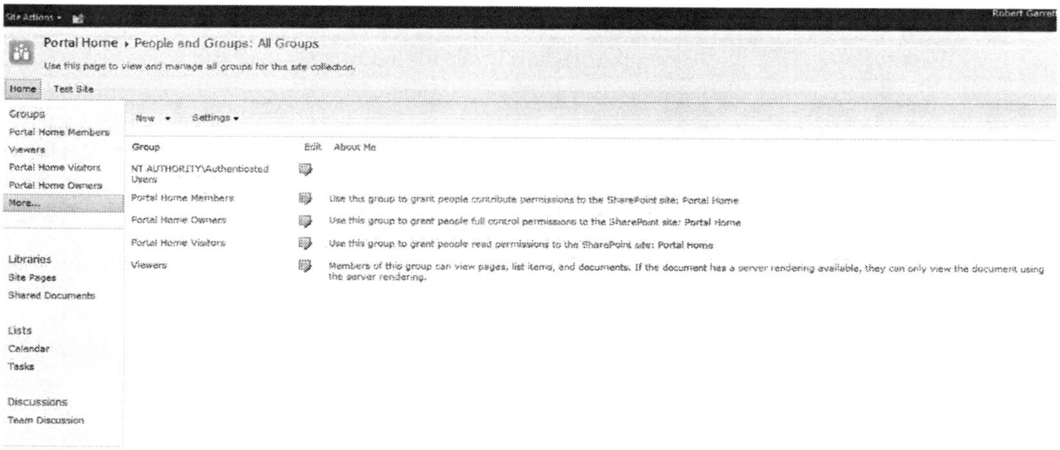

Figure 3-7. Groups in the site collection

Notice, in Figure 3-7, that SharePoint created three default groups, described as follows:

- [Site Name] Members—This group has contribute permission level access to the site; thus any users in this group have contribute access to the site and sub-sites that inherit permissions from this site. Add those users to this group that you wish to allow contributor access, so those users may add, edit, or delete content in lists and containers, and edit pages and other content.

- [Site Name] Owners—This group has Full Control permission level access to the site; thus any users in this group have full control access to the site and sub-sites that inherit permissions from this site. Add those users to this group who have ownership rights, so those users may add, edit, or delete content and change, add, edit, or delete lists, sub-sites and so on.

- [Site Name] Visitors—This group has Read permission level access to the site; thus, any users in this group have read access to the site and sub-sites that inherit permissions from this site. Add those users to this group who have read-only access to see content in lists and sub-sites, but may not change anything.

- Viewers—This group allows view only, and users added to this group may not download documents in document libraries.

Publishing and Enterprise site collections have the following additional default groups:

- Approvers—Users added to this group have approval rights for any lists that have content approval enabled.

- Designers—Users added to this group have design rights (see the previous section in this chapter on permission levels for a description of the Design permission level).

- Hierarchy Managers—Users in this group have hierarchical change rights (see the previous section in this chapter on permission levels for a description of the Hierarchy Management permission level).

- Restricted Readers—Users in this group have restricted read rights (see the previous section in this chapter on permission levels for a description of the Restricted Read permission level).

All security groups in SharePoint work the same way via the SharePoint user interface. For the sake of brevity, the following sets of steps discuss adding and removing users from the members group, via the page in Figure 3-7, but the same steps apply to any other group in SharePoint.

Adding Users to a Group

The following steps detail how to add a new user to an existing group:

1. Click the Members group name title.

2. SharePoint shows a page, listing existing users in the Members group.

3. From the sub-menu (New, Actions, and Settings), click New (or the arrow next to New and select Add Users).

4. SharePoint will show a dialog like that in Figure 3-8. Inside the Users/Groups box you may type the username of a user to add, followed by the tick icon (to validate the user), or click the book icon to bring up the people picker as in Figure 3-9 to choose a user to add.

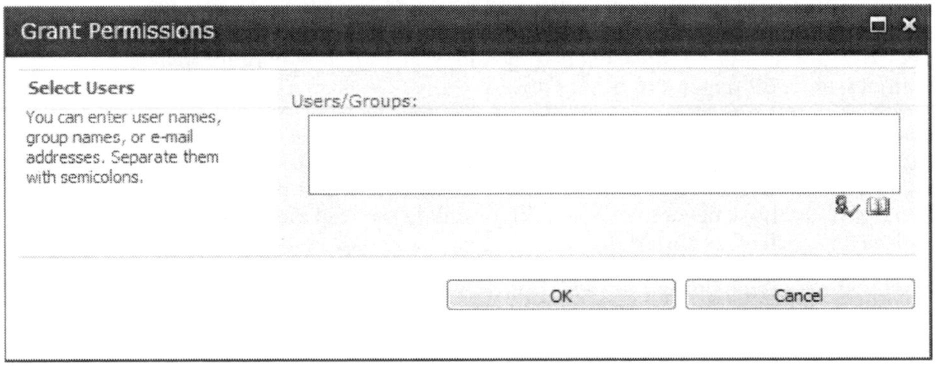

Grant Permissions

Select Users

You can enter user names, group names, or e-mail addresses. Separate them with semicolons.

Users/Groups:

OK   Cancel

Figure 3-8. Adding users to a SharePoint security group

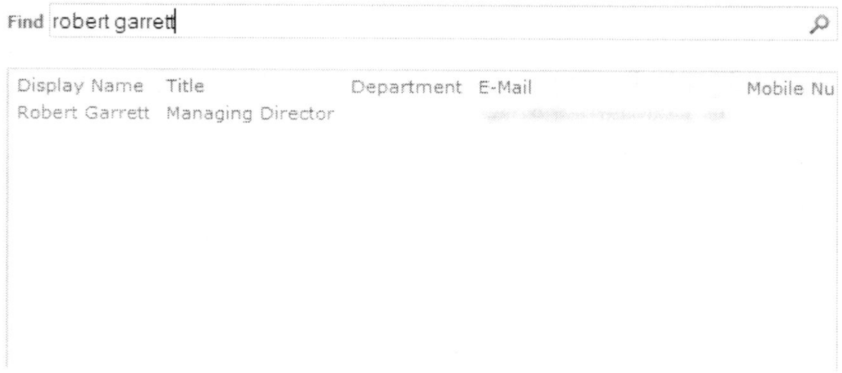

Find robert garrett ⌕

Display Name	Title	Department	E-Mail	Mobile Nu
Robert Garrett	Managing Director			

Figure 3-9. The People picker dialog from adding users to a security group

Removing Users from a Group

The following steps detail how to remove a user from the Members group:

■ **Note** Removing a user from a SharePoint Security Group does not remove the user from the site collection. To remove a user from the site collection, remove the user from the hidden users list, mentioned earlier in this chapter.

---

1. Click the Members group name title.
2. SharePoint shows a page listing existing users in the Members group.
3. Check the check box next to each user you wish to remove from the group.
4. From the sub-menu (New, Actions, and Settings), click Actions, and then click Remove Users From Group
5. Click OK in the warning dialog that appears.

Group Settings and Permissions

From the sub-menu (New Actions, and Settings), click the Settings menu item. The list below describes the various setting options available for the group in context:

- Group Settings—Click this option and SharePoint shows a page like that of Figure 3-10, which details general settings for the group, such as the group owner, who has rights to see into the group for list of users, whether users can request to join or leave the group, and similar actions. The group owner may also delete the group from this page.

  The Name and About Me sections of this page contain the name and description of the group. The Group Owner field is a people field that contains the name of the person who created the group, and is therefore the owner.

  The Group Settings section allows you to specify who has access to view the members in the group and who may edit members of the group. Either all group members have access to see other members of the group or everyone with access to the site collection. You may choose either the group owner or members of the group (thus delegating responsibility of group membership to other members of the group) to allow editing membership of the group.

  The Membership Requests section allows you to control how users may request access to a group and how to leave. By default, SharePoint does not allow requests from users to join or leave the group. Toggle the option to Yes to allow this capability. Once users may request to join a group, the second option tells SharePoint whether to auto-accept all requests. Be careful enabling this option— if you secure areas of your site with group permissions, and then allow anyone to request membership of the group with auto-accept turned on, then any user can gain access to the secured areas to which the group has access.

Figure 3-10. Group Settings

- View Group Permissions—Click this option to see what permission levels this group has and for what securable objects (sites, lists, pages).

- Make Default Group—Makes the group the default "Members" group.

- List Settings—Shows a List Settings page similar to the standard list settings page, in this case the group owner can modify the views and columns shown.

Creating a New Group (and Assigning Permissions)

Site collection administrators may create new custom security groups, and then apply permission levels to these groups within the context of a secured object (site, list, or page). For example, your organization may decide that the default Members, Visitors, and Owner roles are not sufficient, and want to create a specialized group of users, called Steering Committee Members. This group might have contributor access to a site in the collection but not delete rights. Look back at the "Permission Levels" for creating a custom permission level that allows contribute without delete. You'll apply this custom permission level to this custom committee group at the site level (see the next section on granting permissions) to grant this unique set of users the custom permission level.

The following steps detail creating the new group as described:

1. From the root site collection, click the Site Actions menu.

2. Click Site Settings, and then click People and groups in the Users and Permissions area.

3. From the quick launch left navigation area, click the Groups title.

4. You should see a list of groups like that shown in Figure 3-7 earlier.

5. Click New from the submenu (or the arrow next to New, and then New Group in the drop-down).

6. SharePoint displays a page like Figure 3-11.

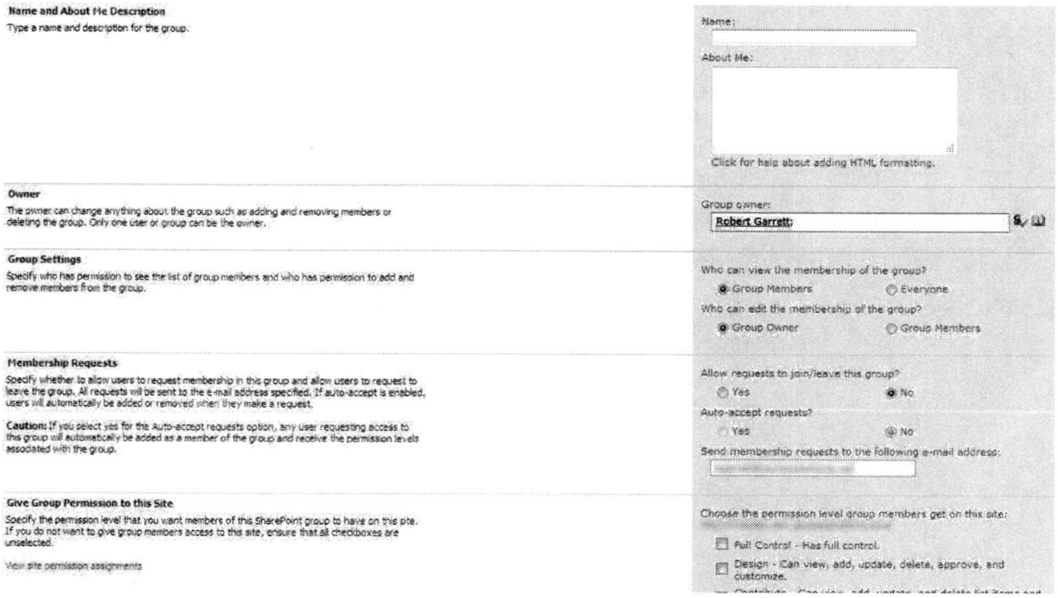

Figure 3-11. The New Group settings page

7. Give the group a new name and description, configure the group settings, and assign the default permission levels.

8. You do not have to assign default permission levels at this stage; you can do so later when applying permissions to a secured object for users contained in this group.

9. Click the Create button to create the group.

Deleting a Group

Deleting a SharePoint Security Group is a straightforward process, summarized in the following steps:

1. From the root site collection, click the Site Actions menu.

2. Click Site Settings, and then click People and Groups in the Users and Permissions area.

3. From the quick launch left navigation area, click the Groups title.

4. You should see a list of groups like that in Figure 3-7 earlier.

5. Click the Edit icon next to the group you wish to delete.

6. SharePoint shows the settings page for the group; at the bottom of the page click the Delete button.

7. Click OK on the dialog box that appears.

Assigning New Visitor, Member, and Owner Groups at Site Creation

The default for a new site collection is to create the Visitors, Members, and Owner groups. When creating a sub-site in the site collection, an administrator or site owner may decide to create a new set of VMO groups and assign permission levels. The following steps details creation of a sub-site and assigning new VMO groups:

1. From the parent site (or root site collection), click the Site Actions menu.

2. Select New Site from the menu.

3. SharePoint presents a dialog box like that shown in Figure 3-12.

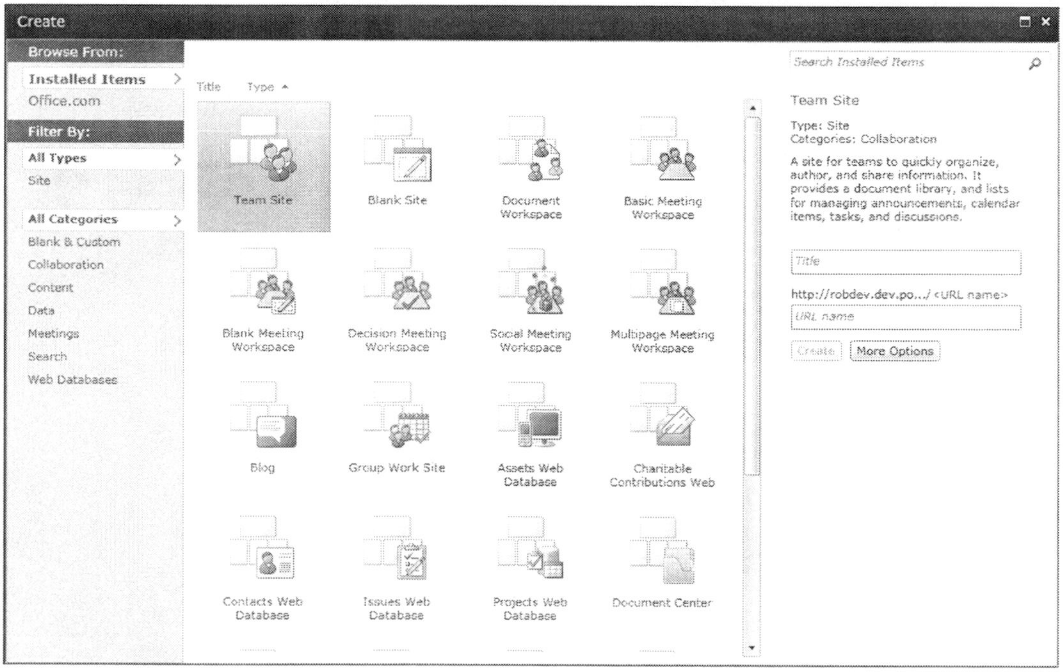

Figure 3-12. *The New Site dialog*

4. Choose a site template, and complete the title and URL name fields.

5. Click the More Options button.

6. You should now see a dialog like Figure 3-13.

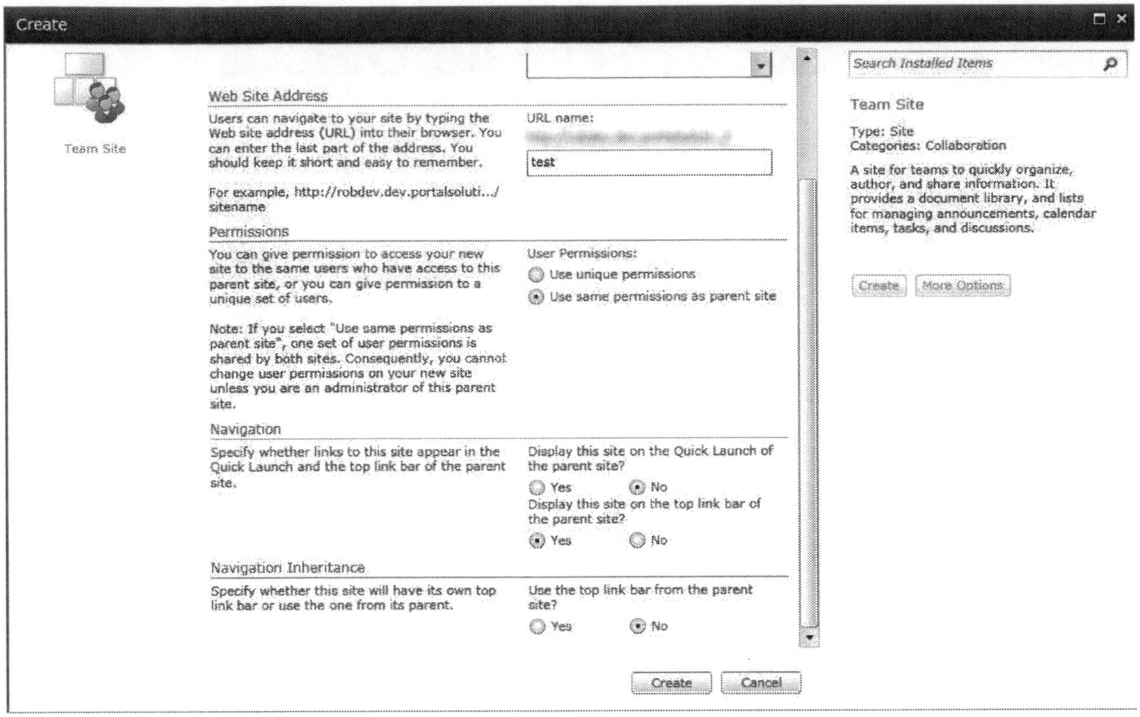

Figure 3-13. The More Options dialog at site creation

7. Scroll to the Permissions section.

8. By default, SharePoint assumes you want to inherit the same site permission level assignments as that of the parent site, change the option to Use unique permissions.

9. Leave all the other options as default, and click the Create button.

10. SharePoint navigates to a page like that shown Figure 3-14.

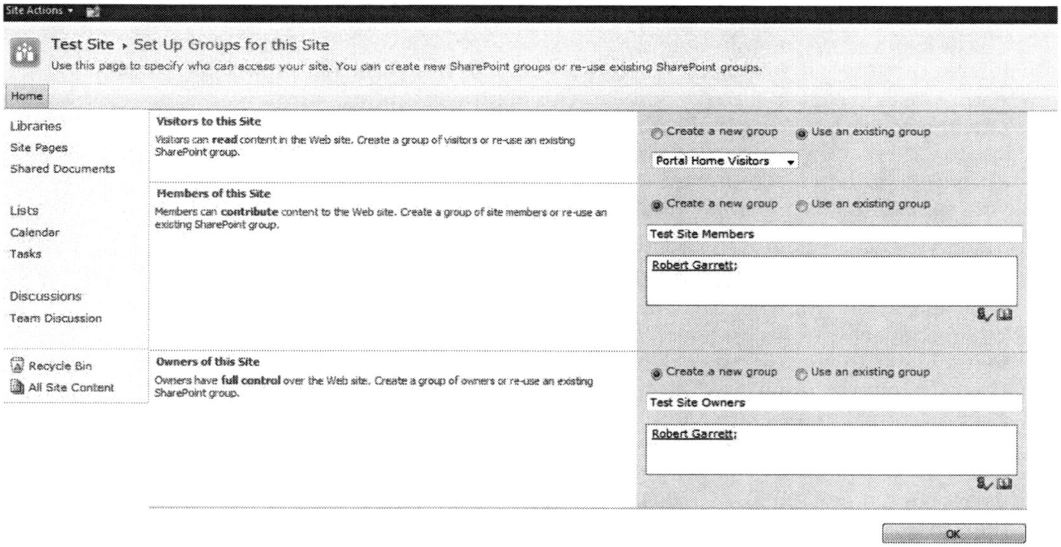

Figure 3-14. *New VMO groups at site creation*

11. On this page, you can specify creation of new groups for the new site created. SharePoint helps you out with the naming by prefixing the site title to the group type, but you may change the VMO groups to anything you like.

12. Click the OK button, and SharePoint creates the new sub-site and new VMO groups. Navigate back to the Groups page and you should see the three new groups created and stored at the site collection level.

Best Practices

When working with clients, I often receive questions about the Microsoft best practices for applying security permissions to sites, lists, and pages in SharePoint. Although there is no hard-and-fast right or wrong answer to configuring SharePoint security, there are some good best-practice rules to follow, which involve the use of security groups:

- Avoid granting permissions (permission levels) to individual users.
  I am sure we have all been there—someone calls the help desk and asks that "Bob" have access to a SharePoint site, list, or document. The quick-and-dirty solution is to find the securable object and grant contributor permission rights to Bob. The problem is what happens when Bob no longer works for the organization and someone else needs to follow on his work. Magnify this issue across multiple users in the organization and in different areas of the site collection hierarchy, and you will have a security management nightmare growing. Adding Bob into a security group and applying permissions to the group is more effective, because you as the administrator can add more users into the group, and/or remove Bob from the group without having to go hunting for areas where Bob has specific permissions.

119

- Avoid too much security group specialization.
  The default visitors, members, and owners group should suffice in most scenarios, but on occasion you may need to create a group for users that have a specific set of permissions in a given security context. This approach is fine in rare circumstances, but if you find yourself managing more than a handful of specialized security groups and needing to remember complicated permission assignments, then I recommend rethinking your security model and clumping your users into more abstract groups.

- Active Directory Groups as Users in SharePoint.
  SharePoint does not really distinguish between AD users and AD groups; both have an identity from the user store, and both may receive permissions for a given secured object (site, list, or page). AD groups are a good thing in general because they allow IT to manage user access to Windows-based services (for example, file shares). However, applying direct permissions to AD groups in SharePoint tightly couples your site collection permissions with IT operations. For example, let us say you assign permissions within your site collection to an AD group called Developers. Somewhere along the line, you want to grant access to your new developer recruit—Bob—to the site collection… Now you have to call IT to ensure that Bob is in the correct AD group. In theory, if IT is religious about putting new employees in the correct AD groups and removing ex-employees from AD groups, then all is peachy, but if not, then you cannot grant Bob access to the site collection until IT commits. Instead, if you add the Developers AD group to a SharePoint Security group, and then assign permissions to the SP group, you can add Bob temporarily to the SP group until IT adds him to the AD group.

- Apply permission levels to collections only.
  Anyone who manages file system permissions will tell you that it is a nightmare managing permissions applied to individual files, simply because there are too many of them. The same theory applies to SharePoint list items. SharePoint administrators will have a much easier time applying permissions to collections (lists, sites, and so on) rather than individual list items.

- Break permission inheritance only when necessary.
  The following section discusses granting of permission and the use of inheritance in more detail. For the purpose of this summary, SharePoint leverages inheritance of security permission levels from the root of the site collection, though sites and sub-sites, into lists and list items. When applying permissions to users (via SP groups) at the top of a virgin SharePoint site collection, the same permissions apply to the user for all sub-sites, lists, and list items. That is, until someone breaks the permission inheritance. Breaking the security inheritance chain in a sub-site, list, or list item means that any change to the permissions at a level above will not affect the permissions configured below the break point. This is often done deliberately when separating sections of the site collection hierarchy from the main site trunk access, but when it happens too often, administrators have a hard time applying new permissions from the top level to all sites and lists below.

Granting Permissions

At this stage of the chapter, we have established how SharePoint 2010 handles groups of related permissions within permission levels; reviewed basic user identity; and discussed security groups and best practices in using them. This section of the chapter discusses granting of permissions (via permission levels) to groups of users for specific securable objects (sites, lists, pages, list items, and so on) in a site collection.

Granting Permissions at the Root Site Collection

The following steps detail granting permissions to the root site in the site collection:

1. From the Site Actions menu, click Site Permissions.

2. Click the Grant Permissions icon from the Ribbon.

3. SharePoint displays a dialog like that in Figure 3-15.

4. Add the user or AD group name in the Users/Groups box and click the tick icon below to validate the name entered. You may also click the book icon and search a user or AD group using the people picker.

5. In the Grant Permissions section, choose the SharePoint security group to add the user or AD group.

6. Alternatively, you can decide to Grant user permissions directly. Look back in the previous section on best practices to see why this is not necessarily a good idea, but SharePoint will let you do it anyway.

7. Decide whether send the new user or AD group an email notification, and then click the OK button.

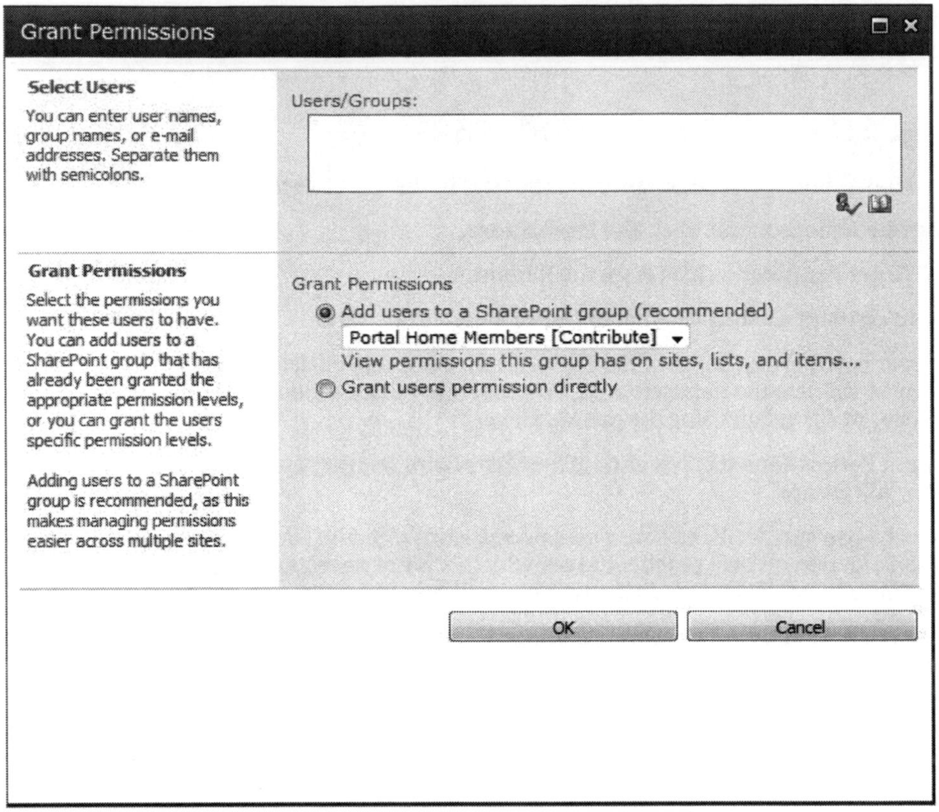

Figure 3-15. The Grant Permissions dialog

Granting Permissions at a Sub-Site (Breaking Inheritance)

Granting permissions to users or AD groups for a sub-site is identical the procedure shown in the previous section, granting permissions at the root site collection—*as long as the sub-site breaks inheritance.* Permission inheritance is an important topic and worthy of a mention here.

By default, permissions granted to users, AD groups, or SharePoint Security groups apply to sub-sites and lists within the current site and sub-sites, as long as site and list owners maintain inheritance. From the landing page of a new sub-site in the site collection, click the Site Permissions menu item from the Site Actions menu. See Figure 3-16 for the different icons in the Ribbon.

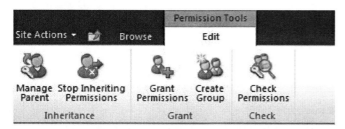

Figure 3-16. Ribbon icons in the Site Permissions page of a sub-site with inherited permissions

1. Click the Grant Permissions icon.

2. SharePoint presents a dialog like that in Figure 3-15, only with the options to apply direct permissions grayed-out.

3. Click Cancel.

4. From the Ribbon, click the Stop Inheriting Permissions icon.

5. SharePoint shows a confirmation dialog, click OK.

6. You should now see the Ribbon change to show more options, including an icon to reestablish permission inheritance and to view permission levels.

7. Now click Grant Permissions, and you see the dialog shown in Figure 3-15.

Permission inheritance works similarly to the way permissions work in the Windows file system. By default, all permissions inherit from the parent. You can add additional users to the SharePoint security groups at the sub-site level, thus providing a greater level of access to users in sub-regions of the taxonomy. However, to change the permissions applied to groups and users at the sub-site level, you must break the permission inheritance chain. Site owners typically break permission inheritance when they wish to revoke access to users or groups of users granted further up the hierarchy. Unlike Windows file system permissions, SharePoint does not provide an "inherit but deny" option for users.

▓ **Note** If you find yourself breaking permission inheritance often, to prevent user access, then this suggests you have too many permission rights applied further up the hierarchy. The best practice is to apply restrictive permissions higher up the chain and less restrictive in specialist sites deeper down the chain.

Granting Permissions to a List or Document Library

For the purpose of this discussion, documents and lists work the same way when it comes to applying unique permissions.

By default, lists inherit permissions from the parent site, just as sites inherit their permissions from their parent. The following steps demonstrate how to view permissions applied to a list, and how to break the inheritance so you can apply unique permissions at the list level:

1. From the Site Actions menu, click View All Site Content.

2. Click the title of any one of the lists or document libraries on the page shown.

3. From the Ribbon, in the List Tools section (or Library Tools if a document library), click the List tab (or Library tab if a document library).

4. Click the List Permissions icon (or Library Permissions icon if a document library).

5. SharePoint displays a page like that in Figure 3-17.

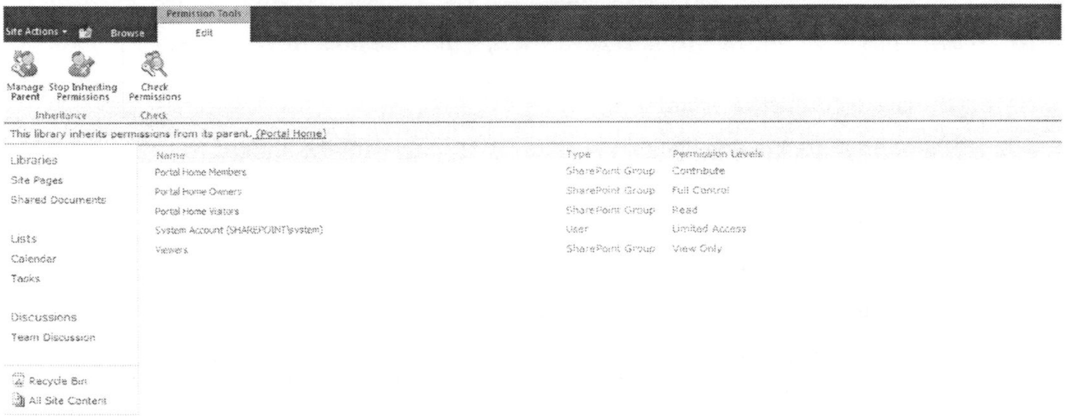

Figure 3-17. *List Permissions*

This permissions page works exactly like the permissions page for a site. To grant unique permissions, break the permission inheritance and assign specific permission levels to new or existing users or groups of users.

Granting Permissions to a List Item or Document

Granting unique permissions to list items or documents in a document library is a process similar to granting permissions at the site and list level. The different is in how to get to the permissions page.

1. From a list view page, hover the mouse over the list item.

2. Select the drop-down arrow that appears.

3. Click Manage Permissions.

4. SharePoint shows a page to manage the permissions of the list item, much like that in Figure 3-17 for the list permissions.

As you did with sites and lists, you must break the permission inheritance to apply unique permissions to the list item.

■ **Note** Try to avoid granting unique permissions to list items and documents in a document library. Doing so is bad practice and may lead to security management difficulties later.

Anonymous Access

By default, SharePoint requires users to authenticate, before gaining access to a site collection. In some cases, the organization may desire to open a site to anonymous users. Anonymous users are those users who visit a SharePoint site without ever authenticating—as far as SharePoint's concerned, there is no user information or user context for the user accessing the site collection anonymously. Typically, anonymous user access does not make a whole lot of sense for team sites and Intranet-like site collections, but it makes perfect sense when used in conjunction with publishing web sites in SharePoint 2010.

■ **Note** A publishing site is a site based on the Publishing Site Collection template, which provides content management services for owners of an organization's public web site.

Anonymous access begins with the web application, which ties configuration to the application in Internet Information Server (IIS). If an administrator does not enable anonymous access at the creation of the web application, or later in the web application settings, then SharePoint does not allow anonymous access at the site collection level. See Chapter 2 for the details of creating a web application and enabling anonymous access. The following steps detail how to enable anonymous access for an existing web application.

1. Open Central Administration.

2. Click the Manage Web Applications option under Application Management on the home page.

3. Select the desired web application from the list.

4. Click the Authentication Providers icon from the Ribbon.

5. Click the title of the zone to change the authorization and enable anonymous access (typically Default).

6. In the dialog that appears, scroll to the Anonymous Access section and check the check box.

7. Scroll to the bottom of the dialog and click the Save button.

You should now have enabled anonymous access for the web application. However, you must now also enable anonymous access at the site collection. The following steps demonstrate how:

8. Open the site collection of the site to enable anonymous access.

9. From the Site Actions menu, click Site Permissions.

10. SharePoint shows a page with site permissions.

11. Click the Anonymous Access icon from the Ribbon. This icon grayed out if anonymous access not enabled at the web application level.

Figure 3-18 shows the three options for anonymous access:

- Entire Web Site—Anonymous users see everything in read mode.

- Lists and Libraries—Anonymous users can only see lists and list items where the owner has explicitly granted permissions to anonymous users.

- Nothing—No anonymous access to the site collection.

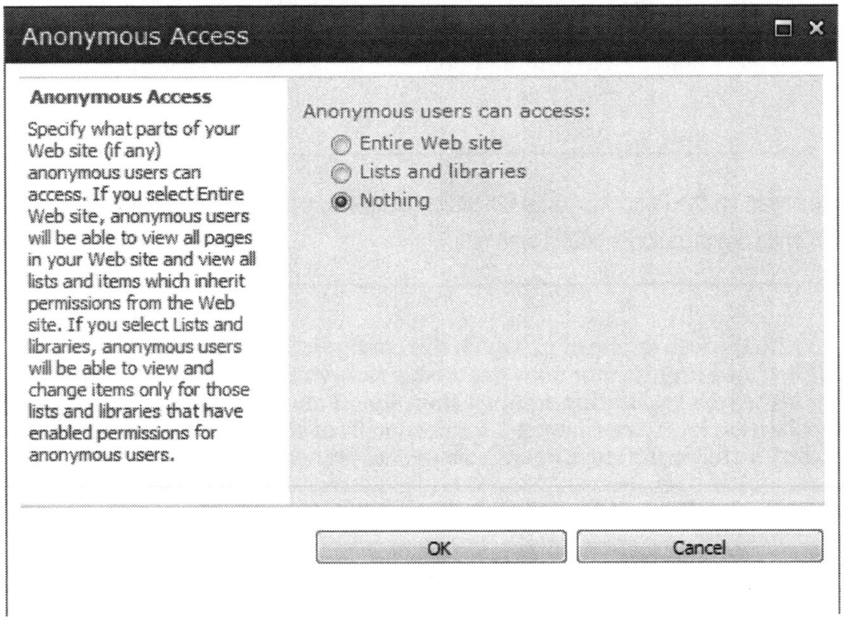

Figure 3-18. *Anonymous access permissions*

Web Application Policies

Site collection security, discussed in the previous sections of this chapter, provide nice granular control of user access to the site collection, sites, lists, and even list items. However, sometimes an administrator needs to grant access to users for an entire web application. SharePoint 2010 provides this capability via the Central Administration web site.

■ **Note** Granting users access to the entire web application via Web Application policy bypasses all security settings applied at the site collection, sub-sites, lists, and list item levels. I strongly recommend you only use this capability under special or rare circumstances, such as troubleshooting, or granting access to Very Important Administrators.

1. Open Central Administration.

2. Click the Security heading from the home page.

3. From the Users sections, click Specify web application user policy.

4. SharePoint shows a page like that in Figure 3-19.

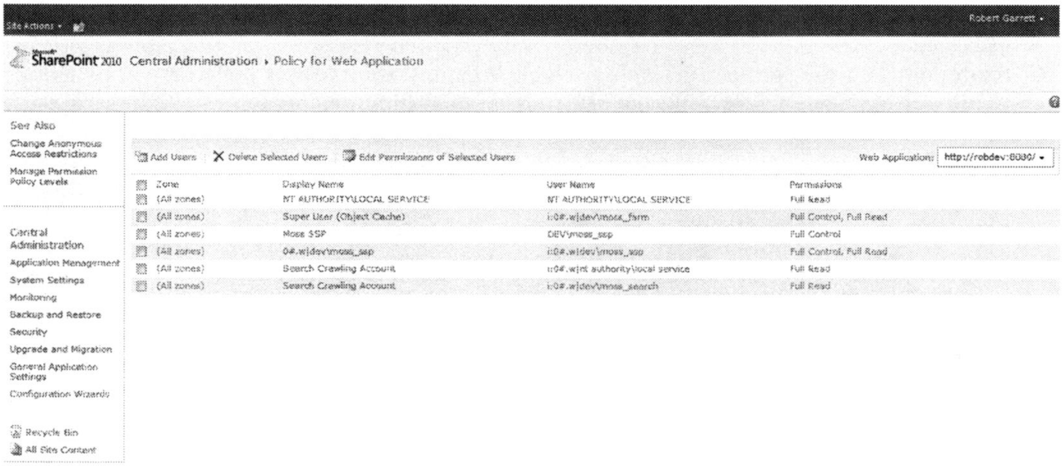

Figure 3-19. Web application security policies

The page displays a list of current user policies for the selected web application in the drop-down on the far right. Notice the strange user names, like 0#.w|dev\moss_ssp, which is how SharePoint stores user identity as part of the claims-based-authentication model (see the next section).

5. Click Add Users from the submenu.

6. From the next page, choose the desired web application from the drop-down.

7. Choose the desired zone or all zones if you want the new policy to apply to all security zones for the application.

SharePoint maintains four zones for each web application - Default, Custom, Intranet, and Internet—the labels are not important but to help administrators assign policy for typical purpose. The drop-down that appears in step 3 shows only those zones in which the administrator has configured an authentication scheme (Windows, Kerberos, or Claims-based).

8. Click the Next button.

9. Enter the users or AD groups in the Users box; then click the tick icon to validate the entered text, or click the book icon to choose users via the people picker dialog.

127

10. Select the appropriate permissions—this is the only place in the SharePoint security model where an administrator may deny access rights. This feature comes in handy if an administrator needs to revoke access for users in the web application, without editing the permissions in site collections.

11. You may choose to operate the account policy as System, meaning the account does not show up in user information lists (it's effectively hidden).

12. Click the Finish button to enact the policy.

Pay close attention to the quick links on the top-left of the page, shown in Figure 3-19. Administrators can change the permission policy levels, and change the anonymous access policy for web applications via these links, as follows:

13. Click the Manage Permission Policy Levels link.

14. SharePoint lists the permission levels available for application to user policies at the web application level. This page provides similar functionality to changing permission levels in the site collection, as discussed earlier in this chapter.

15. Click any of the existing permission level policy names to see a list of permissions maintained by the permission policy level, or...

16. Click the Add Permission Policy Level from the sub-menu to create a new permission policy level.

17. Click the Change Anonymous Access Restrictions link from the See Also section on the left of the page.

18. SharePoint displays a page similar to that for configuring user permission policy for web applications, but this time for anonymous access.

Claims-Based Authentication

Before discussing the new Claims-Based-Authentication (CBA) model in SharePoint 2010, let us quickly visit what we mean by the term *authentication*. Authentication means to provide a set of credentials to a secure system to identify a person, or user, as known to the system. Successful authentication involves a user passing his or her credentials—typically a username and password, after which the system looks up the credentials in a credential store and finds a match, proving that the user known to the system. Unsuccessful authentication occurs when the system cannot match the credentials, passed by the user, against the credential store.

You should also keep in mind the difference between *authentication* and *authorization*. Authentication is the process of determining the identity of the user. Authorization is the process of determining whether a given user (already authenticated) has access to a secured object in the system, based on role-based or user-based permissions.

SharePoint 2007 would authenticate users, using one of three methods:

- NTLM (NT LAN Manager)

- Kerberos

- Form-based

The specifics of each of these authentication protocols are beyond the scope of this book, except to say that NTLM is the standard Windows Challenge-Response authentication scheme, Kerberos a ticket based system, and Forms-based (FBA) custom authentication using an ASP.NET membership provider.

The problem with all of these authentication methods is that they tightly couple the authentication mechanism with the SharePoint system. Both NTLM and Kerberos use Active Directory to authenticate username, domain name, and password. FBA uses the ASP.NET membership provider model (see `http://msdn.microsoft.com/en-us/library/ff648345.aspx`) to authenticate username and password values, sourced via HTML form and HTTP post variables from a login form. However, each of the three authentication methods assumes that the authentication source (credentials store) identifies users via a unique username. This creates problems when switching authentication schemes. SharePoint must leverage some form of identity to bind permissions for access to secured objects, and in SharePoint 2007, the username identity changed depending on the authentication method. Administrators become more aware of the issue when using multiple authentication schemes.

For example, Bob authenticates via NTLM when in the office, but when outside the office he authenticates using FBA. As far as Bob is concerned, he is the same person, accessing the same SharePoint site collection, but SharePoint 2007 sees his identity as either `DOMAIN\username` (NTLM) or `membership_provider:email` (FBA).

Enter SharePoint 2010 and Claims-Based-Authentication (CBA), which abstracts the process of authentication and identifies users with a common token (based on a set of claims about the individual). No matter which authentication method Bob uses to access the site collection, the CBA system generates the same identity token for Bob so SharePoint 2010 can apply permissions no matter what the method of authentication. CBA is not SharePoint-specific, but part of a larger initiative, called Open Identity (see `http://openid.net/`). The process of abstracting the authentication from the secured system is known as *federated authentication.*

■ **Note** Open Identity and the working specifics of CBA are outside the scope of this book, except inasmuch as CBA is relevant to SharePoint 2010 configuration.

The basic principle of CBA is to authenticate a user once a secured system (the *relying party*) knows the identity of a given user, based on the claims that user makes about himself. A claim may consist of any attribute about a user, and multiple claims provide greater level of security because a given user must match all claim answers to be identified as the user they claim to be. Of course, public attributes do not make good claims, as any person could impersonate another by obtaining the correct set of claim values. SharePoint 2010 still uses username and password values as specific claim and claim values, which SharePoint can then pass onto a *trusted identity provider* (Active Directory Federated Services, Live ID and so on).

At the heart of a federated authentication system exists the *Secure Token Service (STS).* Open Identity and CBA assumes the identity of authenticated users in a secure system by their secure token, or just token for short. It is the job of the STS to issue secure tokens in response to successful authentication against a credential store, via the identity provider. SharePoint 2010 hosts its own STS and this STS authenticates users against a choice of Active Directory, Live ID, LDAP sources, and custom membership provider sources.

Configuring CBA in SharePoint 2010

You may remember that in the Chapter 2 section about creating a new web application, early on in the process SharePoint will prompt the administrator for the authentication type—*Claims-Based* or *Classic Mode* authentication. Figure 3-20 shows a screenshot asking the administrator to choose the authentication type.

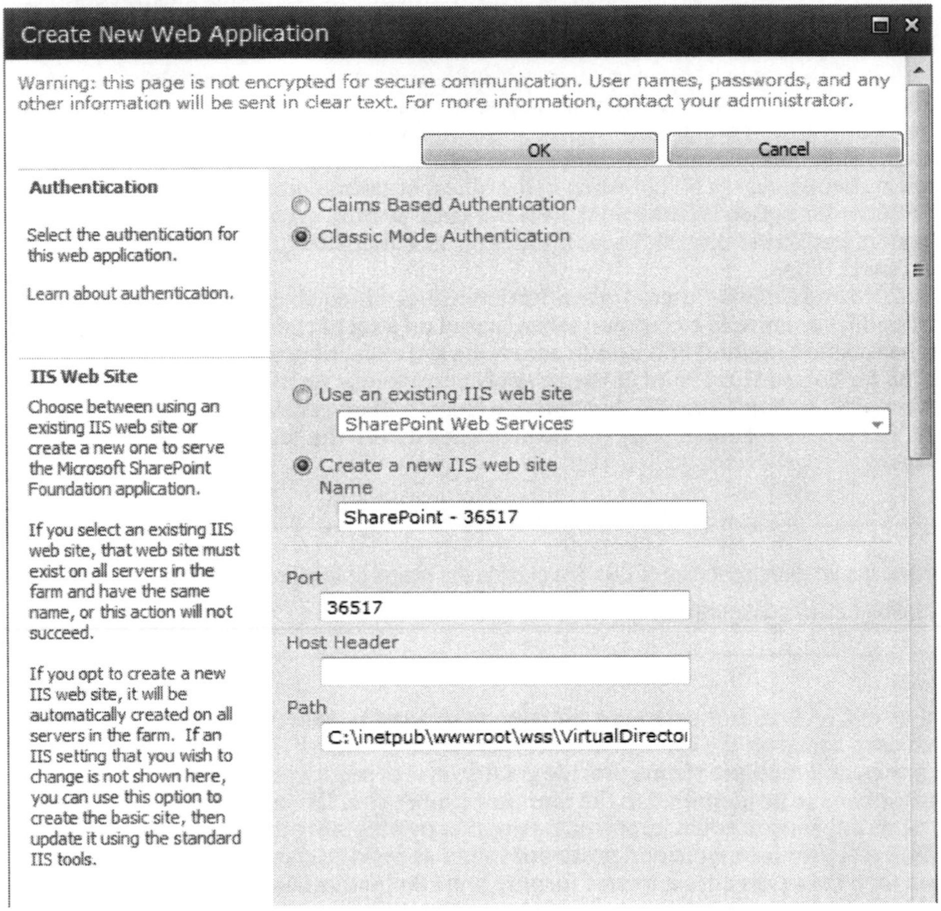

Figure 3-20. Choosing the authentication mode while creating a new web application

Change the mode from classic to CBA, wait for the page to refresh, and you should now see a CBA settings section in the dialog, like that of Figure 3-21.

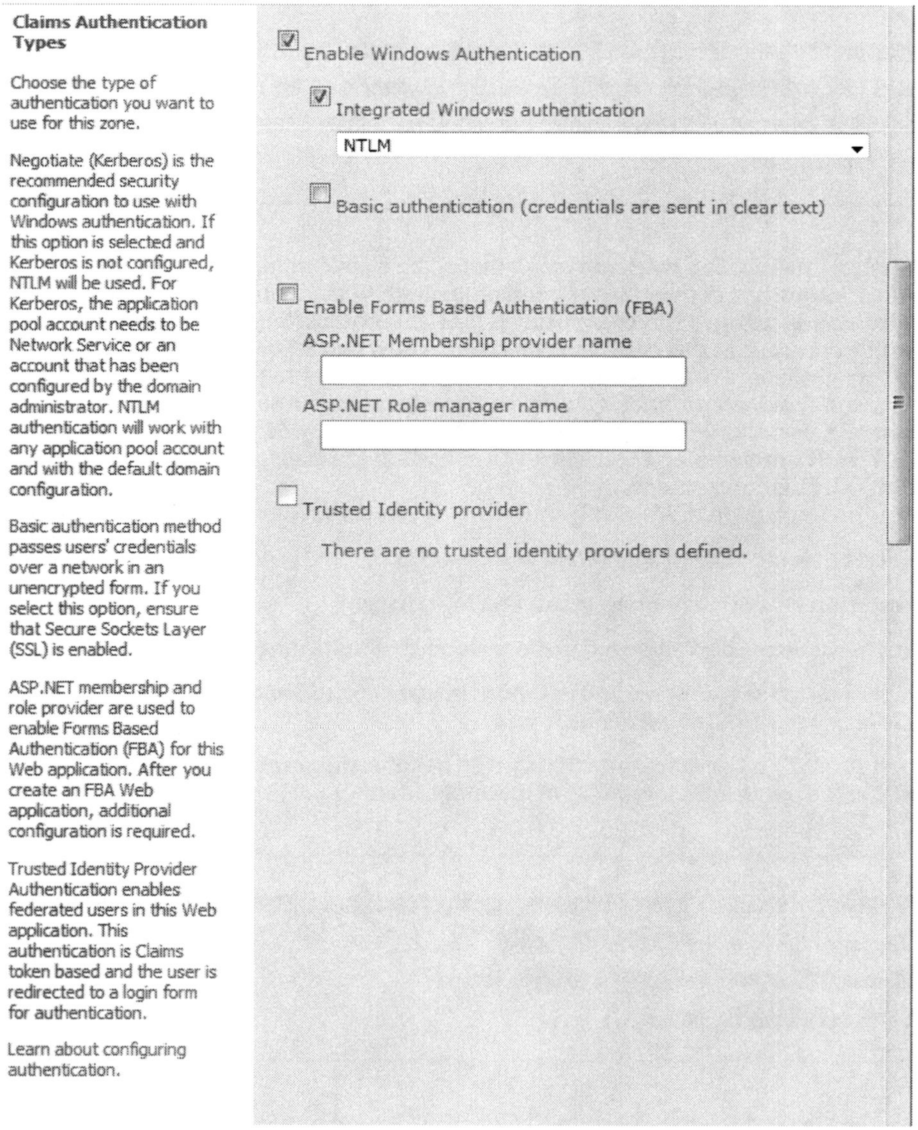

Claims Authentication Types

Choose the type of authentication you want to use for this zone.

Negotiate (Kerberos) is the recommended security configuration to use with Windows authentication. If this option is selected and Kerberos is not configured, NTLM will be used. For Kerberos, the application pool account needs to be Network Service or an account that has been configured by the domain administrator. NTLM authentication will work with any application pool account and with the default domain configuration.

Basic authentication method passes users' credentials over a network in an unencrypted form. If you select this option, ensure that Secure Sockets Layer (SSL) is enabled.

ASP.NET membership and role provider are used to enable Forms Based Authentication (FBA) for this Web application. After you create an FBA Web application, additional configuration is required.

Trusted Identity Provider Authentication enables federated users in this Web application. This authentication is Claims token based and the user is redirected to a login form for authentication.

Learn about configuring authentication.

☑ Enable Windows Authentication

　　☑ Integrated Windows authentication

　　　　NTLM ▼

　　☐ Basic authentication (credentials are sent in clear text)

☐ Enable Forms Based Authentication (FBA)

ASP.NET Membership provider name

ASP.NET Role manager name

☐ Trusted Identity provider

　　There are no trusted identity providers defined.

Figure 3-21. CBA Settings during web application creation

In CBA mode, SharePoint supports three types of federated authentication:

- Windows (NTLM or Kerberos)
- Forms-based-Authentication via ASP.NET membership and role providers
- Another trusted identity provider and external STS

■ **Note** Configuring multiple authentication types in CBA (mixed authentication) will instruct SharePoint to show a choice drop-down on the CBA login page—the authentication action depending on the user's choice. This feature allows multiple authentication schemes on a single domain name URL, something SharePoint 2007 could not accomplish without multiple domain URLs.

The first of the three authentication types works like that of the classic mode—the user sees a Windows popup authentication box in their browser and provides their username, domain, and password to authenticate against Active Directory, using NTLM or Kerberos. Specific details on NTLM and Kerberos are outside the scope of this book, but you should know that NTLM is a challenge–response protocol (server challenges user for credentials in response to user requesting a secured page), and Kerberos is a Microsoft Windows proprietary token based authentication service.

Unlike in classic mode, users authenticating via CBA to Active Directory do so via the built in SharePoint 2010 STS. This STS provides an SAML (Secure Application Markup Language) token with Windows authenticated identifiers contained.

The Forms-based-Authentication (FBA) configuration in CBA works as follows:

1. User requests a secure page in SharePoint 2010, via URL.

2. SharePoint redirects the client browser to a FBA login page.

3. User types in username and password credentials, and submits the page.

4. The browser passes the username and password in plain text to SharePoint (hopefully on a secure SSL connection).

5. SharePoint 2010 STS passes the credentials onto a membership provider, configured in the web configuration file of the application.

■ **Note** Since the STS Service now authenticates FBA users, you must configure custom ASP.NET membership providers in the `web.config` of the STS Service. The location is

`C:\Program Files\Common Files\Microsoft Shared\Web Server`
`Extensions\14\WebServices\SecurityToken`

---

6. The SharePoint 2010 STS passes back an SAML token (assuming successful authentication) to SharePoint 2010, and FBA sends back a cookie to the client browser.

SharePoint 2010 also supports integration of third-party STS to authenticate users. At the end of the day, SharePoint just needs to translate credentials into a secured token, which is the job of any STS. The following steps give a brief overview of how SharePoint authenticates a user with a third-party Trusted Identity Provider (Live ID, Google Accounts, or similar) that hosts its own STS:

7. A user requests a secured page in SharePoint 2010, via URL in the client browser.

8. SharePoint notices that the web application has a custom STS registered (more in this shortly) and redirects the client browser to the identity provider authentication page.

9. The user authenticates with the identity provider.

10. The identity provider performs claims augmentation using its own STS—this is the process, in which a series of claims provided by the user, translate into an encrypted secure token in XML, called an SAML token (. In this case, claims may be any identifiable attributes of the user, including username and password credentials of a known credential store, such as that maintained by the identity provider.

11. The identity provider STS creates and returns an SAML token to SharePoint 2010, which is then passed to the client.

12. The client re-requests the secured page in SharePoint 2010, passing the SAML token. Subsequent requests in the same browser session also pass the SAML token.

13. SharePoint validates the SAML token and then creates an SPUser object in memory for the authenticated session, which contains the SAML token and identity for the authenticated user.

CBA and PowerShell

SharePoint helps the administrator to configure CBA during creation of a web application. However, what if you have an existing web application, operating in classic mode, and you want to change it to CBA? The answer is to use PowerShell.

The following steps demonstrate how to configure an existing web application to use CBA:

1. From the Start menu on the web front-end server, launch PowerShell from Microsoft SharePoint 2010 Products, as SharePoint 2010 Management Shell.

2. Convert your application with the following command (note, you cannot revert a CBA application back to classic mode):
```
$ConvertApp = get-spwebapplication http://<your web application name
$ConvertApp.useclaimsauthentication = "True"
$ConvertApp.Update()
```

Earlier I mentioned adding a new trusted identity provider to SharePoint, so that users of your application may authenticate with external providers, like Live ID and Google. The following series of PowerShell commands configure a new trusted identity provider (IP), which will then show up on the CBA configuration screen when creating a new web application:

3. Create a new X509 certificate for the IP
```
$cert = New-Object
System.Security.Cryptography.X509Certificates.X509Certificate2("path to
cert file")
```

4. Create a claim mapping to use with the IP
```
New-SPClaimTypeMapping
http://schemas.xmlsoap.org/ws/2005/05/identity/claims/emailaddress -
IncomingClaimTypeDisplayName "EmailAddress" -SameAsIncoming
```

5. Create a realm parameter for use with the IP
```
$realm = "urn:" + $env:ComputerName + ":domain-int"
```

6. Create a parameter for the sign in page of the IP
```
$signinurl = "https://test-2/FederationPassive/"
```

7. Register the new IP with SharePoint 2010
```
$ap = New-SPTrustedIdentityTokenIssuer -Name "WIF" -Description
"Windows Identity Foundation" -Realm $realm -ImportTrustCertificate
$cert -ClaimsMappings $map1[,$map2..] -SignInUrl $signinurl -
IdentifierClaim $map1.InputClaimType
```

Summary

In this chapter, I took you on a brief tour of SharePoint security. Following from the previous chapter on installation and configuration, the chapter kicked off by diving into the various administrator types in SharePoint 2010.

SharePoint 2010 uses role-based security, which requires an understanding of the permissions model. We examined the existence of permission levels, how to use them, and the creation of custom levels. We visited best practices and discussed how to leverage SharePoint Security Groups to apply permissions to a particular securable object (sites, lists, pages, list items and so on).

This chapter also introduced *Claims-Based-Authentication*, a new paradigm in SharePoint 2010 that is Microsoft's answer to federated authentication and open identity in the SharePoint world.

In Chapter 4 we look at people and profiles in SharePoint 2010—how user identity expands to profiles so that users take on a persona within a SharePoint-based organization.

CHAPTER 4

People and Profiles

SharePoint 2010 revolves around user collaboration. User collaboration thrives with user adoption of a SharePoint system, and for a SharePoint site to engage users requires integration of user identity in the system. In Chapter 3, I explained security, and focused on user identity as it pertains to authentication in the SharePoint 2010 platform. In this chapter, I will discuss user profiles, which map user identity to the details about said users.

Each user profile in SharePoint 2010 retains metadata about a person using the SharePoint system, such as their role in the organization, photo, summary of skills, office demographics, and so on. After reading this chapter you will know what constitutes a user profile and how an administrator can configure the User Profile Service (UPS) application in a SharePoint 2010 farm, establishing two-way synchronization between user profiles in SharePoint 2010 and that of the organization Active Directory., We will also look at some details about configuring people search.

A User's Profile

A user profile is a collection of data about a person. SharePoint 2010 synonymizes the term "people" with "users," therefore; user profiles in SharePoint consist of data about users of the SharePoint 2010 system. When we think about the profile of a user, we typically think about demographic information—name, address, phone, e-mail, and so on. SharePoint stores this demographic data, and more, as fields in the user profile associated with a user in SharePoint farm. SharePoint terms these fields *profile properties*.

Users of a SharePoint site may view their profile at any time by clicking their name either on the top-left of the Ribbon (followed by My Profile), or next to any document or list item when shown. SharePoint will display a page with main demographic information at the top, your picture (if you have one in your profile), and other information about you—such as the "About me" description, and skills. Below the demographic information is an Edit My Profile link, allowing you to edit your own profile, which SharePoint provides a page with form so that you may provide values for the properties (fields) defined in your profile.

Later on in this chapter, I will demonstrate how you may add profile properties, so that users may add more data about themselves.

Similar to the way you view your own profile, other users of SharePoint may see your public profile information by clicking your name, where it appears next to list items and documents in the site. Your association with a user governs how you see their profile. For example, users can set the visibility of their profile properties to Everyone, Manager, Team, Colleagues, or just themselves; then which group you fit (based on the organization structure) will dictate what profile property values you see.

If you are thinking that user profiles in SharePoint are very much like user records in Active Directory (or any other directory system), you are right. Keeping user profile information in both places may seem like unnecessary work, which is why Microsoft provided the User Synchronization Service in

SharePoint 2010, so you may populate user profiles in SharePoint with those in your directory system. User Profile Sync now also allows you to establish bidirectional sync, so that users may update their profiles in SharePoint 2010 and see the changes reflected in the directory store. The next section of this chapter discusses User Profile Sync.

The User Profile Infrastructure

In this section, my aim is to give you some context for various architectural components that combine to make the User Profile and User Profile Synchronization infrastructure. Figure 4-1 shows a pictorial overview of the components, and provides a logical view of the services and service applications involved. Following the infrastructure overview, we'll configure a new User Profile Service and Sync in a virgin SharePoint 2010 farm.

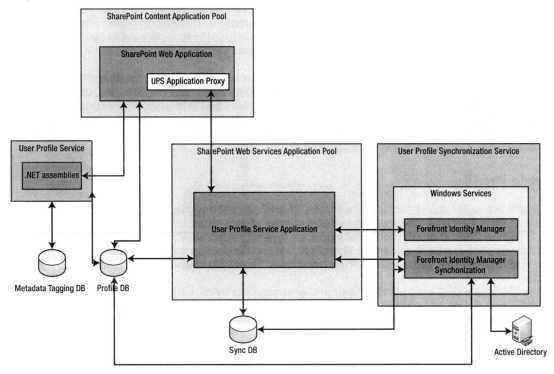

Figure 4-1. User profile infrastructure overview

■ **Note** Although most deployments of User Profile Synchronization use Active Directory, there is no reason why you cannot configure UPS to another directory store, such as an LDAP service.

The User Profile Service Application

A SharePoint 2010 Service Application exists in a context similar to that of a SharePoint web application—it resides in Internet Information Services (IIS) and offers application presence to other SharePoint and non-SharePoint services on the network. Within Internet Information Server Manager 7.0 (INETMGR), expand the SharePoint Web Services application to see a list of IIS applications, some with GUID names—these are the service applications hosted on the current server of your farm. See Figure 4-2.

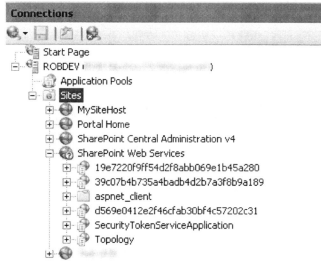

Figure 4-2. *SharePoint service applications in IIS*

The UPS application is actually a WCF (Windows Communication Foundation) service, which exposes service end-points so that other servers in the farm may leverage the UPS application to access User Profile data. Discussion of WCF is beyond the scope of this book, except to say that all SharePoint Service Applications operate as WCF services and expose functionality via the standard WCF service patterns. The UPS application uses three SharePoint databases to host user profile-related data, which we will discuss in the section on configuration, later in this chapter.

Administrators may configure multiple UPS applications in the farm, but only one UPS Service Application associates with a User Profile Synchronization SharePoint Service.

The User Profile Service

The User Profile Service (UPS) is a *SharePoint* service. Note that a SharePoint service is *not* the same as a *Windows* service. SharePoint services exist only in the SharePoint context and consist of functionality that is abstracted into .NET assemblies within the SharePoint platform and exposed to the administrator in the list of services in the SharePoint farm in Central Admin. Take the following steps to view this list:

1. Open Central Admin.

2. Click the link Manage Services on Server in the System Settings section.

3. Look for the User Profile Service in the list.

Only one server in the SharePoint farm should have the User Profile Service running, which is the Service Machine instance for the User Profile role.

The User Profile Synchronization Service

Like the User Profile Service, the User Profile Synchronization Service (UPSS) exists as a SharePoint service and lists alongside its sibling UPS on the server in the farm, delegated as the Service Machine Instance for the User Profile role. This particular service provides .NET wrapper functionality to SharePoint, beyond that provided by the Forefront Identity Manager (discussed next).

Only one server in the farm should run the User Profile Synchronization Service, typically the same server running the User Profile Service. This service associates with only one User Profile Service Application and accepts credentials under which the FIM operates.

The Forefront Identity Manager

SharePoint 2010 bundles a lightweight version of the Forefront Identity Manager Application, which has the primary job of managing user and server identity. The FIM consists of two Windows Services—configured by the User Profile Synchronization Service (UPSS) SharePoint Service.

■ **Note** The FIM client tool, part of Windows, does not support customizing the FIM services that bundle in SharePoint 2010, but supports monitoring and troubleshooting.

The topic of Forefront Identity Management is outside the scope of this book, but it is worth understanding its role in the User Profile Synchronization infrastructure as managing identity as it pertains to users in SharePoint 2010.

The FIM client tool for SharePoint 2010 can be found at the following location: C:\Program Files\Microsoft Office Servers\14.0\Synchronization Service\UIShell\miisclient.exe.

Configuring User Profile Synchronization

Configuration of User Profile Synchronization in SharePoint 2010 is a task that seems to give administrators more trouble than any other area of SharePoint 2010 installation and configuration. Configuration of AD sync on MOSS had its issues also, but UPS sync in SharePoint 2010 is vastly more complicated and therefore gives administrators the most trouble when it does not work. So here I'll guide you through the configuration of User Profile Sync on a virgin SharePoint 2010 environment.

■ **Note** The steps in this chapter assume no prior configuration of UPS and no User Profile Service Application existing in the farm. They also assume the use of Active Directory (AD) as source of user profiles, although you may use another directory service.

Establishing Managed Accounts

Establishing the correct credentials and configuring the necessary services and service applications under the correct set of credentials is essential to ensuring smooth installation and operation of UPS. 90% of the time, when UPS and UPS synchronization fails, it is because of incorrect credentials, or credentials with insufficient privileges.

Chapter 2 introduced the notion of managed service accounts in SharePoint 2010—rather than specifying Active Directory account credentials everywhere, we can map these credentials to a managed account name in SharePoint in one central location. Assuming that you have installed SharePoint 2010 and have access to the Central Administration site, the following steps allow you to view a list of managed service accounts in the farm:

1. Open Central Admin.

2. Click the Security section heading.

3. Click the link Configure Managed Accounts in the General Security sub-section.

You should see a page similar to Figure 4-3, although you will likely see a different list of managed accounts from that in my environment.

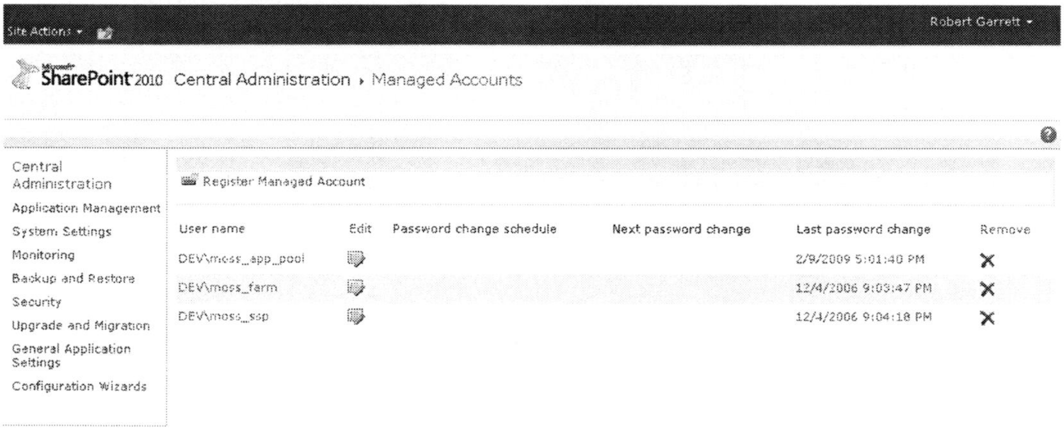

Figure 4-3. *Managed accounts*

Before we begin configuring the UPS infrastructure, make sure the following statements are true:

- SharePoint is installed and configured without a UPS Service Application (you can delete the application and proxy from the managed service applications list).

- You have configured a farm account, e.g. DOMAIN\spfarm as a managed account.

- You are not logged into the server or Central Admin as the farm account.

- The farm account is not a local administrator on the server running UPS.

- Your farm does not use a Fully Qualified Domain Name or IP address to connect SharePoint 2010 with SQL Server—use a SQL alias or NETBIOS name to avoid issues with provisioning services later.

- Your environment has the latest Cumulative Update applied—at least June 2010, preferably August 2010 or later.

With the above provisions met, we are ready to begin configuring User Profile Synchronization in our SharePoint 2010 farm.

Note Follow all steps, from this point on, in sequence. Do not be tempted to skip or attempt steps in a different order, or you will risk failure in the setup.

The first step, and pertinent to this section, is to create some service accounts in your organization's active Directory forest. In a typical SharePoint 2010 configuration, you will need at least the following three domain accounts:

- `DOMAIN\spcontent`

- `DOMAIN\spservices`

- `DOMAIN\spups`

Ensure that these accounts exist as normal users with no password expiration. The `DOMAIN\spups` account must have Replicating Directory Changes permission in the Active Directory. This account does not run any Windows or SharePoint services nor does it run any application pools.

Note Not granting Replicating Directory Changes to the UPS account is typically the first mistake administrators make when configuring UPS synch, and this may lead to issues later.

The following steps detail how to grant replicating directory changes from within the Active Directory Users and Computers configuration snap-in (please note that these steps require AD Security Account Operators right):

1. Right-click the domain name in Active Directory Users and Computers.

2. Choose Delegate Control, and then click Next.

3. Add the `DOMAIN\spups` account and click Next.

4. Select Create Custom Task to Delegate, and click Next.

5. Click Next again.

6. Select the Replicating Directory Changes permission, and click Next.

7. Click Finish.

Next, we configure replicating directory changes on the Configuration Naming Context for the domain:

8. Run `ADSIEDIT.msc`.

9. Connect to the Configuration partition.

10. Select Configuration in the Select a Well-Known Naming Context drop down list.

11. Right-click the Configuration partition and choose Properties.

12. Select the Security tab.

13. Add the `DOMAIN\spups` user to the list and give it Replicating Directory Changes permission.

■ **Note** When running the Domain Controller on Windows 2003 or earlier, add the `DOMAIN\spups` user to the Pre Windows 2000 Compatible Access built-in group.

The SharePoint Farm account must have Logon Locally rights, on the server performing UPS sync. The following steps detail how to configure this:

14. Open either Group Policy editor or the Local Security Policy editor (in Administration Tools).

15. Navigate to Security Settings ➤ Local Policies ➤ User Rights and Assignments.

16. Click Allow Logon Locally.

17. Make sure the farm account is either in one of the groups listed, or explicitly listed.

18. If running SharePoint on a domain controller (this is a bad practice), use `GPMC.msc` to edit the default domain policy.

19. Execute `GPUPDATE.exe` from an elevated command line to refresh the policy.

■ **Note** At this stage, I recommend a server reboot to ensure that the `DOMAIN\spups` account picks up all permission and policy changes—this will help avoid issues with the service provisioning process hanging, later.

Next, register managed accounts for the `DOMAIN\spcontent` and `DOMAIN\spservices` accounts:

20. Open Central Admin.

21. Click the Security section heading.

22. Click the link Configure Managed Accounts, in the General Security sub-section.

23. Click Register Managed Account and provide details for the two domain accounts to register.

24. You can register the DOMAIN\spups account, if you like, but UPS does not use managed accounts and expects a Windows domain account, so there is little point.

With windows domain accounts and managed accounts configured, now create two web applications—one to host your site collection, and another to act as the My-site host. Use the content account as the application pool account for both web applications. Create a new site collection in the My-site Host, using the My-site Host Template.

■ **Note** As a best practice for large deployment (more than 5000 users), consider hosting a My Site host in a separate web application.

After creating a new host application for My Sites, and provisioning service accounts, in the next section we can now configure the UPS application.

Creating the User Profile Service Application

The following steps assume you have completed the steps in the previous section to establish managed service accounts. This is very important; failure to establish correct accounts and permissions affects the steps in this and following sub-sections. Assuming you've completed the prior steps with no errors, or issues, follow the steps below to provision the User Profile Service Application:

1. Open Central Admin.

2. Click the Application Management link.

3. Click the Manage Service Applications link.

4. Make sure no other User Profile Service application or proxy exists in the list. If there are any, delete them.

5. From the Ribbon, click the New icon and then select User Profile Service Application from the list.

6. Give the new service application a name, such as *User Profile Service Application.*

7. Create a new application pool for the application and use the DOMAIN\spservices account.

8. Check the names of the three databases—Profile, Sync, and Social. Either leave the default names, or change them.

9. Enter the name of the My Site host application (the form will validate this entry).

10. Select the managed path and site name scheme.

11. Leave the proxy setting as is.

12. Click Create and wait while SharePoint creates the UPS service application.

13. If the NetBIOS name is different from the Fully Qualified Domain Name, configure the service application with the following PowerShell script:
```
$upssa = Get-SpServiceAplication  -Id <Guid of the UPS Service
Application>
$upssa.NetBIOSDomainNamesEnabled = 1
$upssa.Update()
```

You should now have a working UPS Service Application and proxy in your farm (you may need to refresh the managed services list page). The next section details the steps for starting the necessary SharePoint services for UPS.

Starting the Services

At this point, you should have completed the steps in the previous sections and have a working UPS service application and proxy. Take the following steps to start the User Profile Service and User Profile Sync Service SharePoint Services:

1. Add the DOMAIN\spfarm account to the Administrators group on the server running FIM/UPS.

2. Perform an IISRESET and reset the SharePoint timer service.

3. From the home page of Central Admin, click the System Settings section title link.

4. Click the Manage Services on Server link.

5. If it is not already started, start the User Profile Service, which requires no options.

6. Start the User Profile Sync Service, which displays a page for options, like that in Figure 4-4.

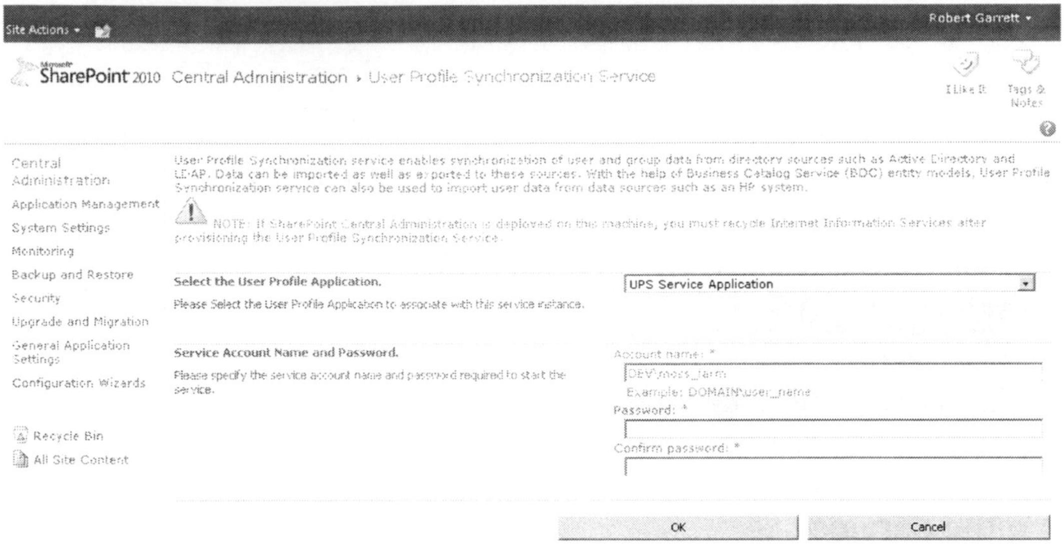

Figure 4-4. *Starting the User Profile Sync Service*

7. Select the UPS Service Application in the drop down.

8. Enter the farm password, and click OK.

9. Now you need to wait. The status of the service will appear as Starting. Do not be alarmed if the status remains in the Starting state for 10 minutes or longer, as SharePoint is doing a lot of work to configure FIM.

10. While you wait, open the services control panel (SERVICES.msc).

11. You should see two Forefront Identity services in the list. The User Profile Sync Service starts these services. *Do not be tempted to start these services yourself—this will break UPS Sync in SharePoint.*

12. Once the User Profile Sync Service is started, remove the DOMAIN\spfarm account from the administrators group on the FIM/UPS server.

13. Perform an IISRESET and reset the SharePoint timer service.

14. If you have a named instance of SQL, you may need to allow inbound connections to MSDTC on the server running FIM.

If all has gone according to plan and you have a green Started status next to both your User Profile Service and User Profile Sync Service in your Services list, give yourself a pat on the back—if something goes wrong, it typically happens before now.

Importing User Profiles from Active Directory

This procedure assumes you have completed the steps in the previous section—and thus have a working UPS Service Application, and the User Profile Service and User Profile Sync Service started in

SharePoint. The following steps demonstrate setting up a connection to Active Directory to perform a profile import for the users in the domain.

1. From the home page of Central Admin, click the Application Management link.

2. Click the link for Manage Service Applications.

3. Find the UPS Service Application, which you created an earlier in this chapter.

4. Click to the right of the name to highlight the row; then click Manage from the Ribbon.

If all is well, you should see a page like that in Figure 4-5.

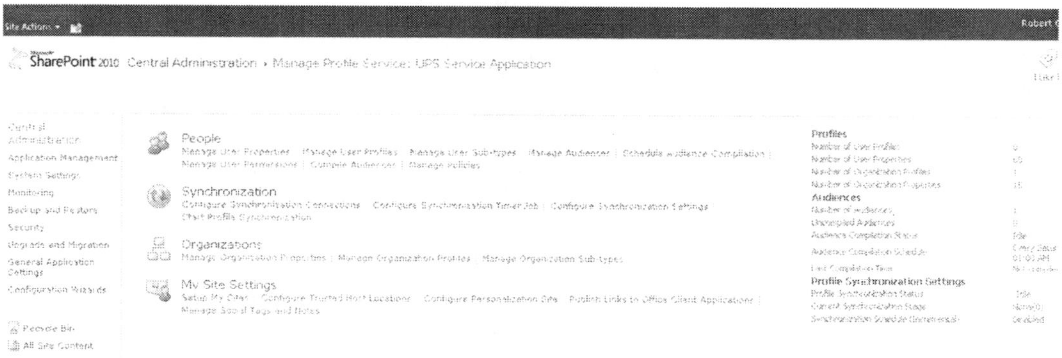

Figure 4-5. The User Profile Service admin page

5. In the Synchronization section, click the Configure Synchronization Connections link.

6. Click the Create New Connection button.

7. Give the connection a name and set the type as Active Directory.

8. Enter the forest name (you can use the domain name for purposes of demonstration).

9. Select the authentication type as Windows.

10. Enter the credentials as DOMAIN\spups and its password; you must use this account as it is the account used by FIM to establish sync with AD.

11. Click the Populate Containers button to get a list of containers, as shown in Figure 4-6.

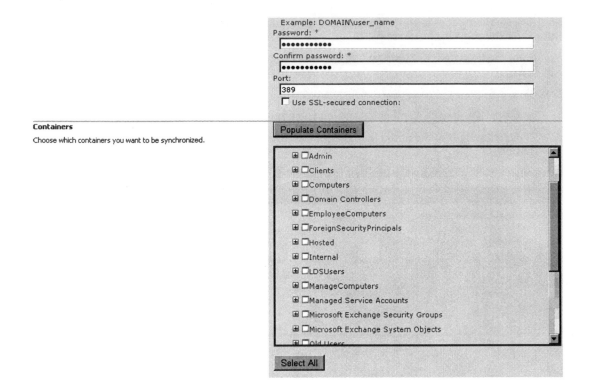

Figure 4-6. *Populated containers for AD connection—import*

12. You might be tempted to click the check box for the entire domain, or hit that Select All button. *Avoid this*; instead, expand the hierarchy, and select the OU that contains the users.

13. Click the OK button, and SharePoint will configure the import connection.

14. Navigate back to the User Profiles admin page (Figure 4-5).

15. Click the Start Profile Synchronization link.

16. On the next page, change the radio button to Full Synchronization, and click OK.

17. Refresh the UPS admin page, and you should see the synchronization status on the right of the page change from Idle to Synchronizing (see Figure 4-7).

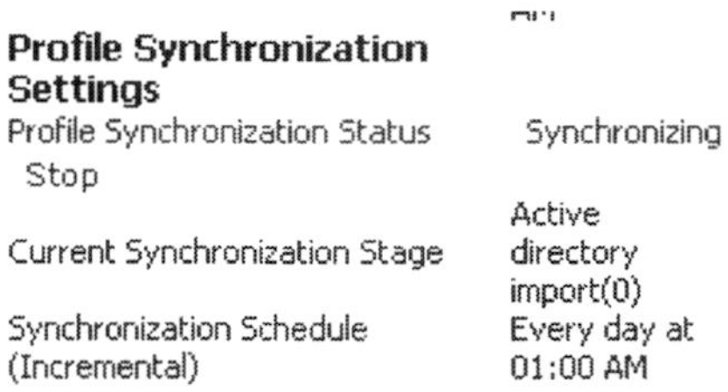

Profile Synchronization Settings

	FIM
Profile Synchronization Status Stop	Synchronizing
Current Synchronization Stage	Active directory import(0)
Synchronization Schedule (Incremental)	Every day at 01:00 AM

Figure 4-7. Synchronization status

The synchronization process is very slow! So be prepared to wait a while.

18. To see the status of the import, you can click the Synchronizing link. For a more verbose view of the import status, run the FIM client tool, available from `C:\Program Files\Microsoft Office Servers\14.0\Synchronization Service\UIShell\miisclient.exe`.

19. Assuming there were no errors, once the synchronization job completes, you can see the number of imported profiles in the top-right of the admin page.

20. In the People section, click the Manage User Profiles link to search and view user profiles for those users imported.

This completes configuration of the User Profile Service and Synchronization for what is the equivalent one-way import that you could do with SharePoint 2007. But the nice thing about SharePoint 2010 is that user profile synchronization works both ways—so users may update their profile in SharePoint and see the changes push back to AD (or other LDAP system). The next section chapter covers the additional configuration steps to write back to Active Directory.

Writing Back to Active Directory

One-way synchronization from Active Directory to SharePoint is fine, but better is the ability to allow users to update their profile in SharePoint and update the changes back to Active Directory. Two-way User Profile Synchronization defines true user-profile synchronization as opposed to isolated import, which assumed that Active Directory (or the LDAP server) was the single-point authority for all profile data. The following steps configure Active Directory and SharePoint 2010 to allow write-back of profile changes to AD.

To allow write-back to AD, our `DOMAIN\spups` sync account requires additional directory permissions—Create Child Objects (for the OU we are writing back into):

1. Run `ADSIEdit.msc`.

2. Connect to the default naming context for the domain.

3. Navigate down the tree to the OU that you wish to allow write back.

4. Right click the OU and select Properties.

5. Click the Security tab.

6. At this point, we need to add the `DOMAIN\spups` user and grant Create Child Objects permission and read and write permissions—but wait!

7. The DOMAIN\spups user already exists in this list because we delegated Directory Replicating Changes permission. If you are tempted to add the additional permissions to this user, *do not*. This will result in breaking the profile import.

8. From the dialog shown in Figure 4-8, click the Add button, to add the user again.

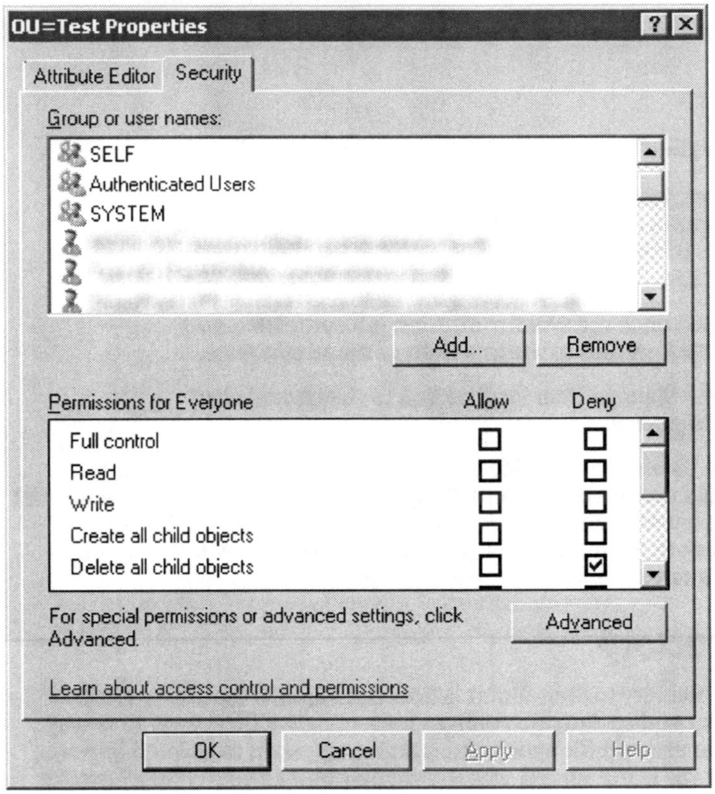

Figure 4-8. Security for the OU

9. *Do not* click OK just yet.

10. Click the Advanced button, and in the dialog that appears, scroll down to the instance of DOMAIN\spups account that has <not inherited>, as shown in Figure 4-9.

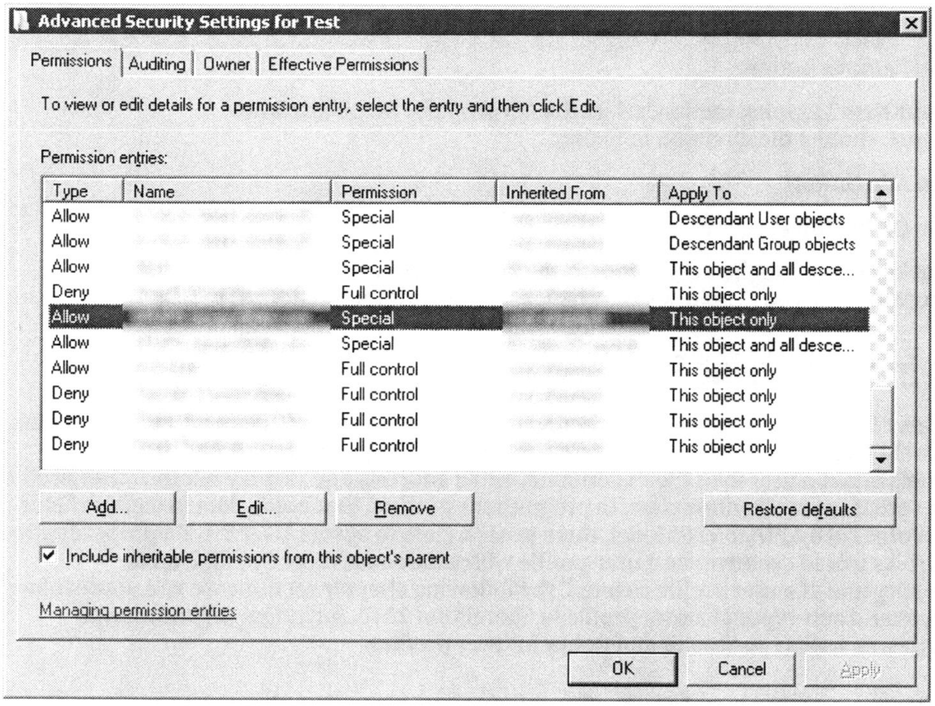

Figure 4-9. Advanced Permissions for our UPS Sync account

11. Click the Edit button.

12. Ensure that the Apply To combo box value is This Object and All Descendent Objects.

13. Click the check box in the Allow column for the permissions: Write All Properties and Create Child Objects.

14. Click OK several times to back to the main ADSIEdit.msc window.

At this stage, the profile import connection, which you established in an earlier configuration stage, imports only! If you think about it, this makes sense—could you imagine how upset HR might be if SharePoint were to overwrite their profile data with user changes, without management control?

The following steps configure the User Profile Synchronization Service for more granular control of properties written back to AD:

15. Go back to the User Profile Admin page.

16. Click the Manage User Properties link.

17. Choose the property, with mapping to AD, to write back (make a mental note of the AD property-mapped field).

18. Click the combo box over the property name and select Edit.

19. Scroll to the section Property Mapping for Synchronization.

20. Click the Remove button.

21. In the Add New Mapping section, select the AD property in the Attribute combo box, change the direction to Export.

22. Click the Add button.

23. Click the OK button to save changes.

You can now make changes to the data in the profile field you changed above, and when the synchronization process runs, you should see the changes for the property reflected in AD.

User Profiles in SharePoint 2010

A user profile consists of a series of attributes that define the profile of a given user known to SharePoint. User profiles effectively give individuals of the system—the users—body in a SharePoint site by providing more details about a user than their username, email address, and display name. A user profile is synonymous to a struct, or methodless class, in programming terms, that holds data in various fields. In fact, in the SharePoint 2010 API/Object Model, there exists a class to access User Profile properties. In a similar vein, DBA folks would synonymize a user profile with a database record or SQL table.

With the basic principle of a user profile covered, the following chapter sections we will now explore the various properties and sub-types of a user profile in SharePoint 2010, including organizational profiles and properties, as well as audiences and policy for user profiles.

User Profile Properties and Sub-Types

Unlike the 2007 version, SharePoint 2010 looks after user profile management via a dedicated managed service application. We will revisit the User Profile Service (UPS) and UPS Application later in this chapter, but at this stage, I can demonstrate view of the user profile properties via the managed service in Central Admin, as follows:

1. Open Central Admin, and click on the Application Management link.

2. Click Manage Service Applications in the Service Applications section.

3. Scroll to the User Profile Service Application—do not worry if you do not see one in the list, I discussed configuring UPS earlier in this chapter.

4. SharePoint shows the UPS admin page (see Figure 4-5 earlier in this chapter).

5. Click the Manage User Properties link and see a page like that in Figure 4-10.

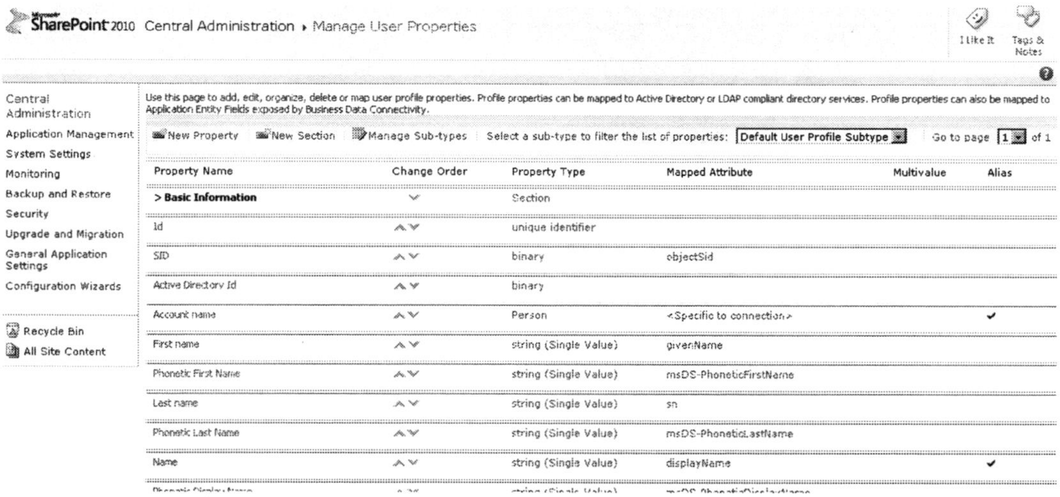

Figure 4-10. User profile properties

In Figure 4-10, notice the Mapped Attribute column, which shows how a profile property maps to an attribute in Active Directory, or other LDAP directory service, configured as part of User Profile Synchronization. Out of the box, SharePoint provides a default set of user profiles to describe an individual in an organization. Not all profile properties map nicely to Active Directory user attributes, which is why not all properties have a mapping.

Each profile property consists of a type, shown in the Property Type column in Figure 4-10. The property type indicates the type of value data a user profile instance might contain for the property. For example, the First Name property is a single String type, because first names typically contain alphanumeric characters and most names have a length less than 255 characters (the SharePoint limit for strings). Other property types used by SharePoint include the subset integers, Booleans, date/time, unique identifiers, person, and binary.

Now we can explore a user profile property. I will start with an easy one—the last name:

6. Scroll down the page shown in Figure 4-10 and find the Last Name property.

7. Hover over the name of the property, and in the drop down combo box, select Edit. You should see a page like that in Figure 4-11.

Figure 4-11. Editing user profile Property Settings

The Property Settings page displays a number of sections for editing specific details about the property. Table 4-1 details the various sections.

Table 4-1:User Profile Property Settings Page Sections

Section Name	Details
Property Settings	Defines the name, display name, property type, length, and whether the property maps to a term set in the term store.
Sub-type of Profile	The sub-type that this property associates (more on sub-types in a moment).
Usage	The number of active profiles in the user profile store that have data values in this property—this is important information because SharePoint Search only indexes user profile properties that have data, if this value is 0, then this property will not show up in search mapping later.
User Description	Description of the property, displayed when users asked to enter data for the property, when editing their profile.
Policy	Policy for the profile property; you'll learn more about policy for user profiles later in this chapter.
Edit Settings	These determine whether users can edit the data in this property or not.
Display Settings	The context of where this property displays.

Section Name	Details
Search Settings	Alias and Index settings for user profile search (more on user profile search later in the chapter).
Property Mapping for Synchronization	I briefly discussed use of this section and the next section, in configuring two-way profile synchronization—this section defines the property mappings to Active Directory and LDAP stores.
Add New Mapping	Section to establish a new mapping to an existing Active Directory or LDAP store connection (configured in User Profile Synchronization).

User Profile Sub-Types

User profile sub-types provide a more granular grouping of property types for a user profile. They allow the creation of different kinds of user profiles, each with its own unique fields, for different purposes. For example, suppose an organization wants a special user profile type for contractors to complete, which has all the attributes of a default user profile but with additional properties. The following steps demonstrate creating the Contractor sub-type.

1. Open Central Admin.

2. Click the Manage Applications link.

3. Click the Manage Service Applications link under Service Applications.

4. Scroll down to the User Profile Service Application, click to the right of the name, and then click Manage from the Ribbon.

5. From the UPS admin page shown in Figure 4-5 earlier, click the link Manage User Sub-types.

Figure 4-12 shows the page for managing user profile sub-types.

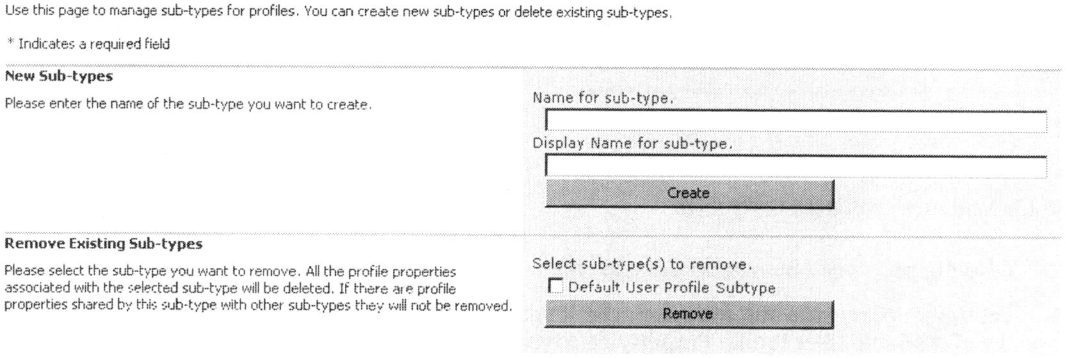

Figure 4-12. Managing user profile sub-types

6. Enter a name in the Name field for the new sub-type, such as Contractor.

7. Enter a display name.

8. Click the Create button; you should now see a new sub-type listed in the section below this button.

9. Navigate back to the UPS admin page.

Next, we can create a new custom property to include in the Contractor sub-type—one that regular profile users need not populate…

Adding Custom User Profile Properties

The SharePoint 2010 User Profile Service allows the addition of custom profile properties, in addition to those provided by SharePoint. The set of user properties that SharePoint 2010 provides is quite extensive, but an organization may require its own custom properties for capturing very specific details about people in the organization. Just like the out-of-box user profile properties, custom profile properties surface in user profile pages, indexes for search, and groups in user profile sub-types. The following steps show how to create a new user profile property and add this property to the sub-type created in the previous subsection:

1. From the UPS admin page, click the Manage User Properties link.

2. Click the New Property button at the top of the page.

3. SharePoint shows a new profile Property Settings page with blank form fields to configure the property (see Figure 4-13).

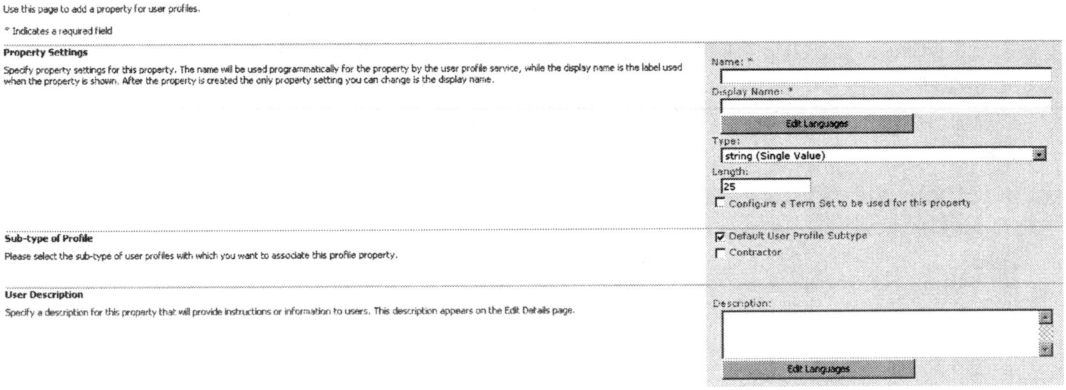

Figure 4-13. New user profile property form

4. Give the property a name and a display name.

5. Set the property type and max character length of the field—see Table 4-2 for a list of available User Profile Property data types.

6. Leave the check box for configure term set unchecked—we will visit term sets in a later chapter—this option effectively couples the property with a term set, so values entered for the profile field map to a term in a term set.

7. In the Sub-type of Profile section, choose the user profile sub-type we created in the previous sub-section, and uncheck the default sub-type.

8. Add an optional description.

9. In the Policy Settings section, set the policy on whether data for the property shall be required by all users and the visibility of the property data with managers and team members.

10. In the Search Settings, leave the check box for Indexed checked to surface data for this property in people search results.

11. You may also map the custom property to a synchronization connection (see earlier on in this chapter).

12. Click the OK button to commit the changes.

13. Assuming there are no errors on the form, SharePoint takes us back to the profile properties list—notice the absence of the new property in the list; this is because we create the property for the Contractor sub-type, and by default the properties page shows those properties for the default sub-type,.

14. At the top of the page, change the sub-type to Contractor.

15. Scroll to the bottom of the page and you should see the new property in the Custom Properties section.

Table 4-2:*User Profile Property Data Types*

Data Type	Description
big integer	Large positive or negative 64-bit number
binary	Binary blog data (usually populated programmatically)
boolean	True or False
date	Date
date no year	Date without the year (ideal for birthday)
date time	Date and time
E-mail	E-mail address
float	Floating point number
HTML	Text with Hypertext Markup
integer	Positive or negative 32-bit number

Data Type	Description
Person	Username of another user in SharePoint or directory system
string (multivalue)	Multiple lines of Unicode text
stirng (single value)	Single line of Unicode text (255 characters)
time zone	Integer value indicating the time zone offset
unique identifier	32-bit unique HEX based identifier
URL	Uniform Resource Locator

A Custom Profile Property and Sub-type in Action

Having completed the steps in the previous two sections, you should now have a new custom user profile property added, and you have contained this custom property in a new Contractor sub-type. Now let's see the Sub-type and custom property in action, as in the following steps:

1. Navigate back to the UPS admin page (see Figure 4-5 earlier).

2. Click the Manage User Profiles link.

For the sake of demonstration, we are going to create a new user profile, by hand.

3. Click the New Profile button.

Figure 4-14 shows the new user profile form.

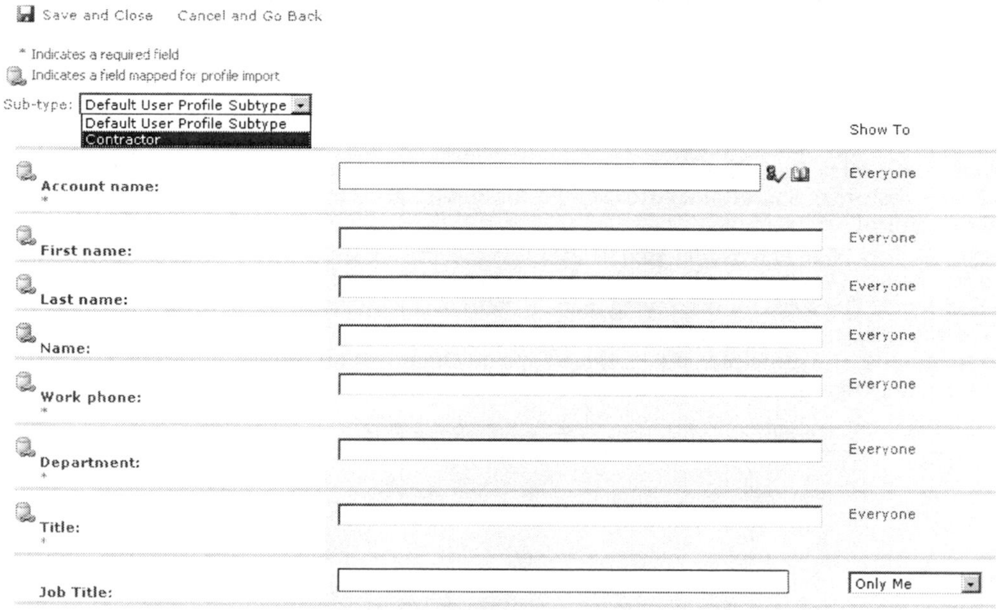

Figure 4-14. *The new user profile page*

4. Notice the combo box at the top of the page that allows you to change the sub-type—select the new Contractor sub-type.

5. Changing the sub-type to Contractor exposes the new property we added a few subsections back, and thus defines this user profile as type Contractor.

6. Scroll to the bottom of the page to see the new custom property; Figure 4-15 shows a portion of my screen with the field for this property highlighted.

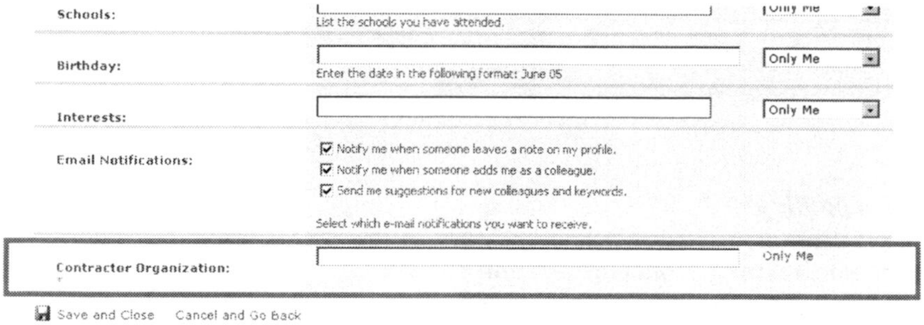

Figure 4-15. *The new custom property in the New Profile form*

Organization Profiles

New to SharePoint 2010 are *organization profiles*. SharePoint 2007 managed organization staff hierarchy via the Manager property of the profile, which was a property of type Person. The main limitation of this approach is that it does not provide much flexibility to arrange an organization chart. For example, if you reported to multiple managers, or your direct report was not necessarily your manager, or if you had managers with multiple roles, then the org chart became unmanageable in SharePoint 2007. The Organization Profile feature of SharePoint 2010 User Profile Service aims to remedy this issue with better control over the organization structure.

Organization profiles work in a similar vein to User Profiles. Within the UPS admin page, you should see three links, to Manage Organization Properties, Manage Organization Profiles, and Manage Organization Sub-types. The steps for displaying management of organization properties, managing sub-types, and creating organization profiles are similar, so I won't repeat them; see the earlier sections of this chapter for details. The principles shown there apply to Organization profiles alike. Figure 4-16 shows the form to enter Organization profile data.

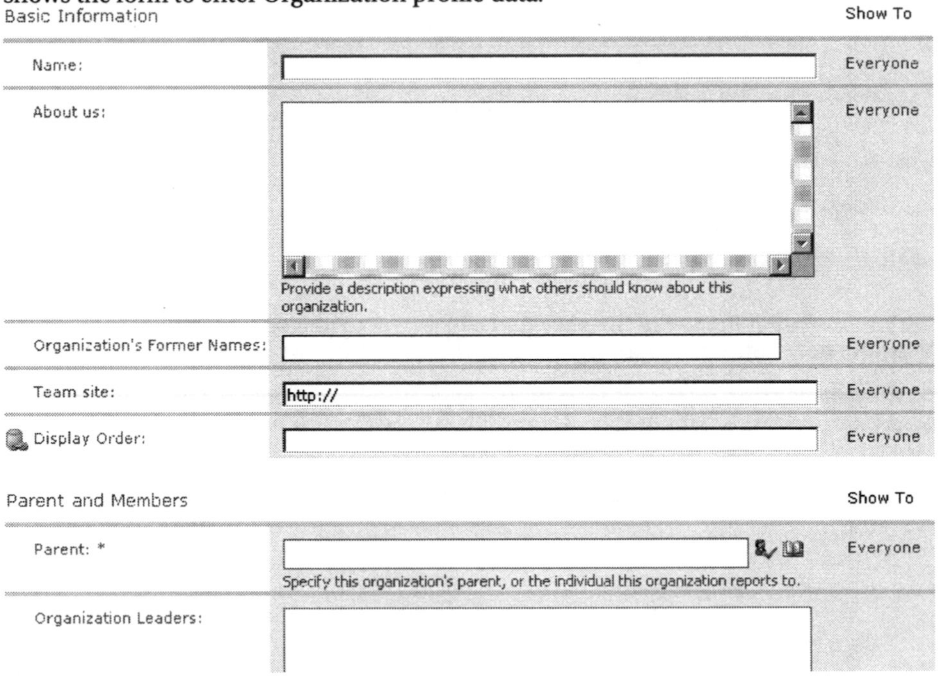

Figure 4-16. A new organization profile form

Following are some points worth noting about Organization profiles:

- Every organization profile may define one or many leaders.

- Every organization profile may include one or many members.

- All direct reports of a leader may be members automatically.

- Every organization profile has a mandatory parent person or group.

- Correct management of your organization chart in SharePoint 2010 allows users of your sites to see a graphical org chart.

Audiences

Audiences in SharePoint 2010 are similar to those of SharePoint 2007. An audience defines a set of people, who see *targeted content*. Do not confuse audiences with SharePoint Security Groups—although both combine a set of users, audiences only define those users who see specific content in lists and list items, and membership of an audience is defined by rule criteria, not explicit inclusion.

For example, a publishing page on a SharePoint 2010 site may include a specific content area that only certain users see. Users who are not in the audience get to see all other content areas on the page, and the page itself, but the specific content area that has a designated audience can be viewed only by those members of the audience. To accomplish this same behavior without audiences would involve multiple page instances with different security permissions and duplicate content across both pages.

Audiences must be compiled by a SharePoint administrator before use, and they can allow targeting of content at the list or list item level. The following steps demonstrate how to create a new audience from the User Profile Service Application and use the audience in targeted areas.

1. Open Central Admin.

2. Click the Manage Applications link.

3. Click the Manage Service Applications link, under Service Applications.

4. Scroll down to the User Profile Service Application, click to the right of the name and then click Manage from the Ribbon.

5. From the UPS admin page (see Figure 4-5 earlier), click the link Manage Audiences.

The page shown in Figure 4-17 displays the total existing audiences and any uncompiled audiences.

Use this page to view audience properties, add and edit audiences, and view audience membership.

Total audiences: 1
Uncompiled audiences: 0
Find audiences that start with:

[   ] [Find]

📁 New Audience   ✖ Delete   View: [All ▼]   Go to page [1 ▼] of 1

Audience Name	Description	Last Compiled	Last Compilation Status	Members
All site users	All users who can access the site	Not applicable	Not applicable	Not applicable

Figure 4-17. Audience list

6. Click the New Audience button.

7. Give the audience a name, description, and owner.

8. Decide whether members of the group are those that meet all the audience criteria or some, and set the radio button accordingly.

9. Click the OK button.

10. In the next screen, shown in Figure 4-18, create a rule based on the value of a user/group property or user association.

Use this page to add a rule for this audience. Learn more about audience rules.

	Select one of the following: *
Operand	○ User
Select **User** to create a rule based on a Windows security group, distribution list, or organizational hierarchy.	⊙ Property
Select **Property** and select a property name to create a rule based on a user profile property.	[Department ▼]

	Operator: *
Operator	[= ▼]
Select an operator for this rule. The list of available operators will change depending on the operand you selected in the previous section.	

	Value: *
Value	[work]
Specify a single value to compare.	

[OK] [Cancel]

Figure 4-18. Rule creation for a user audience

11.   Click the OK button.

The resulting page, shown in Figure 4-19, displays the new audience—still not compiled.

Use this page to view and edit the properties of this audience.

Audience Properties

Name:	Employees
Description:	
Owner:	i:0#.w\ ....
Create Time:	6/5/2011 4:31 PM
Update Time:	6/5/2011 4:33 PM
Compiled:	No
Number of members:	Not compiled
Membership:	Members satisfy all of the rules
Last compilation:	Not compiled
Compilation Errors:	No error

▣ Edit audience
▣ View membership
▣ Compile audience

Audience Rules

Click on audience rules to edit them. Learn more about managing audience rules.

Operand	Operator	Value
Department	=	Work

▣ Add rule

Figure 4-19. Audience details page

12.   Click the Compile Audience link, SharePoint will now include members in the audience that satisfy the audience inclusion criteria.

13.   Once compilation completes (without error), click the View Membership link to see all those members in the audience.

> ■ **Note** SharePoint updates audience membership based on a schedule, which you may change from the Schedule Audience Compilation link in the main UPS admin page.

Once you complete the compilation of an audience, you may then use this audience to target content to those members for list items, and web parts. The following steps configure audience targeting for a list:

14. For a list in your site collection, click the List Settings from the Ribbon.

15. Click the Audience Targeting settings link in the General Settings section.

16. Check the check box to enable audience targeting for the list, and then click OK.

To apply audience targeting for a specific list item, follow the steps below:

17. View the properties of the list item.

18. Find the item field named Target Audiences.

19. Choose a compiled target audience and save the item.

People Search

People Search has always been a popular tool for finding individuals in an organization via a company SharePoint-based Intranet. SharePoint 2007 introduced people search around the user profile paradigm and allowed administrators to configure the SharePoint search engine to surface profile data by indexing User Profile Property field data (see previous sections of this chapter for more on User Profiles and Properties). People search is a powerful tool in an organization, which SharePoint 2010 improves by including tagging and enhanced profile capabilities into the search mixture.

I did not overembellish search configuration and administration in this book, because the subject of SharePoint Search is one that justifies a whole book of its own (and I bet you will find one on the shelves of your local bookstore).[1] However, I felt that People Search deserved a mention.

Since People Search assumes certain knowledge of Search configuration, I will do my best to give you a quick overview of Search in SharePoint 2010. First, however, I want to mention FAST search, which is a new Enterprise Search Platform. FAST provides more scaling and extensibility to SharePoint search, and is very much out of the scope of this book, so when I discuss search concepts I am talking about the standard SharePoint Enterprise Search offering.

SharePoint Search—A Primer

Like almost every other service-based functionality in SharePoint 2010, search exists as a Service Application in the farm. For brevity, I will assume that your farm has search configured and running. The following steps detail how to gain access to the search admin page:

---

[1] For instance, *Pro SharePoint 2010 Search* by Josh Noble, Robert Piddocke, and Dan Bakmand-Mikalski (Apress, 2010).

■ **Note** You can find details on installing and configuring SharePoint 2010 Search at the following location: http://technet.microsoft.com/en-us/enterprisesearch/ee441229

---

1. Open Central Admin.

2. Click the Manage Applications link.

3. Click the Manage Service Applications link, under Service Applications.

4. Scroll down to the Enterprise Search Service Application, click to the right of the name, and then click Manage from the Ribbon.

Figure 4-20 shows a preview of the Administration page for Search.

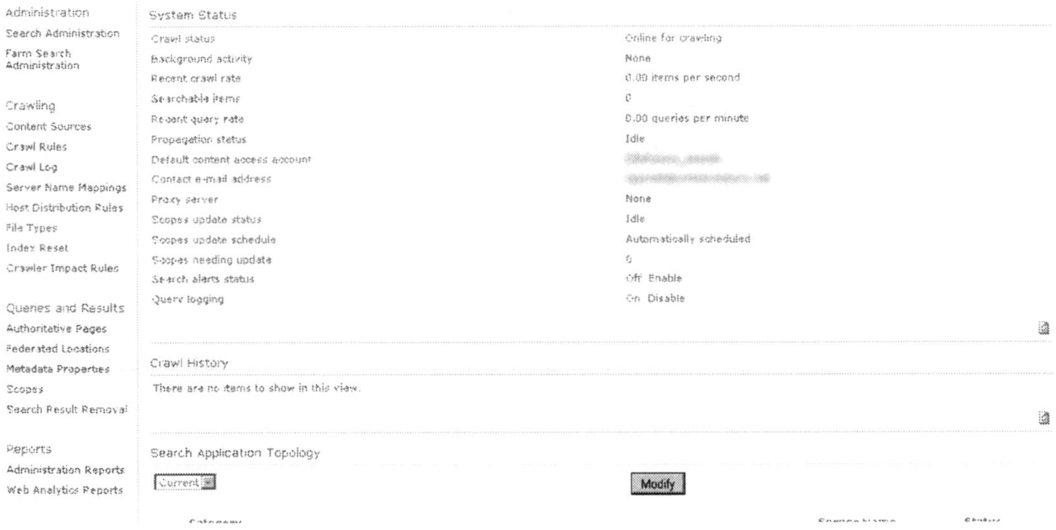

Figure 4-20. The Search Administration page

Content Sources

Let us first look at the crawling configuration, which defines the process in which SharePoint Search crawls for content. SharePoint 2010 Enterprise Search provides Federated Search, meaning that it can crawl and index content from various sources, not just the content in the SharePoint farm (site collections). The following steps demonstrate configuration of a *content source* for People content in the SharePoint User Profile store.

1. Click the Content Sources link in the left navigation.

2. SharePoint displays a page of configured content sources. You should see one already configured, called Local SharePoint Sites.

3. Hover over the name of the content source, click the combo box, and select Edit.

SharePoint shows a page like that in Figure 4-21.

Use this page to edit a content source.

* Indicates a required field

Name

Type a name to describe this content source.

Name: *

Local SharePoint sites

Content Source Details

This shows the current status of the Content Source.

Content Source Type:	SharePoint Sites
Current Status:	Idle
Last crawl type:	N/A
Last crawl began:	N/A
Last crawl duration:	N/A
Last crawl completed:	N/A

View Crawl History

Start Addresses

Type the URLs from which the search system should start crawling.

Type start addresses below (one per line): *

```
http://intranet
http://robdev
http://robdev:24147
http://robdev:4444
http://robdev:8080
sps3://robdev:8080
```

Example:

Figure 4-21. Search Content Source configuration page

- Important to note in Figure 4-21 is the start addresses, and the line that reads sps3://*domain*:*port*—this tells the SharePoint crawler to crawl the people store.

Scopes

SharePoint *search scopes* are effectively filters for content prior to indexing. A scope consists of one or more rules that determine whether the crawler throws out some content or includes it in the index. The content will be indexed if it matches the rule(s).

1. Click the Scopes link in the left navigation of the Search Admin page.

2. Hover over the People scope name and in the drop down combo select Edit Properties and Rules.

SharePoint displays a page like that in Figure 4-22.

3. See the rule that includes people data in the index: contentclass = urn:content-class:SPSPeople.

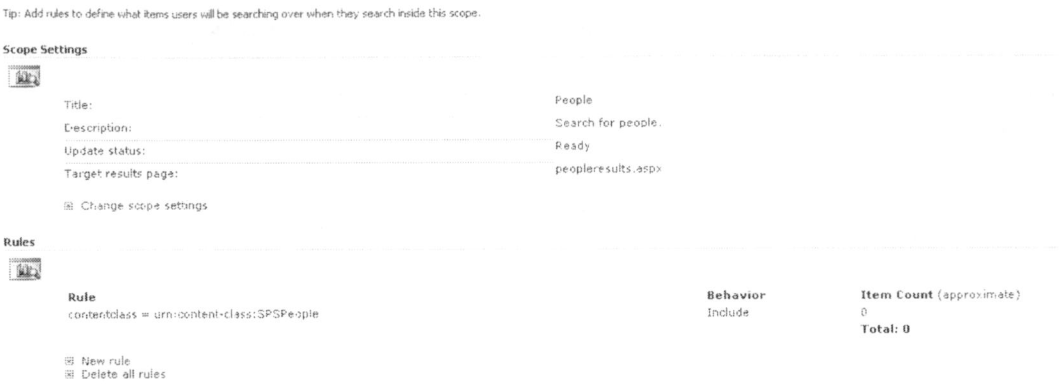

Tip: Add rules to define what items users will be searching over when they search inside this scope.

Scope Settings

Title: People

Description: Search for people.

Update status: Ready

Target results page: peopleresults.aspx

⊞ Change scope settings

Rules

Rule	Behavior	Item Count (approximate)
contentclass = urn:content-class:SPSPeople	Include	0
		Total: 0

⊞ New rule
⊞ Delete all rules

Figure 4-22. *Scope for People*

People Search in Action

With the brief search primer and configuration out of the way, this section demonstrates People Search in action. The following steps detail how to run a people-scoped search from within a SharePoint site collection:

1. From the top right of any of the site pages, change the scope in the search area to People, and type the name of the person (or wildcard) in the adjacent search box.

2. Alternatively, you can perform a people search from a Search Center, using the advanced search box.

3. Click the magnifying glass search symbol to kick off the search.

Figure 4-23 shows an example page of people search results.

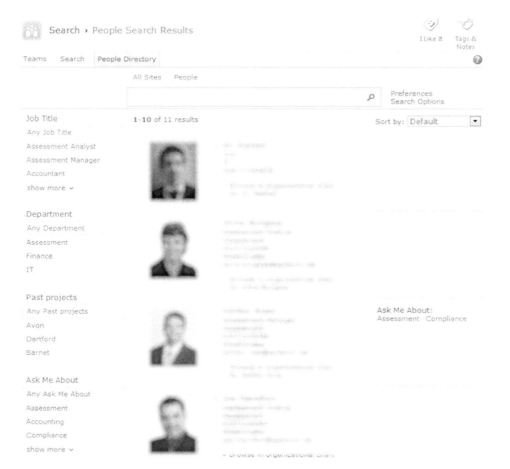

Figure 4-23. *People search results*

Summary

In this chapter, we took an in-depth look at configuring the User Profile Service in SharePoint 2010—one of the most troublesome areas to configure. You read about user profiles, along with their properties and user sub-types, and we looked at organization profiles in brief. Another key concept is audiences— administrators can generate groups of people based in inclusion rules and then apply those audiences to targeted content areas. At the end of this chapter, we had a quick look at people search and the configuration in the overarching SharePoint Enterprise Search Service Application.

In Chapter 5, we will visit social networking, My Sites, and the Managed Metadata Service Application for taxonomy and folksonomy tagging.

Social Networking

Social networking, also referred to as *social computing,* is the practice of many people collaborating and sharing information about their lives, preferences, thoughts, and feelings online. The IT industry and personal computing space has seen a prolific increase in the adoption of social networking, through community-based web sites like Facebook.com and Twitter.com, and collaboration via blogs and wikis. SharePoint has always been about collaboration in the workspace, and with the large drive in social networking from the home and personal computing space, corporations and non-corporate organizations are waking up to the benefits that social networking provides.

If you ask any computer -savvy person today to define their understanding of social networking, they will most likely mention Facebook. In recent years, Facebook has become a household name in the social networking space because it provides an intuitive means for anyone who can use a computer and the Internet to share information about themselves and collaborate on this information with others. Prior to Facebook, those with writing skills, and something to write about, hosted blogs on sites like blogger.com and livejournal.com. In fact, the livejournal.com site today is very different from what it was a few years ago; it embraces collaboration and user adoption through information sharing, and is no longer a space to write a monolithic stream of thought.

SharePoint has always provided a level of personal space in the platform, from as far back as SharePoint Portal Server 2003, with My Sites, which allow users in an organization to store documents and lists, and disseminate their own content to others in the organization. SharePoint 2007 went the next step and introduced wiki and blog site definitions, and with the addition of public -facing web site capability via the publishing infrastructure, SharePoint could participate in the public blogosphere world. What can you expect from SharePoint 2010 social networking features?

SharePoint 2010 now includes many of the information -sharing and content -tagging features that we have come to expect from other social networking platforms. SharePoint 2010 provides the Managed Metadata Service, which allows organizations to build managed taxonomy of tags and allow user self-expression tagging—*folksonomy*—with custom tagging capabilities. Tagging content in the platform assists the SharePoint 2010 search engine to provide richer search results and more relevant content for given search queries. The new Tag Cloud web part gives users a pictorial sense of content that has more relevance—the best part of tagging is that no single body of people in the organization must manage content proliferation, since the audiences of this content determine the relevance based on their view and categorization of the content. SharePoint 2010 introduces *rating controls,* so users can rate documents and pages from zero to five stars.

Blogs and *wikis* still exist in SharePoint 2010, only better—to name one feature, they now include the ability to host rich media in the form of video and audio content in their pages. The User Profile Service, discussed in Chapter 4, underwent enhancement and adopts the managed service infrastructure, and People Search provides greater level of detail when searching for users in the organization. Finally, user My Sites adopt a Facebook-like newsfeed model of ongoing events for a person in the organization. To start the exploration into the administration of social networking in SharePoint 2010, the next section introduces My Sites.   .

My Sites

Each My Site in SharePoint exists as a personal site collection for individuals in the organization. My Sites provide a space for users to store documents, host custom and stock lists, access their profile information, show their news, contribute thru a blog, feed, and so on.

■ **Note** SharePoint 2010 does not require users to have a My Site to view their User Profile information.

Creating the My Site Host Site Collection

In the previous chapter, I included brief details to create a My Site Host application, which is the main IIS-based application to which all My Site collections bind. It is not necessary to have a My Site host application, but I recommend you do for large deployments of more than 5000 users. If you did not create one in Chapter 4, the following steps detail creating such an application:

1. Open Central Administration.

2. Click the Manage Web Applications link from the home page.

3. On the next page, if you see an application with a name that looks like it might be a My Site Host, then the My Site Host application may already exist.

4. Click the New icon from the Ribbon, and then complete the new web application dialog and click OK to create the new application. See Chapter 2 for details on creating new web applications.

5. Return to the Central Admin home page.

6. Click the Application Management link.

7. Under the Site Collections heading, click the View All Site Collections link.

8. Make sure the correct Web Application is selected in the combo box (at the far right) for the My Site application.

You might see at least one site collection—the root ("/"), and possibly others if you have My Sites established (see Figure 5-1).

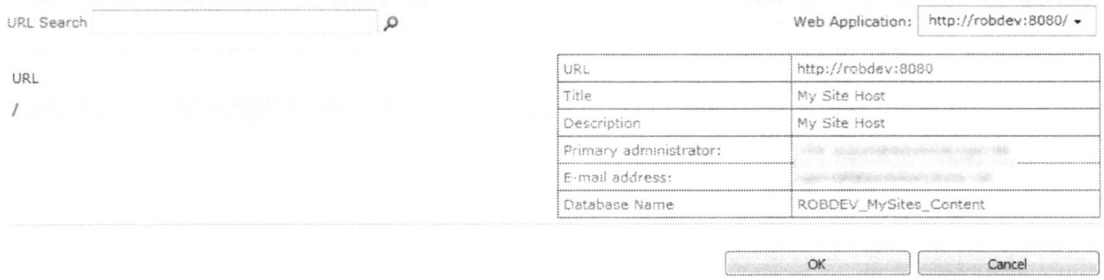

Figure 5-1. List of site collections on the My Site Host application

If you see the My Site Host root site collection, then you have no need to create a new site collection; scroll down to the steps for configuring managed paths.

Creating the Site Collection

If you need to create a site collection, go back to the Application Management area of Central Admin and take the following steps:

1. Click the Create Site Collections link.

2. In the next page, select the correct web application in the drop -down box at the top left of the page.

3. Give the site collection a name and description.

4. Choose the My Site Host template.

5. Provide a DOMAIN\name username for the primary and secondary site collection administrators.

6. Leave the quota option default.

7. Click OK to create the site collection.

Configuring Managed Paths

When you are ready to configure managed paths, go back to the Application Management area of Central Admin and take the following steps:

1. Click the Manage Web Applications link from the home page.

2. Click to the right of the name of the new My Sites host application.

3. From the Ribbon, click the Managed Paths icon.

4. Add two managed paths: personal as a wildcard, and my as explicit.

At this stage, you should have a working My Site host application and root site collection; you also have a managed path to host all user site collections (personal) and the host application path (my). The next set of steps assumes a working User Profile Service (see Chapter 4).

1. From the Central Admin home page, click the Application Management link.

2. Click the Manage Service Applications link.

3. Click to the right of the existing User Profile Service Application name listed.

4. Click the Manage icon in the Ribbon.

5. Scroll to the My Site settings section.

6. Set the My Site Host Location to http://myhostapplication:port/my. This is the location of the My Site host application and contains pages to show profile information of users on the site for example, http://myhostapplication:port/my/Person.aspx?accountname=DOMAIN\rgarrett.

7. Set the Personal Site Location to http://myhostapplication/personal. This is the location where all personal My Sites belong, such as http://myhostapplication/personal/rgarrett.

8. Optionally, click the Configure Trusted Host Locations link to configure other trusted host locations. *Trusted host locations* are other My Site host locations in which users of a specific audience host their My Site collection. For example, if you have an audience (see Chapter 4) for all contractors in your organization and want their My Sites to be hosted in a separate location to all other users, then Trusted My Site Locations are what you need.

With all the above steps complete, you can now begin hosting My Sites—the easiest way to test this is to open up a basic site collection in the farm, log in, and then click the name of the logged -on user in the top right. In the drop-down, click the My Site menu item. If SharePoint does not find a My Site collection for the logged -on user, it will create one before navigating to the My Site.

The My Site Settings section in the User Profile Service application provides a few other options that administrators may deem useful in the organization—Personalization Site Links and Publish Links to Office Applications.

Personalization site links are additional links added to each user My Site, based on audience membership (see Chapter 4). For example, say your organization has a series of committees, and each user belongs to zero, one, or many committees, stipulated by a profile property. When each user visits their My Site, they should see links to their committee sites in the organization. The following steps assume the existence of committee audiences and demonstrate configuration of personalization site links:

9. Navigate to the My Sites settings section in the User Profile Service application Manage Settings page (see the previous procedure).

10. Click the Configure Personalization Site link.

11. Click the New link.

12. Provide the URL to the landing page of the committee, the committee name in the description field, the owner, and the target audience.

Published links to Office Applications are a feature that SharePoint 2010 provides to expose known locations in your portal that users may access in Microsoft Office 2010 applications. For example, if a user wishes to save his Microsoft Word document to a common location in SharePoint, and the location is available as a published link, the user may select Save to SharePoint from the Share tab under the File menu of Microsoft Word 2010. Users may similarly save to SharePoint published links in other Office 2010 applications. The following steps demonstrate configuration of published links in SharePoint 2010:

13. Navigate to the My Sites settings section in the User Profile Service application Manage Settings page.

14. Click the Publish Links to Office Client Applications link.

15. Click the New link.

16. Provide the URL for the published link and description.

17. Select the publication end point type in the drop-down.

Capacity Planning for My Sites

My Sites are individual site collections, supporting document libraries, lists, and sub-sites. By default, the owner of a My Site has full control over the collection, and carte blanche on what they may store in the collection. This suggests that the size of the default content database for the My Site host application may grow quite large, as the number of users in an organization (with a My Site) grows. Furthermore, SharePoint 2010 provides much more compelling incentive for users to store content and track events in their My Site, thus increasing user adoption and the need for better capacity planning.

It is good practice to ensure portability of the content databases and dispersal of My Sites across many content databases in the host application. You may recall from Chapter 2 that each site collection may occupy at most one content database, but a content database may host multiple site collections. Since each user's My Site is a site collection, we need to make sure that as more users sign up for My Site space, SharePoint ensures creation of new content databases as the number of site collections grow.

How many content databases do you need, and what limit should I set for the number of My Site collections per database? This depends on the expected amount of content in each My Site (site collection). Microsoft now allows database sizes up to 4 terabytes with SharePoint 2010 Service Pack 1. Depending on your need for portability and desire for smaller database sizes, the number of site collections in a given database and the expected size of these site collections will roughly define the size of your database. Quota management (see the settings of the My Site Host Web Application, in the Web Application List ➤ Manage) will allow administrators to restrict the amount of content that users upload to their personal My Site. If you have the luxury of multiple SQL servers, you may decide to host My Site content databases on a different server   than other areas in your SharePoint 2010 farm.

The following steps demonstrate restricting My Site collections in a content database to 50 instances:

1. Open Central Admin.

2. Click the Application Management link.

3. Click the Manage Content Databases link.

4. Select the content database for the My Site host application.

5. In the Database Capacity Settings section, change the maximum number of sites to 50, and set the warning 10% less (45). This ensures that the administrators receive a warning when the number of sites in the current content database grows to 45 and when at 50 SharePoint will create a new content database.

A Tour of SharePoint 2010 My Sites

My Sites in SharePoint 2010 look and function very differently than in SharePoint Server 2007. Figure 5-2 shows the landing page of a My Site in my corporate network. Assuming you have My Site enabled on your SharePoint 2010 farm, and have completed the steps in the previous sections of this chapter to provision My Site functionality, you can invoke your own My Site by the following steps:

1. Click the name of the logged on user in the top right corner of the page (assumes standard SharePoint 2010 branding).

2. In the drop-down that appears, click the My Site link.

Figure 5-2. The My Site landing page

My Newsfeed

Figure 5-2 shows the landing page for My Site, which opens to show the Newsfeed. The Newsfeed is akin to those seen on Facebook and Twitter, and shows a feed of current activity of my colleagues and me. Activities on the Newsfeed consist of a list of SharePoint tracked events, configured in each personal profile. Figure 5-3 shows a snapshot of the list of activities to follow, as it appears in my edit profile page.

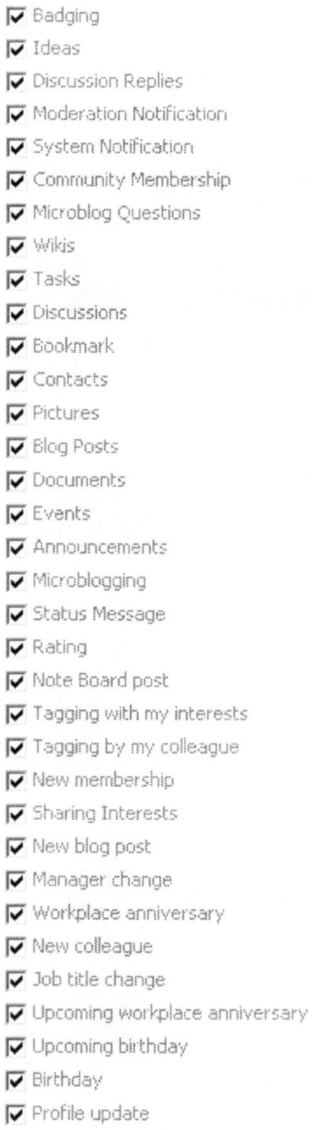

☑ Badging
☑ Ideas
☑ Discussion Replies
☑ Moderation Notification
☑ System Notification
☑ Community Membership
☑ Microblog Questions
☑ Wikis
☑ Tasks
☑ Discussions
☑ Bookmark
☑ Contacts
☑ Pictures
☑ Blog Posts
☑ Documents
☑ Events
☑ Announcements
☑ Microblogging
☑ Status Message
☑ Rating
☑ Note Board post
☑ Tagging with my interests
☑ Tagging by my colleague
☑ New membership
☑ Sharing Interests
☑ New blog post
☑ Manager change
☑ Workplace anniversary
☑ New colleague
☑ Job title change
☑ Upcoming workplace anniversary
☑ Upcoming birthday
☑ Birthday
☑ Profile update

Figure 5-3. *Activities to track in my Newsfeed*

Clicking the name of any of my colleagues in the Newsfeed takes me to that colleague's profile page, which includes a Newsfeed filtered to that person's activities.

My Profile

I discuss user profiles in detail in Chapter 4, and from an administration perspective, a user profile consists of a collection of properties about a particular user. Refer back to the previous chapter to read more about user profile properties and administration of user profiles with synchronization to LDAP sources, like Active Directory.

From any page in your My Site, click the My Profile link in the top horizontal navigation. Figure 5-4 shows a screen capture of a My Profile page, currently populated with data. The My profile page consists of various sections and tabs for displaying information about a user, sourced from the User Profile properties, discussed in Chapter 4.

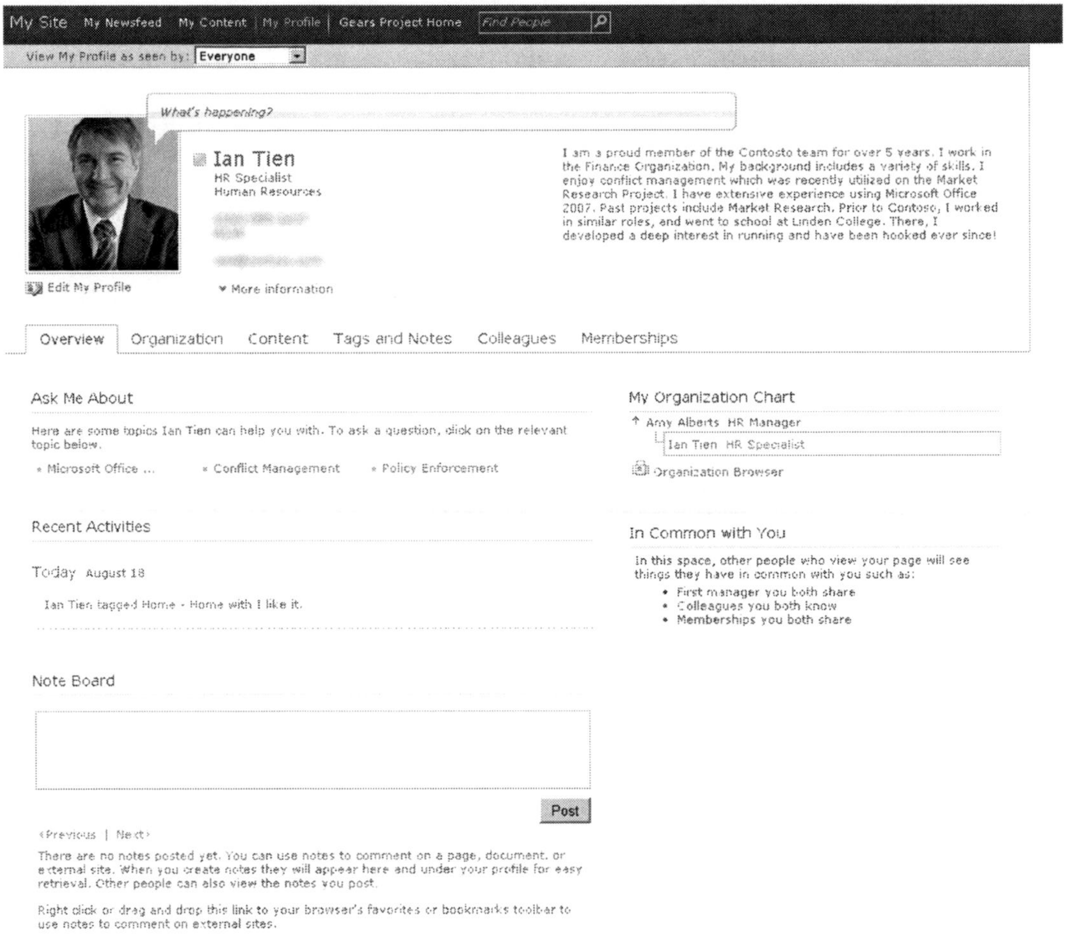

Figure 5-4. *A My Profile page*

Similar to the user profile page of my colleagues and peers, shown when clicking the name of one of my colleagues, team members, manager, or whoever, my profile page shows a news feed—in this case filtered by *my* recent activities. You can see my demographic information and picture, shown at the top of the page. Over on the right is a small organization chart, showing my position in the organization (sourced from Active Directory). Toward the bottom of the page (not shown in Figure 5-4) is my notes board—showing notes I have made on external web sites, pages in SharePoint, and so on

---

■ **Note** A user does not need to have a My Site to have a profile page. Users without My Sites still show a profile page to others.

From your own profile page, click the Edit My Profile link under your photo.

Figure 5-5 shows a partial screen capture of the profile-editing page. Chapter 4 discusses editing of user profiles in more detail and synching user profiles with LDAP stores, such as Active Directory, to automatically populate profile details in SharePoint and send edits, made in SharePoint, back to the LDAP store.

At the top of the page in Figure 5-4   is an option to view your own profile from the perspective of your Manager, Team, Colleagues, or Everyone—this relates to the profile properties visibility, shown in Figure 5-5, where users may designate certain profile properties as viewable by members of the list above. SharePoint determines your colleagues, team, and manager based on property settings in your profile and designation of colleagues in your profile area.

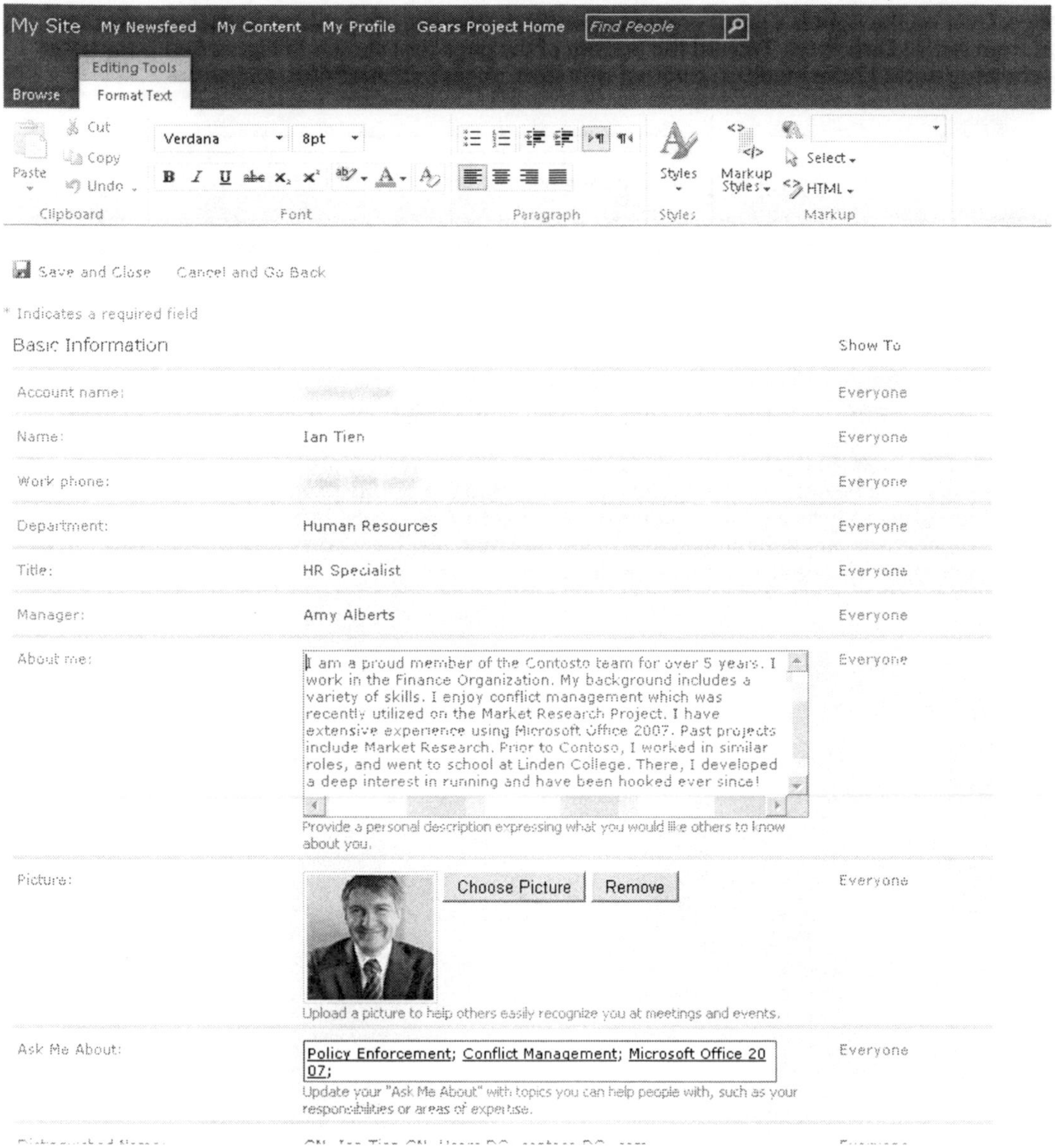

Figure 5-5. Profile Edit Page

Navigate back to the landing page of My Profile. The page opens showing various sub-navigation horizontal tabs, as follows:

- **Overview**—Shows recent activities from your newsfeed, status of profile completion, number of colleagues, your notes, and a summary of where you reside in the organizational chart.

- **Organization**—Shows a new graphical organization chart (see Figure 5-6), implemented in Silverlight. The chart includes people you report to, people who report to you, and colleagues, all shown pictorially and driven by the manager field in the profile and colleagues associated. Users without Silverlight can view an HTML -only view of the org chart by clicking the link in the lower -left corner of the control.

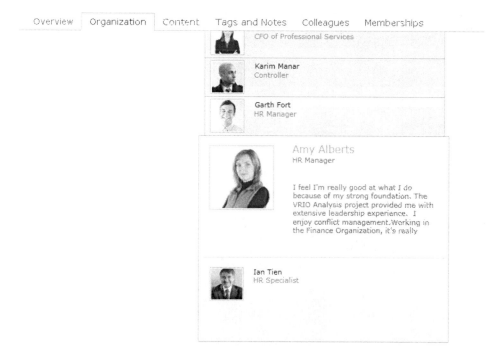

Figure 5-6. Silverlight Organization Chart

- **Content**—The Content tab shows a summary of document libraries, lists, and blog posts, viewable publically by others in the farm. The data in this tab is a subset of that in the content area, accessed from the My Content link on the top My Site navigation.

- **Tags and Notes**—This section of your profile consolidates notes and tags made of internal and external content. At the bottom -left of this tab is a link that you may drag to the links bar in your browser (Internet Explorer) so that you may tag and make notes of external sites outside that of SharePoint when you surf the Internet. This feature behaves very much like the Facebook feature of leaving a status that includes a link to an external site—only much better. The Tags and Notes tab also contains a tag cloud and the ability to scroll through tags and notes by month.

- **Colleagues**—The Colleagues tab shows a list of colleagues you associate with—a great idea, which promotes social networking within the SharePoint farm. Colleagues may either be part of your team, or part of a particular group, and may elect to show you colleague association to everyone, your other colleagues, your manager, your team, or keep your association to yourself. Figure 5-7 shows the dialog for editing one or many colleagues.

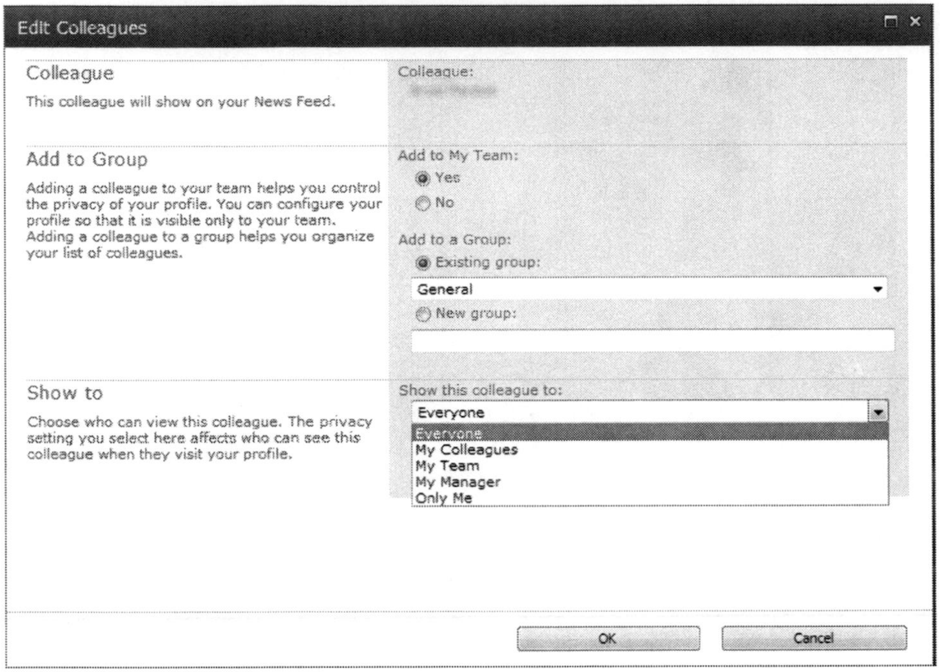

Figure 5-7. The Edit Colleagues dialog

- **Memberships**—The Memberships tab displays a list of all Active Directory distribution groups and SharePoint sites that you are a member of. This tab allows you to edit the visibility of these memberships to Everyone, your Colleagues, Team, Manager, or to just you.

Most of the content sections displayed in the My Profile page and tabs of the My Profile page exist as web parts. Users of My Sites may decide to host these same web parts on other pages. The My Profile page itself is a dedicated page in the hive, and so only administrators may change the layout, but since most profile data is web -part based, users can get creative with their own profile views in their own My Sites.

Customizing My Profile Tabs

You may wonder how to add additional content tabs. The default tabs are links that point to the pages in Table 5-1.

Table 5-1: *Default Tabs in My Profile*

Tab Name	URL
Overview	/my/Person.aspx
Organization	/my/OrganizationView.aspx
Content	/my/PersonContent.aspx
Tags and Notes	/my/_layouts/thoughts.aspx
Colleagues	/my/_layouts/MyContactLinks.aspx
Memberships	/my/_layouts/MyMemberships.aspx

As an administrator in the farm, follow the steps below to add a new tab:

1. Navigate to the Person.aspx page in the My Site Host application.

2. From the Site Actions menu, click the Site Settings menu option.

3. Under Look and Feel, click the Quick Launch link.

4. SharePoint provides a navigation settings page to add new navigation links to other pages and configure existing tabs.

These steps easily allow addition of a new tab link, which is fine for linking to another non-profile page, but what if you want to give the user the feel that there is another tab in the My Profile page? The secret is in the way SharePoint constructs the default pages.

Each page listed in Table 5-1 has the same layout and same navigation component, but with different tab highlighted. Clicking through the tabs gives the illusion that the user is in the same page but opening different tabs, where in fact the URL in the browser shows the physical page changing. To add a new tab under the profile page, create a new page with the same markup as the Person.aspx page. Link to the new page, using the steps just shown, and then edit the page in SharePoint Designer 2010 to select a different tab:

Look for the following markup in your new page, which shows the Tab navigation control. The CSS class depicts the selection of the tab and the uniqueness of the tab against the sibling tabs.

```
<SharePoint:AspMenu
    ID="MySiteSubNavigationMenu"
    Runat="server"
    EnableViewState="false"
    DataSourceID="MySiteSubNavDS"
    AccessKey="<%$Resources:wss,navigation_accesskey%>"
    UseSimpleRendering="true"
    UseSeparateCss="false"
    Orientation="Horizontal"
    StaticDisplayLevels="1"
    MaximumDynamicDisplayLevels="0"
    PopOutImageUrl=""
```

```
      SkipLinkText=""
      CssClass="s4-sn">
  </SharePoint:AspMenu>
  <SPSWC:MySiteDataSource
      ShowStartingNode="False"
      SiteMapProvider="MySiteSubNavProvider"
      id="MySiteSubNavDS"
      runat="server"/>
```

My Content

The My Content page of your My Site is synonymous with the legacy My Site paradigm of SharePoint 2007. The landing view for the My Content page shows a Shared Documents document library and Personal Documents document library, My Links list and Note Board. Not unlike most other pages in SharePoint, this page layout consists of various web part zones, and owners of a My Site (content) may move web parts around the page. Figure 5-8 shows the My Content page on my company Intranet.

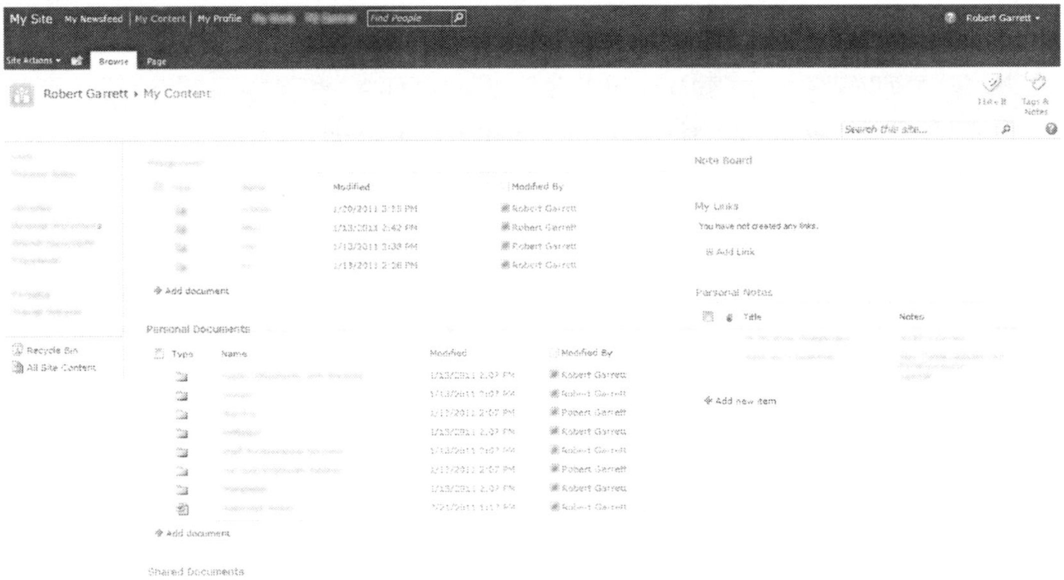

Figure 5-8. A My Content page

Unlike profile pages, pages in the My Content—the actual true My Site collection—do not require SharePoint Designer for the site owner to edit them. The following steps demonstrate editing of the My Content page, and movement and addition of web parts.

1. From the My Content page, click the Page tab in the Ribbon section at the top of the page.

2. From the Ribbon, click the Edit Page icon.

3. Figure 5-9 shows the same My Content page in edit mode, with the web parts shown.

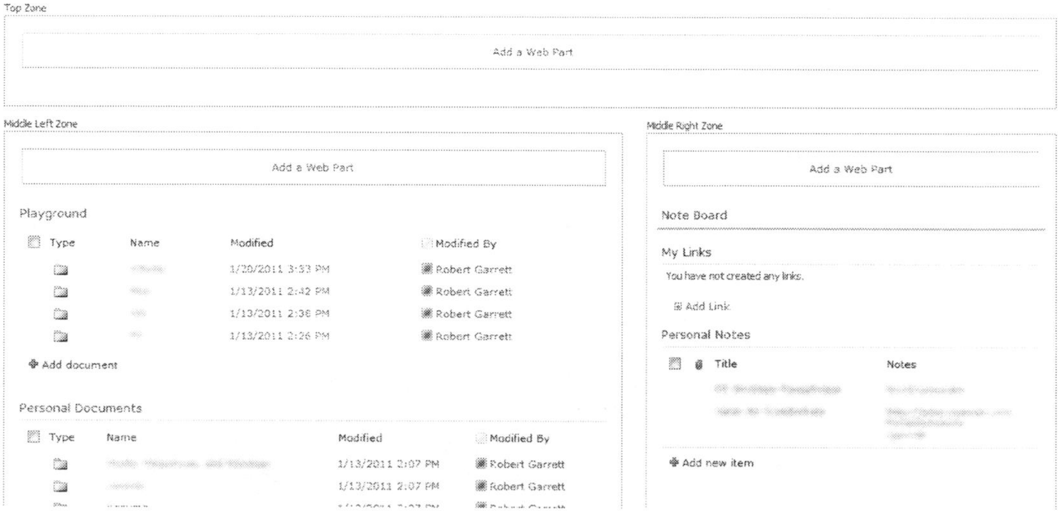

Figure 5-9. Edit view of the My Content page

18. Choose one of the zones and click the Add a Web Part link.

19. SharePoint shows the web part gallery at the top of the page. Spend a few minutes looking through the various web parts and choose one that you like, before selecting the web part and clicking the Add button.

20. SharePoint then adds the web part to the page.

21. Drag the web part to another open web part zone by left-clicking the title area of the web part and dragging the web part to the other zone.

22. Hover the mouse over the web part title, click the small arrow on the right, and select Edit Web Part to display the web part settings.

23. From the web part settings, expand the layout area and you may change the destination zone of the web part by changing the value in the zone drop-down combo box.

Adding new pages, sub sites, new lists, and so on, works identically in a My Site to any other site collection in the farm, where you have full control permissions in the collection. With My Sites, users can get quite creative, and build a complete web site hierarchy of their own within SharePoint, to share information and collaborate with their peers.

My Site Lockdown

Although My Sites are wonderful for promoting user collaboration and marketing of self-identity in the enterprise, they may not fit in all organizations. Say for example, your organization has policy about what data employees may share in the organization, or perhaps you want to restrict My Site and social network features to select groups of individuals. The following steps demonstrate changing the Personalization and Social Networking policy in the User Profile Service application:

1. Open Central Admin.

2. Click the Manage Service Applications link in the Application Management section.

3. Scroll down the list to the User Profile Service Application.

4. Click to the right of the name and then click the Manage icon in the Ribbon.

5. In the UPS application landing page, click the Manage User Permissions link in the People section.

SharePoint displays a dialog like that in Figure 5-10.

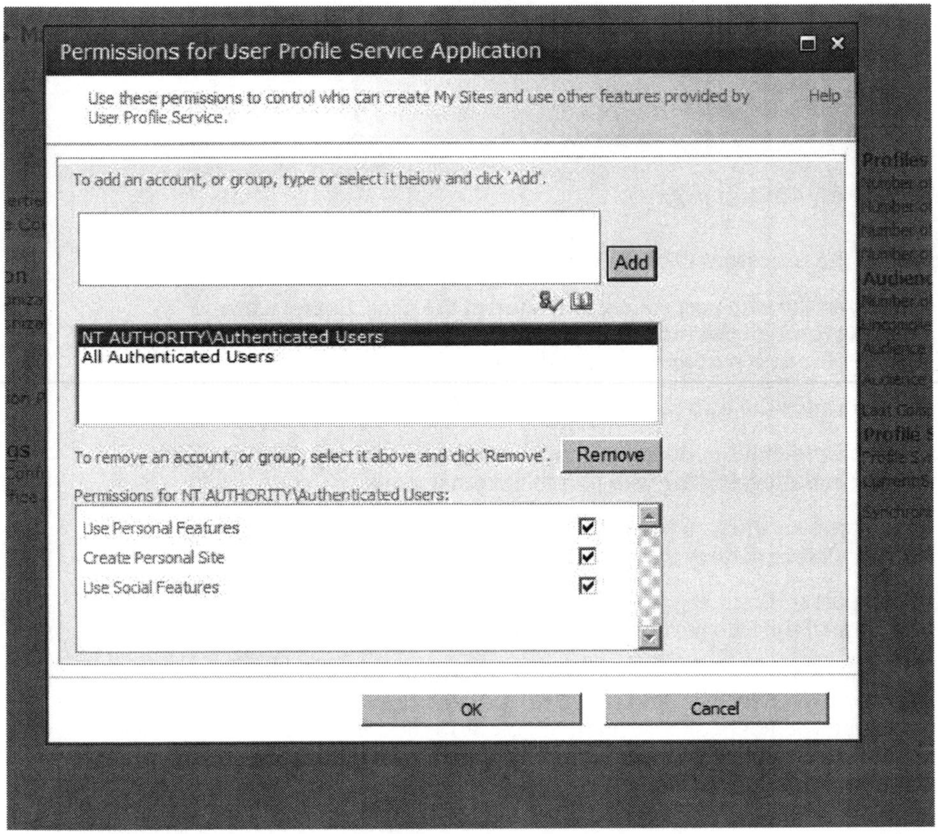

Figure 5-10. User personalization permissions dialog

For each user or AD group in the middle box of the dialog, SharePoint shows the policies for personalization. These policies are available:

- Use of Personal Features—User profiles, et al.

- Create Personal Site—The ability to create a My Site.

- Use Social Features—The ability to tag, add notes, and like content.

Notes and Tagging

Tagging is the flavor of the Internet these days. With the explosion of social networking, and sites like Facebook, everyone is in the mode to tag and "like" content. SharePoint 2010 is on the tagging bandwagon and offers users the ability to perform extensive tagging using the Managed Metadata Service application.

When discussing SharePoint 2010 tagging, notes, and social networking capabilities, the topic of metadata will invariably come into play. Metadata is "data about data." For example, a database schema defines the structure and properties of SQL tables—this is metadata for the actual row data in the table. In the world of SharePoint 2010, tags are metadata, because they give the reader of certain content some level of categorization and thus context. SharePoint bakes metadata into the platform, and surfaces it in basic lists, document libraries, document and records management, publishing, and social networking. The topic of metadata is vast enough that I cover it in Chapter 6.

A Brief Segue on Taxonomy and Folksonomy

Tags are more than just lists of strings that categorize the data/content to which they are applied. In a typical enterprise, tags follow a strict hierarchical structure, called the *taxonomy*. Taxonomy is a synonym used to define the structure of tagging and promotes dynamic browsing and filtering of content.

If you have visited any consumer electronics store web site recently, then the site has most likely leveraged taxonomy to narrow your product selection. For example, sites like Best Buy allow you to browse for a new TV and filter on brand, size, and other key features. Search for a new computer on the same web site and the filter selections differ. This capability likely involves some level of taxonomy hierarchy with the main product category at the top of the tree.

Organizations that adopt taxonomy typically enforce a strict set of rules on the available tags and their place in the taxonomy. This strict behavior promotes accurate tagging of data (in the case of Best Buy, data about their products) and avoids miscategorization because of a misspelled tag or tag of similar nomenclature as another. SharePoint 2010 implements strict taxonomy management in the Managed Metadata Service application, and allows administrators to define groups, term sets, and terms (SharePoint terminology for a tag name). You'll learn more about taxonomy in Chapter 6.

Folksonomy addresses a different requirement of tagging, commonly referred by users of social web sites as *user-based tagging*. Instead of a predefined set of tags, folksonomy is the practice of user self-tagging. When a user sees a particular piece of content on the site that he/she wants to tag, they simply apply a tag name of their choice. If the tag name already exists, the folksonomy model does not create a new tag and instead uses the existing tag name, but if the tag name is new then a new tag begins its life in the folksonomy infrastructure. SharePoint 2010 implements folksonomy via the Enterprise Keywords site column (a metadata field), which also utilizes the Managed Metadata Service application to track tags.

Tagging in SharePoint 2010

Tagging is ubiquitous throughout the entire site collection. At the top-right of any standard SharePoint page you will see the I Like it and Tag & Notes icons. (I say "standard SharePoint page" because publishing pages follow templates defined by site designers and may not include these icons, except as part of the Ribbon when editing the page.) See Figure 5-11 for an example of these icons.

Figure 5-11. *The Tags & Notes and I Like It icons*

SharePoint 2010 allows tagging of various objects in the platform, as shown in the following list:

- Lists
- Libraries
- List Items
- Documents and Images
- Pages
- External Web Sites

The last item is interesting—SharePoint allows you to like an external web site, which then shows up in your newsfeed, so that others may visit the site, if they are related to you and see your newsfeed as a colleague, team member, or manager. The Tags and Notes tab in your profile provides a link to drag to your browser links bookmarks, so that you may click the link from any external web site to like it in your SharePoint My Site.

■ **Note** New content tagged or new notes added to your SharePoint do not show up in your Newsfeed immediately. The Activity Feed Job in the Central Admin ➤ Monitoring ➤ Timer Jobs ➤ User Profile Service Application updates newsfeeds on a schedule.

Document libraries do not enable the tagging capability on contained documents by default. The following set of steps detail how to enable tagging for a document library:

1. From any document library view page, click the Library tab from the Ribbon.
2. Click the Library Settings icon from the Ribbon.
3. Click the Enterprise Metadata and Keywords Settings link.
4. Check the Add Enterprise Keywords check box to add the Enterprise Keywords Metadata column to the document library. SharePoint will not allow you to opt out of this option once it is checked and the settings page saved. The Enterprise Keywords Metadata column allows folksonomy behavior for documents in the library.

5. Check, the Metadata Publishing checkbox to allow any folksonomy tags entered for a document to appear in your newsfeed, profile pages, tag cloud, and so on, as a social tag.

■ **Note** When saving a document from Microsoft Word to a SharePoint 2010 Document Library, with an Enterprise Keywords column, the Save-As dialog displays a Tags text box to save entered tags to the Enterprise Keywords column in the library list item, associated with the document.

To demonstrate the Tag & Notes and Like social icons' capabilities in SharePoint 2010, follow the steps below:

6. Open a page in your site collection with the social icons in the top right corner.

7. Click the I Like It icon.

8. The Tags & Notes icon changes color to show you like this page.

9. Click the Tag & Notes icon. SharePoint displays a dialog like that in Figure 5-12.

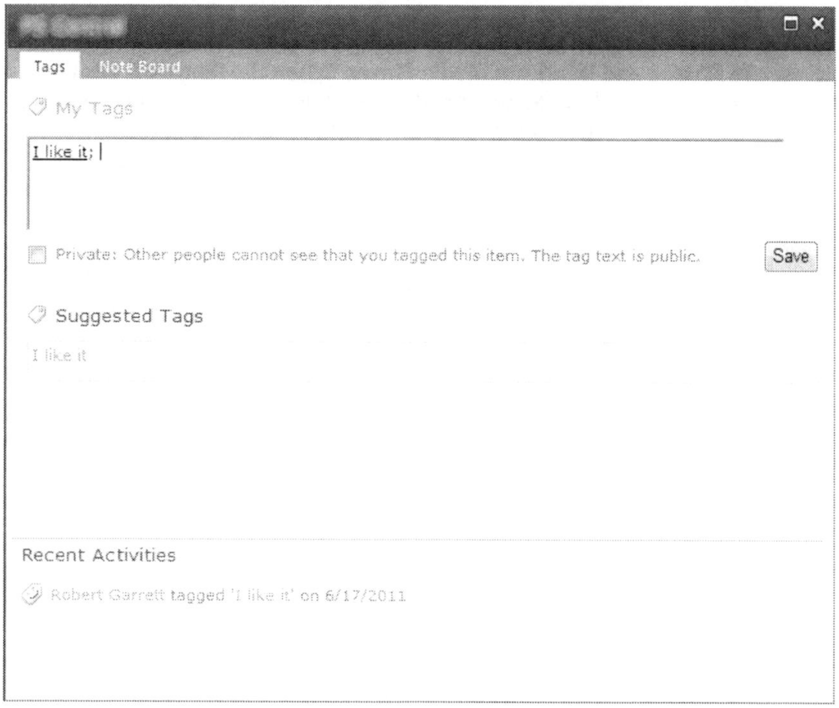

Figure 5-12. The Tag & Notes dialog

10. Notice that the dialog shows the I Like It tag, which is a SharePoint built-in social tag/term for liking content in the site farm.

11. Start typing a tag name in the My Tags section, and SharePoint will show existing folksonomy/social tags that match what you typed (if any exist).

12. Checking the Private check box means that other users do not see that you tagged the current page. Leaving the box unchecked shows an entry in your newsfeed.

13. Navigate to the My Newsfeed page in your profile/My Site to see an entry for the page you just tagged, assuming you did not mark it private.

14. Navigate to a different page in your site collection with the social icons available.

15. Click the Tag & Notes icon again.

16. Click the Notes tab.

17. Enter a note in the space provided.

Other users who pull up this same dialog will see the notes you leave about the current page.

Ratings

New to SharePoint 2010 are ratings. SharePoint 2010 adds another method to collect user feedback with star ratings—similar to ratings seen in iTunes and Windows Media Player. When the feature is enabled for a list or library, users can apply their rating for the list item or document and SharePoint keeps track of all user ratings to display a collective ranking. Figure 5-13 shows an example of ratings in action.

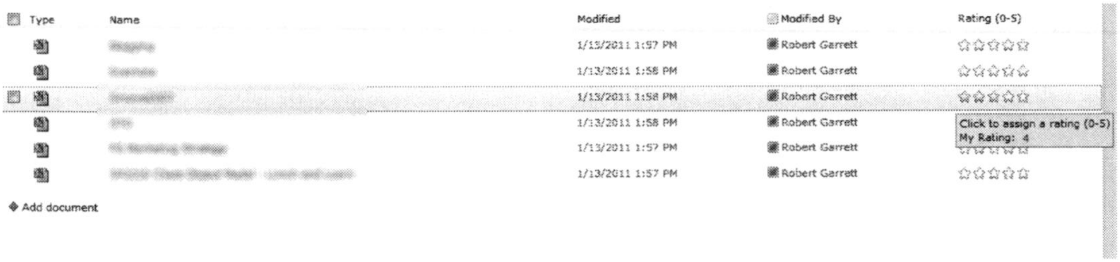

Figure 5-13. Ratings

SharePoint 2010 does not enable rating on lists or document libraries by default. The following steps demonstrate how to enable rating functionality for a document library:

1. From any document library view page, click the Library tab from the Ribbon.

2. Click the Library Settings icon from the Ribbon.

3. Click the Rating Settings link.

4. Set the radio button option for Allow Items in This List to Be Rated, as Yes.

▓ **Note** If you are trying to find the Rating Settings and not seeing it (perhaps you are attempting the above steps for a document library on your My Site), then ensure you have enabled the Site Collection Publishing feature.

Follow the steps below to enable the Site Collection Publishing feature on your site, if the rating settings are not available:

1. Make sure you are at the root of the site collection (if in your My Site, click the My Content item in the main navigation).

2. Click the Site Actions menu.

3. Click Site Settings menu item.

4. Click the Site Collection Features link in the Site Collection Administration section.

5. Scroll down the list and find the feature named SharePoint Server Publishing Infrastructure.

6. If it is not activated, click the Activate button.

In Figure 5-13, I'm hovering the mouse over the rating for a document in one of my document libraries. SharePoint indicates that I have rated the document with four stars. SharePoint keeps current track of my rating but collates all user ratings for the document at specific time intervals using a timer service. The current time service for rating update is one hour. Follow the steps below to set it to one minute to demonstrate how SharePoint collects all user ratings for list items and documents:

7. Open Central Admin.

8. Click the Monitoring link from the left navigation.

9. In the Timer Jobs section, click the Review Job Definitions link.

10. Find the UPS Service Application—Social Rating Synchronization Job—you may need to navigate to subsequent pages using the paging links at the bottom of the current page. The timer job may have a different name, depending on the name of your User Profile Synchronization Service Application, but will end with Social Rating Synchronization Job.

11. Click the timer job definition title.

12. On the settings page, change the schedule to run every minute.

13. Give SharePoint time to run the job.

14. Refresh the document library/list and see the current rating for the item/document you rated earlier.

Rating Control and Publishing Pages

SharePoint allows ratings on any document library where the feature is enabled; this includes publishing pages. How do page content owners display a rating control on publishing pages so that public web site users may rate the content of the page? The following steps show how:

1. Enable rating for the Pages document library, using the steps shown earlier in this chapter section.

2. Looking at the metadata (list settings) for the Pages document library, you should see two site columns: Number of Ratings and Rating (0–5).

3. In your page layout, using SharePoint Designer, add the following field control:
   `<SharePointPortalControls:AverageRatingFieldControl`
   `FieldName="Rating_x0020__x0028_0_x002d_5_x0029_" runat="server"/>`

The `FieldName` attribute contains the internal static name of the `Rating` (0–5) field.

Blogs

Long before sites like Facebook and Twitter, blogs (short for Weblogs) existed for those people who had something to share with the Internet. Initially, techy and literary folks had blogs and wrote articles for select pockets of readership. Around the year 2000, the blogosphere evolved and people woke up to the fact that they could easily host a blog and say whatever they wanted to the world via the Internet. It seemed that everyone had a blog, ranging from intellectual ideas to ramblings of his or her personal life and social sharing. Sites, like Live Journal, promoted personal blogging, and were part for the beginnings of social networking.

Microsoft acknowledged the demand for blog engines and incorporated the blog site definition in SharePoint 2007. SharePoint 2010 continues with the blogging capabilities and offers more integration with My Sites and social sharing of self-authored content in the enterprise. Let us begin with blogs in My Sites:

1. From your My Site, click the My Profile link in the main navigation.

2. Click the Content tab.

3. Scroll to the bottom of the page and click the link to create a new blog, if you see the Recent Blog Posts web part then you already have a blog.

4. Your My Site blogs exists at the following location, by default:
   `/personal/<username>/Blog/default.aspx`.

See Figure 5-14 for a typical newly created blog in My Site.

Figure 5-14. *A personal blog in My Site*

Blogs are not just limited to My Sites; administrators and site owners may add them into the site collection anywhere as sub sites. Follow the steps below to create a new blog underneath a site of your choice in your site collection:

5.   From the Site Actions menu, click the New Site menu item.

6.   SharePoint displays a new dialog, like that in Figure 5-15.

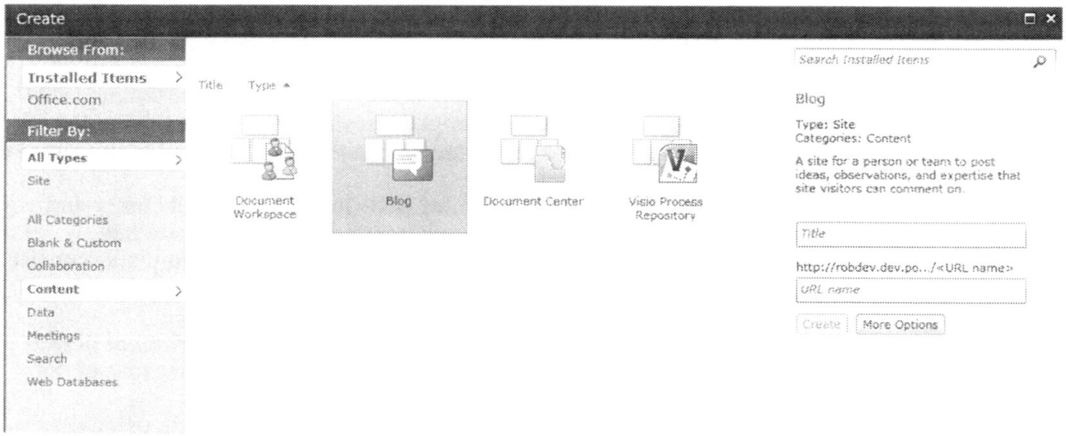

Figure 5-15. *New Site Dialog*

7.   Select the Content category, and SharePoint filters site types to content-based sites.

8. Click the blog site, and give the site a title and URL suffix.

9. You may click the More Options button to supply more options at blog site creation, including inheritance of security permission settings.

10. Click the Create button to create the new blog site.

Blog posts are effectively a collection of list items in a dedicated list, called Posts, in the blog site. From the blog landing page (shown in Figure 5-14), click the Site Actions menu and then select the menu item View All Content. In the List section, you should see the Posts list. Also, notice the Comments and Categories lists, which store—you guessed it—the comments and categories of blog posts.

Wikis

A *wiki* is a web site that allows users to create and edit any number of interlinked pages. Wiki pages typically render as HTML, and users edit text and image content on wiki pages using WYSIWYG (What-you-see-is-what-you-get). The purpose of wiki sites is to foster collaboration of content creation and editing by allowing any user to edit the content, regardless of their security access. Wiki sites, like Wikipedia.com, have become a trusted source for information on the Internet because readers constantly vet and update the content.

Microsoft designed wiki sites in SharePoint 2010 for ease of use for the content owners and contributors. Like most other content containers in SharePoint, a wiki exists as a list in a site, and the pages of a wiki exist as the list items in the wiki library.

In SharePoint 2007, wiki lists were more of an afterthought, whereas in SharePoint 2010 wikis are baked into the platform. For example, the new Team and Blank site definitions now default to use wiki libraries and pages for all content pages. This replaces the legacy Web Part Pages of SP2007, in which content owners would have to drop content web parts into specific zones of the page to host content. Content contributors now have free rein to place text content anywhere on the page, and still use web part zones—determined by site designers in the page layout—thus wrapping text and image content around typical functional web parts.

Users create wiki sites in SharePoint 2010 much like any other site, and I shall demonstrate the steps in just a moment. Before doing so, I must distinguish between SharePoint Enterprise Wiki sites and Blank or Team sites.

SharePoint 2007 blank and team sites used web part pages, which are ASPX pages containing HTML markup and web part zones for users to drop web parts. Site designers would need to use the Publishing features and site templates if they wanted to provide page customization and Web Content Management capabilities in SharePoint 2007.

Sites created from the Enterprise Wiki template, in SharePoint 2010, include a special library and publishing features, typically associated with publishing sites—page ratings, managed metadata, customization capabilities, and so on, whereas sites created from Team and Blank site templates consist of the standard collaboration features, offered in the Foundation platform, and a Site Pages library, to contain wiki pages.

SharePoint 2010 blank and team sites allow wiki-style editing of content and the placement of web parts without the need for web part zones, and rudimentary customization of the page, because of the free flow of content editing that wiki pages provide.

Enterprise wiki sites, in SharePoint 2010, provide users with greater control of content, using the publishing features, and adhere more to Web content management. Wiki pages in an Enterprise Wiki site use page layouts and master pages, so designers may customize metadata on wiki pages, much like publishing pages.

Administrators may create wiki libraries, by creating a new wiki site, or adding a wiki library to an existing site. The following steps demonstrate both approaches.

New wiki site:

1. Click the Site Actions menu, and click the New Site menu item.

2. Click the Collaboration category to filter the site types.

3. Click the Enterprise Wiki site.

4. Provide a title and URL suffix, and you may click the More Options button to apply additional options before SharePoint creates the wiki site.

5. Click the Create button when ready to create the wiki site.

New wiki library:

6. From within any existing site, click the Site Actions menu, and then click the More Options menu item.

7. In the Filter By section, click the Library filter.

8. Click the Wiki Page Library list type.

9. Give the library a title, and click the More Options button if you wish to apply more options before SharePoint creates the library.

10. Click the Create button.

A wiki site is really just a team site with a default wiki library, with the site welcome page pointing to the main landing page in the wiki library.

Since both blogs and wikis consist of list/library containers to store content, site owners and collaborators may make use of all the tagging, notes, and rating social networking tools in the platform in conjunction with blog and wiki content.

Outlook 2010 Integration

Outlook 2010 now integrates with SharePoint 2010, using the Social Connector. This tool shows user profile information of people included in your email to/from address lines, including their picture. To enable the Social Connector in Outlook 2010, follow the steps below:

1. Open Outlook 2010, and click the View tab.

2. Click the People pane button.

3. Click Account Settings.

4. On the Social Networks account screen, click the checkbox next to My Sites.

5. Supply the URL of your My Site, and your username and password.

6. Click the Connect button, and then Finish.

If all is well, you should see a message about successful integration.

With the social connector configured, you can now see your SharePoint Newsfeed in Outlook in the left navigation pane. You may also add other users into your network, and truly embrace social networking without ever having to leave the comfort of your email client.

Summary

In this chapter, I introduced the fundamentals of social networking. We started by looking at how Microsoft implemented social networking capabilities into SharePoint 2010. Users are central to any social network and collaborative system, so I covered user profiles and user personalization via My Sites.

My Sites provide individual users in an organization the capabilities to host their own content and disseminate content to peers in the organization. You read about how SharePoint 2010 envelops the social network features—tagging, notes, liking, taxonomy, and folksonomy into user My Sites.

My Sites are not the only mechanism for publishing content to your peers in the enterprise—you also read about blogs and wikis, which carry from SharePoint 2007 and now integrate better in the SharePoint 2010 platform.

In Chapter 6, we discuss the large topic of content types and metadata, and I include details on the Managed Metadata Service application, which maintains the tagging/taxonomy/folksonomy infrastructure in SharePoint 2010.

CHAPTER 6

Site Content and Metadata

Metadata is data about data, and is essentially the categorization of the content within a content management system. A good example of metadata is in the classification of documents in a Content Management System (CMS) or Document Management System (DMS)—a proposal document might have some essential attributes associated, aside from the actual content in the proposal document, such as Proposal Number, Client, Date, and so on. These attributes are the metadata associated with the document.

Why is metadata important? Simply, metadata allows rapid search of content in a system and grouping of content when browsing. Sophisticated search engines—such as the one included in SharePoint 2010—allow searching inside the content of documents, but sometimes a user wants to navigate quickly to a document without dealing with the search result noise typically associated with keyword searching. Metadata and categorization assist users to *retrieve* content without a lot of hunting and pecking into document or file content.

Metadata also assists a search engine. Search Engine Optimization (SEO) algorithms assign more relevance to data stored in metadata, because content owners typically provide metadata explicitly.

In the previous chapter, we looked at social networking, and you saw how taxonomy and folksonomy play an important part in categorization of content. Continuing from this theme, in this chapter we explore metadata in SharePoint 2010, the Content Type Model, and the Managed Metadata Service—the central hub that manages metadata in SharePoint 2010.

The SharePoint 2010 Content Type Model

If metadata is data about data, then a *metadata model* is a system that allows the creation, editing, and management of metadata. SharePoint 2010 has a metadata model—called the Content Type Model.

The SharePoint Content Type Model consists of metadata types—*content types*, which themselves consist of metadata fields—Columns, and the management of these types in the core of the SharePoint platform. I cover SharePoint *metadata types* in the next section of this chapter, but first I'll present the SharePoint 2010 Content Type model at a high level.

What Are Content Types and Site Columns?

A SharePoint content type is a grouping of fields that describe a data entity in the SharePoint site collection or site—such as a document, calendar event, task, or any other list item. Each content type consists of one or multiple fields, which are known as *columns*.

Content types exist at either the root site collection or sub-site level. Lower sites in the hierarchy may use content types from parent sites to define data elements. In both cases, content types reside in the Content Type Gallery of the site or site collection.

The fields of content types exist as centrally managed *site columns*, at the same level as the containing content type or at parent levels to it. For example, a content type defined at a sub-site level may contain site columns that reside in the root site collection or parent site in the hierarchy. Sites may not leverage content types and site columns at lower sub-site levels to the current site—just up the hierarchy chain.

There is a difference between centrally managed site columns and list columns. When creating a custom list, the user may define columns specifically for the new list, meaning the columns bind only to that list. By contrast, site columns reside in the Site Column Gallery, and users may reuse these columns in lists (Add an Existing Column) and content types.

Content types may inherit from other content types at the same level in the site hierarchy or a parent level. Even the most basic content types, at least, inherit from the stock Item content type, which contains the Title site column. Through inheritance, users may customize content types by defining new types that have the same columns as the parent, with additional columns to complete the specialization. For example, if you want to customize task list items with new columns, rather than creating a new content type, you can inherit the existing task content type and add the new custom columns. Inheritance provides the added benefit that any changes to a parent content type apply to content subtypes.

■ **Note**: Never change stock content types and site columns; always inherit from content types, and then specialize.

New Content Type Model Functionality

SharePoint 2007 included lists, libraries, content types, site columns, and list columns. Just as you would expect, SharePoint 2010 includes them, too. This version brings new functionality, either as a direct enhancement to the Content Type Model or as an associated metadata or document management feature. Following are some of the more noteworthy additions to SharePoint 2010:

- Content types and lists that use lookup site columns may now specify additional columns of the lookup list to include, in addition to the primary lookup column.

- Referential integrity between lists for lookup columns and list items that reference the lookup parent list items. For example, when you delete a list item from a lookup list, SharePoint 2010 will either delete list items that look up the parent list item to the one just deleted, prevent the deletion of the parent, or do nothing, depending on a referential integrity setting.

- Document sets, a new content type and feature that allow collection of documents in one list item. They are ideal for collecting multiple documents that combines to a single finished entity, such as a proposal.

- A new Managed Metadata column type that maps to term sets in the Managed Metadata Service term store.

- A new Enterprise Keywords column, which allows users to add their own tags.

- Metadata extracted from the EXIF of images.

- Auto tagging of list items, based on their placement of list item in a folder of a list or library.

- Shared content types via a content type hub.

- Access to the external data via the Business Connectivity Service, and external data surfaced via an External Content Type.

- In-place records management (discussed further in Chapter 7) and information policy, down to the folder level.

- Introduction of a Rating site column.

- Advanced routing of documents via Content Organizer and policy rules.

SharePoint Metadata Types

Microsoft embraced metadata in SharePoint 2007—SharePoint 2003 incorporated "categories" for list data, but this was a far cry from deserving the title of metadata. SharePoint 2007 introduced the concept of the *content type*, which is a grouping of related attributes that describe a piece of content. Using the example in the preface of this chapter—a content type for a "proposal" document would typically contain all the attributes that content owners may assign to a proposal document.

SharePoint 2007 managed content types at the site collection level and enabled site collection administrators to create new content types in the Content Type Gallery, for use in the site collection hierarchy. Site owners of sub-sites in the hierarchy could elect to use content types defined at parent sites or the top-level site collection, or they could define new ones for their site and sub-sites below. Content types also make inheritance possible, so site owners could inherit from a site collection content type and add additional attributes for the specific site instance.

The new Managed Metadata Service application provides a central hub in a SharePoint 2010 farm for management of metadata across site collections and web applications in the farm. Centralizing metadata in this fashion releases content owners from the shackles of the site collection, and it allows for content types shared across multiple site collections—very useful if the enterprise site consists of multiple site collections, as it should according to best practices for content distribution.

Before we dig into the specific details of the Managed Metadata Service, let us review the principle metadata components in SharePoint 2010—site columns and content types.

Site Columns

SharePoint maintains a list of site columns, which represent attributes for metadata. If you have created a custom list, or looked an existing list defined, in SharePoint, then you will have seen the site columns in action as the "columns or fields" of the list.

For example, a list of contacts in a site maintains names and addresses of project members. The list retains the first name, last name, street address, city, state, ZIP code, and DOB of the contact. Each of these attributes exists as site columns in SharePoint and when applied to a list definition they constitute the columns or fields of the list.

Site columns have attributes of their own: title, description, and type. Table 6-1 lists the various types of site column in SharePoint 2010.

Table 6-1: *Site Column Types in SharePoint 2010*

Site Column Type	Description
Single line of text	String of text up to a maximum of 255 characters.
Multiple lines of text	Multiple lines of text; content owners specify how many lines to show in edit forms.
Choice	Single choice of fixed values; choices are defined with the site column and displayed as radio buttons or drop-down list.
Number	Floating-point number.
Currency	Two- decimal place number with currency symbol.
Date and Time	Date, Time, or both.
Lookup	Single or multiple-choice lookup of value from another list in the collection (or context at or below the location of the site column in the hierarchy).
Yes/No	Boolean value, shown as a check box in edit forms.
Person or Group	Selection of people or groups from user credential store (Active Directory or other user store, such as LDAP).
Hyperlink or Picture	Either a link to another location or link to an image to display; the content owner chooses at site column creation.
Calculated	Site column value calculated from formula (Excel-like) from other columns in the list row.
Full HTML (Publishing)	HTML field available with the Publishing feature. Allows rich text or full HTML markup.
Image (Publishing)	Image only field available with the Publishing feature.
Hyperlink (Publishing)	Hyperlink only field available with the Publishing feature.
Summary Links (Publishing)	Allows collection of Hyperlinks by the end user. When this column is added to a page layout and publishing page content type, page editors may add links to show as a collection on the page.
Rich Media (Publishing)	Inclusion of movie, audio, and image media on publishing pages.

Site Column Type	Description
Managed Metadata	New to SharePoint 2010. These columns surface terms from a term set in the Managed Metadata Service Term Store and are further discussed later in this chapter.

The following steps show how to access the Site Column Gallery in a site collection, and how to add a new column for use in the site collection:

1. Click the Site Actions menu.

2. Click the Site Settings menu item.

3. From the Site Settings page, in the Galleries section, click the Site columns link.

SharePoint displays the Site Column Gallery, like that in Figure 6-1.

Figure 6-1: *Site Column Gallery*

The page in Figure 6-1 shows a list of the site column names, the type, and the location. If you access the Site Column Gallery from a sub-site, the location values show where the site column resides in the hierarchy.

4. Click the Birthday column. SharePoint displays the edit screen as in Figure 6-2.

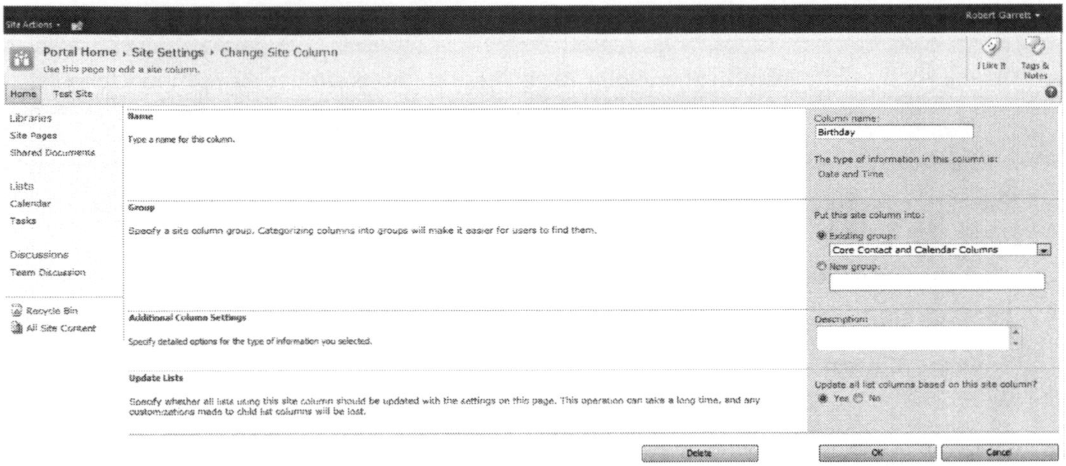

Figure 6-2: Edit site column properties

Here you may change the column name, contained group, description, and whether existing list columns, based on this column will update with changes. To change the column type you have no choice but to create a new column, as follows:

1. Navigate back to the Site Column Gallery, showing the list of site columns.

2. Click the Create link.

3. SharePoint shows a new edit form to populate with site column properties. (Note: The page posts back automatically when you select different site column types, since different types warrant additional properties.)

4. Change the type to Person or Group.

5. Wait for the page to post back and then scroll to the bottom.

6. See the options to allow selection of people only, people and groups and a SharePoint Security Group to limit choice of person.

7. Complete all mandatory properties on this page and then click OK to create the new site column.

Content Types

Content types provide content owners with the powerful capability to manage metadata content in SharePoint. The basic anatomy of a content type is that of a group of site columns (fields) that represents a content object in the content management system. For example, a content type may include several site columns that constitute a person's contact details—name, address, telephone, and so on.

Understanding the use of content types is important when discussing content and metadata management in SharePoint, because SharePoint uses content types practically everywhere there is categorization or definition of content schema. These are some of the areas in which SharePoint employs the use of content types:

- Column definitions in lists and list items

- Document metadata (document properties) in document libraries

- Content fields in publishing pages

- External data definition via Business Connectivity Services

- Search filtering and scopes

Content types incorporate *inheritance* in the SharePoint Metadata System, which provides for greater level of flexibility in metadata modeling and abstraction of content definition. Content owners may define basic content types and then sub-class these content types to define new content types with greater refinement of metadata.

As an example, Table 6-2 defines a Bio-Page content type for a publishing page, containing biographic information for staff members on an organization's public web site.

Table 6-2*: Site Columns (Fields) for a Bio-Page Content Type*

Site Column Name	Column Type	Description
First Name	Single line of text	First name of staff member
Last Name	Single line of text	Last name of staff member
Abstract	Multiple lines of text	Small blurb about the staff member
Biographic Text	Full HTML	Complete bio of the staff member
Biographic Image	Publishing Image	Headshot image of the staff member

When this content type is coupled with a page layout, SharePoint 2010 allows content owners to define new page instances, with the defined site columns, to contain data about a staff member. The page layout defines HTML markup, which tells SharePoint how to render the page content. The actual content of the page resides in a list item that is the page instance in a Pages document library.

The organization, hosting the web site, decides one day to provide a new advanced biographic page type that not only shows the standard details on a staff member, but also includes education information. To achieve this new advanced bio page implementation, the site designers provide a new page layout, based on the standard bio page layout, with placeholders for the new education fields. Rather than create a completely new content type to associate with the page layout, SharePoint allows the content owners to sub-class the standard Bio Page content type and add the additional fields.

Using content type inheritance, users may create elaborate metadata models with basic content types at the root of the model, and more specification of content types throughout the branches of the model. Figure 6-3 illustrates the concept of content type inheritance. Both the MSA and SOW content types exist as separate document content types, which inherit from the common Contract content type parent. The Contract content type inherits from the stock Document content type, which itself inherits from the stock Item content type. All the columns in each content type of the chain exist in the leaf content type, so the SOW content type includes the following columns: Project, Contact, Customer, Size, and Filename.

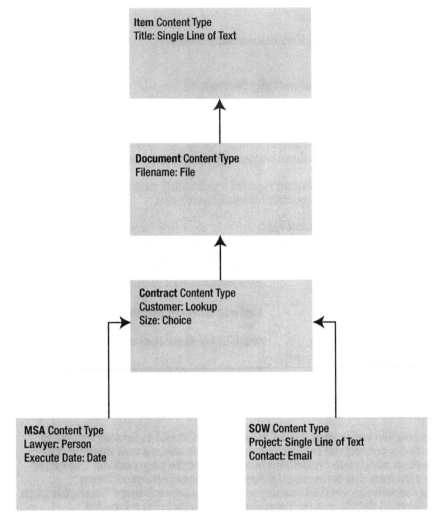

Figure 6-3: Content Type Inheritance

SharePoint 2010 defines a basic content type, called *Item*, which contains the site column Title. Examples of content types that sub-class the Item content type include Document, which adds the Name column for the filename, and Announcement, which includes columns for the Body of an announcement and a date field for Expiration. SharePoint 2010 ships with many stock content types in Basic and Team site definitions, and even more in publishing site definitions.

As it does with site columns, SharePoint maintains a list of content types in a site. The following steps demonstrate how to create a new content type for our Bio Page (Table 6-2).

> ▦ **Note**: Even though SharePoint will allow you to create content types and site columns at any sub-site level in the site collection, as a general best practice, define all content types and site columns at the root of the site collection.

1. From the root of the site collection, click the Site Actions menu.

2. Click the Site Settings menu item.

3. On the site settings page, under Galleries, click the Site Content Types link.

SharePoint shows all the content types defined in the site collection, as in Figure 6-4. There you can see that each content type belongs to a group and specifies both a parent and the source location in the site collection hierarchy.

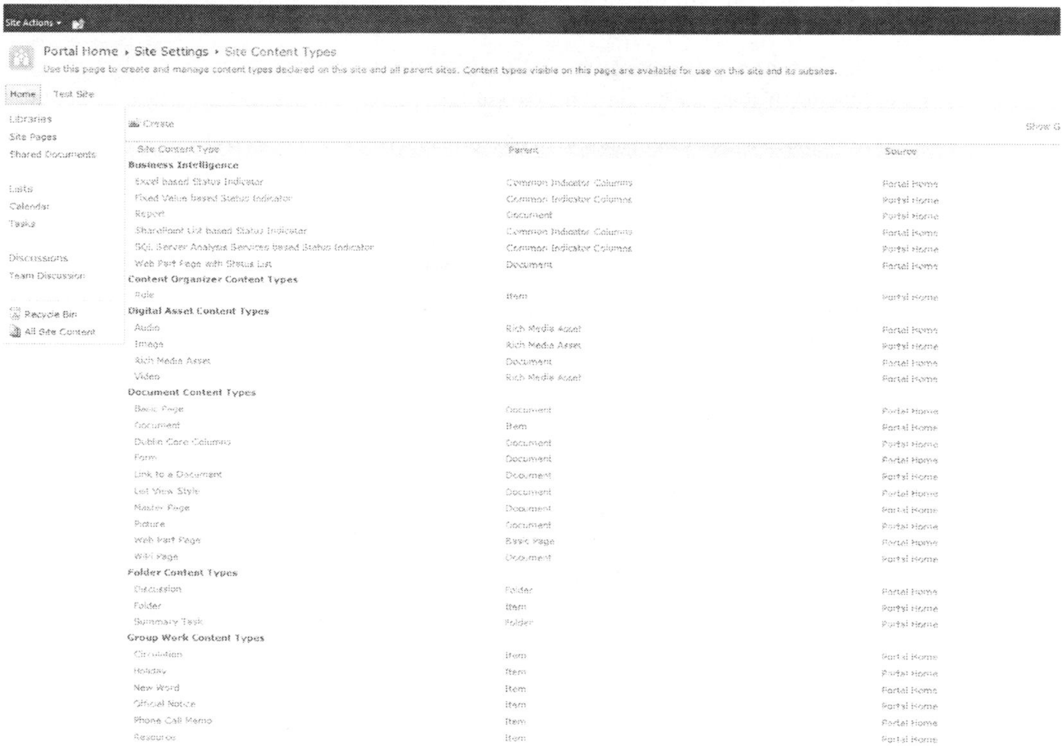

Figure 6-4: Site Content Types

> ▦ **Note**: Every content type inherits from a parent, even if it is just the base Item content type.

1. Click the Create link at the top of the page.

2. Give the new content type a name, and a description.

3. Specify the parent content type. SharePoint helps you out here by providing a drop-down to restrict the choices by group.

4. Provide either an existing group or a new group name to file the new content type.

5. Click the OK button.

SharePoint should now show you the settings page for the content type created. SharePoint allows you to attach workflow and information management policy and to change general settings for the content type in the Settings section of this page.

6. Scroll to the Columns section.

You should see those columns present from the parent content type. In my case I inherited from the Item content type, and so I see the Title column only.

1. SharePoint indicates the parent content type under the Source heading (linked). You may click this link to visit the settings of the parent content type.

2. Click the Add from Existing Site Columns link to navigate to a page to choose from existing site columns at the current site and above (if not at the root of the site collection).

3. Click the Add from New Site Column link to create a new site column for the content type—any new site column created resides in the Site Columns Gallery.

Content types provide for powerful, yet flexible definition of the metadata. Like most things in life, this power and flexibility comes with caveats, as follows:

- You cannot delete a content type once it is in use by a container, list item, page, or inherited by another content type.

- Once a content type is created, you may not change its inheritance relationship with the parent. You must delete the content type and recreate it to inherit from a different content type. This restriction, coupled with the first caveat, can make for difficulty in restructuring an existing metadata model in use by content. Design your model with flexibility at the onset.

- Deleting an inherited column from a content type is ill advised. Instead, make the column *hidden*.

- Avoid modifying stock content types. Instead, create a new content type and add customization to your new type—content owners expect standard behavior when using stock content types.

- You may not delete any content type deployed via a custom-developed feature.

Content types not only define metadata for documents in libraries and list items in lists; they also provide additional functionality, outlined in Table 6-3.

Table 6-3: *Functionality Associated with Content Types*

Content Type Functionality	Description
Templates	You may associate a document template with a document content type, such as a Contract content type that associates with a Word document, containing the skeleton of a contract document. When users create a new list item, using the content type, SharePoint will open the template so the user may begin editing the document.
	You may also specify an ASPX page in the SharePoint site collection as the template, so SharePoint opens a web page when a user creates a new content type.
Document Information Panel (DIP)	This panel appears in Office 2010 applications to show users the metadata associated with a document they opened from SharePoint. Chapter 9 covers the DIP and templates.
Workflow	You may associate a workflow with a content type, so when users create a new list item, based on the content type, SharePoint starts the workflow.
Management Policy	Management Policy applies to content types. You may audit events on list items that use a content type, apply retention rules, and do similar tasks. Chapter 7 covers records management and auditing.

Metadata in Lists

In a previous chapter, we looked at creating lists, which contain columns. By default, new custom lists do not maintain columns with content types. Changing a list to allow the management of content types provides for greater control of content in the list—for one, a list may associate with multiple content types, and thus have list items with different columns. The following steps demonstrate adding content types to a document library, and assume the existence of a site collection based on the Team site template:

1. In the left navigation, click the Shared Documents link in the Libraries section.

2. From the Ribbon, click the Library tab.

3. From the Ribbon, click the Library Settings icon.

4. Under General Settings, click the Advanced settings link.

5. Toggle the option to Allow Management of Content Types to Yes.

6. Scroll to the bottom of the page and click the OK button.

The Library Settings page should now show a Content Types section, as shown in Figure 6-5.

Content Types

This document library is configured to allow multiple content types. Use content types to specify the information you want to display about an item, in addition to its policies, workflows, or other behavior. The following content types are currently available in this library:

Content Type	Visible on New Button	Default Content Type
Document	✔	✔

Add from existing site content types
Change new button order and default content type

Figure 6-5: *Content Types section in the Library Settings page*

Here you see that my document library has one content type—Document—and this content type is the default for all new items added to the list. Farther down the page, in the Columns section notice the Title column, sourced from the Document content type. SharePoint adds the special Modified By, Create By, and Checked Out columns to each list, and are not associated with any content type.

7. Back in the Content Types section, click the Add from Existing Site Column Types link.

8. In the content type section page, change the drop-down to display Document Content Types group.

9. Select the content type Picture, and click the Add button.

10. Click the OK button.

In the Library Settings page, within the Content Types section, you should see the addition of the Picture content type

11. Scroll to the Columns section, notice the presence of new columns, as used in the Picture content type.

12. Navigate back to the default view of the Shared Documents library (hint: you can use the breadcrumb at the top of the page).

13. Click the Documents tab in the Ribbon.

14. From the Ribbon, click the New Document (lower part of the icon), as shown in Figure 6-6.

Figure 6-6: *Creating a new document*

You may apply the above series of steps to regular lists so that content owners and contributors may add list items to a list with different column data. This practice greatly comes into play when creating multiple content types for different publishing pages within a single Pages document library of a publishing site.

One area of confusion I have seen with lists and content types is in the inheritance chain. When adding a content type to a list, SharePoint makes a new content type at the list level, which inherits from the site content type of the same name. The purpose of this action is to provide a degree of abstraction from changes applied to content types at the site level that differ from specific changes at the list level. The following series of steps demonstrates this thinking:

1. In the left navigation, click the Shared Documents link under the Libraries section.

2. From the Ribbon, click the Library tab.

3. From the Ribbon, click the Library Settings icon.

4. Scroll to the Content Types section.

5. Click the Document content type.

SharePoint shows the content type settings page for the Document content type. At the top of the page, notice that the parent of this selected content type is Document also. The heading at the top of the page shows as List Content Type Information.

6. Click the parent Document content type.

7. SharePoint now shows a page for the site version of the Document content type.

The page heading changes to show Site Content Type Information.

8. Click Add from New Site Column to navigate to the new column page.

9. Scroll to the bottom of the page and notice the setting for Update All Content Types Inheriting from This Type.

10. If you toggle this option to No and then add a new column to the site version of the content type, then the list version of the content type does not receive the new column. With the option toggled to Yes, then the list content type also receives the new column added.

Metadata in Publishing

We touched on metadata in the SharePoint 2010 Publishing features within the previous sections of this chapter. In this section, here I will elaborate further on how site columns and content types play a part in the Publishing infrastructure of the SharePoint platform.

For most intended purposes, you can consider the core platform of SharePoint as a list management system, which leverages site columns, content types, and list containers to house data. No matter whether the data in discussion are documents in a document library, forms data entered through an InfoPath form, a calendar event, or a publishing page on a public SharePoint hosted web site, they all rely on the basic premise of lists, content types, and site columns—metadata.

Publishing pages in SharePoint consist of the ASPX files that live in a Document Library—called *pages*. Unlike regular web part pages and wiki pages in non-publishing sites, publishing pages contain no data or markup, just references to a page layout in the Master Page Gallery, and metadata associated with the page file. Next time you open the Pages Library in SharePoint 2010 for a publishing site, try downloading one of the page files to your local computer and opening the file with Notepad. You should see that the file consists mainly of XML references for the page layout and other publishing infrastructure data—the page will not contain any layout markup or content.

Figure 6-7 defines the component parts of a publishing page.

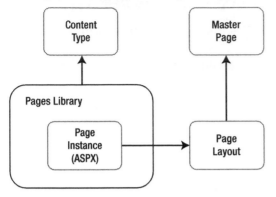

Figure 6-7: *Components of a publishing page*

In Figure 6-7, the content type defines the fields that content owners of the page may edit (either in WYSIWYG mode or as page instance properties in the list item). The content type is associated with the Pages Library—a list—and the page instance file resides in the library with applied metadata property values. The page layout resides in the Master Page Gallery, as another ASPX file, and contains HTML markup for the presentation of the page. Embedded in the markup are field controls that map metadata fields in the content type to the layout. When SharePoint renders the page instance, the platform replaces these field controls in the layout with the content stored as metadata and associated with the page instance file in the Pages Library.

Without going too far into the specifics of Web Content Management and the publishing infrastructure in SharePoint 2010, the diagram in Figure 6-7 and the previous discussion give a high-level overview of how metadata works with publishing pages. The purpose of the model is to abstract content from presentation, so that content owners may influence content without concern for presentation (editing the metadata properties of a page list item), and page designers may work on one or multiple flavors of page design without requirement to embed content in their templates. Use of the publishing infrastructure and metadata model promotes not only content abstraction but also reuse of page design—using the same template for multiple pages—and the ability to change the visual design of the site without having to change the content.

Before we leave the topic of metadata in the publishing infrastructure, the Publishing feature includes a number of new site column types and content types, worth mentioning. Table 6-1, listing the available site columns, described the following columns:

- Full HTML

- Image

- Hyperlink

- Summary Links

- Rich Media

These additional site column types (fields) provide for richer content on publishing pages, aside from the typical single/multiple lines of text, image, and hyperlink columns in the core platform. The Full HTML column type is interesting in that it allows content owners to embed full HTML in content areas on the page. A word of caution not to break best practices here—try not to embed layout or branding elements with content in full HTML fields, as this tightly couples content with formatting, which is exactly what page layouts and content abstraction try to avoid.

The Managed Metadata Service

Up to now, this chapter has introduced concepts that already exist in SharePoint 2007 (with a few exceptions). Content types, site columns, and the publishing features operate in SharePoint 2010 pretty much the way they do in the previous version of SharePoint. This section of the chapter introduces the Managed Metadata Service, which many associate with tagging and taxonomy, but is essentially the central hub for managing metadata across site collections and applications in a SharePoint 2010 farm (and potentially across farms, using the service and service proxy components).

The Managed Metadata Service exists as a managed service application in a SharePoint 2010 farm and acts as a central hub for the management of metadata. In SharePoint 2007, site collection owners could only define content types as far up as the site collection. Sharing of content types across multiple site collections was only possible via deployment of site collection features, containing custom content type and site column definitions. The Managed Metadata Service now allows for the centralization of metadata for sharing across multiple site collections, applications, and SharePoint 2010 farms.

Initial Setup

Chapter 2 discusses managed service applications, and the Managed Metadata Service is one such application, among others in the farm. Typically, the Managed Metadata Service already exists in a working SharePoint 2010 farm. Since the majority of readers of this book are administrators, it would be a disservice not to present the steps for provisioning the Managed Metadata Service. The following steps demonstrate how to create a new Managed Metadata Service from Central Admin.

1. Open Central Administration.

2. Click the Manage Service Application link under the Application Management heading on the Central Admin home page.

3. In the list of service applications, if you see the Managed Service Application (or something like it), leave it alone—for the purpose of this demonstration we will just create another.

4. Click the New icon from the Ribbon, and select Managed Metadata Service from the drop-down list. SharePoint opens a dialog for the service provisioning properties, as shown in Figure 6-8.

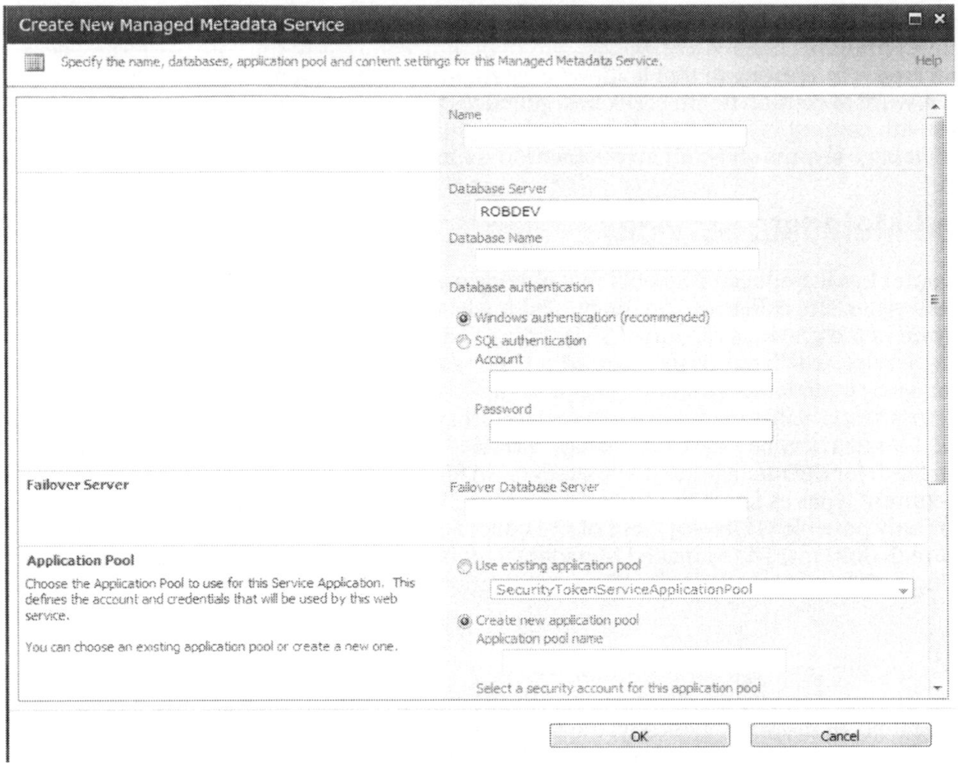

Figure 6-8: The New Managed Metadata Service settings dialog

5. Give the application a name and database details for storing the metadata service data.

6. The Managed Metadata Service is an application, hosted in SharePoint via IIS, and therefore requires an application pool account, so provide the credentials.

7. The content type hub is an existing site collection that acts as the central store for all shared content types, so provide the site collection URL for a new hub for this managed metadata service application.

8. Check Report Syndication Report Errors if you want the service to report synchronization errors.

9. Check Add this Service Application to the Farm's Default List if you want all sites to use this service by default.

10. Click the OK button to provision the new Managed Metadata Service.

11. From the Managed Service Applications list, click to the right of the name of the new Managed Metadata Service application and then click the Manage icon in the Ribbon.

SharePoint displays the Term Store Management Tool, shown in Figure 6-9.

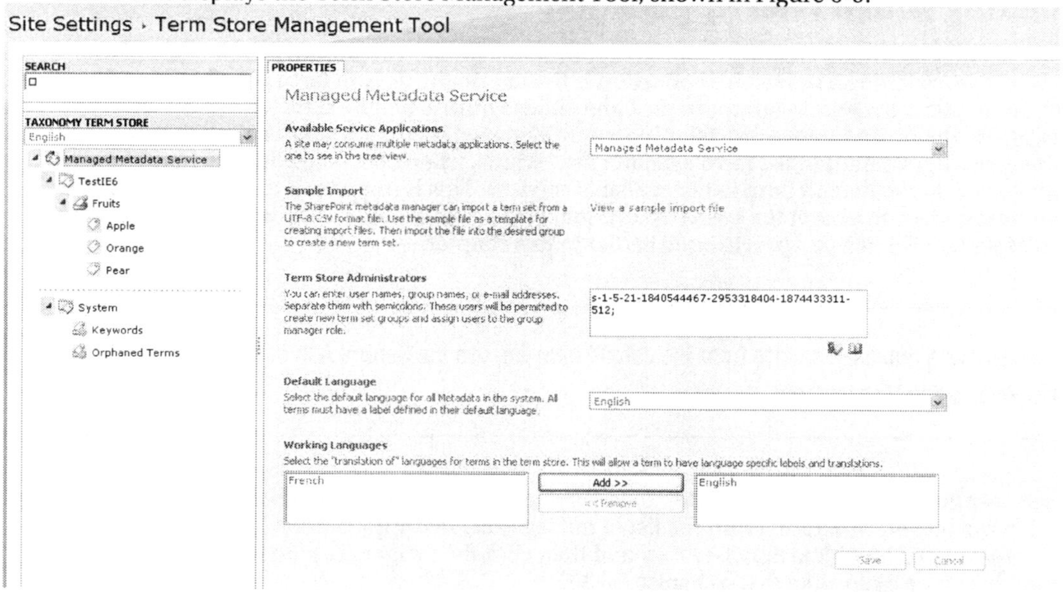

Figure 6-9: The Term Store Management Tool

What is a *term store*? Each Managed Metadata Service contains at least one term store, which consists of a hierarchy of term sets, or groups of term sets. I cover this terminology in more depth shortly, so for now you only need to know that a new provisioned Managed Metadata Service contains a default term store, which is the beginning of your tagging taxonomy.

The Term Store Management Tool enables administrators (and users with access rights to the service) to manipulate settings for the Managed Metadata Service. Table 6-4 identifies the various settings in Figure 6-9.

Table 6-4: Settings on the Landing Page of Term Store Management Tool

Setting	Description
Available Service Applications	Drop-down list of provisioned Managed Metadata Service applications in the farm.
Sample Import	Click the sample link to see a sample CSV file so that you may create your own to import tags into the term store.
Term Store Administrators	Users who have full control over the term store.
Default Language	The Managed Metadata Service supports multilingual terms; this setting stipulates the default language.
Working Languages	Specifies the languages available for terms in the term store.

Associating with a Web Application

In Chapter 2, I demonstrated creating new web applications (in IIS) via Central Admin. One of the options when provisioning a new web application is to opt into the default farm list of managed service applications, or allow the administrator to pick and choose from available services.

Recall from the procedure for provisioning a new Managed Metadata Service the check box option "Add this service application to the farm's default list," which, when checked, adds the new Managed Metadata Service to the default farm list of available services. This is important to note, because if administrators choose to accept the farm defaults for service applications, they will include the new Managed Metadata Service you provisioned earlier in this chapter.

■ **Note**: To remove a managed service from the default farm list, use the Central Administration Farm Association Page under Application Management.

Worth mentioning is the Managed Metadata Service properties page, which differs from the settings discussed in the previous section. From the list of managed service applications, click to the right of the name of the Managed Metadata Service Proxy and then click the Properties icon in the Ribbon. SharePoint displays a dialog like that in Figure 6-10.

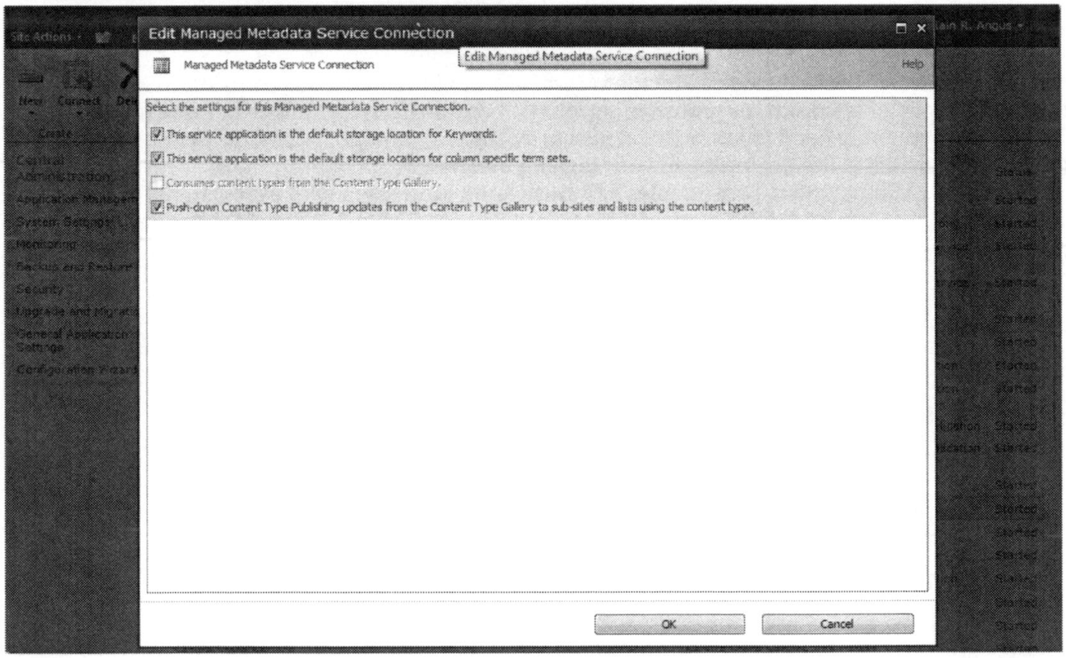

Figure 6-10: *Managed Metadata Service properties*

The first two check boxes tell SharePoint 2010 whether this Managed Metadata Service is will be the default for Enterprise Keywords (Folksonomy) and for term sets (Taxonomy). Only one Managed Metadata service may act as default storage location for tags of either type. The other two properties involve the use of content types and a hub, which I cover later in this chapter.

Taxonomy—Managed Metadata

In the Chapter 5 section "A Brief Segue on Taxonomy and Folksonomy," I discussed the differences in taxonomy and folksonomy, involving tags in social networking. Here is a quick recap, since both principles apply to tagging in the Managed Metadata Service.

Taxonomy is the hierarchical structure of terms and terms sets, where a term is what SharePoint calls the definition of tag. For example, "USA" might be a term identified in a term set called "Countries." This term set may likely include other terms. When tagging content for specific country, users in SharePoint may select the term "USA" to identify the content as belonging to or originating from the USA. The term set "Countries" may exist within a sub-hierarchy, perhaps under "Regions." You can quickly see how easy terms and term sets constitute a hierarchy, which is the taxonomy. In Figure 6-9, the taxonomy features are in the left panel of the Term Store Management Tool.

Whereas taxonomy is structured, and typically predetermined by a term store or taxonomy administrator, folksonomy evolves as users of a content management system invent tag names (terms) for content. Folksonomy provides for only a flat and ad-hoc tagging model, but it is effective because tags evolve as more users participate in tagging of a piece of content. *Tag clouds* are a classic example of folksonomy, which show the proliferation of certain tags based on popularity. Clicking the Keywords node under System in Figure 6-9 will display Enterprise Keywords entered by users for folksonomy.

When working with managed metadata, administrators and taxonomy administrators need to understand the following components: term store, groups, term sets, and terms. The following sections cover each of these components individually.

Term Store

The term store is the entry home of the taxonomy and structured tags. Looking at Figure 6-9, you can see that in our Managed Metadata Service, the term store (shown with the house icon) has the same name "Managed Metadata Service." You may create a term store with any name you choose; by default, SharePoint has named the term store.

At the term store level, administrators of the farm may define term store administrators. These users have full control of the term store, to manipulate the taxonomy.

Term store administrators differ from Managed Metadata Service administrators. The first control changes to a term store; the second have access to the entire managed service. Figure 6-11 shows the location for adding Managed Metadata Service Administrators (in Central Administration), and Figure 6-12 shows the location for term store administrators (in the Term Store Management Tool).

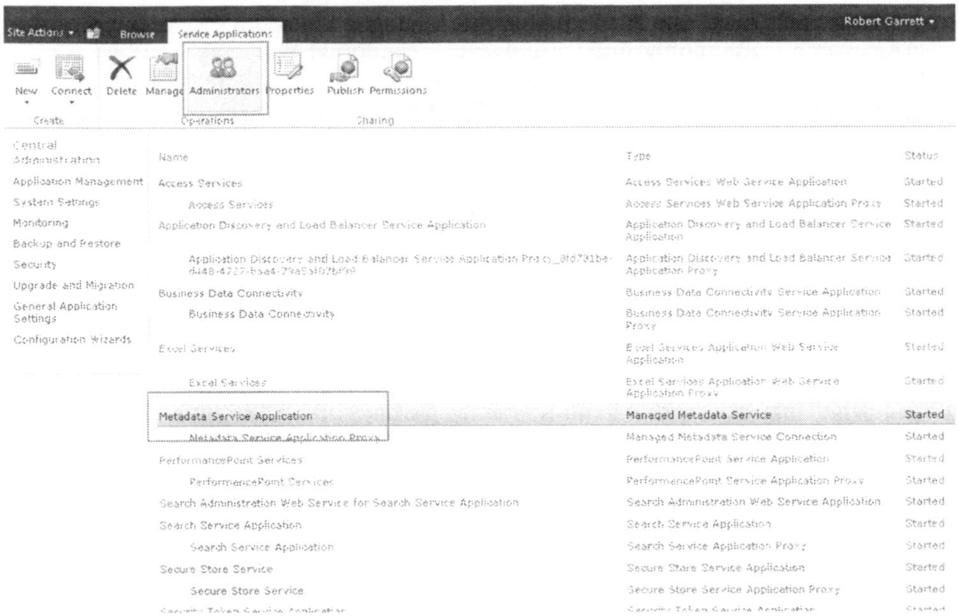

Figure 6-11: *The location for adding administrators for the Managed Metadata Service*

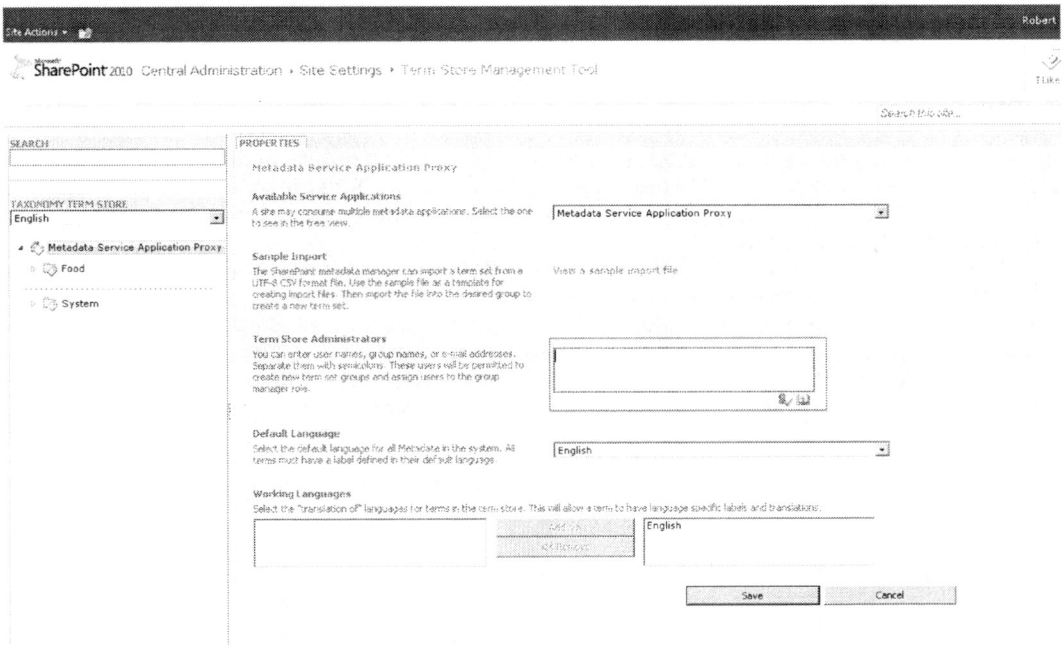

Figure 6-12: *The location for adding term store administrators*

Groups

Groups provide an important role of maintaining a collection of term sets. Groups provide security for the term sets they contain, as both Group Managers and Contributors to the group.

1. Click the drop-down arrow on the Term Store node in the taxonomy tree.

2. Click New Group to create a new group.

3. Provide a name from the group.

SharePoint 2010 displays the group Properties page, as shown in Figure 6-13.

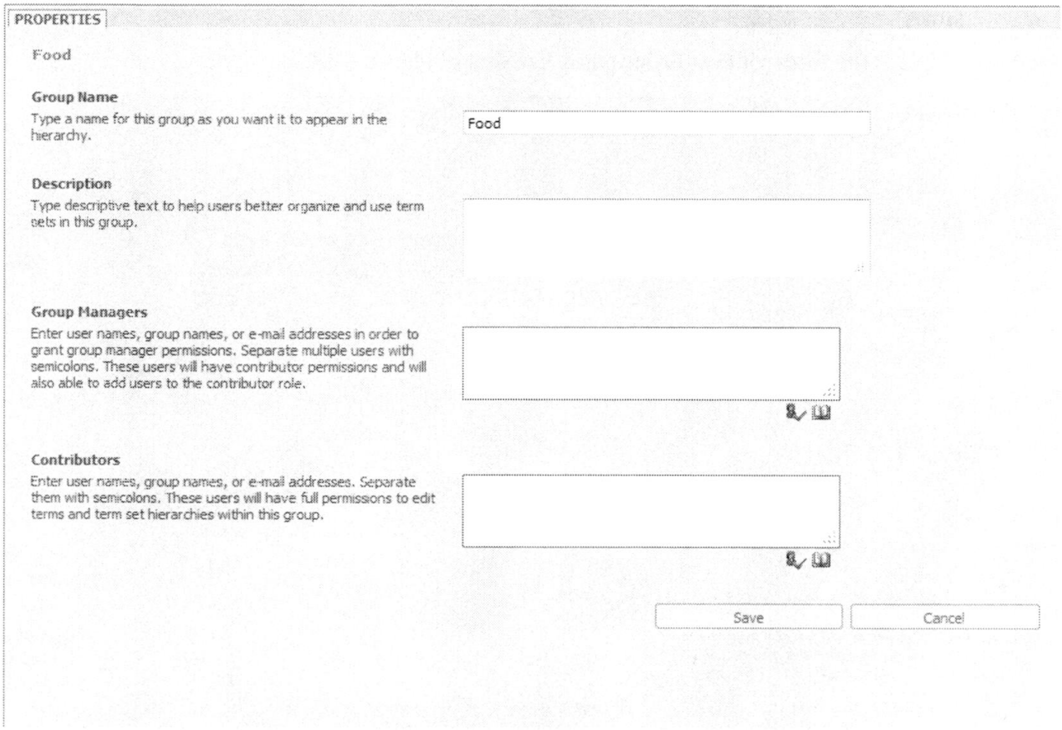

Figure 6-13: Group properties in the Term Store Management Tool—

From within the group Properties pane, you can change the name of the group, give it a Description, and add users to Group Managers and Contributors. Group Managers may add other users as contributors, as well as remove and add new term sets. Contributors may add new terms to term sets and configure group hierarchies.

Term Sets

A term set provides the container for terms. Later in this chapter, we will see how term sets bind to managed metadata columns in content types and lists so that users may choose from a set of term values in a given term set for the data of a column.

1. Click the drop-down arrow on the Group node to contain a new Term Set.

2. Click either New Term Set or Import Term Set menu item.

3. If importing a term set, provide the location of a CSV file with similar format to that of the sample shown in the properties pane of the term store.

SharePoint displays the term set Properties pane, like that of Figure 6-14.

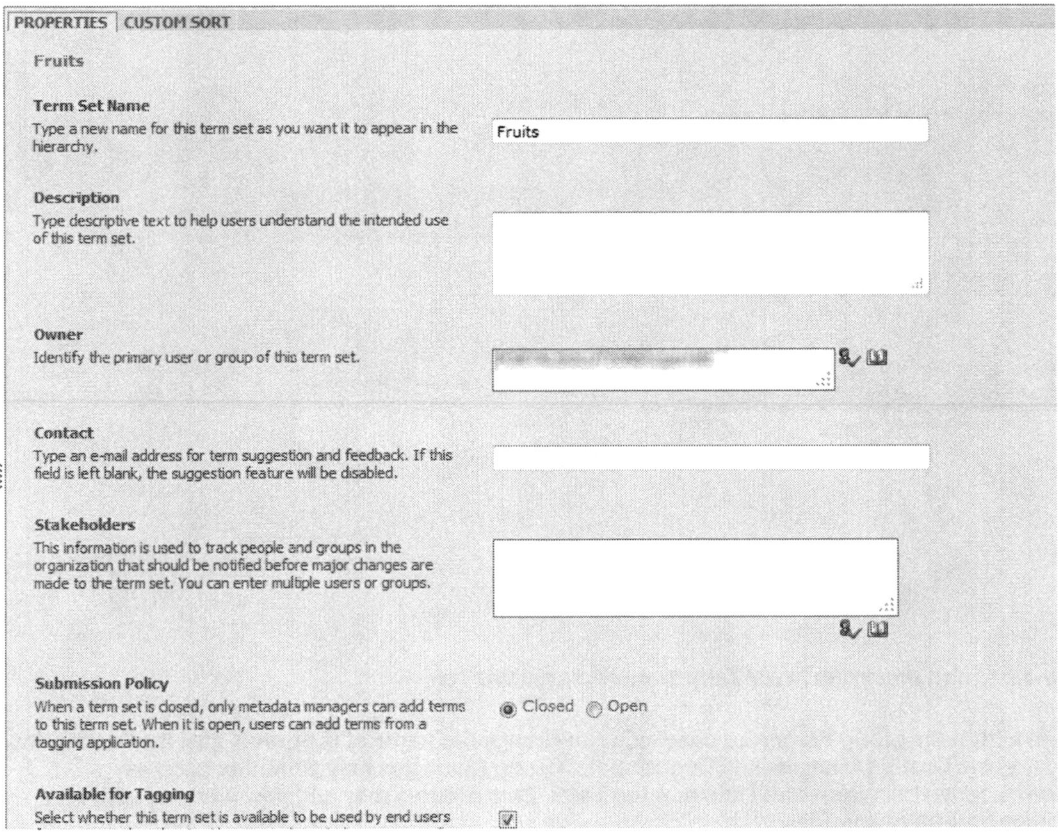

Figure 6-14: Term Store Management Tool—Term Set Properties

On the properties pane of the term set, you may change the name of the term set and the description. The owner (typically the person who created the term set) is the person with full control of the lifecycle of the term set. The term set owner and term store administrators may make significant structural changes to the terms in the term set.

Stakeholders are those users who receive email notification when the term set owner or term store administrator makes changes to the term set. Imagine you have a body of people that want to monitor the evolution of terms for a given term set—these people would be the stakeholders.

The submission policy governs whether the term set allows users to add new terms to the set from managed metadata site columns. By default, SharePoint creates the term set as Closed and assumes the term set owner and stakeholders wish tight management of the terms in the taxonomy term set. Toggling the policy to Open allows users and programmatic addition of terms in the set—edging more to folksonomy than taxonomy behavior.

The property to set the term set as Available for Tagging tells SharePoint whether to show the term values in the managed metadata site column UI when a user starts typing a term value. The Custom Sort property allows the term set owner to custom sort the order of the terms contained in the set— alphabetical order may not always make sense to users for certain term sets.

Terms

Terms are the actual values used in managed metadata site columns for the value chosen from a defined set—the term set. For example, the term set might include terms for food such as fruits. In the site, a user would see the list of fruits to choose from, and the SharePoint UI will limit the list of available terms as the user types the first few letters of a known term. Figure 6-15 shows the term values (the fruits) in the background, and user interface to create, copy, reuse terms, etc.

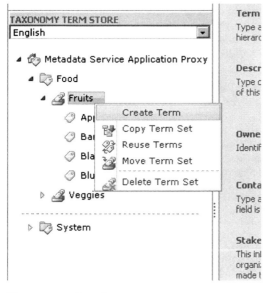

Figure 6-15: Creating a new term

1. Click the drop-down arrow on the term set node to add a new term.

2. Give the term a name.

A term has an expected name and description property, designated language, and option for tagging, and other labels or properties. The language property is important—term set owners may designate certain term values for specific languages. For example, when viewing the site in French, users would see a different set of term values than users viewing the site in English.

The option to make a term available for tagging allows the owner to determine whether a particular term value shows up in the UI of choices for managed metadata site columns.

The Other Labels property provides synonym capability for the term. For example, *MOSS* is a synonym for Microsoft Office SharePoint Server 2007. If a user selects the term value as MOSS in a managed metadata site column, SharePoint understands that the value MOSS corresponds to the Microsoft Office SharePoint Server 2007 term.

Managed Metadata in SharePoint Sites

Terms within a Managed Metadata Service term store surface in a site collection via special site column types. Assuming the administrator has associated a SharePoint 2010 site with the term store contained in the Managed Metadata Service, content owners may add the new metadata columns to lists, content types, and the Site Column Gallery. Table 6-5 details the different Managed Metadata site column types.

Table 6-5: New Managed Metadata Column Types

Managed Metadata Column Type	Description
Managed Metadata	Provides a column mapping to a term set in the site-associated term-store; depending on the configuration of the term set, this type will depict whether users see all available term sets when selecting a term, have the ability to submit feedback to the term set owner, or add new terms.
	Use the Managed Metadata column type when you wish to provide users with a choice of tags from a given term set in the term store.
Enterprise Keywords	A special column type added to a list when users enable Enterprise Keywords in the Enterprise Keywords and Metadata Settings section of the list settings page. Terms entered by users in Enterprise Keywords columns appear under the System/Keywords node in the term store.
	Use the Enterprise Keywords column type when you want to allow users to tag with their own tag values.

Earlier in this chapter, I demonstrated how to create a new site column. Follow the same steps here, except choose the Managed Metadata column type this time. After your browser posts back to display available properties for the selected column type, scroll to the section on Term Set Settings, as shown in Figure 6-16.

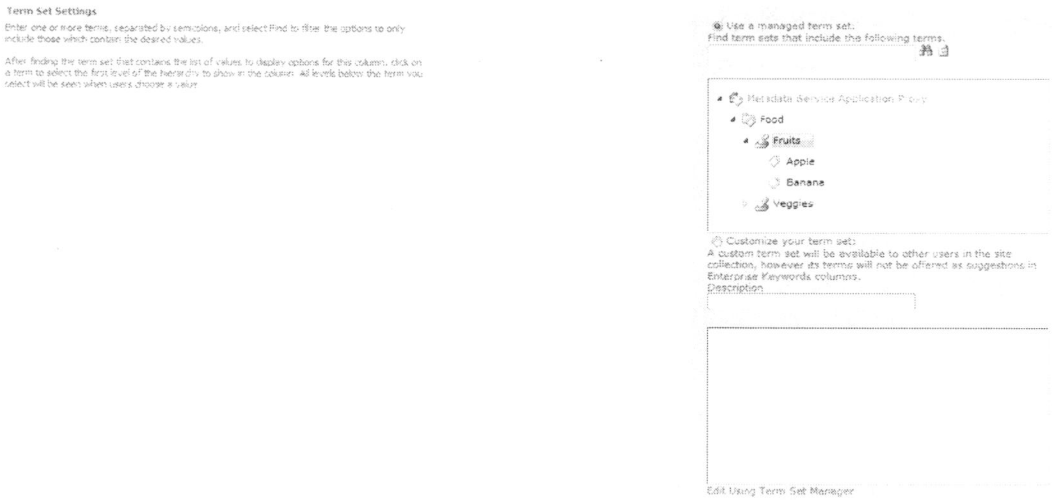

Term Set Settings

Enter one or more terms, separated by semicolons, and select Find to filter the options to only include those which contain the desired values.

After finding the term set that contains the list of values to display options for this column, click on a term to select the first level of the hierarchy to show in the column. All levels below the term you select will be seen when users choose a value.

⦿ Use a managed term set.
Find term sets that include the following terms.

▲ 🗂 Metadata Service Application Proxy
  ▲ 🗁 Food
    ▲ 📑 Fruits
      ◇ Apple
      ◇ Banana
  ▷ 📑 Veggies

◇ Customize your term set:
A custom term set will be available to other users in the site collection, however its terms will not be offered as suggestions in Enterprise Keywords columns.
Description

Edit Using Term Set Manager

Figure 6-16: *Term Set Settings in the Create New Site Column page*

The Term Set Settings section includes the option to bind the new Managed Metadata column to a particular term set in the term store. In Figure 6-16, I created a simple group called *Food* and a term set called *Fruits*. In the next section of this chapter, we will see how SharePoint presents the available terms under this term set to the user via the user interface.

If the term set has an *open* policy, users can add new terms to the set from the column user interface. If the administrator specified the feedback email address, then users also have the option to suggest terms via a feedback email (see Figure 6-17).

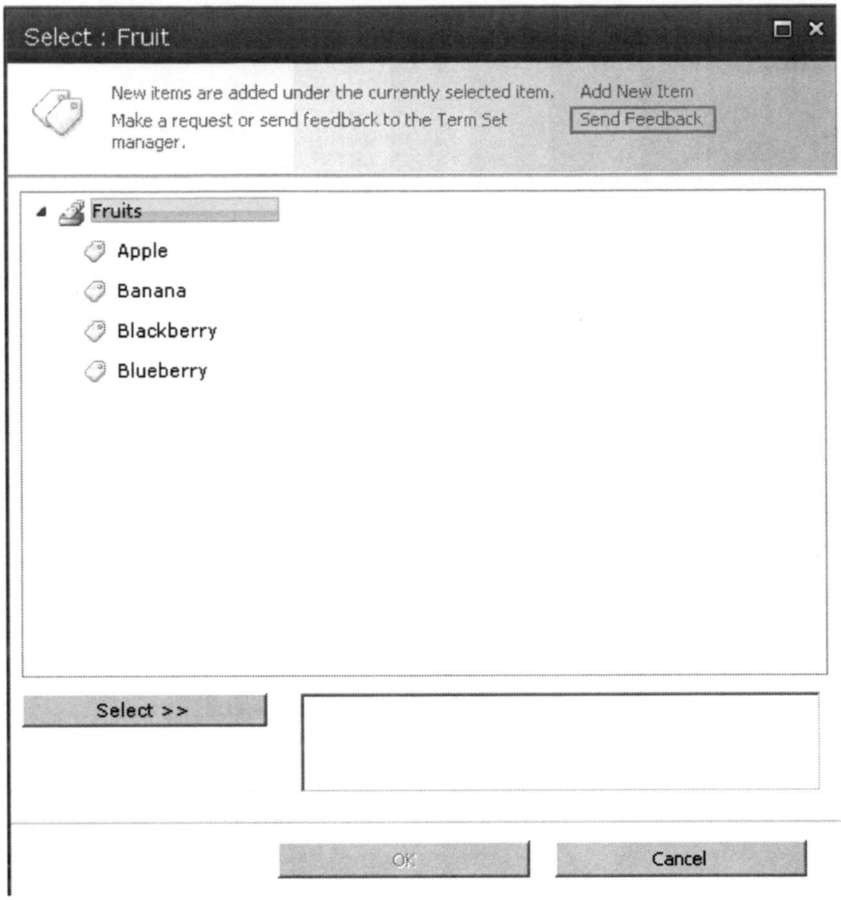

Figure 6-17: Link to send feedback via email

Owners of a site column can choose to create a customized term set, rather than use an existing term set in the term store.

■ **Note**: If SharePoint displays an error message that there is no default term store associated with the site, ensure the check box for default term store is checked, as in Figure 6-10 earlier.

The Enterprise Keywords column type is a special SharePoint 2010 type. The following steps demonstrate how to enable Enterprise Keywords on a list:

1. From a list page, click the List/Library tab on the Ribbon.

2. Click the List/Library Settings icon.

3. Click the Enterprise Keywords and Metadata Settings link.

4. Enable the Enterprise Keywords option.

5. Go back to the List/Library Settings page and you should see a new Enterprise Keywords column added to the list columns definition.

In the next section, we will see how both Enterprise Keywords and Managed Metadata columns appear to end users in the user interface.

Tagging User Interface

To demonstrate the user interface for Managed Metadata columns and Enterprise Keywords, I performed the following steps as a precursor:

1. Created two term sets—Fruits and Veggies (as in Figure 6-18).

2. Set the policy for Fruits as open and for Veggies as closed.

3. Created a custom list with two Managed Metadata columns, each bound to one of the Fruit or Veggies term sets.

4. Enabled Enterprise Keywords on the custom list

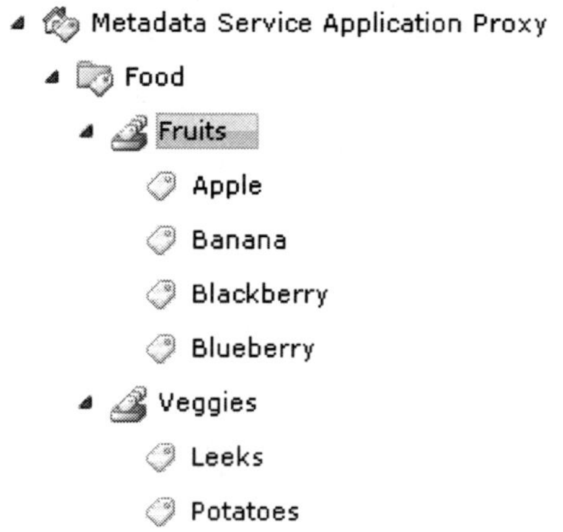

▲ 🗐 Metadata Service Application Proxy

  ▲ 🗐 Food

    ▲ 🗐 Fruits

      🏷 Apple

      🏷 Banana

      🏷 Blackberry

      🏷 Blueberry

    ▲ 🗐 Veggies

      🏷 Leeks

      🏷 Potatoes

Figure 6-18: My Term Store to demonstrate Managed Metadata User Interface

Adding a new list item to my custom list produces a dialog as shown in Figure 6-19.

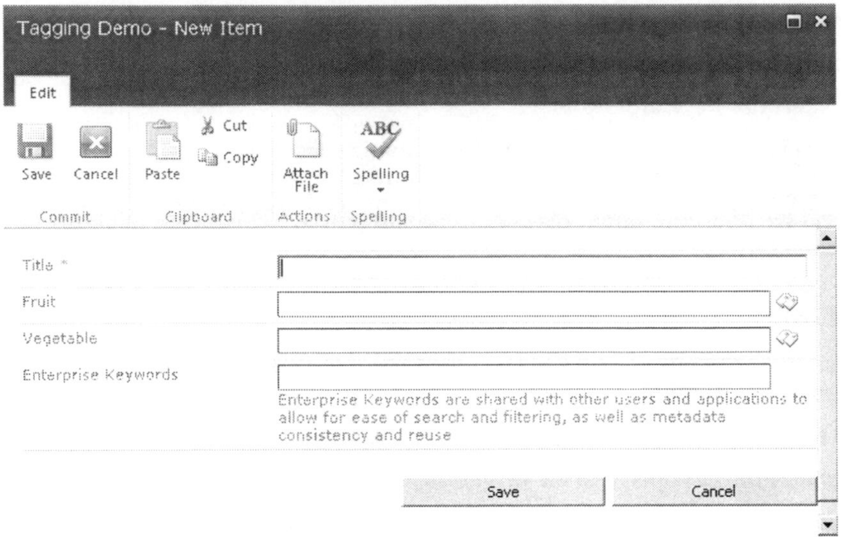

Figure 6-19: New list item dialog with metadata columns

With the dialog displayed, as in Figure 6-19, start typing the name of a fruit in the Fruit field. Start with the letter B (hint, hint) and SharePoint will show suggestions of all fruits beginning with the letter B. You can try the same test on the Veggies fields, although, if use the letter B you should notice that SharePoint has no suggestions because I did not create any vegetable terms starting with the letter B.

Switch to the Enterprise Keywords field and begin typing the name of a fruit that exists in the Fruit term set. Even though the term is part of another term set, SharePoint allows the Enterprise Keywords column to query terms in term sets of the same term store. Before leaving this field, type the name of another food that is neither a fruit nor a vegetable, save the list item, and then come back to this dialog to enter another item. Back in the Enterprise Keywords field, you can now start typing the name of the new food item (I chose donut) and see that SharePoint saved the new term.

■ **Note**: To prevent Enterprise Keyword fields from offering suggestions from a term set, uncheck the setting Available for Tagging in the term set settings.

Before leaving the New Item dialog, click the small tag icon to the right of the Fruit field. This icon links the user to the dialog for browsing terms, as shown in Figure 6-20. From this dialog, users may visualize all terms in a term set and select the appropriate term. Notice in the top-right of the dialog a link to Add a new Item (term). Remember that I configured the Fruit term set as Open, meaning that users can add new terms. Compare this dialog to that of the browse term dialog for the Vegetable field—the Add New Item link is missing because the veggies term set has a Closed policy.

The Send Feedback link is a standard mail-to link that will open your mail application with the email address configured in the Feedback setting for the term set.

Figure 6-20: *Browseing for a term*

Navigation

Managed Metadata navigation in SharePoint 2010 is about the process of filtering list data (at least in the context of this chapter). In the previous section in this chapter I set up a new demo list and add a couple of Managed Metadata site columns to the list. In this section, I will demonstrate how to add taxonomy navigation and keyword filtering to a list or document library.

1. From the list page, click the list tab on the Ribbon, and then click the List Settings icon on the Ribbon.

2. From the list settings page, click the Metadata Navigation Settings link.

SharePoint shows a page like that in Figure 6-21.

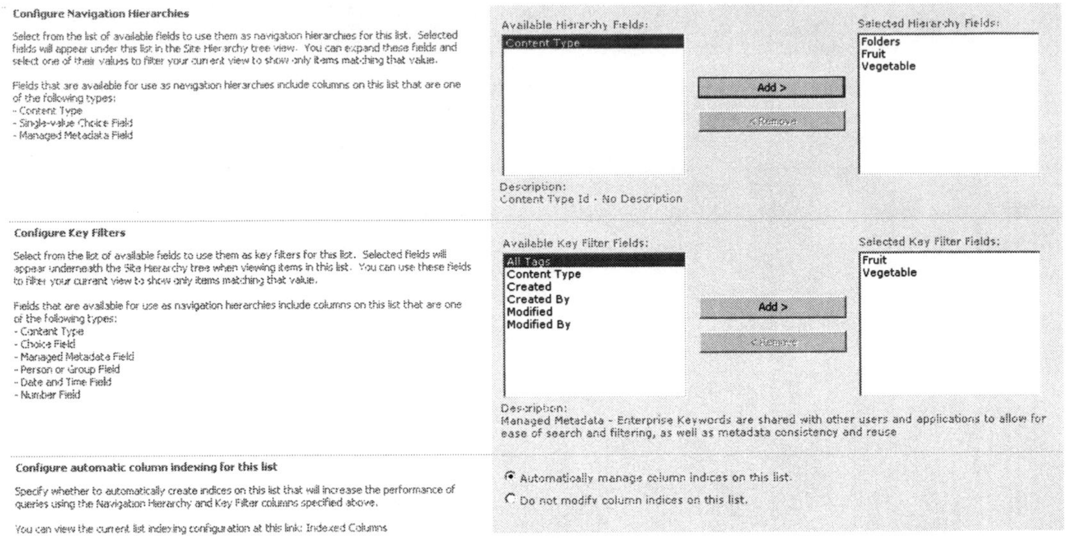

Figure 6-21: *The Metadata Navigation Settings page*

1. Choose one or multiple Managed Metadata fields from the list for the navigation hierarchy. Do the same for the key filters.

2. Navigate back to the list page, and add some list items.

3. From any of the list view pages, glance to the left under the quick navigation links, and you should see something like in Figure 6-22.

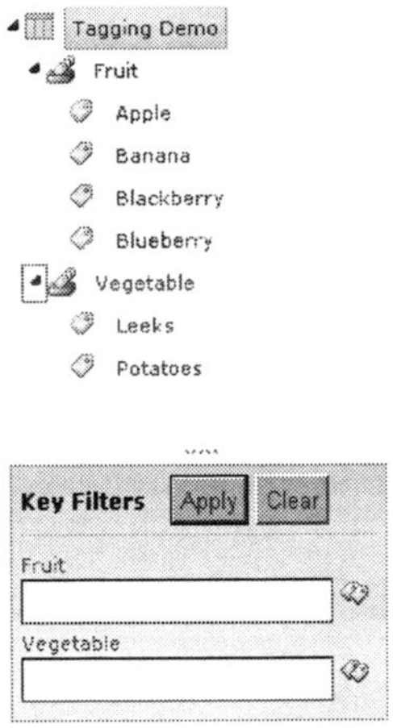

Figure 6-22: *Navigation Hierarchy and Keyword Filters*

Here you can see that SharePoint has added a hierarchy tree for both *Fruit* and *Vegetable* fields in my list. Selecting one of the terms in the tree filters the list of items, similar to filtering lists the traditional way from the list column in the view. The Key Filters feature also provides filtering but it does so via typed keyword, with a UI similar to that of adding values to Managed Metadata fields.

Tagging in Office Applications

Office 2007 and 2010 applications understand metadata when applied to documents opened from a SharePoint source. With the introduction of Managed Metadata site column types and the Managed Metadata Service in SharePoint 2010, Office 2010 can now access term sets and term data from the Document Information Panel (see Figure 6-23).

■ **Note**: Only Office 2010 applications (and later) understand Managed Metadata site column types. Older Office applications cannot update these columns.

Figure 6-23: Managed Metadata in Word 2010

Content Type Hubs

Content types provide a powerful classification of content in SharePoint, whether it's a document, list item, publishing page, or external data. Pretty much all content in SharePoint involves content types somewhere. SharePoint 2007 introduced content types, and users of SharePoint have never looked back since. However, in SharePoint 2007, content types had a major limitation—the scope of a content type went no higher than a site collection. SharePoint best practice is to use multiple site collections in large content systems to distribute content across content databases. This made for a major headache in managing content types in a large enterprise content management system. SharePoint 2010 solves this issue with *content type hubs*; read on.

Earlier in this chapter, I described the steps for creating a new Managed Metadata Service application. During the creation process, SharePoint allows the administrator to specify the site collection as a content type hub. As long as the Managed Metadata Service administrator has Site Collection Administration rights to a site collection, they can specify this site collection as the hub for all new content types. The content type hub is effectively the authoritative site collection for the management of content types, and all other content types that subscribe to the same Managed Metadata Service may share content types from the hub.

▒ **Note**: When delegating a site collection as a new content type hub, I recommend leaving the option to Report Syndication Errors so that the log contains important errors if content types fail to synchronize across site collections.

The following steps confirm the existence of a content type for an existing Managed Metadata Service application, or the option to delegate a site collection as a content type hub:

1. From Central Administration, click the Manage Service Applications link.

2. Scroll down to the Managed Metadata Service (or name you gave when you created it).

3. Click to the right of the name of the service (not the proxy) and then click the Properties icon from the Ribbon.

4. Scroll to the bottom of the dialog that appears to the Content type hub section.

5. Ensure that a URL of a site collection exists in the field and that the check box for Report Syndication Errors checked.

6. If it is blank, populate the field, and then click OK.

With the hub established, let us head over to the site collection content type hub and see the introduction of new site collection settings:

1. Navigate to the content type hub site collection URL in your browser.

2. Access the Site Settings page and scroll to the Site Collection Administration section.

You should notice two links: Content Type Publishing and Content Type Service Application Error Log.

SharePoint 2010 manages publication of content types from the hub and subscription to published content types from consumers of the hub via two timer-jobs. The Content Type Hub job publishes all new content types from the hub where the site collection administrator has marked a content type for publishing. This job also manages the syndication error log. The Content Type Subscriber job exists for all applications where a contained site collection subscribes to the hub for a published content type. In the next subsection of this chapter, I discuss publishing a content type from the hub and consuming the content type in another site collection—the consumer.

Publishing, Unpublishing, and Republishing

The creation of a content type for publication in the content type hub is identical to that of creating a content type in a non-hub site collection. However, when a site collection administrator creates a content type in the hub, SharePoint 2010 displays additional configuration options in the content type settings page. Once you've completed the steps in the previous section to designate a content type hub, the following steps demonstrate creating a new content type for publication to another subscriber site collection.

1. From within the Content Type Hub Site Collection, navigate to the Content Type Gallery from the site collections settings page.

2. Click the Create link at the top of the page.

3. After creating the content type, see the content type Settings page, like that in Figure 6-24.

Figure 6-24: Content type settings page with publishing options

4. Click the Manage Publishing for This Content Type link.

5. The next page shows three options: Publish, Un-publish, and Re-publish (update). Choose Publish and click OK.

■ **Note**: If you get an error about an incorrect proxy at this stage, then either your site collection hub in the Managed Metadata Service is incorrect (if it's a root site collection, use the / on the end of the URL), or you need to change the URL using the following PowerShell command (see Chapter 2 for instructions on launching PowerShell commands):

```
Set-SPMetadataServiceApplication "Managed Metadata Service" –HubUri
http://site_collection_hub
```

---

6. From the consumer site collection, navigate to the Site Settings page.

7. In the Site Collection Administration, click the Content Type Publishing link.

SharePoint 2010 displays a page like that in Figure 6-25.

Figure 6-25: *Content type publishing page*

8. If you do not see your published content type in the Hubs section, check the error log by clicking the link in the section above

---

▨ **Note**: By default, the consumer timer job runs every hour and the hub timer job every 15 minutes. The consumer timer job looks after creating and updating shared content types in consumer site collections; the hub timer job notifies consumers of changes to existing shared content types or the existence of new shared content types.

- To unpublish the content type at the hub, continue with the following steps:

9. From the hub site collection, navigate to the Content Type Gallery from the Site Settings page.

10. Select the published content type to view the settings for the content type.

11. Click the Manage Publishing for This Content Type link.

12. Click the Unpublish option, and then the OK button.

▨ **Note**: You cannot delete a published content type. In addition, changes to a content type in the hub do not update the consumers until you republish the content type.

Once a site collection administrator publishes a content type, the timer jobs complete, and the content type is available to consumers, who may use the content type as if defined locally. Site collection administrators of the consumer site collection may inherit from the content type or use the content type in the sites and lists of the site collection.

1. Navigate to the Content Type Gallery in the consumer site collection.

2. Scroll to find the Consumed content type in the gallery.

3. Click the name of the consumed content type to view the settings page.

4. Click the Advanced Settings link.

5. By default, the consumed content type is read-only; to allow change to the consumed content type, change the read-only setting.

The Error Log

When either the Content Type Syndication Consumer or Publisher timer job encounters an error, it reports an error in the Syndication error log—a list available under the Site Administration section of the site collection site settings page. Administrators may also access the error log from the link on the Manage Publishing for This Content Type link page.

Assuming the administrator did not disable the setting to report syndication errors in the managed Metadata Service, SharePoint 2010 tries to be as verbose as possible in the syndication log. Table 6-6 depicts the columns in the error log.

Table 6-6: Columns in the Content Type Syndication Error Log

Column Name	Description
Title	Error title
Taxonomy Service Store ID	GUID of the term store in the Managed Metadata Service
Taxonomy Service Name	Name of the Managed Metadata Service
Content Type Subscriber Site	Link to the consumer site with syndication error
Syndication Item	Content type that failed to synchronize
Syndication Failure Stage	Stage at which the syndication failed
Syndication Failure Message	Specific details about the error
Syndication Failure Time	Timestamp that the error occurred

Sometimes the error log may report no errors and after successful execution of syndication timer jobs, the consumer site collection has no content types from the hub. The following list identifies a few reasons I have encountered during my research.

- The document ID feature enabled on either hub or consumer, and not on the other—either both require this feature enabled, or both disabled

- The Managed Metadata Service Proxy is not configured to consume content type publications—enable by right-clicking next to the Proxy name in the Managed Service Applications list, clicking Properties, and then checking the option Consumes Content Types from the content type hub.

- I came across one instance where the consumer failed with an error in the log about unknown site ID. This occurred when I checked the option to consume content types in the properties of the Managed Metadata Service proxy, post creation of the consumer site collection. I remedied the issue by recreating the site collection, once the Consumer Web Application MMS Proxy allowed the content type consuming option.

Summary

In this chapter, I introduced the reader to basic metadata—site columns and content types—as they exist since SharePoint 2007, and today in SharePoint 2010. This chapter included details on how site columns and content types operate in sites, lists, and how content owners can build a metadata model via content type inheritance.

With the basics understood, we dove into the specifics of the Managed Metadata Service—a new service application in SharePoint 2010 that handles taxonomy, folksonomy, and use of both for content tagging.

The Managed Metadata Service provides content type synchronization capabilities across site collections in the farm (and across farms), using the service and service proxy model of the Managed Service architecture. I demonstrated how to designate a site collection as the Content type hub, for Published Content Types. I then demonstrated how other consuming site collections (within a consumer web application) consume published content types from the hub. We briefly covered the syndication error log that SharePoint utilizes when a failure occurs to synchronize published content types.

Metadata and the Managed Metadata Service are important topics in the land of SharePoint 2010. Of all the chapters in this book, this chapter is one I recommend revisiting, especially if you are deploying a Content Management System in SharePoint 2010 across the Enterprise.

In Chapter 7, I cover Document and Records Management, which assumes that you have read and understood this chapter.

Documents and Records Management

Walk into many enterprise organizations and ask someone in a department to describe their document storage and processing operations, and they will likely give you a story about how management of documents and data is far from ideal.

In the time that I have been working with SharePoint and various clients looking to implement an information management system in SharePoint, the situation is typical—documents and files scattered on a shared drive or file share, no categorization, multiple copies of the same document floating around in emails. Even the more organized groups have issues with multiple document and information silos.

Document Management Systems (DMS) and Records Management Systems (RMS) are about the "management" of documents and data at an Enterprise level. This chapter focuses on the SharePoint 20101 DMS and RMS features, and how you can configure and apply these features to alleviate business pains with document collection.

Before diving into the topics of document management and records management, I should mention that both of these fall under the umbrella of Enterprise Content Management (ECM). Microsoft includes DMS and RMS with Web Content Management (also mentioned in this chapter) and Managed Metadata (see the previous chapter) to constitute ECM.

Note Microsoft provides an overview of ECM in SharePoint 2010 at the following URL:

http://technet.microsoft.com/en-us/sharepoint/ee263905.aspx

What Is a Document Management System?

Even though the name implies management of documents in an organization, Document Management is really about empowering users, who create and collaborate around documents, to do so with more structure and control. Consider the following questions:

1. How many documents does your organization produce in a year?

2. Are these documents stored on a central file-share with any form of structure?

3. How do users search and browse for particular documents?

4. Does your organization suffer from multiple versions of the same document in your document store?

5. Do users email copies of documents, or links to documents stored in a central location?

6. Are any documents in your organization security-sensitive? If so, how does your organization secure them?

7. Does your organization have a business policy or practices for the location of documents, movement of documents, and archival?

8. How does your IT department back up the organization document silo?

9. Does your organization use documents of non-Microsoft Office types?

10. Do you know of any approval or manual workflow for documents, such as proposal management?

The above questions are a small subset of those that I send new clients looking to move from a file-share document silo to a Document Management System. A DMS aims to provide a secure, central location for storage of all documents in an organization. Typical features of a DMS include the capabilities to:

- Apply meta-data to categorize documents

- Promote browsing and searching of documents based on document content or meta-data

- Manage versions and change control of documents

- Secure sensitive documents to groups of users without intervention of the IT department

- Provide a consistent reference link to a document, so that despite the location of the document in the DMS, users can still access the document from a shared link

- Scale to handle growth of document and meta-data content

Any good DMS provides features/functionality to address some or all of the questions raised above. The next section introduces the features of SharePoint 2010 document management.

Document Management in SharePoint 2010

At the core of the SharePoint 2010 platform, SharePoint provides document libraries for storage of documents. This feature addresses an immediate need to prevent emailing of multiple copies of a document under construction. Instead, users can email a link to the most recent document in a SharePoint site.

Beyond SharePoint Foundation, SharePoint Server 2010 offers many more features in the document management suite. The best way to get started exploring these features is to create a new site collection with the Document Center features installed, as in the following steps:

1. Open Central Admin.

2. If you need to create a new IIS web application, see Chapter 2 for instructions.

3. Click the Application Management heading on the Central Admin home page.

4. Under Site Collections, click the Create Site Collections link.

5. SharePoint displays the Create Site Collection page. Change the web application to the application you want to host the new site DMS site collection.

6. Give the site a name and a URL suffix if it is not a root site collection.

7. In the Site Templates section, click the Enterprise tab and then select Document Center as the template type.

8. Provide the primary and secondary (optional) site administrators.

9. Click the OK button and wait for SharePoint 2010 to finish creating the Document Center, which is our DMS.

■ **Note** You may install/activate all the features, available in the Document Center, in other site templates, but for the purpose of this chapter, it is easier to create a Document Center site collection. The Document Center site template is an easy way to create a new site collection with all the document management features included, but you may activate these features in any other existing site collection. Some document management features default to document libraries, so users may make use of these features in any site that uses document libraries.

---

10. Navigate to the new Document Center site, and you should see a page like Figure 7-1.

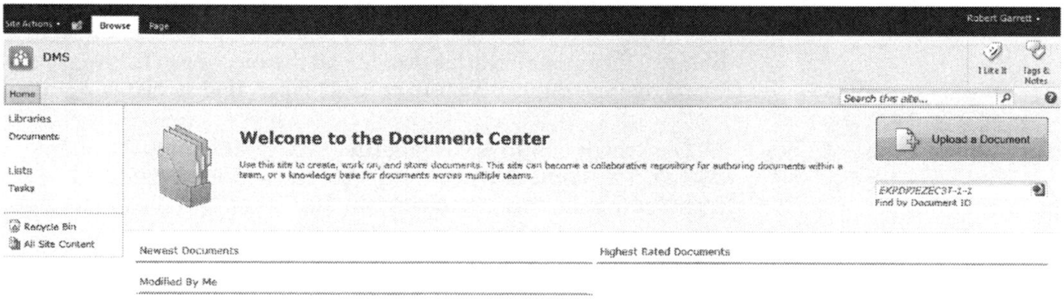

Figure 7-1. Document Center home page

The page consists of various content web parts, some content query web parts, to display recent documents, and the Find Document by ID web part. You may arrange these web parts differently by editing the page, and you may place these web parts on any other page in the site collection that has web part zones.

Overview of SharePoint 2010 DMS Features

With the Document Center created in the previous section, you are now ready to explore the document management features in SharePoint 2010. The first place I would like you to look is in the Site Collection Features page:

1. Click the Site Actions menu.

2. Select Site Settings from the menu.

3. In the Site Collection Administration section, click the Site Collection Features link.

4. Notice the activated Document ID Service and Document Sets features.

Table 7-1 describes the DMS features in SharePoint 2010 at a high level, and I will discuss each feature in greater depth in the following chapter sections. Some of the features listed are not specific to DMS but part of the core functionality and list behavior in SharePoint.

■ **Note** Not all the features listed in Table 7-1 exist as individual SharePoint Features; some combine as part of the core platform, and some are part of specific document center features. The term *feature* as it pertains in the table denotes a piece of functionality, not a SharePoint feature.

Table 7-1. DMS Features in SharePoint 2010

Feature Name	Description
Document Libraries	Available in the core, document libraries derive from a basic list and allow users to upload, edit, and manage documents (files) to a library. Document libraries provide all the niceties of lists—workflow, versioning, custom content types, and so on.
Document Content Types	All Document Libraries contain the Document content type, by default. This content type inherits the Item content type and includes the site column to contain the filename of the document.
Document Sets	New to SharePoint 2010, document sets provide a special content type that allows users to encapsulate multiple document files in a single Document Library item. Document sets apply nicely to those documents that constitute multiple parts, such as proposal documents, where users need to work on the component parts as documents in their own right. Document sets allow users to assign document components their own content type.

Feature Name	Description
Document IDs and Barcodes	The Document ID Service assigns newly uploaded documents a unique ID (included in the document URL on the site). If a document moves location within the site collection then SharePoint keeps track of the location and the Document ID still allows users to access the document. This feature allows users to email links to documents without worrying about the links breaking because another user moved a document or changed the document library structure. This feature gives users of the DMS peace of mind in uniquely identifying a document link. SharePoint 2007 included the barcode feature, which assigns a unique barcode footprint on the document, so when in print form users can track the document.
Workflows	SharePoint 2010 Server includes a number of out-of-the-box workflows, which users may apply to lists, libraries, and sites. Notable is the Approval workflow, which routes tasks to users for document approval, either serially or in parallel. Other workflows, including Collect Signatures, Collect Feedback, and Disposition Approval, execute on documents library items.
Document Versions	Document libraries and lists maintain versions and change (when enabled) so users may roll back to prior versions of a list item in time. SharePoint supports Major Version numbers, in which each major version constitutes publication of the list item for non-approver users, and Major/Minor Versions, in which a minor version denotes draft version, and users need to publish the item as a major version to make the changes available to non-approvers. In addition to versioning, SharePoint lists and libraries also support check in/out, so any one user may ensure another does not change a document while they have it checked out for edit.
Document Workspaces	Document workspaces provide user collaboration for a document. At any time, a user with collaboration rights to a document, and site creation rights, may elect to create a new document workspace site, which contains lists and libraries to collaborate on the document. For example, a proposal document may require a team of people to complete, who meet regularly and keep detailed notes and managed tasks for their work on the document.

Feature Name	Description
Drop-off Libraries	Drop-off document libraries are new to SharePoint 2010. Rather than leaving users the arduous task of deciding or knowing where to upload/save documents to a library in a site collection hierarchy, a drop-off library provides a single upload point for all documents. Based on metadata and document content, administrators of the drop off libraries may then apply rules to uploaded documents to move them to correct locations automatically.
Search within Documents	SharePoint 2010 Standard and Enterprise Search (and FAST) index the content of typical Microsoft Office documents (Word, Excel, PowerPoint, Access, Visio, and so on). SharePoint 2010 can access other non-MS document types as long as an I-Filter exists, such as that for Adobe PDF. When users search for documents by keyword, SharePoint will use the data found in documents, as well as the metadata applied to each document list item, to provide search results.
Document Conversion Service	The Document Conversion Service is a SharePoint 2010 Managed Service Application, which handles the load balancing and conversion of documents; converted from one format to another.

Document Content Types and Document Sets

In Chapter 6, I discussed content types at length. I showed you how to create new custom content types and how to use them in lists and libraries. If you are new to content types, I recommend taking a quick look back at the previous chapter to familiarize yourself with creation of content types.

Document Content Types

Why are content types important in a Document Management System? Any good DMS must allow users to distinguish one document type from another, without expecting users to open documents. Metadata and thus content types provide the baseline functionality to allow content owners to categorize their content with properties—the fields of content types.

The action of creating a content type and applying a content type to a document constitute basic categorization—without even adding fields/properties to the aforementioned content type. For example, in my project management system I may need documents for Project Plans, Statement of Work, Client Presentation, Invoice, and so on. Creating custom content types, which derive from the stock Document content type, and then adding these content types to a document library allows users to upload Office documents of the designated aforementioned type. In this example, a good practice is to remove the stock Document and Item content types from the document library, forcing users to choose a content type that classifies the document.

The following lists some best practices to consider when creating new content types for documents in your DMS:

- **Avoid overarching or high-level content type names** that cause ambiguity. Ironically, "Document" itself is a bad example of a content type name because it is too generic, but it suffices as a base type.

- On the other hand, **try not to create content types too specific to context**—for example, "*Customer Name* Weekly Meeting Notes" restricts the content type to a particular client and meeting context. A better example (in this case) is "Meeting Notes."

- **Create content types at the root site collection**, so that you may repurpose them throughout the DMS site collection.

- **Avoid adding too many properties/fields to any one content type**, which suggests that the content type is too specific to context. Abstracting properties to a base content type is more effective and manageable.

- **Use Choice, Lookup, and Manage Metadata fields when possible** to ease the population of metadata for the end user. If you insist on too many string or text fields, users will likely skip filling them in when uploading or saving a document, thus defeating the point of metadata. Recent best practice with SharePoint 2010 is to use the Managed Metadata fields because the Managed Metadata Service gives the greatest flexibility to manage taxonomy and tagging.

- **Use just the right blend of required and optional fields** in your content types. SharePoint will insist that users provide values for all required fields before allowing them to upload/save a document. If you specify too many required fields, users will become frustrated; no required fields, and some users will not populate any necessary metadata.

- **Limit the choice of content types for your document library to a finite amount** (a good rule of thumb is 10 or fewer). Too many content types, especially when they are similar, will cause your users confusion.

Once a user adds a document to a document library in SharePoint, and then applies metadata via content type, subsequent editing of the document from SharePoint integrates the field/properties in Microsoft Office applications. Office 2007 and 2010 support visibility of document metadata in the application, Office 2010 supports the managed metadata types only, and Office 2003 and prior does not support visibility of metadata in the application.

Let us say I create a content type for a Statement of Work document, including properties for client, contract type, and cost estimate, and then upload an SOW document to a library and then classify the document as an SOW. When I open the same document from SharePoint, I can see and edit the properties directly from the Office application. The following series of steps demonstrates this example:

1. Navigate to the Document Center site we created earlier.

2. Click the Site Actions menu.

3. Click the Site Settings menu item.

4. From the Site Settings page, click the Site Content Types link under Galleries.

5. Click the Create link.

6. Give the new content type the name Statement of Work.

7. Inherit from the parent Document content type in Document Content Types group and click OK.

8. Add a new Choice column to the content type, called Estimate Range. Assign the Choice column the values: Less than $50k, $50k to $100k, Over than $100k.

9. Add a Single Line of Text column, called Client Name.

10. This concludes the creation of our content type.

11. Navigate to the Documents library from the left navigation.

12. Click the Library tab on the Ribbon.

13. Click the Library Settings icon on the Ribbon.

14. Scroll to the Content Types section, notice the presence of the Link to Document and Document Set content types—we will discuss these later.

15. Click the Add from Existing Site Content Types link.

16. Add the Statement of Work content type.

17. Navigate back to the All Documents view of the Documents library.

18. Click the Documents tab on the Ribbon; then click the *lower portion* of the New Document icon; see Figure 7-2.

19. Do not be tempted to click the Add document link, because this assumes the default content type and does not demonstrate our Statement of Work content type.

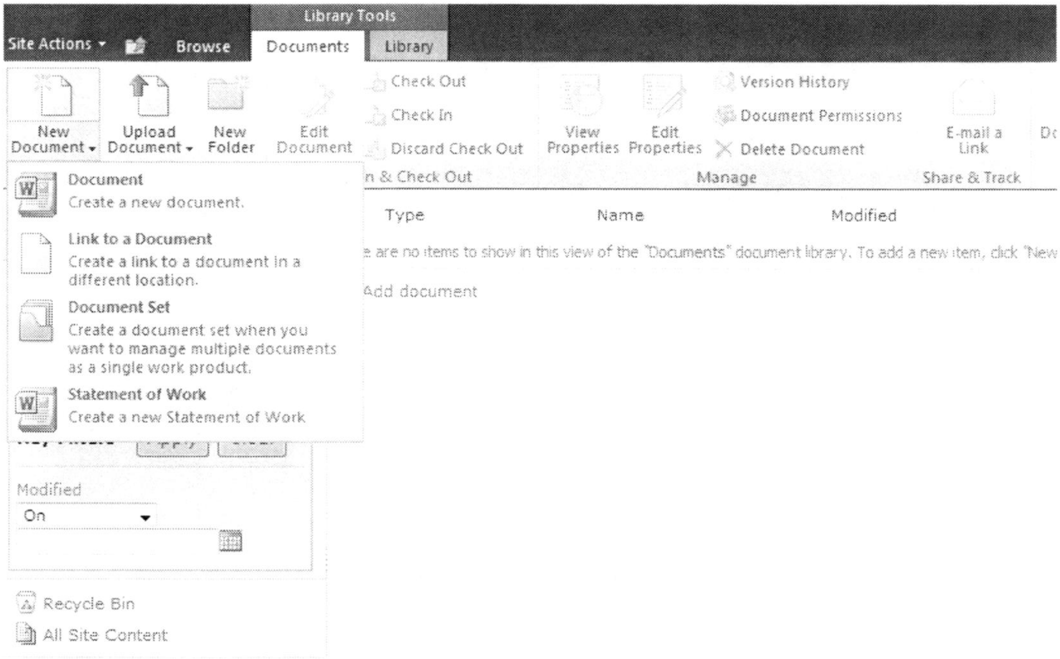

Figure 7-2. New Documents, based on content types

20. Click the Statement of Work menu item.

21. Acknowledge the warning displayed by your browser about the danger of uploading files.

Microsoft Word opens with a new document.

22. Notice the Document Information Panel in Word, as shown Figure 7-3 (Office 2007 and 2010 versions only).

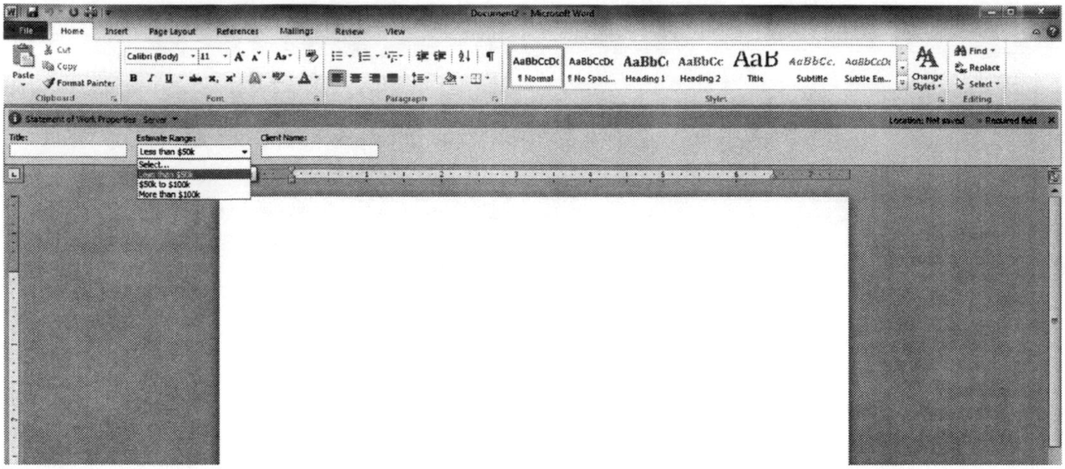

Figure 7-3. *Microsoft Word with Document Information Panel*

How did SharePoint know how to open a Word document? Navigate back to the Statement of Work content type in the Content Types Gallery to see.

23. In the settings page of the content type, click the Advanced Settings link

SharePoint displays a page like Figure 7-4. The Document Template section governs the document template to use when creating a new list item of this content type. Figure 7-4 shows the template as blank; thus SharePoint defaults to Microsoft Word.

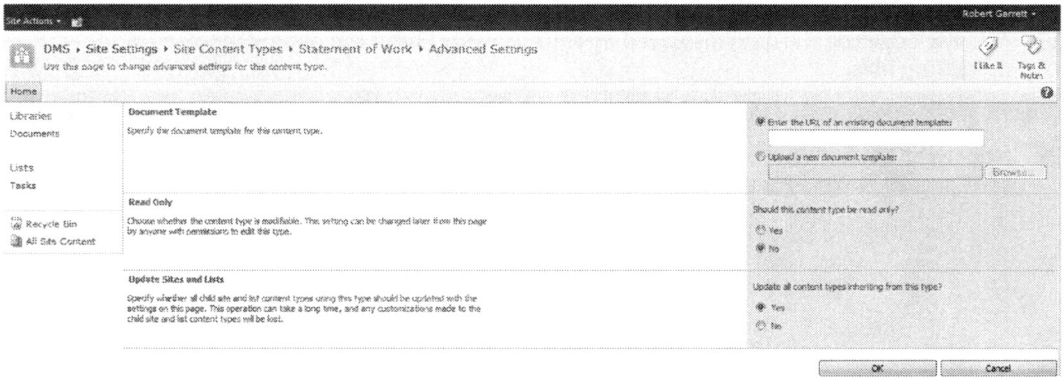

Figure 7-4. *Advanced Settings page for our custom content type*

24. Compare this setting with that of other stock content types to see how this setting influences the default document.

25. Before leaving the content type Settings page, click the Document Information Panel settings link.

26. In this settings page, SharePoint allows you to specify the XSN of a custom InfoPath form, or the URL location of a custom page to render from the Office Application.

▓ **Note** Document Information Panel requires at least Office 2007, and ideally Office 2010.

Uploading a Document

Perhaps you have a document on disk and want to upload it to a SharePoint document library. How does SharePoint know which content type to assign? It asks you...

1. Navigate back to the All Documents view of the document library.

2. Click the Documents tab on the Ribbon.

3. Click the Upload Document icon (if your browser supports it and your SharePoint site in the Intranet or Trusted Sites zone, you can upload multiple documents).

4. Navigate to a document on disk, and click OK.

After a brief moment during the document upload, SharePoint displays a dialog like that of Figure 7-5.

5. Change the drop-down to the desired content type and fill in the fields.

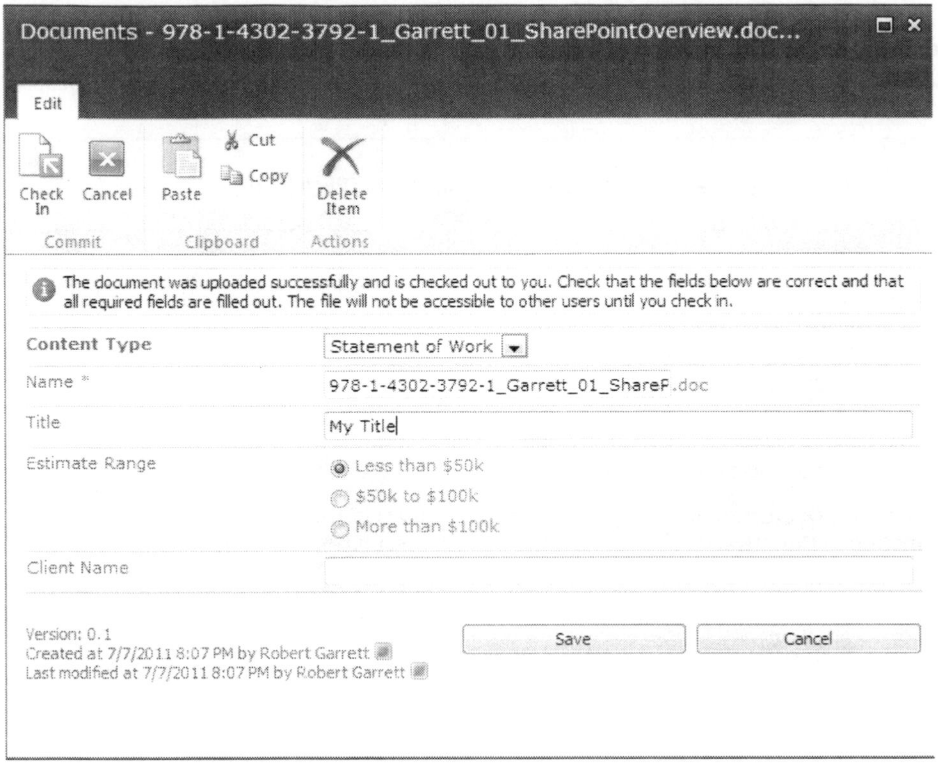

Figure 7-5. Select document content type after upload

6. Using the Save-As feature in an Office application and then specifying the location as a SharePoint document library renders a similar dialog to choose the content type (Figure 7-6).

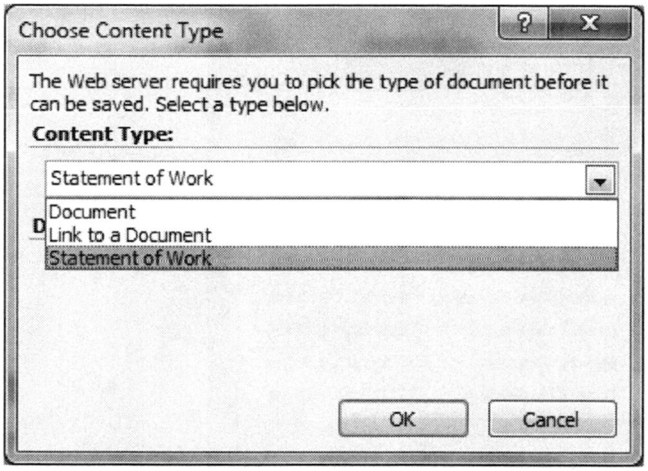

Figure 7-6. *Choose Content Type from Microsoft Word*

Saving a Document to SharePoint from Office

Office 2007 and 2010 applications allow you to save directly to a SharePoint location from within the application. The following steps demonstrate how to save an open Word 2010 document to an existing document library in SharePoint 2010:

1. From inside Microsoft Word 2010, click the File tab in the top left corner of the application.

2. Click the Save As tab from the left navigation.

3. In the Save-As dialog provide the URL of the document library in the location field, and click Enter.

■ **Note** The easiest way to get the URL of a document library is to navigate to the library page in your browser and then strip off the `/Forms/AllItems.aspx` part from the URL. For example: `http://server/site/DocumentLibName/`.

Word will think for a few seconds as it tries to access the document library in SharePoint 2010. The dialog should show the document library (see Figure 7-7).

4. Provide the filename in the appropriate text box.

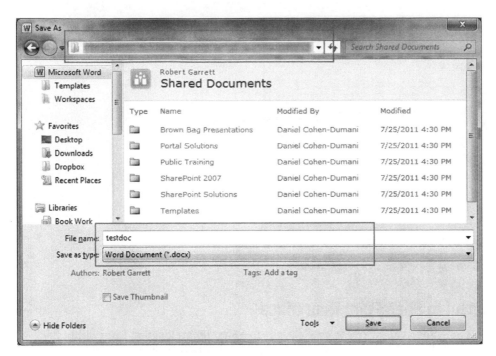

Figure 7-7. *Save As dialog in Microsoft Word 2010*

5. Click the Save button.

6. Word displays a dialog to choose the destination content type, like Figure 7-6.

7. Click OK to complete the save operation to SharePoint.

Linking to Other Documents

SharePoint 2010 allows users to add links in a document library to another document in a different document library. SharePoint achieves this with a simple content type that contains a URL field and an ASPX page that allows a user to enter the name and URL of the linked document.

1. Navigate back to the All Documents view of the document library.

2. Click the Documents tab on the Ribbon.

3. Click the lower portion of the New Document icon.

4. Choose the Link to a Document menu item.

SharePoint pops up a dialog, asking for the name and URL of the remote document.

5. Looking at the template for the Link to Document content type (advanced settings), the URL is /_layouts/NewLink.aspx, which renders the dialog.

Document Sets

You can think of a *document set* as a mini-document library or folder that lives in the context of a list item of a parent document library—a library within a library. Document sets consist of collections of documents, which when combined represent a finalized full document.

A good example of the use of document sets is a proposal document. Typically, in business, a proposal is a large document and requires effort from many authors to complete. One way to accomplish the creation of the proposal is to have authors write independent documents for the various sections and then combine these documents into a finished proposal document at the end. I have seen this approach in action on SharePoint 2007, and the authors maintained the document pieces in a folder of a larger project document library. Document sets now allow users to continue to work on document pieces but manage them together in a document set of a document library. Since a document set is a special content type, each document set has its own metadata, in addition to the metadata specified by the content types of the documents contained inside the document set.

Using our Document Center and default Documents document library, the following steps demonstrate how document sets operate:

1. Navigate back to the All Documents view of the document library.

2. Click the Documents tab on the Ribbon.

3. Click the *lower* portion of the New Document icon.

4. Choose the Document Set menu item.

■ **Note** If you do not see the Document Set menu item, follow the steps at the bottom of this section, for adding document sets to existing document libraries.

---

5. SharePoint displays a dialog and asks for the name and description for the document set, give the document set the name Proposal and click OK.

6. SharePoint displays a document set page, like that in Figure 7-8.

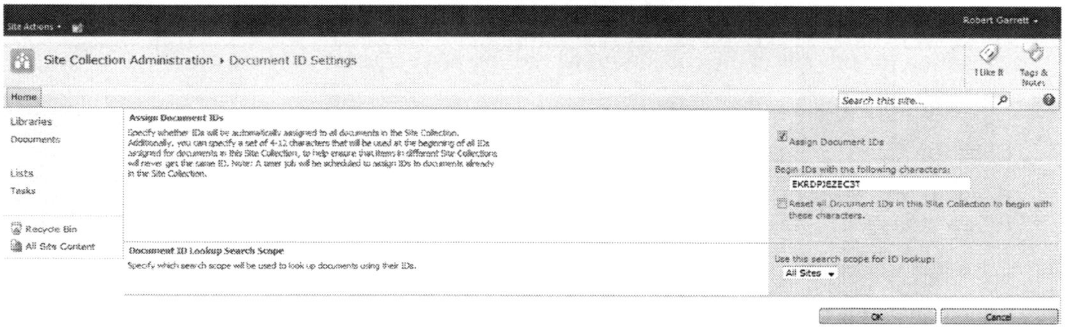

Figure 7-8. Document Set Page

7. The Document Set page provides a similar interface to that of a regular document library. On the Ribbon you should see the familiar Documents and Library tabs.

8. Clicking the Library tab and then the Library Settings icon displays a setting page for the main document library.

9. Click the Manage tab in the Ribbon (Document Set).

The Ribbon shows various options for the document set, such as:

- **Properties**—Populate the fields, defined in the Document Set content type.

- **Permissions**—Permissions for the document set.

- **Delete**—Delete the document set.

- **E-mail a Link**—Send a link of this document set to a colleague.

- **Version History**—See the history of changes.

- **Capture Version**—Create a version label of documents in the set.

- **Workflows**—Apply workflow to the document set.

Adding Document Sets to an Existing Document Library

You are not required to use the Document Center site template to use document sets. Document sets exist as a feature at the site collection level, and as a content type, which you must add to your document library as follows:

1. Open a site that is *not* a Document Center.

2. Click the Site Actions menu and select Site Settings.

3. Click the Site Collection Features link, under the Site Collection Administration heading.

4. Activate the Document Sets feature.

5. Navigate to the default page view of your document library in the site collection (or sub-site of the collection) where you just activated the feature.

6. Click the Library tab in the Ribbon.

7. Click the Library Settings icon in the Ribbon.

8. If you do not see the Content Types section on the Library settings page, then follow steps 9–11; otherwise, skip to step 12.

9. Click the Advanced settings link.

10. Toggle the Allow Management of Content Types setting to Yes.

11. Scroll to the bottom of the page and click OK.

12. Click the Add from Existing Site Content Types link.

13. On the next page, add the Document Set content type, and then click OK.

14. Navigate back to the default view of the document library, and you can now add document sets, per the information above this sub section.

Document Workflows

Like many of the topics in SharePoint 2010, *workflow* is the subject of whole books. A workflow is a process, either automated by computer or manual with human intervention. Workflow may consist of both human and automated elements, but the premise is the same—a workflow management system keeps track of the steps in a process (the *activities*) and alerts different actors in the process of tasks to complete an activity/step in the process chain. Microsoft workflows come in two flavors: sequential, meaning that each step succeeds the next; and state machine, in which the workflow system tracks overall state at any time and transition from state via activities.

SharePoint uses the Microsoft Workflow Foundation (WF) to provide business process on documents, web pages, forms, and list items. SharePoint allows attachment of workflow to lists, libraries, and content types.

Since workflow in SharePoint 2010 uses WF, developers may create custom workflows to automate the process of documents and list items. SharePoint Designer allows developers to create sequential workflows, with drag-and-drop ease, and Visual Studio 2010 provides for creating more elaborate coded workflow. Even though SharePoint 2010 allows for the adoption of custom workflow, the platform provides out-of-the-box workflow for use of document approval, signature collection, disposition approval, and so on. Table 7-2 describes the out-of-the-box workflow.

Table 7-2. SharePoint 2010 workflow

Workflow Name	Description	Available in SP2010 Foundation
Collect Feedback	Sends a document for review	No
Approval	Sends a document for approval, typically before publishing	No
Disposition	Handles document expiration and disposition	No
Collect Signatures	Routes a document for signatures	No
Translation Management	Handles the translation of a document into other languages	No
Three-State	Track the business state of a document through three different phases	Yes

In the days of SharePoint 2007, users could only apply workflow activation to lists[1], which limited reusability. SharePoint 2010 allows application of workflows to sites and content types. Since content types provide portability of metadata in a site collection, applying workflow now means that users can provide business process with the portability. If a content type exists for a proposal document in an organization site collection, the organization can attach the workflow process whenever someone creates a new proposal document—anywhere in the site collection, not just a particular list instance.

Adding a Workflow to a Library or List

Take the following steps to add a workflow to a library or list:

1. Browse to the list or library.

2. Click the List or Library tab on the Ribbon.

3. Click the Workflow Settings icon in the Ribbon.

4. On the Workflow settings page, click the Add a Workflow link.

5. Select the workflow, set the tasks and history lists, and apply the appropriate options.

Adding a Workflow to a Library or List Content Type

Take the following steps to add a workflow to a library or list content type:

1. Browse to the list or library.

2. Click the List or Library tab on the Ribbon.

3. Click the List Settings or Library Settings icon.

4. Scroll to the Content Types section (if it is missing, enable Content Types under Advanced Settings).

5. Click the name of the content type to associate with the workflow.

6. Click the Workflow Settings link.

7. On the Workflow settings page, click the Add a Workflow link.

8. Select the workflow, set the tasks and history lists, and apply the appropriate options.

Adding a Workflow to a Site Content Type

Take the following steps to add a workflow to a site content type:

---

[1] Developers could attach workflow to content types in SharePoint 2007, but they had to develop workflow in Visual Studio.

1. Click the Site Actions menu.

2. Choose the Site Settings menu item.

3. Click the Site Content Types link under Galleries.

4. Click the name of the content type to associate the workflow.

5. Click the Workflow Settings link.

6. On the Workflow Settings page, click the Add a Workflow link.

7. Select the workflow, set the tasks and history lists, and apply the appropriate options.

Editing and Developing Custom Workflow

With a whole workflow platform and plenty of ideas to automate business process, it is natural that users will want to create their own custom workflows. Creation of custom workflow falls under development and is therefore out of the scope of this administration book. However, I do wish to mention some of the new enhancements that SharePoint brings to workflow in the platform.

- SharePoint Designer 2010 allows editing of out of the box workflow.

- SharePoint Designer 2010 deploys custom workflow as WSP (SharePoint Package) files, which developers may then open and edit in Visual Studio 2010.

- SharePoint 2010 brings many more SharePoint-based activities, for inclusion as workflow steps.

- SharePoint 2010 provides more events to subscribe workflow.

Document Tracking

Any good Document Management System allows users to reference documents from the system, without concern about other users changing the location of such documents in the DMS. The blog sphere addressed this very topic with permalinks—links that do not directly link to blog articles, but provide virtual links, which the blog engine translates into the physical link. SharePoint 2007 pretty much ignored the issue of document link tracking, but fortunately, SharePoint 2010 now provides this functionality.

The Document ID Service

SharePoint 2010 incorporates a Document ID Service feature for keeping track of the location of documents and providing users with virtual URLs for documents with unique ID. By default, the platform does not enable the Document ID Service feature, although the Document Center template does enable it. To confirm the existence of Document ID tracking, follow the steps below:

1. From the root of the site collection, click the Site Actions menu.

2. Click the Site Settings menu item.

3. Click the Site Collection Features link in the Site Collection Administration section.

4. Scroll down the list and see if the Document ID Service feature activated.

5. Navigate back to the Site Settings page for the site collection.

6. Click the Document ID Settings link in the Site Collection Administration section.

SharePoint displays a page like that in Figure 7-9.

Type	Name	Modified	Modified By	Rating (0-5)	Barcode	Barcode Value
▣	SharePtServUpgrade ⑨NEW	7/7/2011 10:59 PM	Robert Garrett			1395531176

1395531176

◆ Add document

Figure 7-9. Document ID Settings page

7. Ensure that the box for Assign Document IDs is checked.

8. You may optionally change the prefix for all document IDs and change the scope for lookup search.

9. Upload a new document to one of the Document Libraries in the site.

10. From the All Documents view, hover over the name of the document you just uploaded.

11. Click the drop-down arrow and select View Properties from the Edit-Control-Block (ECB) that appears.

12. In the dialog that appears, look for the Document ID field and assigned Document ID.

13. Hover over the Document ID and get the properties of the hyperlink from your browser, it should look something like this:
    `http://server/sites/dms/_layouts/DocIdRedir.aspx?ID=EKRDPJEZEC3T-3-7`

Notice that this link does not reference any particular document library, just a common redirection page and the document ID.

14. Move the document to another document library and repeat the steps to get the Document ID—notice that the link remains the same. Users may email this link around the organization without fear of the link breaking because the document has moved.

15. Try deleting the document and then accessing the Document ID link from the earlier step. Notice that the user receives a nice message about no document, not a 404 or convoluted error message.

Barcodes

SharePoint 2007 introduced the feature for adding unique barcodes to documents, so users may track documents when printed or part of a manual processing workflow. As you would expect, SharePoint 2010 also includes this feature. The following steps detail how to enable barcodes at the site collection level and then for a particular document library. You may also apply information policy at just the list/library level.

1. From the root of the site collection, click the Site Actions menu.

2. Choose the Site Settings menu item.

3. Click the Site Collection Policies link under Site Collection Administration.

4. Click the Create link to create a new policy.

5. Give the policy a name and policy statement.

6. Check the option to Enable Barcodes and click OK.

7. Navigate to the list to apply the new policy.

8. Click the Library tab on the Ribbon.

9. Click the Library Settings icon on the Ribbon.

10. Click the content type to apply the policy (ensure that content types are applied to the library under Advanced Settings).

11. Click the Information Management Policy Settings link.

12. Change the radio button option to Use a Site Collection Policy, and select the new policy you created and click OK.

13. From the desired view for the document library, add the Barcode and Barcode Value columns (Modify this View from the Breadcrumb).

14. Upload a document and select the correct content type, and see that SharePoint assigns barcodes. Figure 7-10 shows an example.

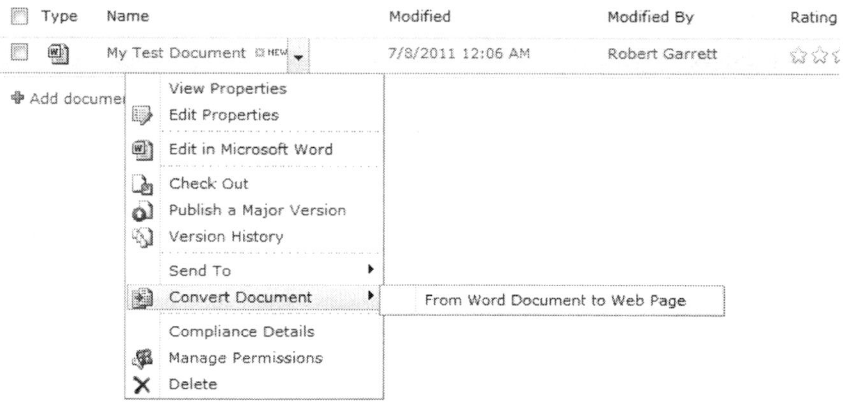

Figure 7-10. Barcodes added to document library

Document Conversion

SharePoint 2010 includes a Document Conversion Service for converting documents of one type to another, such as Word Document to PDF. Document conversion is important in any DMS because it allows user to upload documents of a type and allow other users to read and edit these documents in another type, typically a common type that most users can access. The new version of Office 2010 uses a new XML format for document data, and the Document Conversion Service converts documents of these types to viewable web pages for those users who do not have Microsoft Office 2010 installed on their desktop.

The Document Conversion Service consists of two parts: a Load Balancer Service and a Launcher Service. SharePoint requires both services configured and running to enable the Documents Conversion Service. The following steps detail how to configure Document Conversion in your SharePoint 2010 farm.

■ **Note** You must start the Load Balancer Service before the Launcher Service for Document Conversion to work. The Launcher Service stops if the Load Balancer Service not started or stopped.

---

1. Open Central Administration.

2. Click the Manage Services on Server link, under System Settings.

3. Click the Start link for the Document Conversions Load Balancer Service.

4. Click the Start link for the Document Conversions Launcher Service.

5. Select the server for the launcher, load balance server and port number and click OK.

6. You may change the settings of either service by clicking the name of the service; options include choosing the server on which the service is running, and port numbers.

The next set of steps demonstrates how to enable document conversion in a web application.

7. Open Central Administration.

8. Click the General Application Settings section title.

9. Click the Configure Document Conversions link under External Service Connections.

10. Select the web application.

11. Flip the setting to Enable document conversion.

12. Specify the load balancer server.

13. Configure schedule for blocks of conversion.

14. SharePoint lists the current installed converters at the bottom of the page as a series of links, click the link to configure the converter.

15. Click the OK button when done configuring.

From the document library, you should see a Convert Document option in the ECB, as in Figure 7-11.

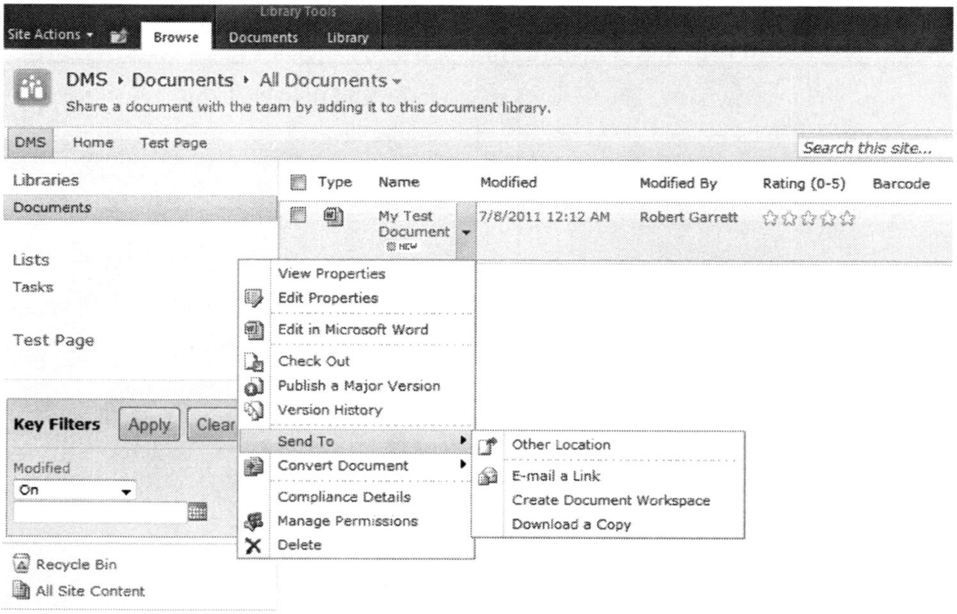

Figure 7-11. *The Convert Document option added*

If you are not seeing the menu option to convert a document, ensure that the following conditions are met:

- The document is in an Office 2007 DOCX format.

- The Document Conversions Load Balancer Service is started.

- The Document Conversions Launcher Service is started (after the load balancer).

- The web application has document conversion enabled.

- The site content type (as opposed to the list content type) allows document conversion.

- Publishing features are enabled at site collection and site level.

Document Workspaces

SharePoint has always been great at providing space for users to collaborate. At the core of the platform—Foundation offers basic and team sites, which include task lists, calendars, document libraries, and so on for users of the space to share and collaborate on a topic of interest.

A *document workspace* is a specific site template, geared for users to collaborate on the construction of a document. Large documents, such as proposals often require much work by several team individuals. The users in the team may need to meet weekly to discuss progress, planning, set agendas, require a place to store notes and so on. This is the purpose of the document workspace.

Starting from our Document Center and draft document in the main Documents library, the following steps detail how to create a Document Workspace:

1. From a view of the document library, such as the All Documents view, hover the mouse over the document title until the drop-down arrow appears.

2. Click the drop-down arrow, select the Send To menu item, and then click the Create Document Workspace link (see Figure 7-12).

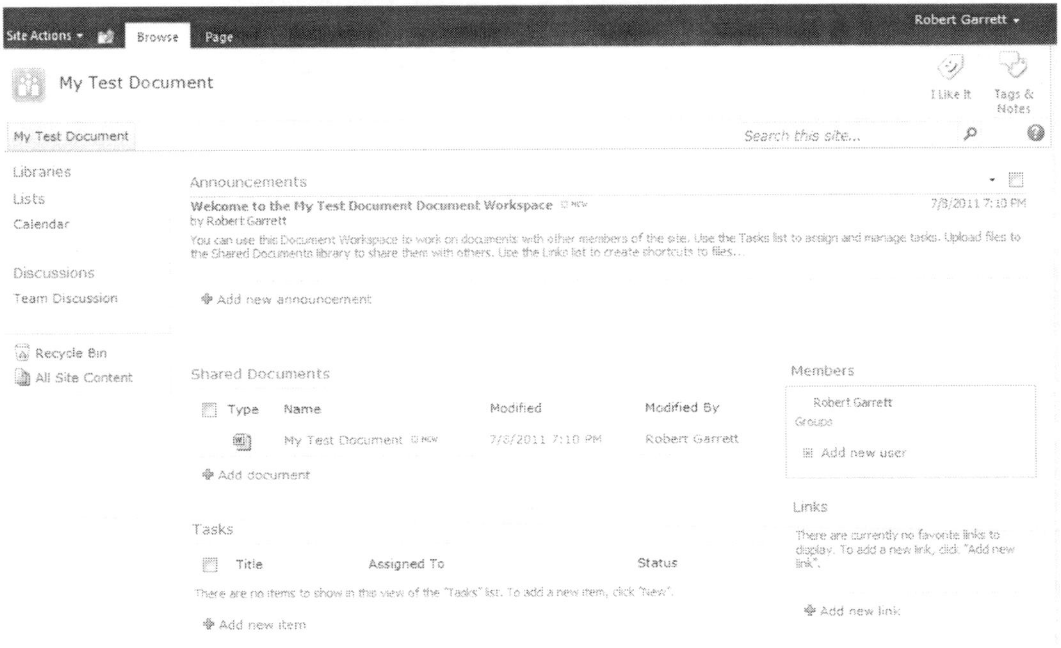

Figure 7-12. Create Document Workspace link

3. SharePoint will display a page asking you to confirm the creation of the Document Workspace. Click the OK button.

4. Once the new Document Workspace is created, SharePoint shows you its landing page. (Figure 7-13). Notice that SharePoint copied over the document itself to the Shared Documents library so members of the team can begin collaborating.

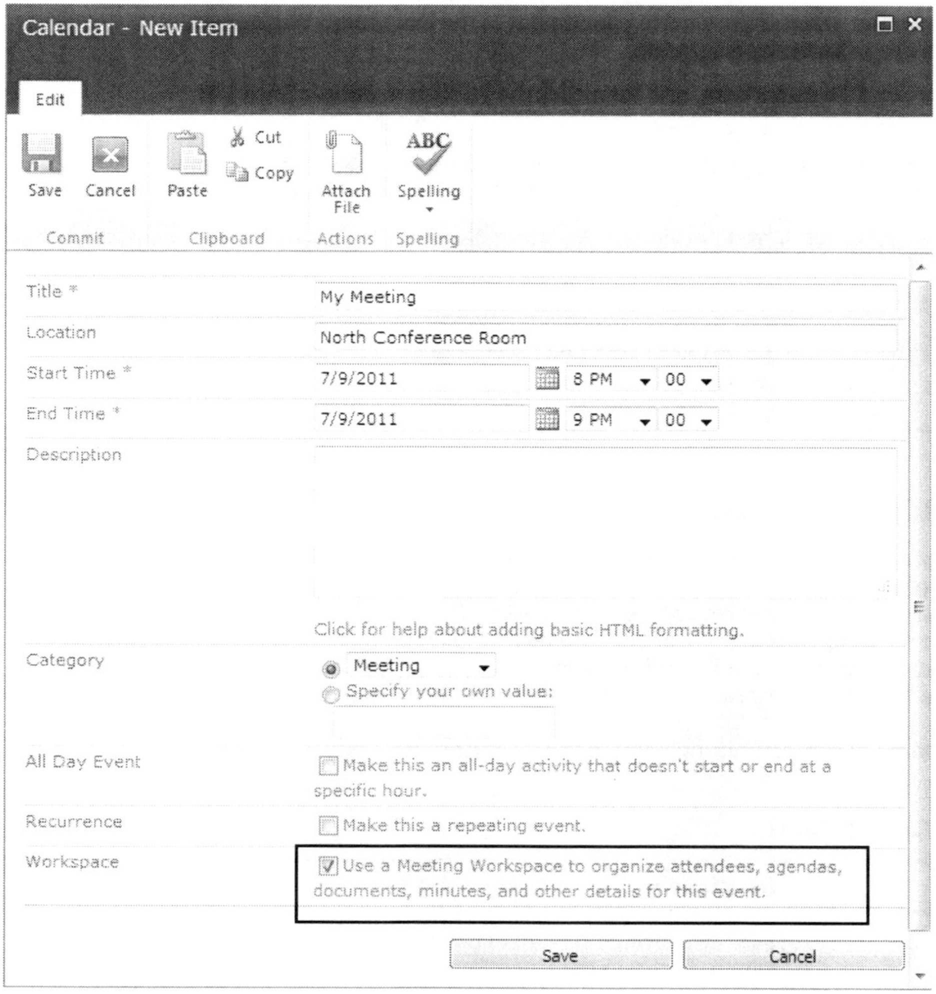

Calendar - New Item ▢ ✕

Edit

Save	Cancel	Paste	✂ Cut / 🗐 Copy	Attach File	ABC Spelling
Commit		Clipboard		Actions	Spelling

Title *	My Meeting
Location	North Conference Room
Start Time *	7/9/2011 ▦ 8 PM ▾ 00 ▾
End Time *	7/9/2011 ▦ 9 PM ▾ 00 ▾
Description	

Click for help about adding basic HTML formatting.

Category	◉ Meeting ▾ ◯ Specify your own value:
All Day Event	☐ Make this an all-day activity that doesn't start or end at a specific hour.
Recurrence	☐ Make this a repeating event.
Workspace	☑ Use a Meeting Workspace to organize attendees, agendas, documents, minutes, and other details for this event.

[Save]   [Cancel]

Figure 7-13. Document Workspace

5. On the right, in the Members box, click the Add New User link.

6. Search for users from your team in the Select Users section, and grant them the appropriate permissions in your new document workspace.

7. Click the Lists heading in the left navigation. SharePoint shows you a page of all the lists in the Document Workspace: Announcements, Calendar, Links, and Tasks.

With your team added to the workspace, and the list containers present, your team may now collaborate on the document. Once the team completes the document, what happens next?

8. Hover over the name of the working document in the Document Workspace, until the drop-down arrow appears.

9. Click the Send To menu item, and then click the Publish to Source Location link.

10. SharePoint displays a page with a quick warning about overwriting the original source document (from which you created the document workspace).

11. Click the OK button (if you are sure).

■ **Note** At this stage, SharePoint may give you an error that the original file is not set as checked out, in which case head over to the source location and check out the document.

Records Management in SharePoint 2010

Records management is about the policy for processing content and routing of documents and data in SharePoint. SharePoint 2007 introduced the Records Center, which was a site collection for centralized collection of documents and content routed based on policy. One of the many jobs of the Records Center is to manage the long-term archive of documents that become records in the Records Center.

SharePoint 2010 also includes the Records Center, with enhancements, but in addition, SharePoint now brings in-place records management. Owners of regular document libraries can now apply policy to their documents.

Table 7-3 lists some of the features included in the Records Center, which we discuss in this section of the chapter.

Table 7-3. Records Center Features

Feature	Description
Document ID	See the previous section of this chapter about document management, which discusses the Document ID feature.
Content Organizer	Routes documents and records in the Records Center based on defined policy.
Drop-off Libraries	Let the user drop documents in the drop-off library and have the Content Organizer route dropped documents, based on policy.
Records Retention	Determines when documents and records expire and how SharePoint handles deposition.
Hold and e-Discovery	Provides auditing and tracking of external actions that might interrupt normal document lifecycle (for example, because of litigation).

Before discussing records management further, I should mention that, like many of the areas in SharePoint 2010, records management and information policy are a huge topic, and so what you read here is simply an overview for administrative purposes. Without further delay, let us create a new Records Center site collection by following the steps below:

1. Open Central Admin.

2. Click the Create Site Collections link (under Application Management). If you need to create a new IIS web application, see Chapter 2 for details on performing this task.

3. Select the web application to create the new site collection.

4. Give the site collection a name (such as Records Center).

5. Populate the URL suffix, if not a root site collection.

6. In the Template Selection, click the Enterprise tab, and then select Records Center.

7. Provide user names for the administrators; then click OK.

8. Once it is complete, navigate to the new Records Center site collection (see Figure 7-14).

Figure 7-14. Records Center in SharePoint 2010

Setting Up the Content Organizer

The Content Organizer feature is responsible for routing documents, found in drop off libraries, to other areas in SharePoint. In the next section, we will configure the Records Center, which you created in the previous section. Before doing so, we need to configure the Content Organizer and send-to locations for document routing.

1. In the Records Center site collection, click the Site Actions menu.

2. Click the Site Settings menu item.

3. Click the Content Organizer Settings link, under the Site Administration heading. SharePoint shows a page like that in Figure 7-15.

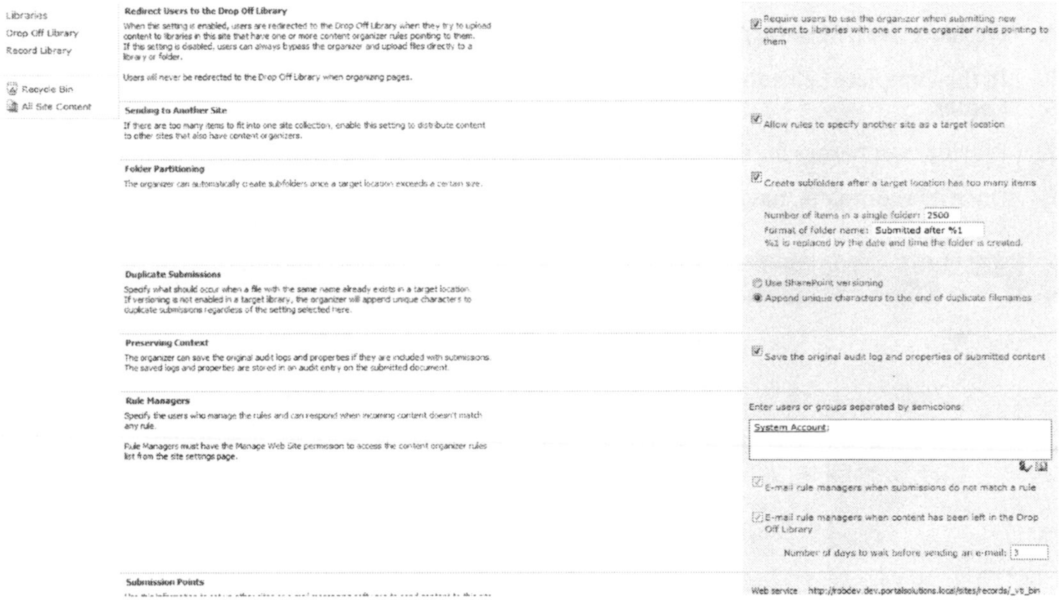

Figure 7-15. The Settings page for the Content Organizer

The Content Organizer Settings page provides the following settings:

- **Redirect users to the Drop-off Library**—Ensures that users cannot upload documents to document libraries that have content organizer rules. This forces the user to comply with using the drop-off library to route content, rather than decide manually.

- **Sending to Another Site**—Check this option if you would like to submit documents to another location. Check it for this exercise so you can try this capability later.

- **Folder Partitioning**—Ensures that target document libraries do not become too large.

- **Duplicate Submissions**—Tells the Content Organizer how to handle repeat submissions of the same document.

- **Rule Managers**—Specifies the users who can execute rules for incoming content.

- **Submission Points**—Provide points so that other sites can submit documents to this site collection.

Ordinarily, when configuring Content Organizer rules in a Records Center, you would likely want documents routed to a document or record library. For the purpose of demonstration, I am going to show you how to specify our Documents Center site collection as a destination location. Once it is configured, users can submit a record (document) and have the document routed to the Document Center.

4. Open Central Administration.

5. Click the General Application Settings link from the left navigation.

6. Click the Configure Send To Connections link, under External Service Connections.

7. Add a new connection to a documents library in the Document Center, such as `http://server/sites/dms/_vti_bin/officialfile.asmx`

▪ **Note** the URL `http://server/sites/dms/_vti_bin/officialfile.asmx` is specific to the structure of the target site.

---

8. Navigate to the Document Center site collection.

9. Navigate to the site that has the target location to route documents, in my case the root of the site collection.

10. Click the Site Actions menu, and then click the Site Settings menu item.

11. Under Site Actions, click the Manage Site Features link.

12. Activate the Content Organizer feature (if not already activated).

Setting up the Records Center

Assuming you followed the steps in the earlier section, you now have a new Records Center site collection. The following steps detail setting up the records center to accept documents as records.

1. Click the Site Actions menu.

2. Notice the new menu item Manage Records Center; click it.

The Manage Records Center page provides high-level steps for establishing tasks and file plans so the new Records Center may accept documents as records.

3. Click the Step1: Create Content Types link, and SharePoint navigates you to the site collection Content Type Gallery. Create content types for all documents you wish to store as records in the Records Center. Please review Chapter 6, on metadata, for steps to creating content types.

4. Navigate back to the management page from the Site Actions menu.

5. Click the Step2: Create Records Libraries link. SharePoint navigates you to a page to create new libraries.

6. Under Libraries, click Record Library. In the resulting page, give the new library a name and click the Create button.

■ **Note** The Records Center has a default Record Library and Drop-Off library.

---

7. Navigate back to the management page from the Site Actions menu.

8. Click the Step3: Create Content Organizer Rules link.

SharePoint navigates you to a list of rules. Each contains a list item based on the Rule content type. Let us take this opportunity to create a new rule.

9. Click the Add New Item link.

10. Give the rule a name, and make sure the rule is active.

11. Choose the content type; rules apply to documents added to the records list with designated content type. In this case, choose the default Document content type.

12. Add any conditions, based on the properties of the content type, name, or title.

13. Specify the target location for the document. I chose the Documents library in my Document Center site—shown in the drop-down, if you completed the steps in the previous section.

14. Click OK.

15. At this stage, we have a Content Organizer rule to route all documents submitted to the Drop-off library to the Document Center Drop-off library. We now need a similar Content Organizer rule to route documents in the Document Center.

16. Head over to the Document Center.

17. Click the Site Actions menu and click the Site Settings menu item.

18. Click the Content Organizer Rules link, under Site Administration.

19. Repeat the earlier steps to create a new rule to route documents from the Document Center Drop-off library to the Documents library.

This procedure is a lot to digest, so allow me to recap. We provisioned a new Records Center site collection, set up the Content Organizer to allow routing of documents to our Document Center site collection, and created a rule to route documents with content type Document in both the Records Center and the Document Center.

Assuming all is well, we can now click the Submit a Record button, on the home page of the Records Center, specify a document, and see the document route to the Document Center.

20. Click the Submit a Record button on the home page of the Records Center. This effectively is the same process as dropping a document in the Drop-off library in the Records Center.

21. Choose a document from your computer.

22. Click OK.

23. SharePoint shows a dialog to provide a title and confirm the file name.

24. Click the Submit button.

25. SharePoint pauses to think and then shows a dialog with status. If all worked, then the status indicates that the Content Organizer routed your document to the Drop-off library in the Document Center.

26. Head over to the Document Center Drop-off library, and notice that it is empty; this is because the Content Organizer rule in the Document Center routed the document to the Documents Library. The net effect here is that the document passed from Record Center Drop-Off Library, to Document Center Drop-Off Library, and then to a final document library in the Document Center.

Hold and e-Discovery

Any organization that maintains a large enough collection of documents, and defines policy that warrants the use of Records Management, may need to locate documents and put policy on hold. One common example in US business is that of litigation—when a court wants to review an organization's documents, the organization may want to isolate documents from typical routing, and retention polices—this is where the Hold and e-Discovery feature of SharePoint 2010 comes in handy.

The Hold and e-Discovery feature activates for each site in a site collection and is enabled by default in Records Center site. To verify that you have this feature enabled, follow the steps below:

1. Click the Site Actions menu for the site.

2. Select the Site Settings menu item.

3. Under the Site Actions heading, click the Manage Site Features link.

4. Scroll down the features and see if the Hold and e-Discovery feature activated.

5. Head back to the Site Settings page, and look for the Hold and e-Discovery heading.

At this stage, we have enabled the Hold and e-Discovery feature for the current site; the following steps detail how to make use of this feature to hold documents in the site. Before proceeding with the steps, upload a number of documents to the Records Library in the Records Center (which we are using for this demonstration).

259

6. From the Site Settings page, under Hold and e-Discovery click the Discover and Hold Content link.

7. Select the site to search for documents to hold.

8. Provide search terms to search for documents to hold, click the Preview Results button.

9. Choose to hold locally or export and then hold. Local hold consists of locking the record in the current place, whereas export and hold involves copying the content to another location (such as a records repository) and then holding.

10. Select or create a hold for all the documents in the result set.

11. Click the Add Results to Hold button to hold documents in the result set.

You may also hold documents directly from the Record/Document library, as follows:

1. Navigate to the Records library in the Records Center.

2. Upload a document.

3. Hover over the name of the document, and click on the drop-down arrow.

4. Click the Compliance Details link from the ECB.

5. Click the Add/Remove from Hold link.

6. You may add or remove the document from hold, using the resulting screen.

The following steps demonstrate how to create a hold, which you may then apply to a document in the preceding steps:

1. Navigate to the Site Settings for the Records Center.

2. Click the Holds link under the Holds and e-Discovery header.

3. Click the Add New Item link to add a new hold.

4. A hold consists of a Title, Description, and Manager of the hold; define these in the dialog that appears.

Records Retention

Records Retention and Deposition is the process of managing the lifecycle of a document, from inception to deprecation. SharePoint 2010 handles document retention by default at the content type level, but it also permits retention schedules at the library and folder level. The following steps detail how to set up Records Retention on a document library in the Records Center.

1. From the root of the Records Center site collection, click the Site Actions menu.

2. Select the Site Settings menu item.

3. From the Site Settings page, click the Site Content Types link under Galleries.

4. Click the content type name to add a retention schedule; I chose the Document content type.

5. Click the Information Management Policy Settings link.

6. Check the Enable Retention checkbox (wait for the page to post back).

7. You may establish retention policy on documents as records, and non-records.

8. Leave the default for non-records as not to expire (this exercise demonstrates retention stages in records).

9. Change the setting for Records to Define Different Retention Stages for Records.

10. Click the Add a Retention Stage for Records link; see Figure 7-16 for the resulting dialog.

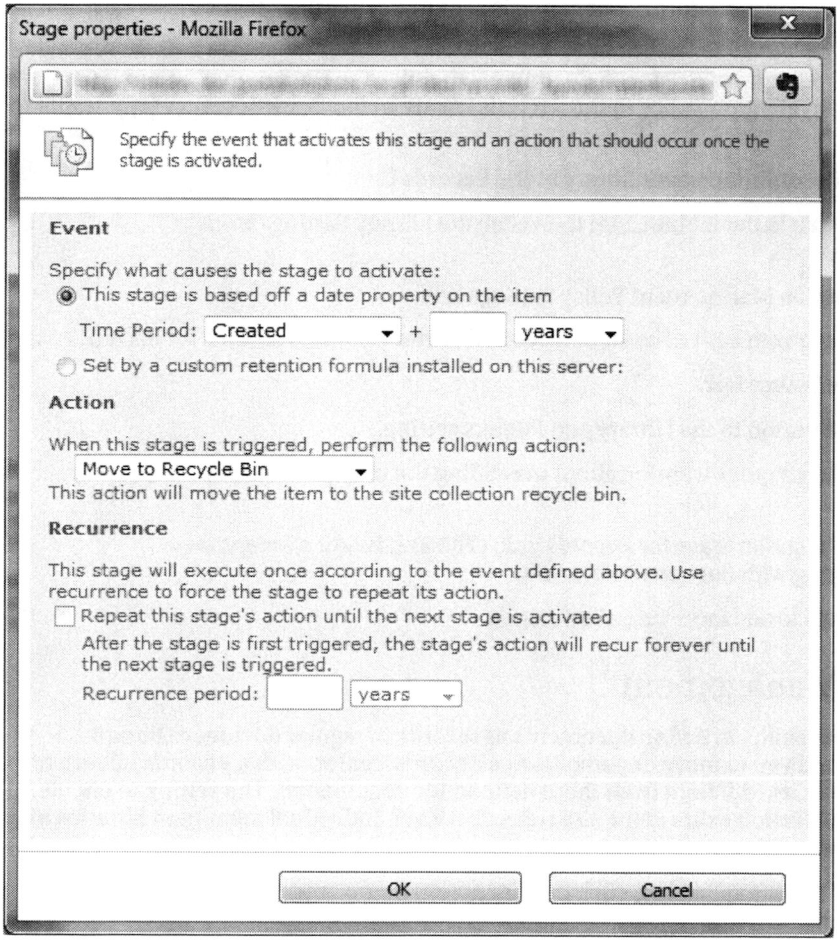

Stage properties - Mozilla Firefox

Specify the event that activates this stage and an action that should occur once the stage is activated.

Event

Specify what causes the stage to activate:
- ◉ This stage is based off a date property on the item

  Time Period: Created ▾ + [   ] years ▾

- ○ Set by a custom retention formula installed on this server:

Action

When this stage is triggered, perform the following action:

Move to Recycle Bin ▾

This action will move the item to the site collection recycle bin.

Recurrence

This stage will execute once according to the event defined above. Use recurrence to force the stage to repeat its action.

☐ Repeat this stage's action until the next stage is activated

After the stage is first triggered, the stage's action will recur forever until the next stage is triggered.

Recurrence period: [   ] years ▾

[OK] [Cancel]

Figure 7-16. The Add retention stage for a record

11. In this dialog, set the time period and action.

12. Click OK to save the stage.

13. You may create additional stages for different periods and set the action to move to the next step.

■ **Note** You can only set a custom retention formula from custom code.

---

14. Click t OK at the end of the Information management policy settings page to save the new policy.

We have now created a retention policy for all documents that use the Document content type. Continue the steps to assign a retention policy to the Records library in the Records center (applicable to any document library).

15. Navigate to the Records document library in the Records Center.

16. Click the Library tab in the Ribbon, and then click the Library Settings icon from the Ribbon.

17. Click the Information Management Policy Settings link.

SharePoint displays a page with a list of content types and current policies defined for each (if any).

18. Click the Change Source link.

19. Change the radio button to the Library and Folders setting.

20. SharePoint displays a quick warning about overriding the policy of content types.

21. Click the Add a Retention Stage for Records link. (The link is Add a Retention Stage when working with document libraries).

22. Repeat steps 11–23 to add more retention stages.

In-Place Records Management

New to SharePoint 2010 is the ability to define documents as records in regular document libraries. SharePoint previously required you to move documents to a Records Center, with a Records Library to use records retention and policies (different from those defined for documents). The setting to enable automatic or manual record creation exists at the site collection level. Individual document libraries may override the site collection setting.

1. From the root of the site collection, click the Site Action menu, and then click the Site Settings menu item.

2. Click the Site Collection Features link, under the Site Collection Administration heading.

3. Ensure that the In Place Records Management feature is activated.

4. Navigate back to the Site Settings page.

5. Click the Record Declaration Settings link, under Site Collection Administration, to display the window shown in Figure 7-17. This page defines settings for the edit/delete restrictions once a document becomes a record, whether in place records management available globally in the site collection, and the user roles that may turn a document into a record and back again.

Record Restrictions

Specify restrictions to place on a document or item once it has been declared as a record. Changing this setting will not affect items which have already been declared records. Note: The information management policy settings can also specify different policies for records and non-records.

- No Additional Restrictions
  Records are no more restricted than non-records.
- Block Delete
  Records can be edited but not deleted.
- Block Edit and Delete
  Records cannot be edited or deleted. Any changes will require the record declaration to be revoked.

Record Declaration Availability

Specify whether all lists and libraries in this site should make the manual declaration of records available by default. When manual record declaration is unavailable, records can only be declared through a policy or workflow.

Manual record declaration in lists and libraries should be:
- Available in all locations by default
- Not available in all locations by default

Declaration Roles

Specify which user roles can declare and undeclare record status manually.

The declaration of records can be performed by:
- All list contributors and administrators
- Only list administrators
- Only policy actions

Undeclaring a record can be performed by:
- All list contributors and administrators
- Only list administrators
- Only policy actions

[OK] [Cancel]

Figure 7-17. *Records declaration settings*

6. Navigate to the document library in the site collection, in my case the Documents library in my Document Center site collection.

7. Click the Library tab on the Ribbon, and then click the Library Settings icon from the Ribbon.

8. Click the Record Declaration Settings link.

9. In the next page, you may override the setting at that site collection level to enable/disable in place records management. You may also check the setting so that all documents added to the library become records.

10. Enable manual declaration of records for the document library.

11. Navigate to the default view page of the document library.

12. Select one or many documents in the view, and then click the Documents tab in the Ribbon.

13. Check out the document, and then click the Declare Record icon in the Ribbon.

The document icon now has a padlock, meaning that SharePoint has protected the document as a record, which now subscribes to all record retention policies and stages. How to undeclared the document as a record (assuming you have rights)?

14. Select the document in the view.

15. Click the drop-down arrow and click the Compliance Details link from the ECB.

16. Click the Undeclared Record link.

Auditing

SharePoint 2010 provides basic auditing for events in a list or document library. Similar to the way we configured barcodes in a document library, a list owner may configure auditing at the content type level.

1. Navigate to the List/Library Settings page.

2. Click the Information Management Policy Settings link.

3. Click the content type in the list to audit.

4. Change the setting to Define a Policy (unless one already exists in the site collection, in which choose the last option and select the policy).

5. In the next page, give the policy a name and policy description.

6. Check the Enable Auditing checkbox.

7. Select your choice from the available events to audit and Click OK to save the policy.

8. To view audit reports, navigate to the site collection Site Settings page.

9. Click the Audit Log Reports link.

Web Content Management

Web Content Management came about with SharePoint 2007. What the industry calls WCM, Microsoft refers to as *publishing features*, in the SharePoint platform. The publishing infrastructure in SharePoint allows creation of public facing web sites, built upon the content management features of SharePoint. The major capabilities of any good WCM system include the following:

- It provides web site and web page infrastructure with typical CMS capabilities for content owners.

- Content experts may add new content and edit existing content in the system without knowing HTML, or web presentation technologies.

- Allows web site and page designers to create sophisticated design without content context.

- The entire system drives from one or many web servers and the end users—viewers and content owners may use the site from a web browser.

The SharePoint publishing features, coupled with many of the core features in the Enterprise Content Management System, meet the objectives stipulated above.

Publishing Sites

In the previous chapter, we looked at metadata—content types, site columns, and so on—and I introduced you to publishing page layouts and master pages that use metadata. In this chapter, (I want to discuss content deployment, which we have not visited in this book until now. Before doing so, Table 7-4 provides a recap of the common features in the publishing infrastructure.

Table 7-4. Publishing Infrastructure Common Features

Publishing Feature	Description
Master Pages and Page Layouts	Chapter 6 shows how page layouts meld with content types and page instances to render a web page to users. Master pages provide common branding for all pages contained in a web site (in fact, SharePoint uses master pages in all site definitions). Page layouts define the templates for page instances, based on associated content type.
Metadata	Available in the core of the platform, the publishing features make use of content types to define page content and the fields displayed in page templates.
Versioning, Publishing, and Content Approval	Page libraries are document libraries and therefore benefit from all the same features as regular document libraries, which include versioning, content approval, and publish to view.
Multi-language	The publishing infrastructure manages multiple language versions of pages and site hierarchy through *variance*, a topic outside the scope of this book. Variance relies on alternative site structures, workflow, and timer services to synchronize change of default language content, so that other language content changes at the same time.
Content Deployment	Discussed in the following section.
Searchable	Like all other content in SharePoint, web site and page content includes in SharePoint search indexing. Administrators may configure content sources to search web site content as SharePoint content (fields, metadata, and so on) or as a complete web page (like Google).
WYSIWYG Editing	Content owners may edit page content within the page design, as they would see the published page. This gives content owners some context when editing their content.

Content Deployment

In most organizations, the public web site is of significant importance. The web site presents an organization's public image, along with the products and services it offers to the public audience, and is susceptible to criticism if the site breaks or is offline for any duration. Therefore, when it comes to the infrastructure that hosts a web site, typically the organization will maintain a production, staging, and perhaps a development copy of the site. Open any good book on best practice web site deployment, and you will most likely find reference to staging and production environments.

Microsoft developed the web publishing aspects of SharePoint with content integrity in mind. Content owners may edit and add new content to the web site, free from worry that the public audience sees their changes until new and changed content undergoes an approval and publish process. The content approval process and versioning/publish features in SharePoint allow complete confidence that the public may view an approved version of content and design while editors and designers can work on the same infrastructure without jeopardizing the public view. Even so, management and the IT group would often balk at the idea of making changes to the production web site. This is where content deployment comes in.

Content deployment allows content owners to work on one SharePoint farm—completely independent from the production farm—and then deploy published changes to the production environment on a schedule. The following instructions provide high-level configuration of content deployment from Farm A to Farm B.

■ **Note** Content deployment only deploys user content from one SharePoint Farm to another—sites, list, list items, documents, metadata and so on. I will not deploy customizations (such as code deployed via features and package solutions).

Configuring the Destination Farm

Take the following steps to configure a destination farm for content deployment:

1. Open Central Admin on the destination farm.

2. Click the General Application Settings link in the left navigation.

3. Scroll to the section on Content Deployment.

4. Click the Configure Content Deployment link to allow the destination farm to accept incoming content deployment.

5. Configure the farm to Accept Incoming content deployment. Also set the import server in the destination farm to accept the import content (see Figure 7-18 as an example).

Central Administration ▸ Content Deployment Settings

These settings apply to all content deployment paths and jobs.

I Like It   Tags & Notes

❓

| OK | Cancel |

Accept Content Deployment Jobs

Specify whether you want to permit this server farm to receive content deployment jobs from another farm. Even with this setting enabled, the remote farm will need to authenticate to Central Administration to deploy content.

◉ Accept incoming content deployment jobs
○ Reject incoming content deployment jobs

Import Server

Specify the server you want to receive incoming content deployment jobs. This server must have enough available disk space to store the incoming jobs, and it must be running an administration web application for the farm.

This server will experience additional load when a content deployment job runs.

Server you want to use to manage import of content deployment jobs

SPS ▾

Export Server

Specify the server to which you want to send outgoing content deployment jobs. This server must have enough available disk space to store the outgoing jobs, and it must be running an administration web application for the farm.

This server will experience additional load when a content deployment job runs.

Server you want to use to manage export of content deployment jobs

SPS ▾

Connection Security

By default, content deployment can only occur if the connection between source and destination farms is encrypted by using the HTTPS protocol.

If you deploy content over a connection that is not encrypted, the user name and password you use to authenticate with the destination farm could be intercepted by malicious users, as could the content you are deploying.

○ Require encryption (recommended)
◉ Do not require encryption

Temporary Files

Specify where you want to store temporary files for content deployment jobs. These files are automatically deleted when the deployment job is finished.

This folder must have enough available disk space to store all the content that is deployed at one time.

Path:

C:\ProgramData\ContentDeployment

Reporting

Specify the number of reports you want to keep for each content deployment job that originates from this farm. The oldest reports will automatically be deleted to make room for new ones.

Number of reports to retain for each job:

20

| OK | Cancel |

Figure 7-18. The Content Deployment Settings page

Configuring the Source Farm

Take the following steps to configure a source farm for content deployment:

1. Open Central Admin on the source farm.

2. Click the General Application Settings link in the left navigation.

3. Scroll to the section on Content Deployment.

4. Click the Configure Content Deployment link.

5. Configure the export server for this farm, by providing a path for the export files, and specifying whether you want to use encryption (in case you are deploying across network security boundaries).

6. Navigate back to the General Application Settings page.

7. Click the Configure Content Deployment Paths and Jobs link (see Figure 7-19).

Central Administration ▸ Create Content Deployment Path

A path defines a relationship between a source site collection and a destination site collection.

I Like It   Tags & Notes

OK	Cancel

Name and Description

Specify the name and description of the content deployment path.

Type the name of this path:

WCM to Destination

Type the description of the content deployment path:

Source Web Application and Site Collection

Specify the web application and site collection on the source server.

Source web application:

wcm.sp2010.com

Source site collection:

/

URL: **http://wcm.sp2010.com/**

Destination Central Administration Web Application

Specify the URL for the destination Central Administration Server.

Type the URL of the destination Central Administration Server:

http://sps:40023

⚠ You have specified a URL that begins with http://. Communication to this URL will not be secure and can be intercepted by malicious users.

Authentication Information

Specify the authentication method and credentials you want to use for the destination server. The specified account must have SharePoint Central Administration credentials on the destination server.

Click **Connect** to connect to the destination server and specify settings for this path.

Specify the authentication method and credentials you want to use to log on to the destination server:

Authentication Type:

◉ Use Integrated Windows authentication

○ Use Basic authentication

User Name:

sp2010\administrator

Password:

••••••••••

Connect   Connection succeeded

Destination web application and site collection

Specify the URL for the destination web application and site collection.

Destination web application:

destination.sp2010.com

Destination Site Collection:

/

URL: **http://destination.sp2010.com/**

User Names

Specify whether or not to deploy the user names associated with content. Show me more information.

☑ Deploy user names

Security Information

Specify whether you want to deploy security information (such as ACLs, roles, and membership). Show me more information.

Security information in the content deployment:

All

OK	Cancel

Figure 7-19. Configuring a content deployment path

8. Paths tell SharePoint what to deploy; click the New Path link.

9. Give the path a name and description, and specify the source web application and source site collection.

10. Provide the URL of the Destination Central Admin site.

11. Provide the authentication (I recommend using the Farm account on the destination farm), click the Connect button and make sure you see the Connection succeeded message.

12. Select the destination web application and site collection.

13. Check the checkbox to deploy user names (typically a good idea if you want the users to persist in the site collection, unless your production farm allows now user login).

14. Set the security information for the content deployment and click OK.

With the path defined, we now need to configure a job to deploy on a schedule.

15. Click the drop-down next to the name of the path to show the ECB, and then click the Create Job link (see Figure 7-20).

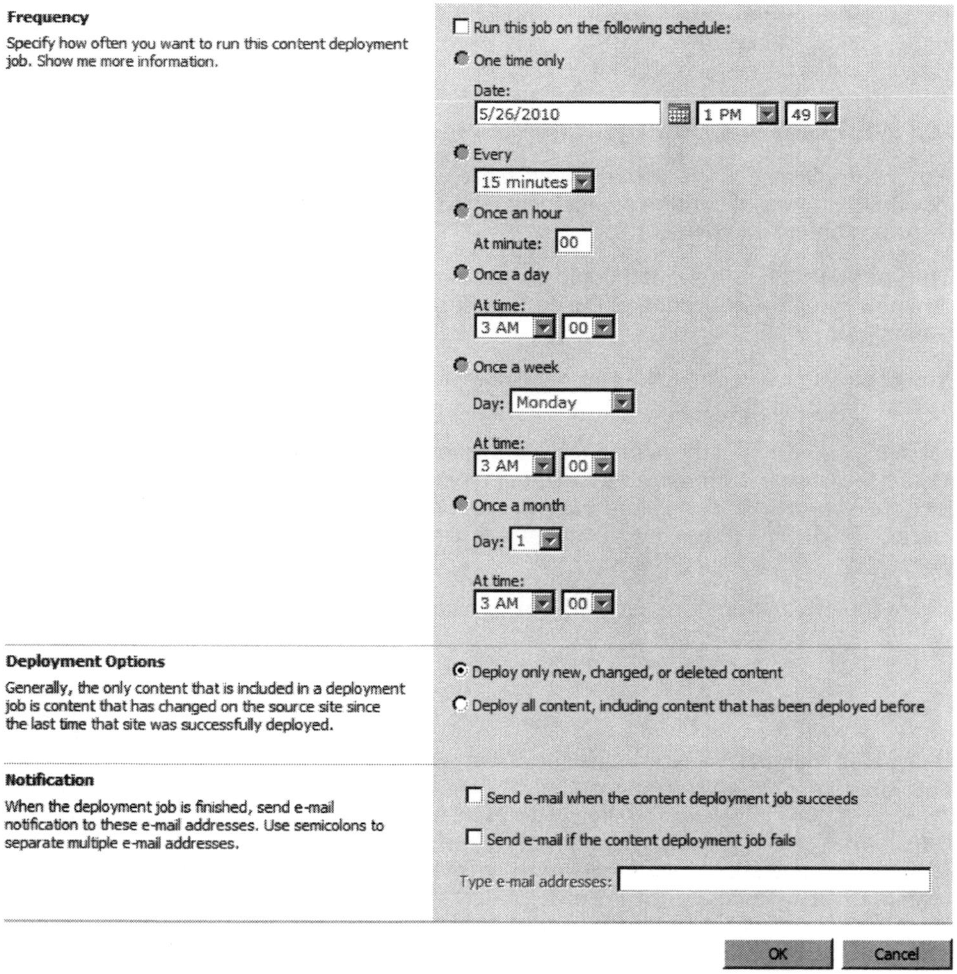

Frequency

Specify how often you want to run this content deployment job. Show me more information.

☐ Run this job on the following schedule:

○ One time only

Date:

| 5/26/2010 | 🗒 | 1 PM ▾ | 49 ▾ |

○ Every

15 minutes ▾

○ Once an hour

At minute: 00

○ Once a day

At time:
3 AM ▾ 00 ▾

○ Once a week

Day: Monday ▾

At time:
3 AM ▾ 00 ▾

○ Once a month

Day: 1 ▾

At time:
3 AM ▾ 00 ▾

Deployment Options

Generally, the only content that is included in a deployment job is content that has changed on the source site since the last time that site was successfully deployed.

◉ Deploy only new, changed, or deleted content

○ Deploy all content, including content that has been deployed before

Notification

When the deployment job is finished, send e-mail notification to these e-mail addresses. Use semicolons to separate multiple e-mail addresses.

☐ Send e-mail when the content deployment job succeeds

☐ Send e-mail if the content deployment job fails

Type e-mail addresses: [   ]

[OK] [Cancel]

Figure 7-20. A content deployment Job

16. Provide a schedule and scope for the deployment job.

17. You can use a SQL snapshot, but since my SQL install is not Enterprise SQL Server 2008, this option is disabled for me.

18. Provide email addresses for notification.

19. Select the deployment type—deploy all content is a full deployment, new or changed content is an incremental deployment and Click OK.

20. From the same page where you created the deployment path—Manage Content Deployment Path and Jobs page—you can view the status of current jobs and paths.

21. Click the Status column of running and completed jobs to see the status of content deployment jobs.

Common Issues with Content Deployment

Content deployment is complicated to get working right. SharePoint 2007 addressed a number of the bugs that frustrated administrators of content deployment jobs. However, there are some known points to note when configuring content deployment:

- The first time you configure content deployment to your production environment, provide a new blank site collection as the destination. Then run a full content deployment job.

- Once you complete a successful full content deployment job, only run incremental jobs from then on.

- Try to avoid deleting metadata elements from the destination farm—content deployment balks when it cannot find a content type on the destination farm that it finds on the source. This issue often comes about when deploying content types via features, and deployment of the feature on the destination farm has differences to that of the source farm.

- Ensure that the destination farm has all the same features deployed as the source farm.

Summary

In this chapter, we explored the various features for document management, including some of the new features provided by SharePoint 2010—Document ID, Content Organizer, Document-Sets, and so on. I demonstrated how some of these new features allow your users to organize their document content better—often the lifeblood of any organization that processes information.

We covered some of the interesting areas of records management—a behemoth of a topic, which included Information Management Policy, the Records Center, Holds and e-Discovery, and Auditing Records Management is all about maintain the lifecycle of documents and data in SharePoint in adherence with organization or business policies.

At the end of this chapter, you learned about content deployment and its use as part of the Web Content Management features of SharePoint. We discovered how content deployment provides administrators with the ability to deploy content from one farm to another, such as staging to production.

In Chapter 8, I will tackle another large topic in SharePoint 2010—*business intelligence,* which is about providing intelligent business decision making for your users by providing dashboard and reports of their data. Stay tuned.

CHAPTER 8

Business Intelligence

Business intelligence is all about allowing organizations to make intelligent business decisions based on collected data. The subject of business intelligence (BI) is vast, and you probably won't be surprised to hear that whole books have been written about it. So why include BI in a book about SharePoint 2010 administration? Simply because SharePoint Server 2010 contains many new BI offerings, including integrated PerformancePoint Services, which used to exist as a stand-alone Microsoft product. Although you will not find much information about the implementation of BI concepts or the use of OLAP cubes and data warehouses in this book, you can expect to read about configuration of SharePoint 2010 to support implementation of BI practice.

In this chapter, we will take a journey of discovery, installing PerformancePoint Services (PPS), Visio Services, and Excel Services. We will also take a tour of Business Connectivity Service (BCS)—the successor to the Business Data Catalog in SP2007.

Before diving in to BI, I want to point out that most if not all the BI features in SharePoint 2010 require an Enterprise license, although in some cases, you can get away with Standard. If you are using a Foundation version of SharePoint 2010, many of the steps and examples in this chapter will not work.

Business Intelligence Features in SharePoint 2010

SharePoint 2010 includes some great new BI features, as follows:

- **PerformancePoint Services and the Dashboard Designer**
  PPS is about providing data analysts and business experts with dashboards of real-time data, hosted within pages of SharePoint 2010. With PPS and Business Connectivity Services, users can hook up their OLAP cube and OLTP table data to dashboards that allow users to drill down into data and explore axes. The Dashboard Designer is a stand-alone application that installs into Windows and provides the mechanism of implementing rich dashboard technology, which SharePoint can then host for data reviewers.

- **Business Connectivity Services (BCS)**
  BCS replaces the Business Data Catalog of SharePoint Server 2007 and provides sophisticated integration of external data. BDC integrated external data via BDC web parts, which provided limited control of the view of the data. By contrast, BCS integrates external data via external content types and presents external data to users just as if they were looking at regular list data. New in SharePoint 2010, BCS provides bidirectional data exchange—BCS can update the external source data as well as aggregate. This is a large improvement over SharePoint 2007 BDC, which did not provide updating and could only aggregate external data.

- **Visio Services**
  Also new in SharePoint 2010; —Visio diagrams need no longer remain static, and can show real-time data *live*. The power of Visio Services provides this capability, and the best part is you do not need to install Visio on client machines for your users to take advantage of the rich diagrams Visio may provide.

- **Excel Services**
  As it did with Excel Services in SharePoint 2007, SharePoint provides hosted Excel data, complete with graphing capabilities, without requiring users to deploy the Excel Office application. SharePoint 2010 includes Power Pivot, so you may take advantage of the Excel web application in SharePoint to render multiple-axis data contained in OLAP cubes.

- **Reporting Services**
  SharePoint 2010 makes the inclusion of SQL Server Reporting Services in the platform simpler. Reporting web parts allow users to surface report data on SharePoint pages, and the Report Builder facilitates creation of complex reports with data stored in SQL Server.

- **Secure Store Services**
  Although Secure Store Services is not directly about BI, the replacement of the Single Sign-on Service in SharePoint 2007 allows integration of multiple channels of data, handling multiple authentication methods. The Secure Store Service is claims-authentication aware. The Secure Store Service is a critical element of the BI offering in SharePoint 2010 and is required in most cases.

PerformancePoint Services

PerformancePoint used to stand alone as a Microsoft product, called PerformancePoint Server 2007. New to SharePoint 2010 is PerformancePoint Services (PPS), which integrates in SharePoint 2010, as a service application (see Chapter 2 for details on service application architecture). Organizations that install an Enterprise license for SharePoint 2010 may provide PPS to their users with Client Access Licenses (CALs).

PPS provides graphical dashboards, scorecards, and key performance indicators within SharePoint, based on real-time data, integrated via Business Connectivity Services. A Windows tool called the Dashboard Designer allows users to design elaborate dashboards around their data, and then publish these dashboards for rendering in SharePoint 2010. Users viewing these dashboards no longer see static images of data, but live graphical views of data that they may interact with and drill-down into.

PPS makes use of objects, called *first class objects (FCOs)*, which are stored in lists and document libraries in SharePoint and categorized via content types. Since PPS now integrates with SharePoint, PPS may take advantage of the SharePoint security model, collaboration, and search, to immerse user data in with the new interactive aspects of the platform. Table 8-1 lists the various FCOs in PPS with a brief description of each.

Table 8-1. FCOs in PPS

FCO	Description
Reports	PPS provides various charts to summarize data visually—known as reports, which include Excel Services, SQL Server Reporting Reports, Analytic Chart and Grid, Strategy Map, and so on.
KPI	Key Performance Indicator: Provides a status against a known metric and typically displays value based on certain thresholds. Red/Amber/Green indicators are one example of the visual representation of a KPI.
Scorecard	Collection of KPIs on a dashboard, used for tracking status and comparing multiple performance indicators.
Filter	Provides a limited view of a dashboard, as the display is filtered, similar to the way you filter data in Excel by column filters.
Indicator	The visual indicator of a KPI, such as the Red/Amber/Green light—the indicator is what displays based on the value of the KPI.
Dashboard	The actual display of reports, scorecards, and KPIs in SharePoint to provide a business intelligence view of data.
Data Source	The source that PPS uses to pull in data for dashboards, reports, KPIs. Examples of data sources include SharePoint lists, Excel Services, SQL Server tables, and OLAP cubes.

With a high-level understanding of the role PPS plays, and keeping the terminology of FCO in mind, let us now get into the technical details of installing PPS within our SharePoint environment.

Secure Store Installation and Configuration

The Secure Store Service replaces the Single-Sign-on Service from SharePoint 2007 and stores security credentials for accessing external sources. PPS requires the Secure Store Service to store unattended account credentials for accessing external data sources. The following steps demonstrate setting up the Secure Store Service.

1. Navigate back to the Manage service applications page.

2. Click the New icon in the Ribbon, and then click the Secure Store Service menu item.

3. Give the service application a name, database name, and application pool.

4. Click the Create button and wait for SharePoint to configure the Secure Store Service application and proxy.

5. Click to the right of the name of the new Secure Store Application, and then click the Manage icon from the Ribbon.

6. SharePoint displays a page, asking for generation of a new key.

7. Click the Generate New Key icon, from the Ribbon—this key is what secures the store so that applications and users may not access the store to retrieve usernames and passwords.

8. Provide a passphrase and confirmation; then click the OK button.

■ **Note** Keep a record of the Secure Store Service Passphrase in a secure place, as you may need it later to reconfigure the service.

PPS Installation and Configuration

At this stage, I have to assume that you have installed SharePoint 2010; if not, flip back to Chapter 2, and follow the extensive steps within. During your SharePoint 2010 installation, you may have executed the Farm Configuration Wizard from Central Administration. Of the many operations, this wizard will likely have created a default web application and a site collection, and installed the necessary features for PerformancePoint Services. If, like me, you shy away from the Farm Configuration Wizard, because it makes a mess of databases and makes assumptions about your installation, then the following steps demonstrate installing PPS into your SharePoint 2010 farm.

1. Open Central Admin.

2. Click the Manage Services on Server link.

3. Ensure that the Secure Store Service and PerformancePoint Service are started on one of the servers in your farm (start the Secure Store Service first), most likely your application server.

4. Navigate back to the home page of Central Admin.

5. Click the Manage Service Applications link.

6. Scroll down and make sure the PerformancePoint Service application is not present in the list (if it is not, then read on).

7. Click the New icon from the Ribbon.

8. From the drop-down, click the PerformancePoint Service Application menu item.

9. Give the new service application a name, such as PerformancePoint Services, and choose whether to include the proxy in the farm default list (meaning that PPS is available to all new Web Applications).

■ **Note**: From the Application Management page, click the Configure Service Application Associations link, and then click the default group link to see the default proxy list for the farm.

10. Create a new application pool, click the Create button, and wait a few moments while SharePoint creates the new application and proxy.

11. If you open SQL Enterprise Manager and point this application to your farm DB server, you should see a database for PerformancePoint Services.

■ **Note** Unfortunately, SharePoint will not enable you to create a PPS database without the GUID, except when using the `Set-SPPerformancePointServiceApplication` PowerShell command.

12. From the list, click to the right of the name of the new PPS application, and then click the Manage icon from the Ribbon. SharePoint displays a page with four options, as in Figure 8-1.

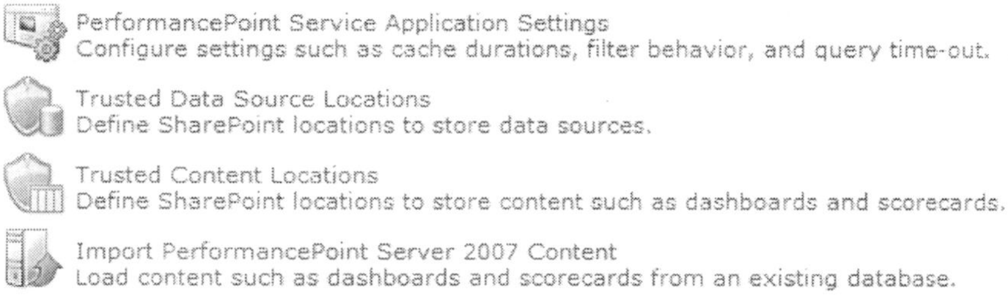

PerformancePoint Service Application Settings
Configure settings such as cache durations, filter behavior, and query time-out.

Trusted Data Source Locations
Define SharePoint locations to store data sources.

Trusted Content Locations
Define SharePoint locations to store content such as dashboards and scorecards.

Import PerformancePoint Server 2007 Content
Load content such as dashboards and scorecards from an existing database.

Figure 8-1. Management of PPS

Before we look at these options, we will next configure PerformancePoint Services to use the Secure Store Service.

Configure PerformancePoint Services to Use the Secure Store Service

Take the following steps to configure PPS for Secure Store Service:

1. Navigate back to the PPS management page, as in Figure 8-1.

2. Click the PerformancePoint Service Application Settings link (see Figure 8-2).

Secure Store and Unattended Service Account

Configure the Secure Store Service which is used to store the Unattended Service Account used for authenticating with data sources.

Secure Store Service Application:

Secure Store Service ⓘ

Unattended Service Account:
User Name: (Domain\Username)

Password:

Comments

Users who have appropriate permissions can annotate scorecard cells (in Dashboard Designer and on a deployed SharePoint site). Multiple comments can be made per annotation.

☑ Enable comments
Maximum number of annotated cells per scorecard:
1000 cells

[Delete Comments by Date]

Cache

Temporarily storing frequently-accessed items, or caching, decreases load times for future requests. Enter the duration for items to remain in the cache.

KPI icon cache:
10 seconds

Data Sources

Set the duration of no response before a data source query is cancelled.

Data source query time-out:
300 seconds

Filters

Enter how long to remember user-selected filter values and how often to clear them when they expire. Set the maximum number of members to retrieve into a filter of type "tree".

Remember user filter selections for:
90 days
Maximum members to load in filter tree:
5000 members

Select Measure Control

Set the maximum number of measures to retrieve into a dashboard Select Measure control.

Maximum measures to load in Select Measure control:
1000 measures

Show Details

Set the limits for the number of rows returned when a user clicks "Show Details".

Initial retrieval limit:
1000 rows

Maximum retrieval limit
◉ Fixed limit:
10000 rows
○ Limit controlled by Analysis Services

Decomposition Tree

Set the maximum number of individual items (per level) returned to the decomposition tree visualization. The minimum value is 0. The maximum is 1,000,000.

Maximum number of items:
250 items

Figure 8-2. PerformancePoint Service application settings page

3. Provide the user credentials for the Unattended Service Account—This account may access external data stores, and the credentials entered here go into the Secure Store Service repository.

Figure 8-3 shows the target application entry in the Secure Store for the PerformancePoint Service's unattended account.

		Target Application ID↑	Type	Target Application Name
Central Administration	☐			
Application Management	☐	d846f7d3-4e02-4868-94a8-b00128904987-PPSUnattendedAccount	Group	PerformancePoint Services
System Settings				
Monitoring				
Backup and Restore				
Security				
Upgrade and Migration				
General Application Settings				
Configuration Wizards				

Figure 8-3. A target application entry for PPS in the secure store

Creating a New BI Center

So far, we have installed the Secure Store Service and PerformancePoint Services applications. To demonstrate Business Intelligence capabilities we can establish a new BI Center site collection, which includes most of the features to deploy dashboard content and first class object containers. The following steps demonstrate creating the BI Center.

1. Open Central Admin.

2. From the home page, click the Create Site Collections link, under the Application Management heading.

3. Select the appropriate web application to install the new BI Center (see Chapter 2 if you need steps for creating a new web application).

4. Give the site collection a name, description, and URL suffix (if it is not the root site collection).

5. In the Template Selection section, click the Enterprise tab and then select the Business Intelligence Center.

▪ **Note** If you do not see the Enterprise tab or the Business Intelligence Center, then you may not have a SharePoint 2010 Enterprise license installed.

---

6. Provide username credentials for at least the primary site collection administrator and optionally the secondary site collection administrator.

7. Click the OK button and wait for SharePoint to spend a few moments creating the site collection.

8. Navigate to the new site collection and you should see a landing page like that in Figure 8-4.

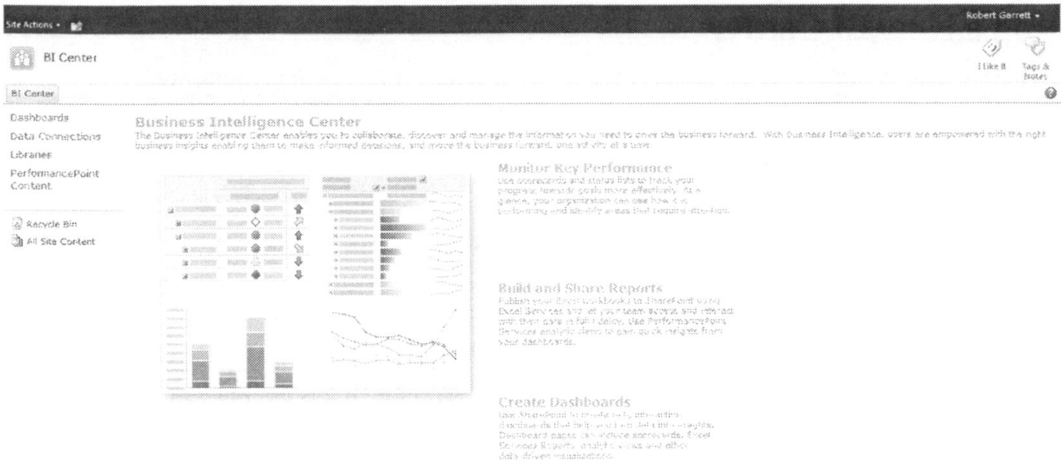

Figure 8-4. Business Intelligence Center home page

Installing the Dashboard Designer

The Dashboard Designer is a Windows application that enables users to create sophisticated dashboards, which they may then deploy to SharePoint 2010. The Dashboard Designer and PerformancePoint Server work together to provide real-time user interaction with data via the SharePoint 2010 web interface. Users who view dashboards, reports, scorecards, and so on do not need the Dashboard Designer, just PPS installed to render these first class objects in SharePoint. Only authors of these FCOs need the Dashboard Designer. Table 8-2 lists the Dashboard Designer prerequisites.

Table 8-2. Dashboard Designer Prerequisites

Prerequisite	Description
Microsoft .NET Framework 3.5 SP1	The Dashboard Designer is a click-once .NET application, which requires the latest version of the 3.5 Framework installed on the client computer to operate.
Visio 2007/2010 Professional	Required to create strategy maps, reports that connect KPI data to Visio shapes.
Report Viewer 2008	Required to create and edit SQL Server Reporting Services reports.

1. From the home page of the BI Center, hover over the section titled Create Dashboards.

2. In the open block on the left, click the Start using PerformancePoint Services link.

3. Click the Run Dashboard Designer button to launch the installation of the Dashboard Designer.

■ **Note** I recommend using Internet Explorer to launch and install the Dashboard Designer.

4. Once it is installed, you should see the Dashboard Designer, as in Figure 8-5.

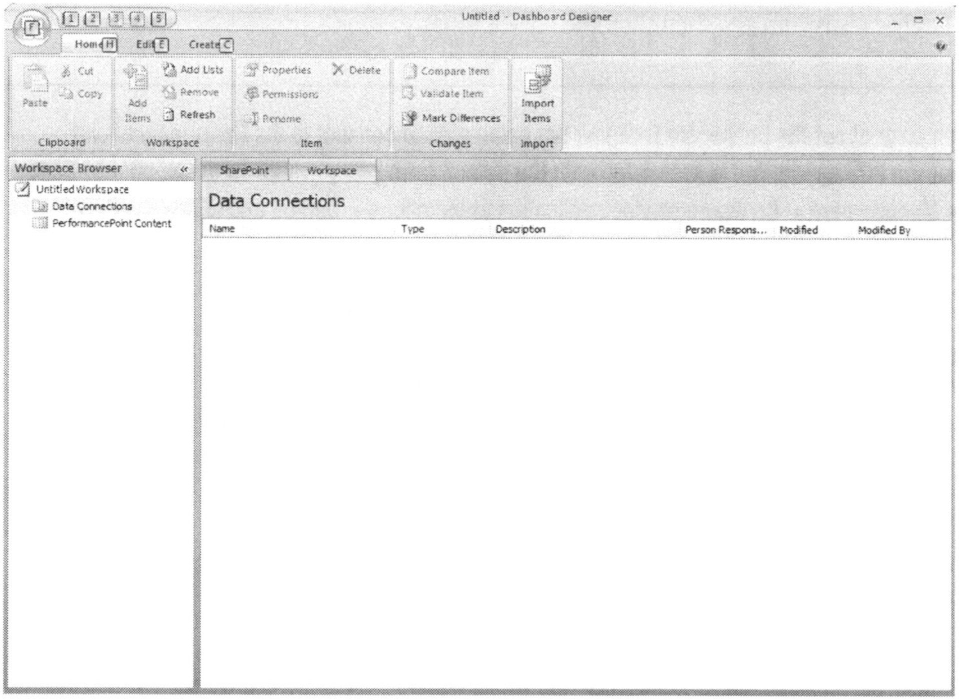

Figure 8-5. *Dashboard Designer*

Creating a Simple BI Dashboard

Although the primary focus of this book is administration, I would be doing the reader a disservice if I did not demonstrate how easy it is to create a simple dashboard in SharePoint 2010, using PPS and the Dashboard Designer. Dashboards can often get quite complicated, and since there is no end to the different shapes and forms that data may take, the same applies to that of data reporting and dashboards.

■ **Note** The following demonstration requires the Adventure Works sample databases and OLAP cubes, available for download at http://msftdbprodsamples.codeplex.com/, and requires SQL Server Analysis Services to be installed and configured.

The following example demonstrates creating a simple dashboard, using an OLAP cube in the Adventure Works sample databases.

1. Follow the steps in the previous section to install the Dashboard Designer.

2. Right-click Data Connections, in the Workspace Browser, and select New Data Source.

3. Click Analysis Services, and then click OK.

■ **Note** If you see an error about the Dashboard Designer not being able to connect to the PerformancePoint Services, ensure that the PPS application is associated with the default farm proxy group. To do so, choose Central Admin Application Management - Configure service application associations - default and check the PPS service application.

---

4. Give the connection a name, and then in the Connection Settings window provide the server, OLAP database, and cube name (see Figure 8-6).

5. Click the Test Data Source button and make sure the connection succeeded, then the Close button.

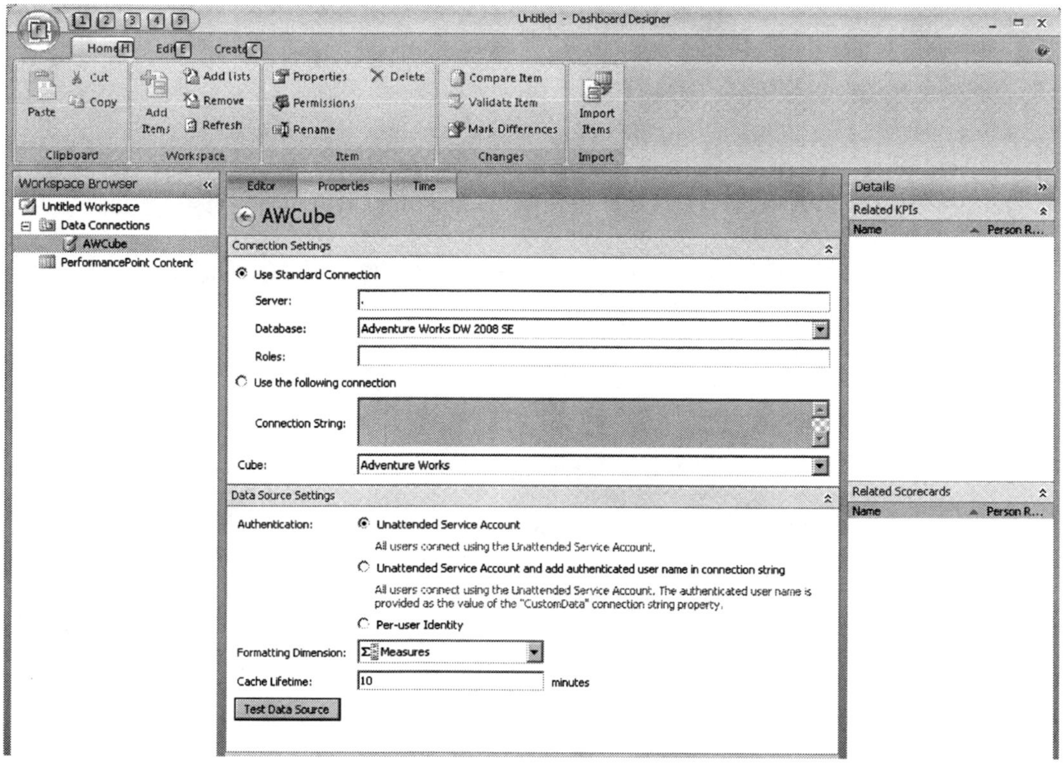

Figure 8-6. Configured connection to an OLAP cube

6. Now is a good time to save the dashboard to disk. Click the Save All icon on the very top bar of the Dashboard Designer, provide a filename and location, and click the Save button.

• We will now create a scorecard that links with the cube data:

7. Right-click the PerformancePoint Content heading in the Workspace Browser, and then click the New menu item, followed by Scorecard in the sub-menu.

8. Click the Analysis Services Template in the popup dialog, and then click OK.

• Click the new Data Connection we created moments ago, and then click Next.

9. Leave the option checked to Create KPIs from SQL Server Analysis Services Measures.

10. Click the Next button.

11. The next dialog allows you to create KPIs; click the Add KPI button.

12. Choose one of the measures from the cube for Actual, such as Gross Profit.

283

13. Choose another measure for the Target, or provide a fixed amount (I provided a fixed amount of 100,000).

14. You may add other KPIs.

15. Click the Next button twice (the default for filters and columns are fine for this demo).

16. Ensure that the KPIs were created in the PerformancePoint Content, and click the Finish button.

17. The Dashboard Designer creates a new scorecard with the KPIs you specified earlier; give it a name.

See the view of my Scorecard in Figure 8-7.

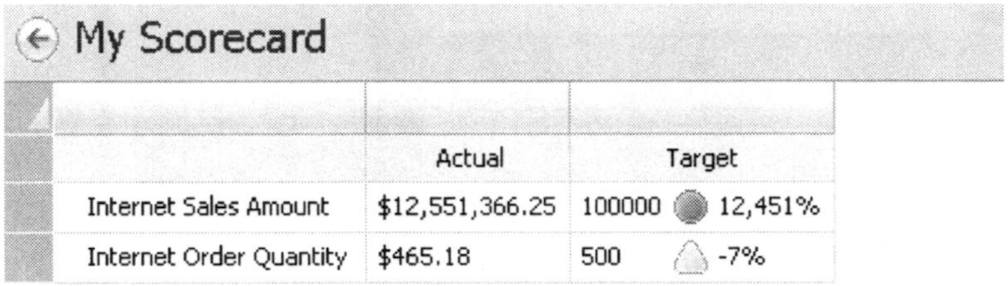

		Actual	Target		
	Internet Sales Amount	$12,551,366.25	100000	●	12,451%
	Internet Order Quantity	$465.18	500	△	-7%

Figure 8-7. My Scorecard

My scorecard is fine as it is, but a little boring—what if I want to see all the sales figures for selected countries? This is where the dimensions come in.

1. In the Details section of the Dashboard Designer, expand the Dimensions heading.

2. Expand Sales Territory, and then click Country.

3. Hold the Shift key (this is important), and then left-click-drag the Country dimension to the scorecard so that all the KPI names in the far left column highlight; then let go of the mouse and Shift key.

Your scorecard should look something like Figure 8-8.

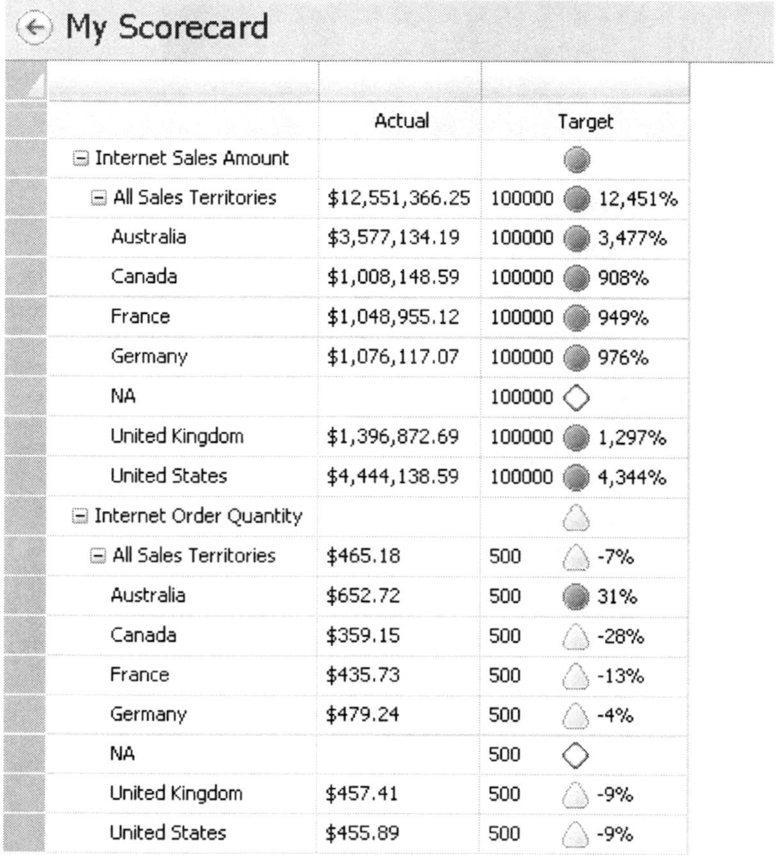

My Scorecard

	Actual	Target		
⊟ Internet Sales Amount		●		
⊟ All Sales Territories	$12,551,366.25	100000	●	12,451%
Australia	$3,577,134.19	100000	●	3,477%
Canada	$1,008,148.59	100000	●	908%
France	$1,048,955.12	100000	●	949%
Germany	$1,076,117.07	100000	●	976%
NA		100000	◇	
United Kingdom	$1,396,872.69	100000	●	1,297%
United States	$4,444,138.59	100000	●	4,344%
⊟ Internet Order Quantity		△		
⊟ All Sales Territories	$465.18	500	△	-7%
Australia	$652.72	500	●	31%
Canada	$359.15	500	△	-28%
France	$435.73	500	△	-13%
Germany	$479.24	500	△	-4%
NA		500	◇	
United Kingdom	$457.41	500	△	-9%
United States	$455.89	500	△	-9%

Figure 8-8. My Scorecard with dimensions

We will now create a report:

18. Right-click the PerformancePoint Content heading in the Workspace Browser, and then click the New menu item, followed by Report in the sub-menu.

19. Choose the Analytic Chart template and the same data connection. Before clicking the Finish button, give your report a name.

20. Drag the Average Sales Amount metric to the Bottom Axis column, and the Sales Territory Country dimension to the Series.

21. Right-click the report and change the Report Type to a Pie Chart, to see something like Figure 8-9.

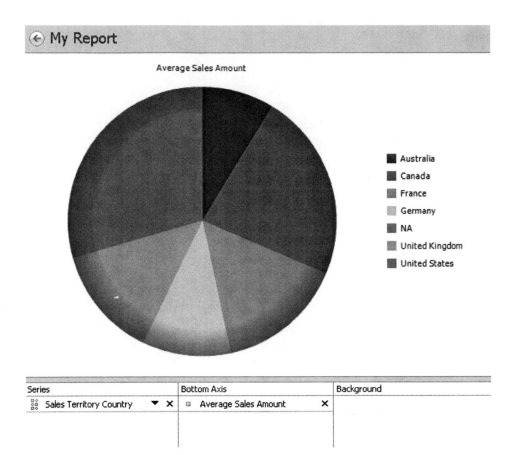

Figure 8-9. *A Pie Chart report*

Next, we will create a filter for our dashboard:

22. Right-click the PerformancePoint Content heading in the Workspace Browser, and then click the New menu item, followed by Filter in the sub-menu.

23. Choose the Member Selection filter, and the same data connection, before clicking the Next button.

24. Click the Select Dimension button to choose a dimension over which to filter—I chose Geography.Country.

25. Choose the members of the dimension, by clicking the Select Members button. Choose some countries for the filter.

26. Click the Next button.

27. Choose the display method for the filter: List, Tree, or Multi-select Tree. I chose the Multi-Select Tree.

28. Click the Finish button, and then give the filter a name.

Finally, it is time to bring our BI components together into a dashboard:

29. Right-click the PerformancePoint Content heading in the Workspace Browser, and then click the New menu item, followed by Dashboard in the sub-menu.

30. Choose the Layout template. Give your dashboard a name. Then click the Finish button

31. Drag the BI components from the Details panel on the right, onto the Zones of your dashboard.

32. To link the scorecard and report to the filter, hover over the filter you dragged to a zone, and then click and drag the Member Unique Name field to the zone containing the scorecard. Repeat for the report.

33. Click the Save-All icon on the top of the Dashboard Designer.

34. Right-click the dashboard we just created, and select the Deploy to SharePoint menu option.

35. SharePoint 2010 opens to a page showing the finished dashboard, like that of Figure 8-10. Try changing the value of the filter to see the pie chart report and scorecard change.

My Filter: **All Geographies, Australia, Canada, Franc...** ▼

My Scorecard

	Actual	Target	
⊟ Internet Sales Amount		🔵	
All Geographies	$12,551,366.25	100000 🔵	12,451%
Australia	$12,551,366.25	100000 🔵	12,451%
Canada	$12,551,366.25	100000 🔵	12,451%
France	$12,551,366.25	100000 🔵	12,451%
Germany	$12,551,366.25	100000 🔵	12,451%
United Kingdom	$12,551,366.25	100000 🔵	12,451%
United States	$12,551,366.25	100000 🔵	12,451%
⊟ Internet Order Quantity		🔺	
All Geographies	$465.18	500 🔺	-7%
Australia	$465.18	500 🔺	-7%
Canada	$465.18	500 🔺	-7%
France	$465.18	500 🔺	-7%
Germany	$465.18	500 🔺	-7%
United Kingdom	$465.18	500 🔺	-7%
United States	$465.18	500 🔺	-7%

My Report

Average Sales Amount

■ All Geographies
■ Australia
■ Canada
▨ France
▨ Germany
▨ United Kingdom
▨ United States

Figure 8-10: A dashboard deployed to SharePoint 2010

What is cool about the preceding demo is that we have managed to create an impressive-looking dashboard, containing a filter and two reports, without writing a single line of code. Using PerformancePoint Services and the Dashboard Designer, BI experts can construct some really neat and exciting reports—the best part is that these dashboards run off live data in the OLAP cube.

Before leaving the demo, I want to demonstrate all the PerformancePoint content stored in the SharePoint BI Center site collection…

36. Navigate to the root of the BI Center site collection.

37. Click the Site Actions menu, select View All Site Content menu item.

38. Scroll down the page and click the PerformancePoint Content library.

Figure 8-11 shows the library in my environment, with all the FCOs we created in the demo.

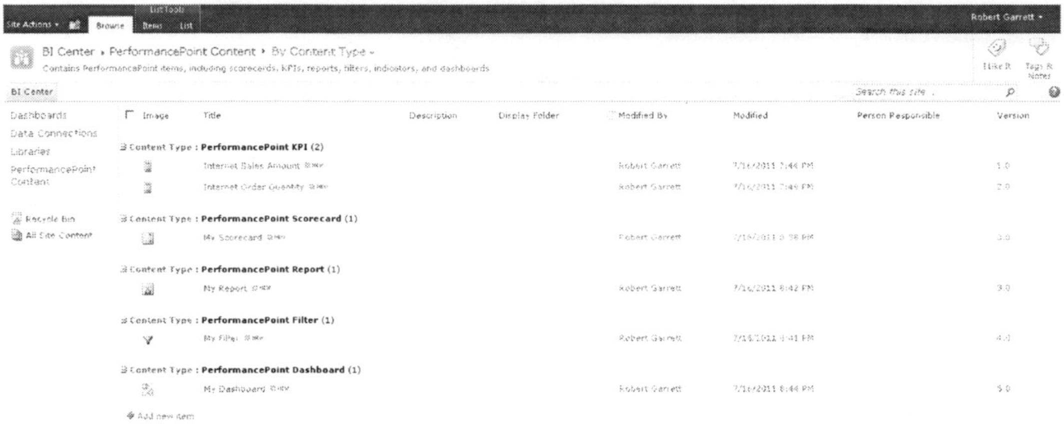

Figure 8-11. FCOs in the SharePoint PerformancePoint Content library

User Permissions in PPS

Like most other areas in SharePoint 2010, PPS requires certain user permissions to perform typical BI tasks. Table 8-3 summarizes these permissions for viewing and creation tasks for Business Intelligence using SharePoint 2010 and the Dashboard Designer.

Table 8-3. User Permissions for PerformancePoint Services 2010

Task Description	User Permission Required in SharePoint 2010
View dashboards.	Read
Create dashboard items and save them in SharePoint 2010.	Contribute
Publish new dashboards from the Dashboard Designer.	Design
Manage user permissions.	Full Control

Deploying to Production

The steps in the previous section, to create a series of reports, filter, and dashboard, are all very well when working in a development environment, but how would you deploy the same business intelligence to production? Aside from site collection backup/restore, which ensures that all site content comes across, the Dashboard Designer provides an approach for deploying the same BI components and dashboards to an environment different from that of the development environment.

Before proceeding with the following steps, you should be aware of three points of note when deploying BI components to another environment:

- Both source and destination SharePoint 2010 farms must have *exactly* the same version number; if one farm differs from another the import will likely have issues with compatibility.

- Make sure you deploy all dependencies with the FCOs (such as Data Connections); failure to do so will result in your dashboards failing in the destination environment.

- If the Dashboard Designer encounters an FCO or Data Connection of the same name in the destination to that of the source, prior to import, the import process will overwrite the version in the destination. This is sometimes desirable for updating an older version of FCOs, but not always the case if the destination contains a completely different FCO of the same name.

With those contingencies noted, let us proceed:

1. Open up the Dashboard Designer from the production BI Center (see the "Installing the Dashboard Designer" section in this).

2. From the Home tab, click the Import Items icon.

3. Navigate to the DDWX file that you created in your development environment to create the initial BI components and dashboards.

4. The file contains references to the development BI Center site collection, so the Dashboard Designer will know how to import the items.

5. When the wizard opens, configure the mapping of importing items to destination locations in the production farm.

6. Decide if you wish to import data sources that already exist in the destination, in which case the Dashboard Designer will replace them, and also decide on importing dependencies (usually a good idea).

7. Click the Next button and SharePoint will provide an import summary once the import completes.

8. Check the checkbox if you want the imported items added to the current open workspace in the Dashboard Designer; otherwise, they just import to the new SharePoint environment only once you click the Finish button.

9. Click the Finish button to complete the import process.

Importing PerformancePoint Server 2007 Content

Users of PerformancePoint Server will be happy to know that Microsoft has not left them out in the cold, and they can import all of their business intelligence content into the new PerformancePoint Services infrastructure, within SharePoint 2010.

Although SharePoint 2010 provides a nice wizard to assist you in importing PerformancePoint Server 2007 content into PPS, administrators should understand various factors that may impact the success in moving the content to SharePoint 2010 PPS.

- **Supported FCOs**: PPS 2010 does not support all of the report types from PPS2007, such as Trend Analysis Charts, Spreadsheets, and Pivot Charts.

- **User Security**: Unlike PPS 2007, local server administrators do not automatically have access to PPS 2010 and permission to upgrade content; you must ensure that the user performing the import is an administrator of the PPS2010 Service Application. In general, the security model of PPS 2010 bases on the SharePoint 2010 security model, whereas PPS 2007 handles its own security model

The following series of steps demonstrates how to import PPS 2007 content into PPS 2010, using the wizard in Central Admin.

1. Open Central Admin.

2. Click the Manage Service Applications link, under the Application Management heading.

3. Scroll to find the PerformancePoint Services application.

4. Click to the right of the application name, and then click the Manage icon on the Ribbon.

5. Click the Import PerformancePoint Server 2007 Content link.

6. SharePoint displays an information page, which is the start of the import wizard.

7. Click the Next button.

8. Provide the security mode (Figure 8-12), as currently configured in your PPS2007 web configurations file—`c:\program files\Microsoft Office PerformancePoint Server\3.0\Monitoring\PPSMonitoring_1\WebService\web.config`.

How was security configured on the original server?　　　　　　　　　Step 1 of 6

For data sources to work correctly, the authentication method used on the
original server must be copied to the data sources being imported.

In PerformancePoint 2007, this was set in the **web.config** file, and applied to
the entire server.

⦿ Default authentication

A single shared user account was used to access all data sources.

◯ Per-user identity *(requires Kerberos Delegation)*

Each user's own account is used to access all datasources.

In the **web.config** files, the **Bpm.ServerConnectionPerUser** property
was set to **True.**

Note: to use this authentication method, a domain administrator must
configure Kerberos Delegation between all instances of the
PerformancePoint Service Application and the data source servers.

◯ Default authentication with user name in connection string

A single shared user account was used to access all data sources, and the
"CustomData" connection string property was used to send the user name.

In the **web.config** files, the **Bpm.UseASCustomData** property was set to
True.

[　　　　Next　　　　]　　[　　　　Cancel　　　　]

Figure 8-12. Security mode in the PPS2007 Import Wizard

9. Click the Next button.

10. Provide connection and credential settings for your PPS2007 instance on SQL
Server, and click Next.

11. Choose the database to import; the default is PPSMonitoring. Click the Next
button.

12. The last wizard page before import is a summary page, and you may click the
Back button to go back to any of the previous pages to make corrections. Once
you click the Import button, you may not interrupt the import process.

13. SharePoint 2010 then shows you a status page with what was imported; check
for any errors. You may click the View List and View Library link to see what
data SharePoint imported. Click the Finish button to exit the import process.

Business Connectivity Services

Business Connectivity Services replaces the legacy Business Data Catalog from SharePoint 2007. BCS
allows administrators to configure external data sources or Line of Business data connectors from
almost any source outside SharePoint 2010. BCS then allows users of SharePoint to interact with external
data via *external content lists,* which for all intended purposes look and behave just like any other
SharePoint list, from the end-user standpoint. This new capability is a major improvement over the BDC
approach of complicated web parts to render external data.

BCS components are packaged with SharePoint 2010 Foundation and allow administrators to configure *external content types* (ECTs) when referencing external data types. These ECTs then shape the data exposed to users via external data lists. Administrators and developers may define ECTs via SharePoint Designer or Visual Studio 2010. By writing them in code, developers have almost limitless capability in exposing external data in SharePoint as long as they can query the external data source via some form of code API.

The following list is an overview of some of the enhancements that BCS brings to the table in SharePoint 2010:

- **True integration:** Users view all external data like SharePoint. SharePoint abstracts the end user from the external data.

- **Read/Write:** Whereas BDC only allowed read-only view of data, BCS allows write-back. Users can make changes to data in external data lists, and BCS will update the external data source.

- **Office Application Integration:** Since external data is surfaced via SharePoint lists, any Office application that understands SharePoint list technology may query the external data. Developers may access external data via the same API they would use to open any standard list in SharePoint.

- **Offline Data:** BCS caches data in SharePoint, so if the external data source goes offline, as soon as it is back online any changes sync back to the source.

- **Support for BLOBs:** Unlike BDC, BCS supports source content in the form of Binary Objects (BLOBs).

- **Extensive security control:** BCS provides greater security over data pulled into SharePoint, as well as the various authentication methods required to access external data sources.

Although BCS integrates in the core platform of SharePoint 2010 Foundation, some of the inherent features built atop of BCS are only available in SharePoint Server 2010, as listed in Table 8-4.

Table 8-4. BCS Capability in Foundation and Server

Functionality	Description	Platform
Core BCS	Provides external source data integration into SharePoint 2010.	Foundation
External Lists and External Content Types	Provides the display and categorization of external data via BCS.	Foundation
BCS Connectors	Logic that connects to an external data source. Developers may create their own, and SharePoint 2010 provides a selection of common BCS connectors.	Foundation
Connector Framework	Allows developers to create their own connectors.	Foundation
Search	Indexes external data and includes it in search results.	Server (Standard)

Functionality	Description	Platform
Secure Store Service	Retains a repository of credentials to several external data sources.	Server (Standard)
User Profiles	Includes external data references in user profiles.	Server (Standard)
Rich Client Integration	External data integrates into Office applications, like Outlook and Word.	Server (Enterprise)

BCS Service Installation

Like most architecture components in SharePoint 2010, BCS operates as a service application. In the full server version of SharePoint 2010, BCS makes use of the Secure Store Service. I explained how to install the SSS earlier in this chapter, as part of the PerformancePoint Server installation. The following steps demonstrate how to create a new BCS service application (assuming it is not already installed and operational).

1. Open Central Admin.

2. Click the Manage Services On Server link, under the System Settings heading.

3. Make sure the Business Data Connectivity Service is started on your application server.

4. Navigate back to the Central Admin home page.

5. Click the Manage Service Applications link, under the Application Management heading.

6. Scroll down the list to verify that no BCS application exists.

7. Click the New icon in the Ribbon.

8. Choose the Business Data Connectivity Service menu item.

9. In the dialog that appears, provide a name for the new BCS service application.

10. Provide the SQL server name and the name of the BCS database.

11. Provide a new application pool for the BCS application.

12. Click the OK button to create the service application.

13. After SharePoint tells you that the service application was created without problem, click the OK button to close the dialog.

14. Click to the right of the name of the new BCS service application, and then click the Manage icon from the Ribbon.

15. Confirm that BCS shows a page of empty connections and a search box (Figure 8-13).

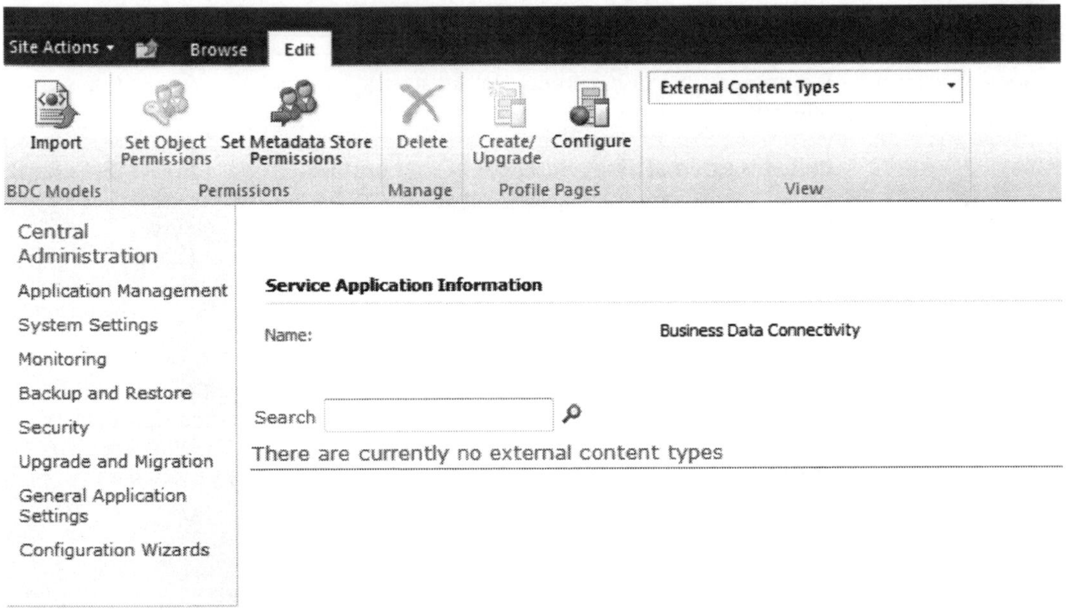

Figure 8-13. The Manage page for BCS

With the BCS service application and the Secure Store Service configured, the next sections take you on a tour of configuring external content within SharePoint 2010, starting with defining an external content type (ECT).

Creating an External Content Type

In this section, I will demonstrate defining an external content type (ECT), using SharePoint Designer 2010. Developers may create ECTs in code, using Visual Studio 2010. Since this is an administration book, I will leave the development aspect to a book on SharePoint 2010 development.

Before we start, ensure that you have a copy of SharePoint 2010 installed on either the application server of your farm or a computer that can access your SharePoint 2010 farm and your SQL Server. Also, install the Adventure Works databases—details at the following link:
http://msftdbprodsamples.codeplex.com/

1. Open SharePoint Designer 2010 (SPD).

2. Open the SharePoint 2010 site collection (click the Open Site button and supply the site URL), where we are going to create an external content type.

3. From the left Navigation pane, under Site Objects, click the External Content Types item.

4. SPD will show any ECTs defined for your site in the right main pane.

5. In the New group of the Ribbon, click the External Content Type icon.

6. SPD shows a page like that in Figure 8-14, in the main pane that allows you to configure your ECT.

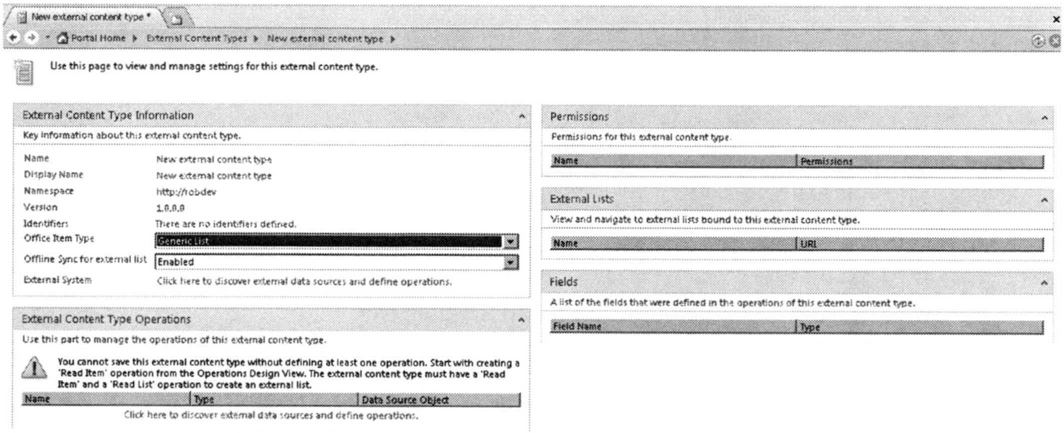

Figure 8-14. Configuring an ECT in SharePoint Designer

7. Click the New External Content Type name to change the name.

8. Click the Click Here to Discover External Data Sources and Define Operations link to open the Operation Designer.

9. Click the Add Connection button to create a new connection to our external data source. In the External Data Source Type popup, select SQL Server. Notice that you can connect using a defined .NET connector or WCF service also.

10. Provide the name of your SQL Server and the name of the AdventureWorks database, and then decide on the security type (I chose the User Identity for this demonstration):

    •   **User's Identity:** Connect to the data source as the user in context, accessing the external data source from SharePoint (pass-through)

    •   **Impersonated Windows Identity:** The identity of another windows user; provide the Secure Store ID of the Windows user.

    •   **Impersonated Custom Identity**: Provide the Secure Store ID of the custom user.

11. Expand the connection to show Tables, Views, and Routines; then expand Tables and right-click one of the tables we will use to create our ECT; I chose the Employee table.

12. You have the option of the various CRUD (Create, Read, Update, and Delete) operations you can create on the data source; I chose to create all operations.

13. A dialog opens; click the Next button, and then select the columns for the ECT (see Figure 8-15).

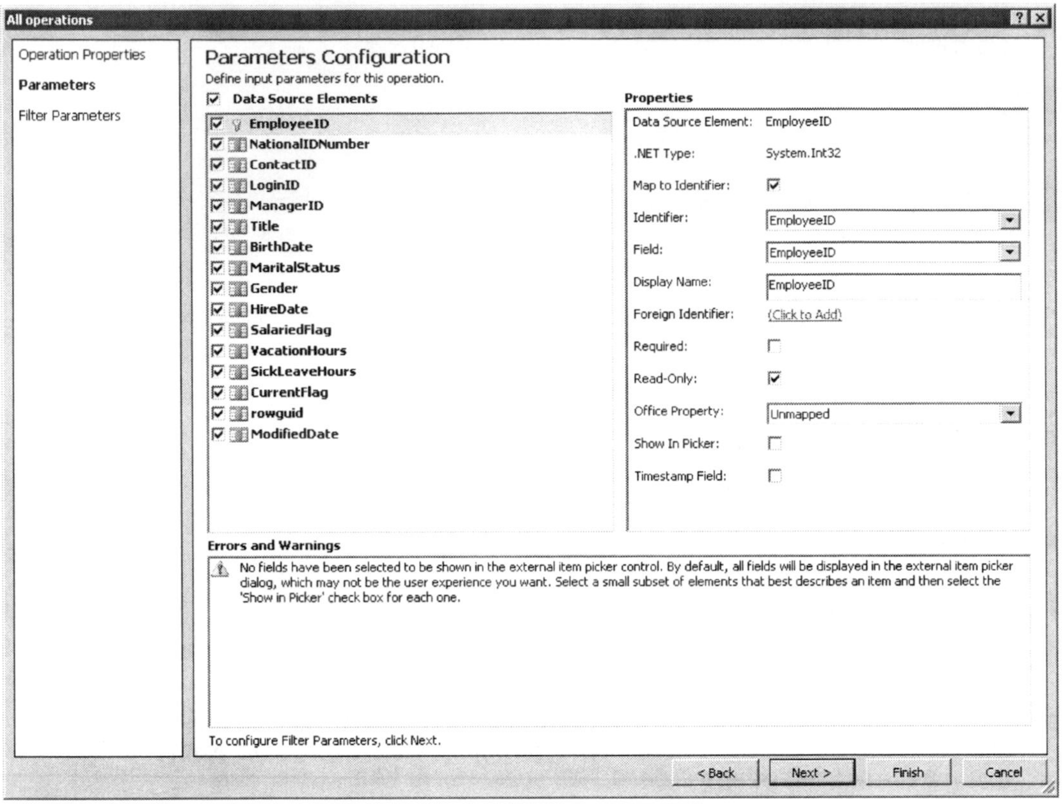

Figure 8-15: Choose fields for the ECT from the Data Source.

14. Click the Next button. In the next dialog you may supply data filters, demonstrated in the following steps.

15. Click the Add Filter Parameter button.

16. Change the Data Source Element to VacationHours (or your choice of field to filter).

17. Click the Click to Add link, and give the filter a name.

18. Leave the default values for the operator, and click OK.

19. Provide the Default Value as 0; my filter will list all employees that have not taken any vacation.

We will now add a row limit—a good idea for read operations:

20. Click the Add Filter Parameter button.

21. Click the Click to Add link, and give the filter a name.

22. Change the Filter Type to Limit, and click OK.

23. Provide the Default Value as 500.

24. Click the Finish button when done.

SPD updates the External Content Type page to appear as in Figure 8-16.

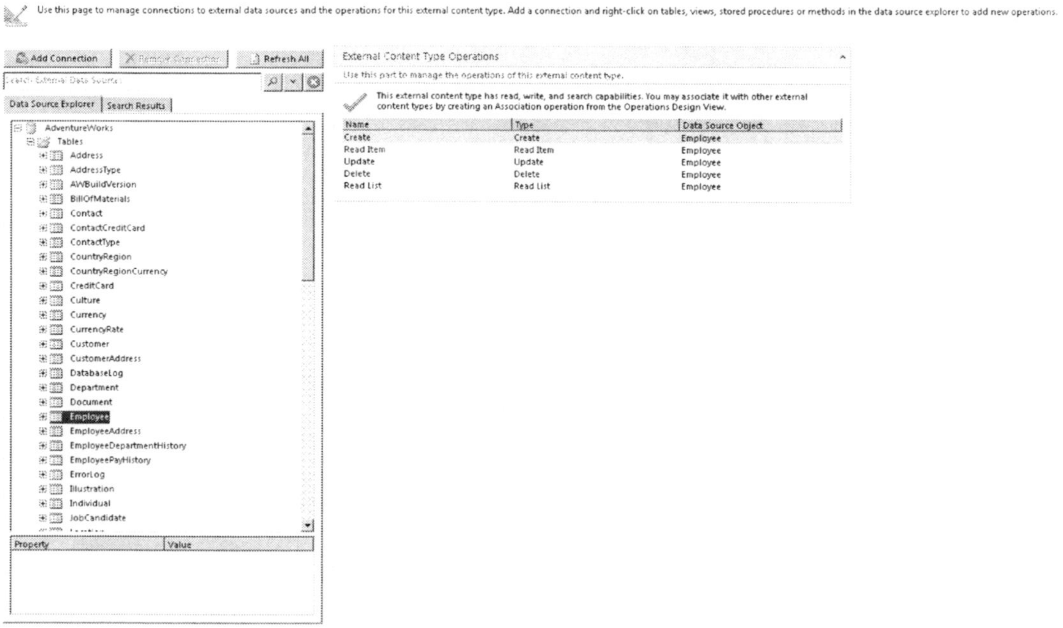

Figure 8-16. Updated External Content Type page in SPD

25. Click the Save icon (the floppy disk) on the very top title bar of SPD, to save our ECT to the site.

26. Open Central Admin.

27. Click the Manage Service Applications link, under Application Management heading.

28. Scroll to the BCS application, click to the right of the title, and then click the Manage icon from the Ribbon to see the BCS Management page.

29. You should see your new ECT in the list; click the name to view its details (see Figure 8-17).

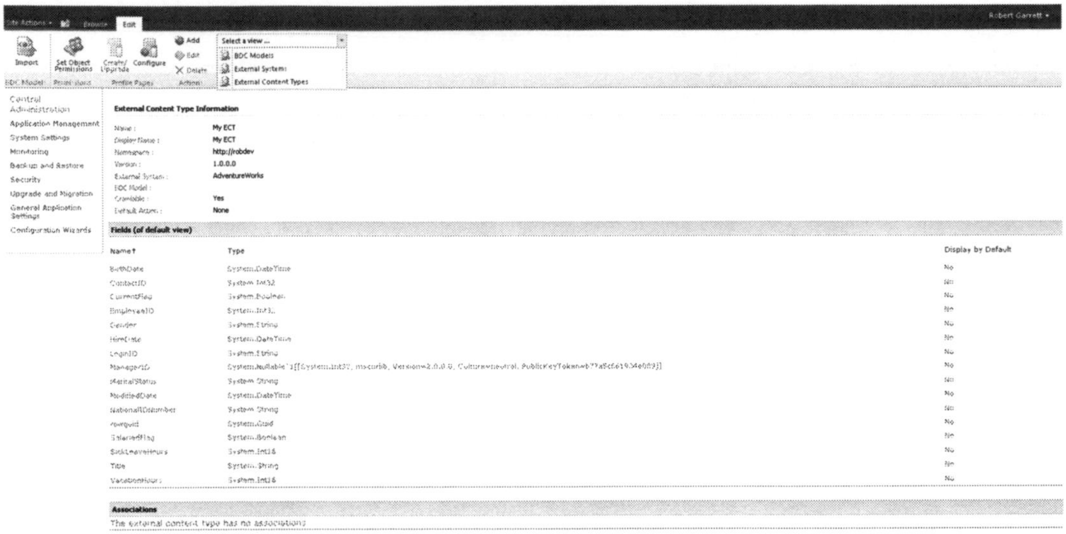

Figure 8-17. ECT Page in the BCS Service Application page

30. Ensure that the page has the Edit tab selected, and then select BDC Metadata from the View drop-down box.

SharePoint 2010 and BCS has done all the heavy lifting and created a BDC XML model, which administrators had to create by hand in SharePoint 2007.

31. Click the BDC model drop-down (if you have more than one, find the model for the ECT you just created).

32. Choose the Export BDC Model menu item.

33. Leave the options on the next page at their defaults, click the Export button, and save the file.

34. Open the file in Notepad—it's an XML file—to view.

In the next section of this chapter, I will demonstrate how to create an external list, using the ECT, we just created.

Creating an External List

If you followed the steps in the previous section, you should have an external content type, pointing to a table in the Adventure Works database in your SQL Server. I created an ECT called "My CT" and configured it around the Employee table. In that procedure, I also added a row limit filter of 500 items and a filter to select only employees with zero vacation hours. With our ECT configured, I will now demonstrate how to create an external list, so that users may interact with the Adventure Works data from the SharePoint UI.

1. Navigate to the SharePoint site collection to host the external list.

2. Click the Site Actions button, and then choose View All Site Content.

3. Click the Create button. SharePoint launches a dialog to create new content.

4. Filter by List and Data, and then choose an External List.

5. Click the Create button.

6. Give your external list a name and description.

7. In the Data Source Configuration section, click the far right icon to choose an ECT. In the dialog that appears, click the ECT we created in the previous section, and then click OK.

8. Click the Create button.

SharePoint 2010 shows you the page of the External List with data populated from the external table in SQL, as in Figure 8-18.

9. If you instead see Access Denied, then you may need to grant permissions to your current user to the ECT. See the following steps: Open Central Admin.

10. Click the Manage Service Applications link, under Application Management.

11. Scroll to the BCS application, click to the right of the title, and then click the Manage icon from the Ribbon to see the BCS Management page.

12. Find the ECT, click drop-down and select the Set Permissions menu item.

13. In the dialog that appears, give the user or group of users permissions to the ECT.

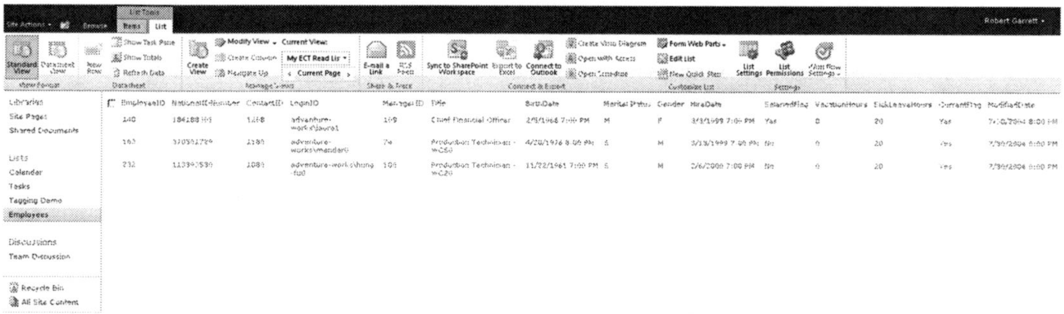

Figure 8-18. *An external list*

In Figure 8-18, you can see that the list looks identical to any other list in SharePoint. Try changing some of the data values in the list and adding new list items. Then head over to SQL Server to see the changes reflected in the database.

Visio Services

Visio Services exist as another service application in SharePoint 2010 and allow users to view Visio drawings in SharePoint 2010 sites, without needing the Visio Office Application installed locally.

Visio Services are not just about providing a view of Visio diagrams in the browser. With this service application installed, users can create Visio diagrams that map to live data in lists. I will cover the specifics of this use of Visio Services later in this section. I detail the configuration of the Visio Graphics Service and promoting Visio Drawings to SharePoint 2010 shortly.

First, we will make sure we have the Visio Service Application installed in our farm.

1. Open Central Admin.

2. Click the Manage Services On Server link.

3. Ensure that the Visio Graphics Service started on one of the servers in your farm, most likely your application server.

4. Navigate back to the home page of Central Admin.

5. Click the Manage Service Applications link, under the Application Management header.

6. Scroll down the list and look for a Visio Services application. If it is not present, then proceed with the following steps.

7. Click the New icon from the Ribbon, and select the Visio Graphics Service from the menu.

8. Give the service a name and configure the application pool. You may also choose to include the proxy in the farm default proxy group.

9. Click the OK button to complete the configuration.

Next, I will demonstrate promoting a Visio diagram to SharePoint 2010 and then rendering it in the browser:

10. Open Visio 2010 and create a drawing.

11. Click the File tab from the Ribbon.

12. Click Save & Send on the left navigation pane.

13. Click the Save to SharePoint button.

14. Change the File Type as a Visio Web Drawing and then click the Save As button.

Visio shows a Save-As dialog.

15. Provide the URL of your document library in SharePoint, and leave the checkbox "Automatically View Files In Browser" checked.

16. Provide a filename and click the Save button.

17. Visio will ask you to select the content type, based on those available in the document library (I chose Document).

18. Click the OK button.

SharePoint 2010 launches in your browser, showing your published diagram in Visio Services (see Figure 8-19).

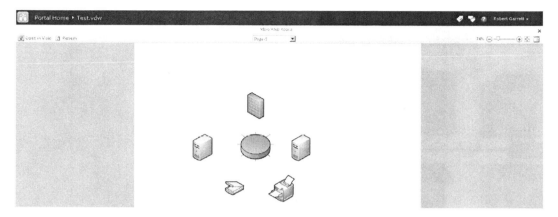

Figure 8-19. A Visio diagram in Visio Services

Creating Visio Drawings from Task and Issues Lists

If you have Visio Professional or Premium 2010 installed, you can take advantage of Visio Services to create Visio drawings from Task and Issues lists in SharePoint 2010. SharePoint 2010 will create drawings that show task flow and contain live references to the data in the SharePoint source list.

1. Create a simple task list in your SharePoint 2010 site collection (see Chapter 2 on creating lists).

2. Add some entries to the task list, and then open the default view.

3. From the Ribbon, click the List tab, and then in the Connect & Export section of the Ribbon, click the Create Visio Diagram icon.

■ **Note** If SharePoint has the icon disabled, check that the Visio Graphics Service is running and the Service Application created. In addition, Visio Services requires a SharePoint Enterprise license enabled in the farm.

---

4. Your browser may pop up a confirmation about opening Visio; click the OK button.

Visio opens with a diagram loaded in three tabs, similar to Figures 8-20, 8-21, and 8-22.

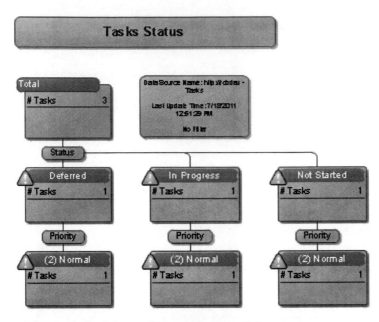

Figure 8-20. *Task Status diagram in Visio 2010*

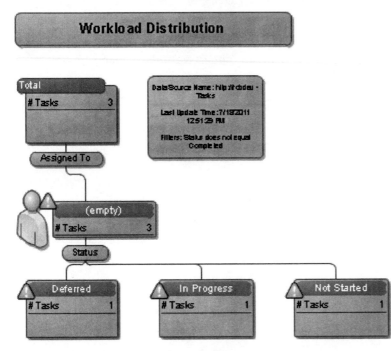

Figure 8-21. *Workload Distribution diagram in Visio 2010*

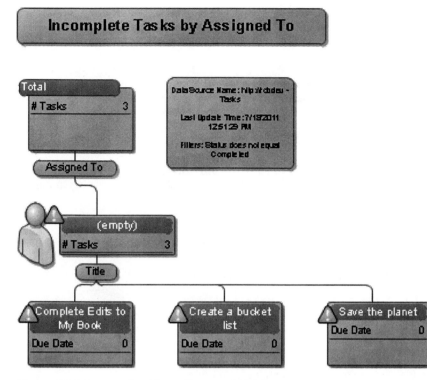

Figure 8-22. Incomplete Tasks diagram in Visio 2010

The diagrams are static, so we need to tell Visio to link the diagrams back to the source lists in SharePoint.

5. From Visio, click the Data tab and then click the Link Data to Shapes icon.

6. In the dialog that appears, change the setting to Microsoft SharePoint Foundation List, and then click the Next button.

7. Provide the URL of the Site in SharePoint that contains the source list, and click Next.

8. Select the List name, specify if the List is a View, and click Next.

9. Click the Finish button. SharePoint shows the list items at the bottom of the diagram where you may drag the items to shapes in the diagram.

Rather than map list items manually, we can ask Visio to perform this task automatically.

10. Click the Data tab, and then click the Automatically Link icon.

11. Choose the option for all shapes (or selected if you have preselected shapes you wish to link), and click Next.

12. The next dialog displayed allows you to map properties of the shapes with the columns in the list. By default Visio shows the ID column and property pair, which is a good choice, since ID fields are unique.

13. Click Next, and then Finish.

14. Follow the steps earlier to promote the diagram to a SharePoint document library, and now you have a diagram in SharePoint that links to live data in the tasks/issue list.

Utilizing the Visio Web Part

The steps in previous two sections demonstrate how to create a dynamic and interactive Visio diagram that links to live data in a task list. In this section, I will demonstrate going a little further in showing the web diagram in a Visio Web Part and configuring connections to filter task list data.

1. Open the site to a standard wiki or web part page.

2. Edit the page. Click on one of the web part zones or rich text areas and add the Tasks list.

3. Add the Visio Web Access web part (from the Business Data folder).

4. Click the Click Here To Open The Tool Pane link in the Visio Web Access web part.

5. Click the browse (ellipses) icon next to the Web Drawing URL text box, and then browse to the document library containing the published Visio drawing.

6. In the text box labeled "Expose the following shape data items to web part connections," enter **ID**.

7. Click the OK button at the bottom of the web part properties tool pane.

8. Click the drop-down arrow on the right side of the web part title bar, click Edit Web Part, and then click the drop-down arrow again and select Connections (see Figure 8-23).

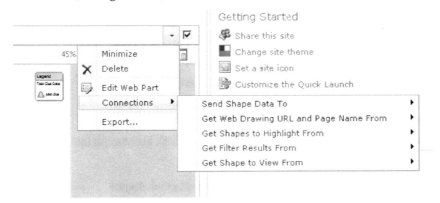

Figure 8-23. The Connections option in the Visio Web Access web part

9. Choose the Send Shape Data To option and then the Tasks list web part.

10. SharePoint displays a dialog. Choose the Get Filter Results From, and then click the Configure button.

11. Set the Shape ID to ID, and click the Finish button.

12. Click the OK button on the web part tool pane, and save the page.

13. From the displayed Visio diagram, select the Workload Distribution diagram and then click Assignee to see the list of tasks filtered by assignee.

Excel Services

If you have read the earlier sections of this chapter (and hopefully the previous chapters of this book), it should be no surprise to you by now that Excel Services is yet another service in SharePoint 2010, exposed as a managed application service (see Chapter 2). Just like the configuration of PerformancePoint Services, Business Connectivity Service, Visio Services, and so on, Excel Services requires configuration of a service in the farm and a service application/proxy to expose the functionality in the farm. The following steps start with the configuration of such service and service application.

1. Open Central Admin.

2. Click the Manage Services On Server link.

3. Ensure that the Excel Calculation Service started on one of the servers in your farm, most likely your application server.

4. Navigate back to the home page of Central Admin.

5. Click the Manage Service Applications link, under the Application Management header.

6. Scroll down the list and look for an Excel Services application. If it is not present, then proceed with the following steps.

7. Click the New icon from the Ribbon, and select the Excel Services Application from the menu.

8. Give the service a name and configure the application pool. You may also choose to include the proxy in the farm default proxy group.

9. Click OK to complete the configuration.

With Excel Services configured in the farm, it is now time to demonstrate creating a simple Excel Services dashboard. Of course, when it comes to dashboards, PerformancePoint Services provides a greater level of sophistication, but if you are looking for simple hosting of Excel sheets and pivot tables, the Excel Service may suffice.

Creating a Simple Dashboard in Excel Services

The following steps details creating a simple dashboard, hosted in SharePoint 2010, originating from data stored in an Excel sheet. Excel Services, like Visio Services, allows users to host sheets and workbooks in SharePoint 2010, without requiring the client to have the full-blown Excel application on their desktop. However, Excel Services is much more than a lightweight Excel sheet-rendering application. Administrators can couple Excel Services to external data, using BCS and the Secure Store Service to render live data. I'll demonstrate a simple dashboard by creating an Excel sheet in the Office application, importing live data from SQL Server, and then promoting it to SharePoint 2010.

■ **Note** The following demonstration requires the Adventure Works sample databases, available for download at `http://msftdbprodsamples.codeplex.com/`.

---

1. Open Excel 2010.

2. Click the Data tab, and then click the From Other Sources icon in the Ribbon to import data into Excel.

3. I chose to import SQL Server data, and from the Employee table in my Adventure Works database. Follow the instructions in the wizard—most of the steps are straightforward. Other than providing the name of my SQL Server, database choice, and table name, I left all options default.

4. When finished, ask the wizard to import the data into an empty Excel sheet as a Table at position A1 (See Figure 8-24).

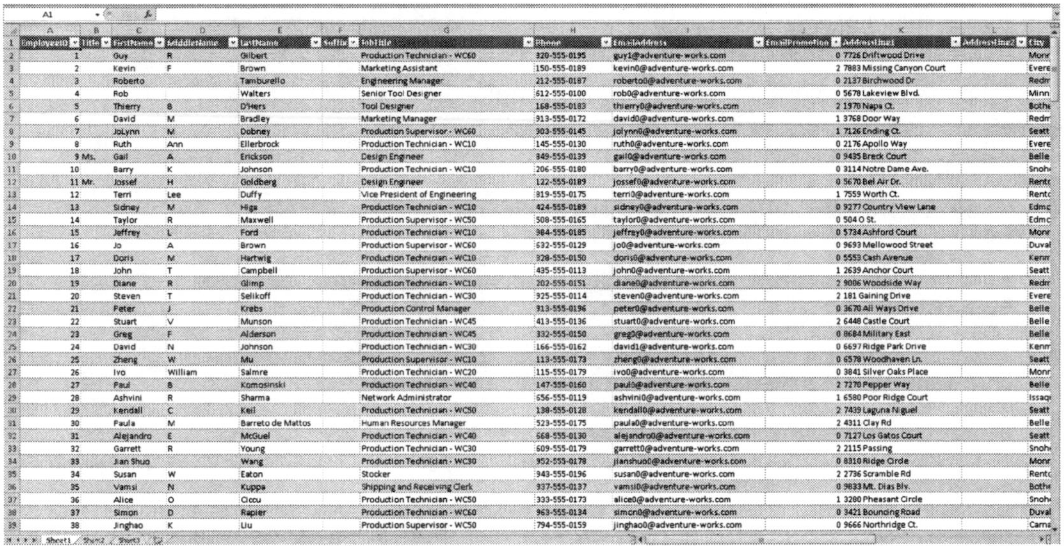

Figure 8-24. Imported data from SQL to Excel

5. Open another sheet in your workbook.

6. In the Data tab, click the Existing Connections icon in the Ribbon.

7. Choose the connection you created a moment ago, and then this time import as a Pivot Chart and Pivot Table Report.

8. Drag the CountryRegionName field to the Report Filter section, and the City to the Row Labels section and Sum Values.

9. Change the filter value to US.

Your pivot table should look something like Figure 8-25.

1	CountryRegionName	United States	
2			
3	**Row Labels**	▼	**Count of City**
4	Bellevue		36
5	Bothell		13
6	Cambridge		1
7	Carnation		5
8	Detroit		1
9	Duluth		1
10	Duvall		10
11	Edmonds		25
12	Everett		18
13	Gold Bar		5
14	Index		5
15	Issaquah		15
16	Kenmore		12
17	Kent		1
18	Memphis		1
19	Minneapolis		1
20	Monroe		14
21	Nevada		1
22	Newport Hills		7
23	Portland		1
24	Redmond		21
25	Renton		17
26	Sammamish		17
27	San Francisco		2
28	Seattle		44
29	Snohomish		10
30	**Grand Total**		**284**
31			

Figure 8-25. *Employees per US City pivot table*

10. Right-click the associated chart and change the type to a line graph, and your graph should look something like Figure 8-26.

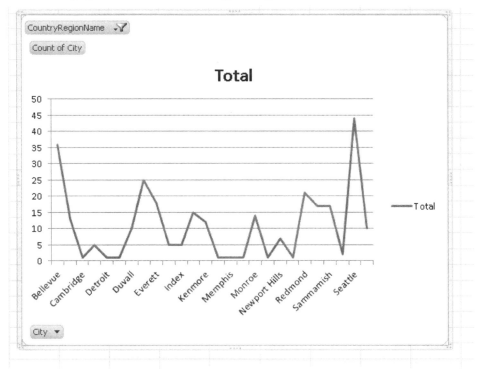

Figure 8-26. *Employees per US City line graph*

11. Click the File tab, and then the Save & Send option from the navigation pane.

12. Click the Save to SharePoint button.

13. In the dialog, provide the URL of the SharePoint document library.

14. Give the workbook a name.

15. Make sure the Open Workbook In Browser checkbox is checked.

16. Click the Save button, after choosing the content type and clicking the OK button. SharePoint 2010 opens in your browser, showing the workbook (see Figure 8-27).

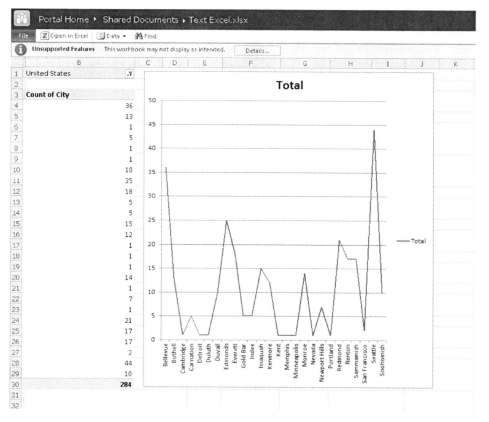

Figure 8-27. An Excel workbook in Excel Services

Summary

In this chapter, we covered a variety of business intelligence topics. Understanding the importance of BI in any modern data-centric organization, and the vast capabilities of BI that SharePoint 2010 provides, I aimed to cover the major topics at a high level.

PerformancePoint Service and the Dashboard Designer are a large and new topic in SharePoint 2010. I demonstrated how to couple PPS 2010 to an OLAP cube in SQL Server Analysis to create an appealing data dashboard in SharePoint 2010, with no code whatsoever.

Also in this chapter, I introduced the reader to Business Connectivity Services and I demonstrated how to create external content types and external lists that host their data in a SQL store.

In the latter part of this chapter, we visited Visio Services and Excel Services to render interactive data (dynamic, not static) in Visio diagrams and Excel Workbooks.

I tried to ensure that the reader of this book grasped a strong hold on the major components of BI in SharePoint 2010, and the administration that SharePoint requires to install and configure these components. I recommend picking up a good book on BI in SharePoint 2010, for those looking for further reading, such as *Pro SharePoint 2010 Business Intelligence Solutions*, by Malik, Sistla, and Wright (Apress, 2010).

CHAPTER 9

Microsoft Office Integration

SharePoint 2010 is a sophisticated web-based information platform, which stands tall alongside many of Microsoft's accomplishments. The SharePoint platform succeeds in being the central storage hub for enterprise and organization data, engages users in collaboration, and integrates external data to facilitate business intelligence in a modern-day organization. However, SharePoint 2010 is not an island, and Microsoft designed the platform to work alongside and integrate with Microsoft Office—one of the most widely used pieces of software installed on office computers today.

In this chapter I will take the reader on a tour of the main Microsoft Office applications (Office Apps for short), and show how they integrate with SharePoint 2010. As in the previous version of SharePoint, Microsoft designed many of the new integration features to work with the latest version of Office—in this case Office 2010. This is not to say that users of Office 2003 and even Office XP cannot integrate with SharePoint 2010, but the feature set and end-user experience are better when working with Office 2010 because Microsoft built Office 2010 applications with SharePoint 2010 integration in mind.

Office 2010 and an Overview of Office 2010 Integration

Pay a visit to any typical corporate or government office today and you are certain to see a number of people in front of computers. Statistically, most of these computers will be running Microsoft Windows, and I would bet you they also have a copy of Microsoft Office installed.

With the exception of software developers, most organization workers use Office applications several times a day. Take Outlook, as an example; despite several rather appealing alternatives, Microsoft Outlook is one of the most popular business applications in use in organizations each day. As another example, Word is the most widely used word processing application, and is the application I chose to write this book.

What are all those users doing with the files that they create from Microsoft Office applications? Sadly, many documents, spreadsheets, presentation decks, diagrams, and so on end up on shared drives (on the network) or embedded in email messages. A typical Microsoft Word document ranges in size from a few kilobytes to megabytes. Now imagine a large Word document floating around the email system—several copies in every recipient's email box, different versions in multiple email messages. Aside from the confusion in ascertaining the most recent version, the IT department has a hard time dealing with Exchange Email boxes that continue to grow over the life of an employee at an organization.

In an earlier chapter, I wrote about the document management features of SharePoint 2010. I demonstrated how SharePoint provides a central location for all documents, to meet the needs of users. This is all good, but how tedious is it if a user working on a masterpiece in Microsoft Word has to exit the application and then remember to upload the document to SharePoint, and what about the nice metadata and categorization of documents in SharePoint? Users would love to access this same metadata in the Office application. Fortunately, Microsoft designed both SharePoint 2010 and Office 2010 applications to communicate with each other.

Users can access SharePoint 2010 features from the comfort of their Office application, and may access their Office application from the web interface of SharePoint 2010. The previous versions of SharePoint 2007 and Office 2003/2007 made similar claims, but honestly, the integration was somewhat half-baked. SharePoint 2010 and Office 2010 go a step further and truly provide seamless integration.

By now, I assume you are familiar with the concept of the SharePoint 2010 Ribbon (see Chapter 1 for an overview). Users of Office 2010 also experience a similar interface— in fact, Office introduced the Ribbon concept first, before SharePoint. Most of Microsoft's newer versions of Office and Office-related products incorporate a Ribbon UI (Figure 9-1) to provide users with contextual access to the vast number of commands available in their applications.

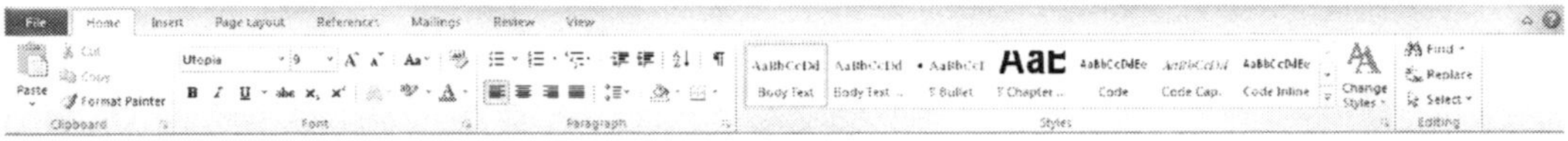

Figure 9-1. *The Ribbon in Microsoft Word*

The Backstage Area

In Figure 9-1, notice the File tab. All Office 2010 applications have this tab, which replaces the legacy File menu of older versions of Office and provides the user to the Backstage area of the application. Clicking the File tab in Microsoft Word shows a page like that in Figure 9-2.

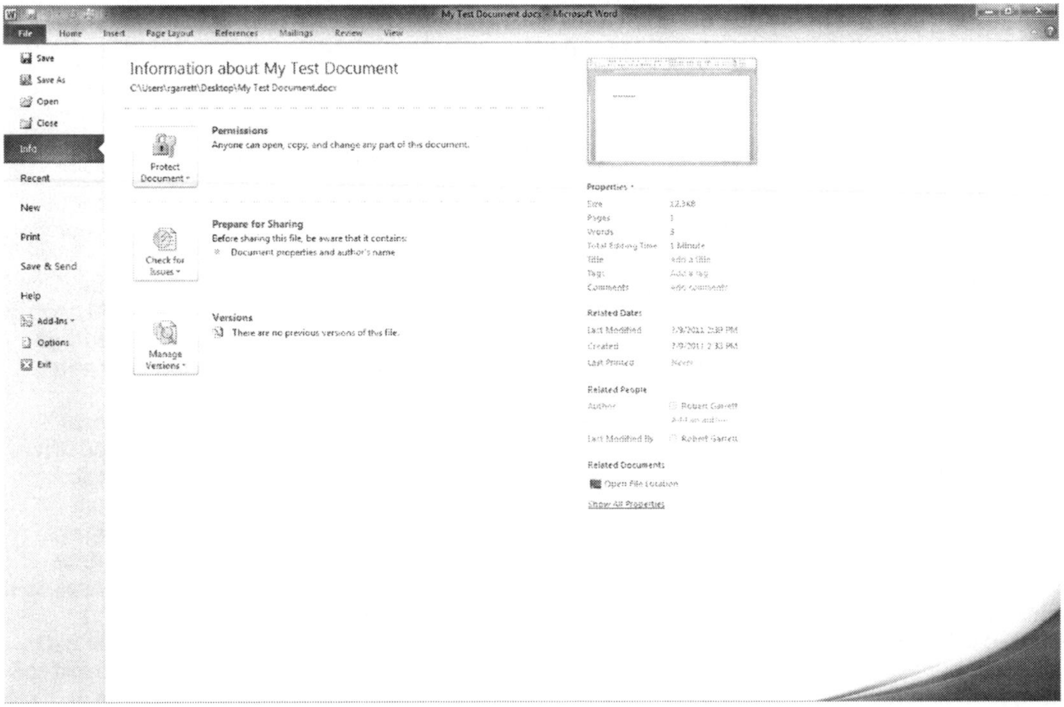

Figure 9-2. *The Backstage page in Microsoft Word 2010*

On the left of the page shown in Figure 9-2, we see the familiar Save, Save-As, Open, and Close options—similar to what we came to expect of the File menu in former versions of Office applications. The Info menu tab provides access to history, permissions, and recent versions. The Recent tab shows all recent documents edited by the application, New shows various templates for creating a new document instance, and Print links to a page for print options for the document. Take a mental note of the Save & Send tab, because we shall visit this page in a moment. The Help item provides help (as you might expect). Toward the bottom of the left navigation of the page are tabs for the Options and Add-on pages, and Exit closes the application.

The middle area of the Backstage page displays operation and action buttons and links for the tab selected on the left. In Figure 9-2, the middle area shows actions for accessing the document permissions, prepare sharing, and access version history, because the Info tab has been selected.

The far-right panel, shown in Figure 9-2, also changes depending on the selected left tab, and currently shows properties of the document, since we have the Info tab selected. Before leaving the Info tab, we shall look at the three buttons:

- The Convert button for Compatibility mode allows authors to convert the document features so that the document may open in the same application in earlier versions of Office (2003, 2007, or both).

- The Permissions button allows the user to protect the document, so other users opening the document may not access or change certain information, as follows:

  - **Mark the document as Final**: Stipulates that editing of the document is complete.

  - **Encrypt with Password:** Requires subsequent users opening this document to provide a password. This option becomes redundant when uploading the document to SharePoint because SharePoint manages access to the document via its own security model. However, if you plan to send this document via email external to your organization, this option provides an added level of security (although weak).

  - **Restrict Editing**: Allows the author of the document to isolate parts of the document for restricted edit by certain users. This feature comes in handy when allowing Live Co-Authoring (discussed later in this chapter).

  - **Restrict Permissions by People:** Makes use of Microsoft Information Rights Management Service: a separate Microsoft product.

  - **Add a Digital Signature**: Adds a digital signature box to the document, used in conjunction with the SharePoint 2010 Collect Signatures workflow, when requiring a signature for the document.

- The Prepare for Sharing button allows the author to inspect the document and check accessibility/compatibility before putting the document out in a shared medium, such as SharePoint.

  - **Inspect Document**: Looks for comments, personal information, and any hidden text. This action comes in handy if you are concerned about damaging comments in Track Changes.

  - **Check Accessibility:** Checks for any content in the document that people with disabilities may not have ability to read.

- **Check Compatibility:** Checks for content in the document that is incompatible with earlier versions of the same Office application (2007, 2003, or both). This option comes in handy when you suspect that the majority of your readers may not have the latest version of Office installed.

- The Manage Versions button allows the author to restore the document to an earlier version. Office attempts to save your document routinely, so in the event of a crash you can go back to a previous version. When your document is sourced from a SharePoint document library, with versioning enabled, this button allows you to maintain versions of the document as stored in the SharePoint document library. The author may check-in, check-out, recover, and delete draft versions, and compare with earlier versions.

Earlier I mentioned we would come back to the Save & Send tab in the Back Stage area. Clicking this tab should show a page like that in Figure 9-3.

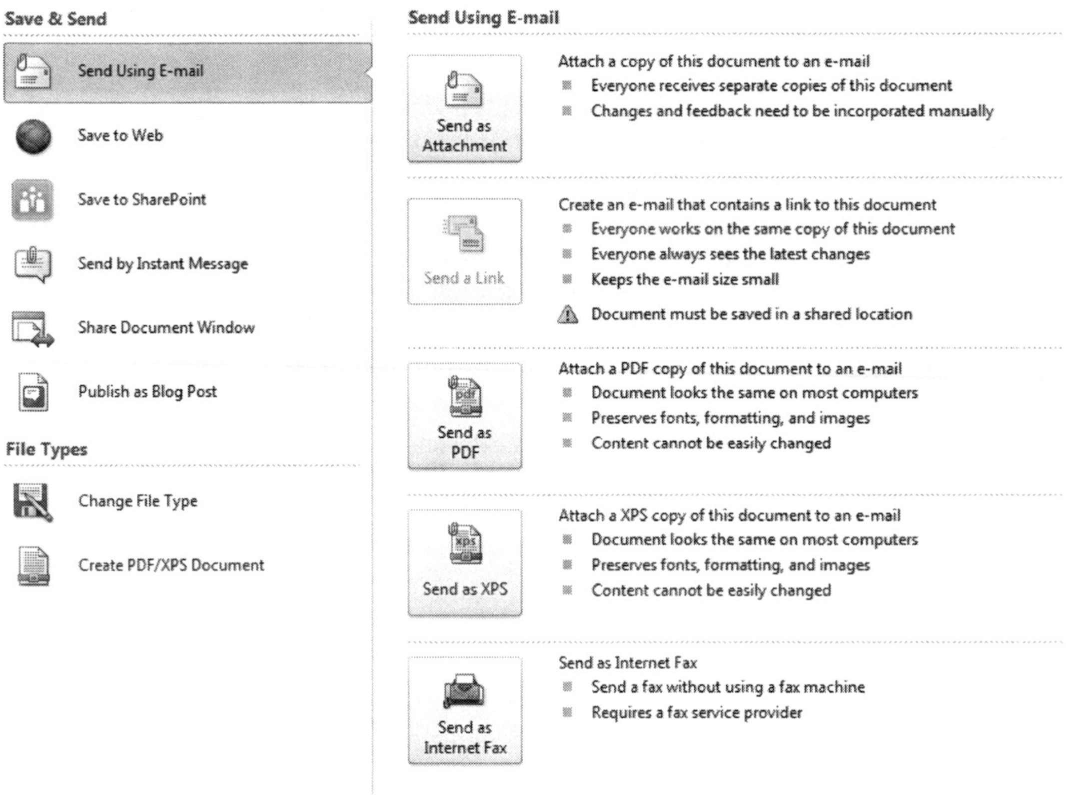

Figure 9-3. *Save & Send actions in Microsoft Word 2010*

- **Send Using E-mail**: Allows the author to send the open document via email to recipients in various formats. The Send a Link option is enabled when the document is sourced from a shared location in SharePoint, and rather than email a copy of the document, recipients receive a hyperlink to the location on SharePoint. At the beginning of this chapter, I mentioned the burden on IT and users when multiple versions and copies of documents float around email. This option goes a step to alleviate this issue because users receive only a small email with a link.

- **Save to Web**: Allows the author to publish the file to a location on the Internet, secured by Live ID.

- **Save to SharePoint:** Allows the author to specify a new SharePoint document library location, or previous location, to save the document. The current user logged into Windows must have Contribute rights to the document library location in SharePoint.

- **Send by Instant Message:** Allows the author to send this document to another user via instant messenger (MS Messenger or Office Communicator).

- **Share Document Window:** If you have Microsoft Live Meeting or MS screen sharing application installed, this operation enables the author to share this document with others.

- **Publish as a Blog Post**: Available only in Microsoft Word, this operation allows the author to post the document to a blog site on SharePoint. Microsoft Word will convert the document so that the text will render as HTML in a SharePoint Blog site.

- **Change File Type:** Allows the author to change the document type to another (for example, Word 2007 to Word 2010 format).

- **Create XPS/PDF:** Allows the author to create a PDF or XPS document, for portability.

- **Workflows:** If sourced from SharePoint in a document library, with workflow enabled, this operation shows the workflows that the author may kick off, such as Parallel Approval.

Live Co-Authoring

Previously, any user wanting to edit a document checked out by another user in SharePoint had to wait until the other user checked the document back in. This situation did not present a big issue in small groups, but when many users collaborated and worked on a large document, checkout on a central document prevented efficient progress.

With the integration of SharePoint 2010, users in Microsoft Word, PowerPoint, and OneNote 2010 may now co-author a document in real time. The following steps demonstrate Live Coauthoring in action:

1. Have User-1 open a Word 2010 document from a SharePoint 2010 document library, and ensure that this user opens the document in Edit mode.

2. Have User-2 open the same document from SharePoint 2010, also in Edit mode.

3. Look to the bottom bar of Microsoft Word 2010 and you should see a small icon, like that in Figure 9-4. You may click this icon to see the users editing the document.

Figure 9-4. *Count of users editing a document in MS Word 2010*

4. Have User-1 enter some text into the document.

5. User-2 receives notification of change, and may refresh the area on their page.

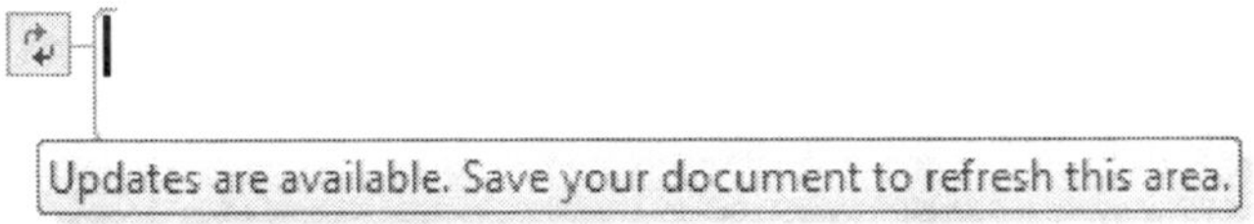

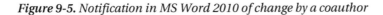

Figure 9-5. *Notification in MS Word 2010 of change by a coauthor*

MS Word will show edits by other users in a different highlighted color; when the document is saved back to SharePoint, Word removes the highlighting.

■ **Note** Co-authoring requires an Office 2010 client or Office Web application. Previous versions of Office do not support co-authoring. See the following URL for more details: `http://technet.microsoft.com/en-us/library/ff718249.aspx#bkmk_sw_version_req`.

Document Information Panel

I mentioned the Document Information Panel (DIP) in Chapter 6, and demonstrated how metadata defined in SharePoint makes its debut in Office Applications. To recap, in this context, metadata is data associated with a document in a SharePoint document library. Metadata exists as site columns (fields) in content types and lists. For example, metadata about a proposal document might consist of the client name and proposal unique identifier.

Microsoft Word, Excel, and PowerPoint 2010 display metadata of documents sourced from SharePoint 2010 via the Document Information Panel (see Figure 9-6).

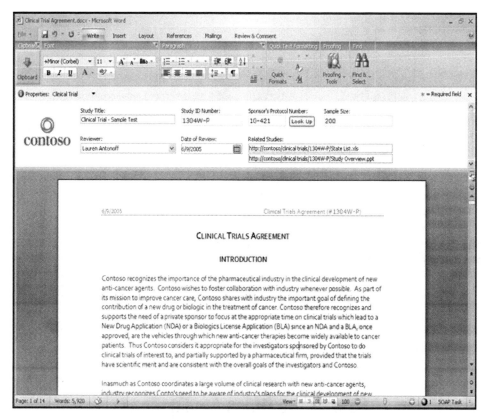

Figure 9-6. The Document Information Panel in Microsoft Word 2010

SharePoint 2010 maintains default settings, per document library, for the DIP for documents of given content types, contained in the document library. The following steps demonstrate accessing these settings and changes administrators may make:

1. Open the document library to the default view.

2. Click the Library tab from the Ribbon, and then click the Library Settings icon from the Ribbon.

3. Click the Advanced Settings link.

4. Ensure that the library allows management of content types.

5. Navigate back to the settings page for the library.

6. Click the name of the content type that classifies documents where we wish to make DIP settings.

7. Click the Document Information Panel Settings link.

SharePoint shows a page like that of Figure 9-7.

Document Information Panel Template

Specify the type of Document Information Panel template to show in Microsoft Office compatible applications.

Note: Creating a custom Document Information Panel template requires Microsoft InfoPath.

☑ Use the default template for Microsoft Office applications

○ Use existing custom template (URL, UNC, or URN)

Edit this template

○ Upload an existing custom template (XSN) to use   Browse...

Create a new custom template

Show Always

Require that the Document Information Panel is displayed automatically for the user under specific conditions.

☐ Always show Document Information Panel on document open and initial save for this content type

OK   Cancel

Figure 9-7. Document Information Panel settings for a document content type

8. The Template section allows you to provide a default document template to use; for example, you may have a proposal document template from which you start all new proposals.

9. Check the checkbox in the Show Always section to ensure that the DIP displays whenever a user opens a document of this content type in the Office application.

■ **Note** Perform the same steps for content types in the site Content Types Gallery if you want to enable DIP settings globally to documents of the content type at the site level.

Integrating SharePoint 2010 with the Office Applications

SharePoint 2010 allows export of most lists and libraries to Office applications. Depending on the list/library type, the Connect & Export section of the Ribbon shows enabled options to export list items to the relevant Office application.

1. Navigate to the default view of any document library.

2. Click the Library tab on the Ribbon.

3. See Figure 9-8 as an example of the Connect & Export section.

Figure 9-8. Connect & Export for a document library

Table 9-1 details the various options available for a given list type.

Table 9-1. *Connect & Export Options for Lists and Libraries*

Export Function	List/Library Type	Description
Sync to SharePoint Workspace	Document Libraries	Synchronizes the current document library with SharePoint Workspace, which is the replacement application for Groove and maintains offline content of documents.
Connect to Office	Lists and Libraries	Creates a favorite link in your own personal list (My Site/User Profile); these links appear in the Backstage area of Office applications.
Connect to Outlook	Document Libraries, Tasks, Contacts, Calendars, Discussion Boards, and External Content Lists	When exporting lists of the available type to Outlook, the list becomes a particular type of folder in Outlook (for example, a Calendar list becomes a Calendar folder in Outlook). Users may read and edit the list items from Outlook.
Export to Excel	Lists and Libraries	Exports all metadata of a list or library to columns and row data in an Excel sheet.
Create Visio Diagram	Tasks	In the previous chapter, I demonstrated exporting tasks as Visio flow diagrams. When exporting a task list, the Visio diagram shows three tabs: Task Status, Workload Distribution, and Incomplete Tasks Assigned.
Open with Access	Lists and Libraries	Opens Microsoft Access and shows the list or library metadata in an Access table. Editing the data in Access updates the list data in real time.
Open Schedule	Tasks	Exports the task list to Microsoft Project.

Thus far, we have seen common and general Office Application integration with SharePoint 2010, both from the Backstage Area of Office and as Export from SharePoint 2010. The following sections of this chapter address the specific areas of Office application integration for each application.

Microsoft Word

In addition to the aforementioned integration features, Microsoft Word works with SharePoint 2010 to allow users to write blog posts, compare versions, and add Quick Parts. The following sections discuss these features.

Writing Blog Posts

Microsoft Word 2007 and 2010 include a template to author blog posts. Microsoft Word works with many blogging engines, not just SharePoint, but since this book is about SharePoint 2010 administration, here I'll focus on creating blog posts for the SharePoint platform.

1. Open Microsoft Word 2010.

2. Click the File tab, and then the left tab item, named New.

3. Select the Blog Post template.

4. Click the Create button.

If you have not registered a blogging service (such as SharePoint 2010), Word will give you the option to do so, with a dialog, as shown in Figure 9-9.

Figure 9-9. Registering a blog account

■ **Note**: You may register new Blogging Service Accounts, at any time, by clicking the Manage Accounts icon in the Blog section of the Ribbon. Then click the New button.

---

5. Click the Register Now button.

6. Change the Blog Provider to SharePoint Blog, and then click the Next button.

7. Enter the URL of the blog site in your SharePoint 2010 site collection.

8. You may click the Picture Options button to configure where Word saves images; by default SharePoint 2010 stores the pictures in the Photos library of the blog site.

9. Click the OK button.

10. After editing the blog post in Word, click the Publish icon on the Ribbon to publish the document to the SharePoint blog.

You may wish to publish a regular Word 2010 document to SharePoint without creating a new blog post document and using copy-and-paste:

11. From an open Word document, click the File tab.

12. Click Save & Send.

13. Click the Publish To Blog Post link.

14. Note: You may launch Word 2010 with a fresh instance of a blog template from within SharePoint 2010 by clicking the Launch Blog Program To Post link.

Compare Versions

Microsoft permits users to manipulate versions of a document opened from a SharePoint 2010 document library, with versioning enabled. The following steps demonstrate how to enable version settings for a document library, and how to compare versions of a document from Microsoft Word 2010.

1. Navigate to the default view of a document library in SharePoint 2010.

2. Click the Library tab in the Ribbon, and then click the Library Settings icon.

3. Click the Versioning Settings link.

4. Under the section Document Versioning History, enable the desired version scheme:

- **Create Major Versions:** Every document version represents a major version; therefore is published for each save or check-in.

- **Create Major and Minor Versions:** Every check-in or save creates a minor version, meaning that the document is in draft mode; users must publish a major version to make the document changes available to other users, which may involve approval workflow.

5. Click the OK button.

6. Navigate back to the default view of the document library.

7. Hover over the name of a document in the document library (click the upload icon on the Ribbon and upload a Word 2010 document if none exists).

8. From the drop-down list, click the Edit in Microsoft Word menu item (you may access the document versions from this same menu).

9. Wait for Microsoft Word 2010 to open.

10. Make some changes to the document.

11. Click the Review tab on the Ribbon in Microsoft Word 2010.

12. Click the Compare icon in the Compare section of the Ribbon.

See Figure 9-10 for the options available.

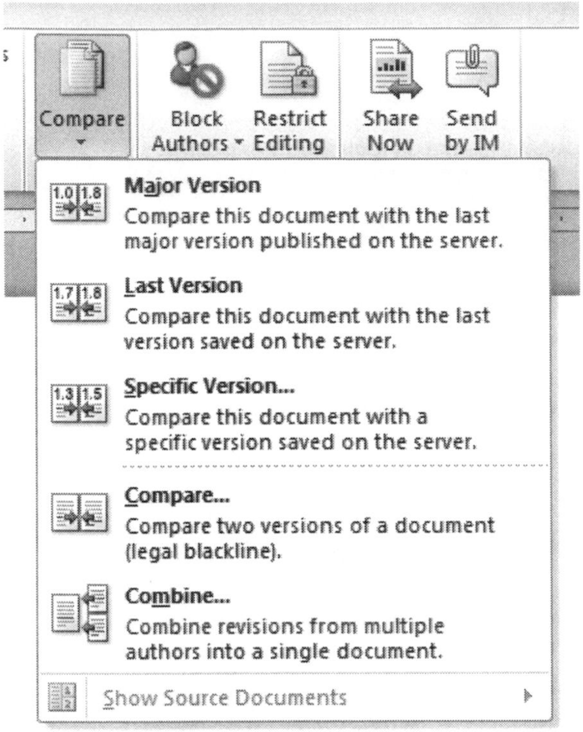

Figure 9-10. Options for comparing document versions in Microsoft Word 2010

Most of the options available in Figure 9-10 are self-explanatory. Users may compare the current open document with another major version, the latest version, or another specific version, and they may combine document versions.

Quick Parts

Microsoft Word documents opened from SharePoint 2010 allow authors to enter Quick Parts, which consist of field values from metadata attached to the document library. The following steps demonstrate adding a Quick Part to our open Word document.

1. Open a Word document from SharePoint 2010; see the previous set of steps.

2. Click the Insert tab on the Ribbon.

3. In the Text section of the Ribbon, click the Quick Parts icon.

4. Select the Document Property menu item, and then select the metadata field from the sub-menu.

Whenever this field value changes in SharePoint the field value changes in the Word document when first opened.

Microsoft Excel

Microsoft Excel does a phenomenal job of managing columns and rows in a sheet. Users can import Excel spreadsheets as custom lists into SharePoint 2010, with the same columns and row data as list items. Users may also reverse the process, exporting existing lists as new Excel sheets.

The following steps demonstrate how to import an existing Excel spreadsheet into SharePoint 2010 as a new custom list. Before starting, ensure that your Excel sheet contains the correct formatting. The first row of the sheet defines the columns (fields) of the new custom list, so make sure to use nice neat and short column names. Start data from row two in the sheet. The first column of the sheet maps to the mandatory Title column in the list, so ensure this contains text data.

▧ **Note** If you have trouble with import and export of Excel data, ensure that your SharePoint site is in the IE browser Trusted Sites Zone or Local Intranet Zone.

---

1. Open the SharePoint 2010 site to import the Excel sheet as a new list.

2. Click the Site Actions menu, and then the More Options menu item.

3. Click the List filter type.

4. Click the Import Spreadsheet list type.

5. Click the Create button.

6. In the next page, provide a name and description, and browse for the XLSX Excel file to import.

7. Click the Import button.

8. Excel 2010 opens with a dialog asking what data to import—Table Range, Range of Cells, or Named Range. I went with Range of Cells and then highlighted the cells in the sheet.

9. Click the Import button on the dialog. After a brief pause, SharePoint will load the page with the default view of the new column.

▧ **Note** SharePoint makes an educated guess about the types of columns to create in SharePoint, based on column formatting and data in the Excel column. For example, ZIP codes may come over as numeric fields unless formatted correctly as text in Excel.

An alternative way to import data into SharePoint 2010 from Excel is as follows:

10. Open Excel and the file to import into SharePoint.

11. Select the cells to import.

12. Click the Format as Table icon from the Home tab Ribbon, and choose a style (it does not matter which you choose).

13. Click the Design tab in the Ribbon.

14. Click the Export icon from the Export Table Data section in the Ribbon.

15. Choose the Export Table Data to SharePoint List menu item.

16. Enter the URL of the destination SharePoint site, in the dialog that appears.

17. Give the list a name and description, and then click Next.

18. Ensure the correct columns and data types in the dialog (see Figure 9-11).

Export Table to SharePoint List - Step 2 of 2

To publish to a SharePoint list, Excel must force columns to use certain recognized data types. All cells with individual formulas will be converted to values.

Verify that each of the columns listed below is associated with the correct data type. If a column is associated with an incorrect data type, click Cancel and confirm that the key cell can be converted to the correct type.

Column	Data Type	Key Cell
Name	Text (single line)	
Address 1	Text (single line)	
Address 2	Text (single line)	
City	Text (single line)	
State	Text (single line)	
ZIP	Number	

Help   Cancel   Back   Next   Finish

Figure 9-11. Export to Excel Table to SharePoint Dialog

19. Click the Finish button.

20. Excel shows a final dialog with export result (hopefully successful) and a link to the new list in SharePoint. Click the link to see the Datasheet view of the new list in your browser.

The following steps demonstrate the reverse of the above—exporting data from an existing SharePoint list to Excel:

21. Navigate to a default view of a list to export to Excel.

22. Click the List tab on the Ribbon, and then the Datasheet View icon (see Figure 9-12 as an example). If this button is disabled, check the settings for the list to make sure Datasheet is permitted, and also check if the site is in either the Trusted Sites Zone or Local Intranet Zone in your browser.

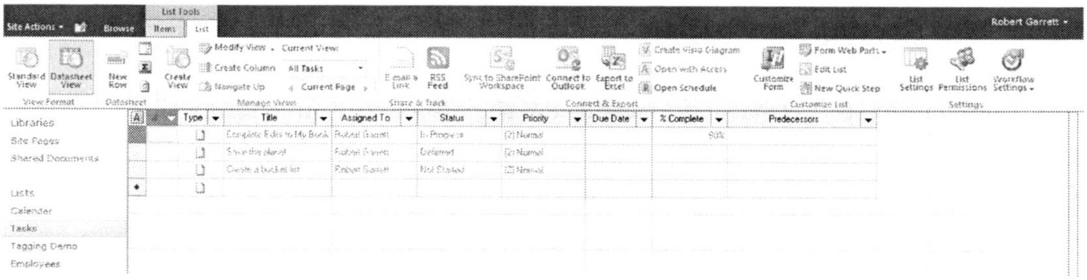

Figure 9-12. *The Datasheet view of a task list*

23. Expand the task pane in the far right of the grid by clicking the thin bar just after the far right cell of the grid.

24. You may click one of the links to export the data as Query List, Pivot Table Report, Chart, and so on.

■ **Note** You might be tempted to click the Export to Excel icon in the Ribbon; this option has the same effect as clicking the Query List with Excel link.

Microsoft PowerPoint

New to SharePoint 2010 and PowerPoint 2010 is Live Coauthoring (see earlier in this chapter). The client/server pair also introduces slide show broadcasting. This feature allows other users viewing the same web broadcast, in SharePoint 2010, to see slide updates as the presenter broadcasts the deck. Think of this feature as a scaled down Live Meeting with a PowerPoint deck.

The following steps demonstrate how to broadcast PowerPoint slides to a SharePoint 2010 broadcast slide show:

1. From an open PowerPoint deck, click the File tab to enter the Backstage area of the application.

2. Click the Save & Send tab on the left.

3. Click the Broadcast Slide Show item, and then click the Broadcast Slide Show button.

4. PowerPoint enables a user to broadcast to a Windows Live Broadcast service, or to a custom broadcast service, such as SharePoint 2010.

5. Click the Change Broadcast Service to change to use SharePoint 2010 (see the next procedure), or Start Broadcast if already configured.

6. PowerPoint provides a link to give to viewers of the broadcast, click Start Slide Show to begin.

The PowerPoint Service Application

The PowerPoint Service Application exists as a specific site collection in a SharePoint 2010 web application. The following steps demonstrate creating this site collection in an existing web application:

1. Open Central Admin.

2. Click the Application Management heading.

3. Click the Create site collections link, under the Site Collections heading.

4. Give the site collection a name, description, and URL suffix—if this is not the root site collection in the web application.

■ **Note** Refer to Chapter 2 for steps to create a new Web Application.

5. In the Template section, click the Enterprise tab, and then select the PowerPoint Broadcast Site template.

■ **Note** The PowerPoint Broadcast site template requires correct installation of Office Web Applications in SharePoint 2010 (see "Office Web Applications" later in this chapter).

6. Choose the site administrators, and then click OK.

7. Once SharePoint 2010 finishes creating the new site collection, visit the new site.

8. Click the People and Groups link in the left navigation pane.

9. Add presenters to the Broadcast Presenters Group, and attendees to the Broadcast Attendees Group. Administrators belong in the Broadcast Administrators group.

From here on, when PowerPoint asks for the URL of the broadcast location, provide the URL of the new site collection you just created.

Slide Libraries

Since the previous version of SharePoint (MOSS 2007), SharePoint has included a Slide Library list type (only available with SharePoint Standard edition). Slide libraries consist of collections of slides, taken from one or many PowerPoint decks. The idea is to collect a repository of popular and commonly used slides for new presentations.

The following steps demonstrate creating a slide library in a SharePoint 2010 site collection.

1. Open your destination site in SharePoint 2010.

2. Click the Site Actions menu.

3. Select the More Options menu item.

4. Click the Library filter on the left.

5. Click Slide Library, and then click the Create button.

▓ **Note** If you do not see the Slide Library Template, make sure you activate the SharePoint Server Standard Features at the site collection level.

---

6. Give the library a name and description, and select whether to display a link on the left navigation and whether to include versioning. Then click the OK button.

Now that we have a slide library, I shall demonstrate how to upload selected slides from a PowerPoint 2010 deck.

7. Open PowerPoint 2010 and a slide deck with a selection of slides.

8. Click the File tab to enter the Backstage area.

9. Click the Save & Send tab on the left, and then the Publish Slides link.

10. Click the large Publish Slides button, and PowerPoint then displays a dialog asking you which slides to publish (See Figure 9-13).

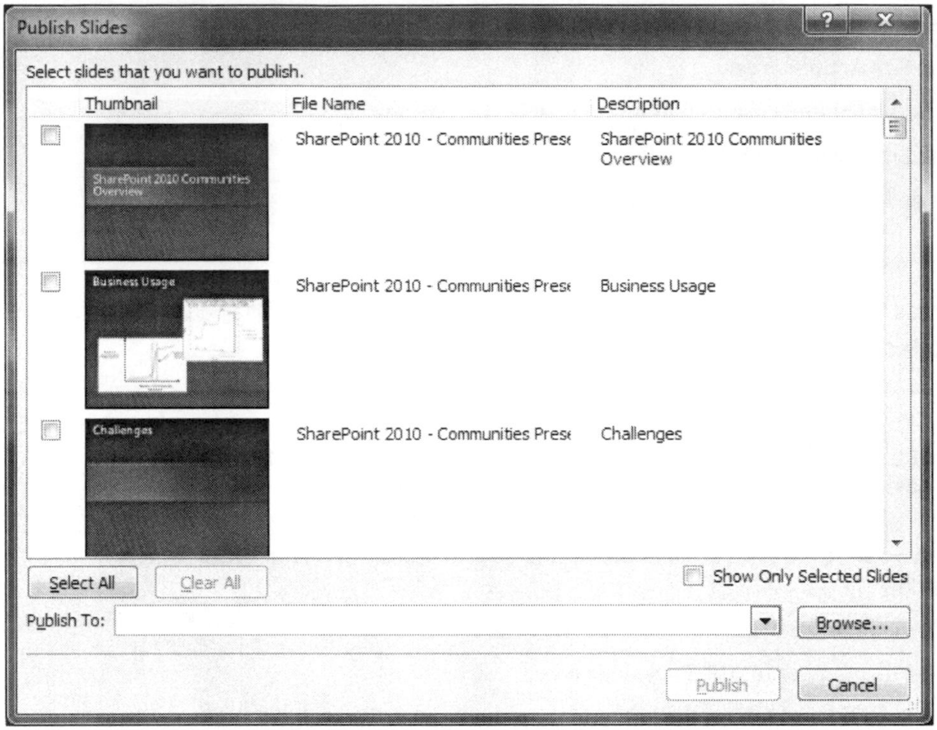

Figure 9-13. Select slides to publish to SharePoint 2010

11. Check the check boxes (or click the Select All button for all) for publishing.

12. Enter the URL of the slide library location in the Publish To box (note that you do not need the `filename.aspx` in the URL, such as `AllItems.aspx`); for example `http://site/ MySlideLib/`.

13. Click the Publish button.

■ **Note** You may need to authenticate with your username and password.

---

14. Head over to your slide library in SharePoint 2010, and you should start seeing the slides appearing (hit Refresh a few times). You may not see all the slides immediately, as SharePoint processes and creates thumbnails for each slide before showing the slide in the library.

With a set of slides in our slide library, I can now demonstrate creating a new PowerPoint deck from a selected number of slides from my new slide library, as follows:

15. Check the checkboxes next to the slides in the SharePoint 2010 slide library that you wish to include in the new presentation (deck).

16. Click the Copy Slide To Presentation link, at the top of the list, just below the Ribbon.

Note You can only copy from a slide library to PowerPoint using Internet Explorer 5.5 or above.

---

17. PowerPoint 2010 opens and presents a dialog, like that shown in Figure 9-14, asking the user whether to copy to a new presentation or an open presentation (if PowerPoint was already open with a deck loaded), with some other options, as shown.

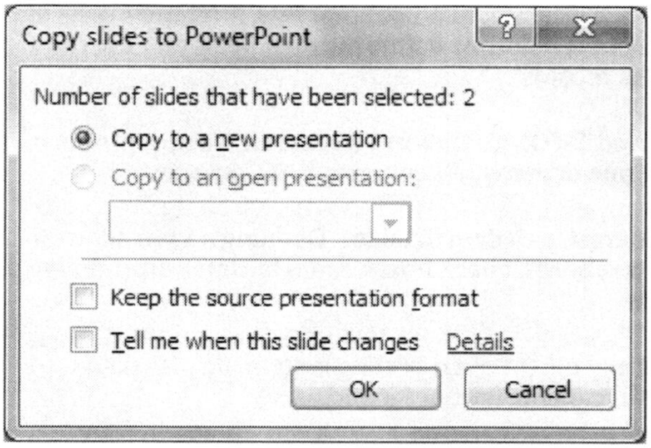

Figure 9-14. The copy to presentation dialog

Microsoft OneNote

Microsoft OneNote is a powerful note-taking application, allowing textual notes, images, media, and handwriting note authoring capabilities. With the integration with SharePoint 2010, OneNote goes beyond a personal note-taking tool and becomes a collaborative tool, much like the rest of the Office suite applications. Similar to Microsoft Word and Microsoft PowerPoint, Microsoft OneNote works with Live Coauthoring—discussed earlier in this chapter.

There is not a whole lot to demonstrate with OneNote's integration with SharePoint 2010, except the following steps to save a new OneNote notebook to a SharePoint 2010 document library from the Backstage area of the application.

1. Click the File tab to enter the Back Stage area.

2. Click the New tab on the left.

3. Choose Network, a filename for the new notebook, and the URL of the SharePoint document library.

4.   Click the Create Notebook button.

Users with collaboration permissions may now co-author content in the new OneNote notebook.

Microsoft Access

Microsoft Access is a small file-based RDMS (Relational Database Management System). Microsoft Access is less powerful and does not scale for performance and enterprise use like SQL Server, but it is portable and ideal for manipulation of small chunks of data in relational form.

Similar to SQL Server and other RDMS applications, Access uses terminology to define certain features and functionality, as described in Table 9-2.

Table 9-2. Microsoft Access Terminology

Terminology	Description
Table	Stores all data, just like SQL Server and SharePoint lists. A table consists of columns and rows, where the columns define the data fields and the rows define the data itself (the records).
Queries	Think of queries like saved T-SQL queries in SQL Server. Queries produce result data by querying one or many tables, using T-SQL syntax.
Forms	Forms allow users to interact with data in tables. Defining a form allows a user to enter data into text boxes, check boxes, radio buttons, drop-down list controls, and the like.
Reports	Reports in Access, as in any other data reporting system, display data queried from Access in a readable format for end users.

With the terminology out of the way, I shall demonstrate how to export data in a SharePoint 2010 list to Access from SharePoint, and how to import lists in SharePoint 2010 to Access.

1.   Open a SharePoint 2010 list at the default view.

2.   Click the Library tab in the Ribbon.

3.   In the Connect & Export section of the Ribbon, click the Open with Access icon.

■ **Note** SharePoint disables the Open with Access button if you do not have Access installed. This icon does not exist at all for document libraries. Instead, follow the Export from Excel steps earlier in this chapter, and use the task pane.

4.   Microsoft Access opens and displays a dialog, asking if you wish to link the table or export the data as a copy.

Link Tables in Access allow users to work with data, as they would any other Access table, except that the data does not reside in Access—in this case, within a SharePoint list. With Microsoft Access, SharePoint 2010, and Link Tables, you could create a lightweight Access application that provides a business-intelligent interface for entering data into SharePoint.

Connecting to SharePoint 2010 from Microsoft Access 2010, and importing data, is just as painless as exporting from SharePoint:

5. Open Access 2010.

6. Click the Create tab in the Ribbon (see Figure 9-15).

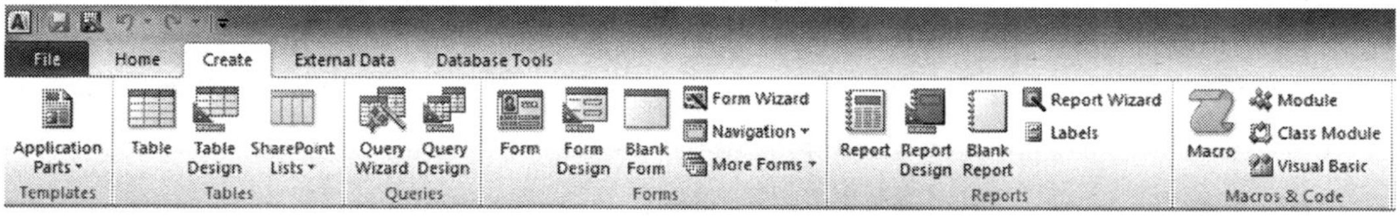

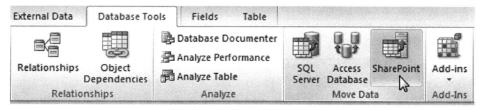

Figure 9-15. The Create tab in the Ribbon of Microsoft Access 2010

7. Click the SharePoint Lists icon to create new SharePoint 2010 lists directly from Access.

8. Click the Database Tools tab, and then the SharePoint icon (see Figure 9-16) to select tables to move into SharePoint 2010 as lists.

Figure 9-16. Move Access tables to SharePoint 2010 as lists

New to SharePoint 2010 is the capability to interact with an Access database from within the SharePoint browser user interface. Simply upload an Access 2010 file to a document library.

Access Services

SharePoint 2010 includes a managed service application for Access—Access Services. With Access Services, users can do much more than just host an Access file in a document library, or link lists with Access tables. Access Services integrates the complete Access functionality into SharePoint 2010, so legacy Access users need not rely on the Office Access application to host forms, run queries, and provide reports.

Access Services provides several benefits to collaborative users of data retained in an Access file, using SharePoint 2010:

*   Access Services locks objects and not the entire file, when users make changes (unlike the full Access application).

- Access Services secures data in an Access database using the same SharePoint 2010 permissions model.

- Access Service is a middle-tier service and web service application, so users can share access to their Access data across the farm and other connecting SharePoint 2010 farms.

- Everything runs in the world of the browser; users do not need the Access Office application on their computer.

The following steps demonstrate how to set up Access Services, via Central Admin, and how to leverage the capabilities of Access Services:

1. Open Central Admin.

2. Click the Manage Services on Server link, under the System Settings heading.

3. Make sure the Access Database Service is started.

4. Click the Manage Service Applications link, under the Application Management heading, from the Central Admin home page.

5. Scroll down the list and see if an Access Services application already exists. If not, continue.

6. Click the New icon in the Ribbon and select Access Services from the menu.

7. In the dialog, give the service a name and create an application pool.

8. Click the OK button, and wait while SharePoint 2010 creates the new Service Application.

9. You may configure the settings for Access Services by clicking the right of the name to select the service application, and then click the Manage icon in the Ribbon.

With the service application running and configured, I shall now demonstrate how to use Access Services, starting with publication from the Access 2010 Office application.

10. Open Access 2010, and an existing Access database application.

11. Click the File tab to access the Backstage area.

12. Click Save & Publish tab on the left, and then click the Publish to Access Services link.

13. Run the Compatibility Checker, and fix any issues that are not compatible with the Web User Interface.

14. The Access application will exist as a new sub-site in SharePoint 2010, so provide the parent site URL or site collection URL, and give the new site a name.

15. Click the Publish to Access Services button.

You may now archive your Access database file, as the new sub-site in SharePoint 2010 becomes the new application.

Before leaving the topic of Access Services, I want to refer you to the New button in the Backstage area of Access 2010. One of the options is to create a new Blank Web Database, which creates a database that is compatible with SharePoint 2010.

Microsoft InfoPath

Microsoft first introduced InfoPath in Office 2003 as an application to visually create forms and deploy them to an audience to fill out. As a stand-alone Office application, InfoPath provides good form design capabilities, and the author of a form has various deployment options.

In 2007, Microsoft Office SharePoint Server 2007 included InfoPath Server as an Enterprise license feature. The purpose of InfoPath Server was to render forms, designed in InfoPath, within the SharePoint environment, to users with a web browser. InfoPath 2007 included the new SharePoint InfoPath Server deployment path.

The problem with InfoPath Server in MOSS 2007 was that the expectation from Microsoft that InfoPath Server would provide site designers the overarching solution for integrating custom forms into the SharePoint platform missed the mark. InfoPath Server came to SharePoint as an additional feature and did not fully integrate into the platform, and so InfoPath-hosted forms in MOSS 2007 looked more like an afterthought.

InfoPath 2010 and SharePoint 2010 now fully integrate. For example, SharePoint 2010 allows administrators to customize any list-based form, via SharePoint Designer 2010, which consists of converting the form to an InfoPath form. Most of the annoying branding that informed the user that InfoPath Server was powering the form rendering is gone, and forms render within the same SharePoint site chrome.

The InfoPath 2010 Office Application itself is in two parts—Designer and Filler. The designer part of the application is used for designing and deploying new forms, and the filler for users to complete forms. Form designers may deploy both browser-based forms and those that are not browser-based to SharePoint 2010. Forms that are browser-based and sourced from a form library with setting to render InfoPath forms in the browser will do so. Forms that aren't browser based or those sourced from a forms library that does not permit browser rendering will open InfoPath 2010 Filler on the client desktop.

SharePoint 2010 supports three different deployment options for browser-based InfoPath forms, as follows:

- **Form-Library**: A SharePoint Form Library is a special type of document library that contains XSN files—the XML definition of an InfoPath form. Form-Libraries work well when deploying forms to a single location at the current site level and the form creator has no expectation of hosting the form in other sites or libraries.

- **Site Content-Type**: Forms may now deploy as content types in SharePoint 2010 to the site or site collection Content Type Gallery. This method supports reuse of the form across sites and libraries in the hierarchy.

- **Administrator-approved Form Template**: This type of form deployment involves deploying the form to the InfoPath Form Services application in the farm (via Central Admin). Administrator-approved forms are reusable across the farm as templates, wherever the farm has access to the InfoPath Forms Services.

Before we dive into the various deployments of InfoPath Forms and seeing InfoPath Forms Services in action, we must first configure InfoPath Forms Services, via Central Admin:

1. Open Central Admin.

2. Click the General Application Settings heading.

3. Click the Configure InfoPath Forms Services link, under the InfoPath Forms Services heading.

SharePoint shows a page like that in Figure 9-17.

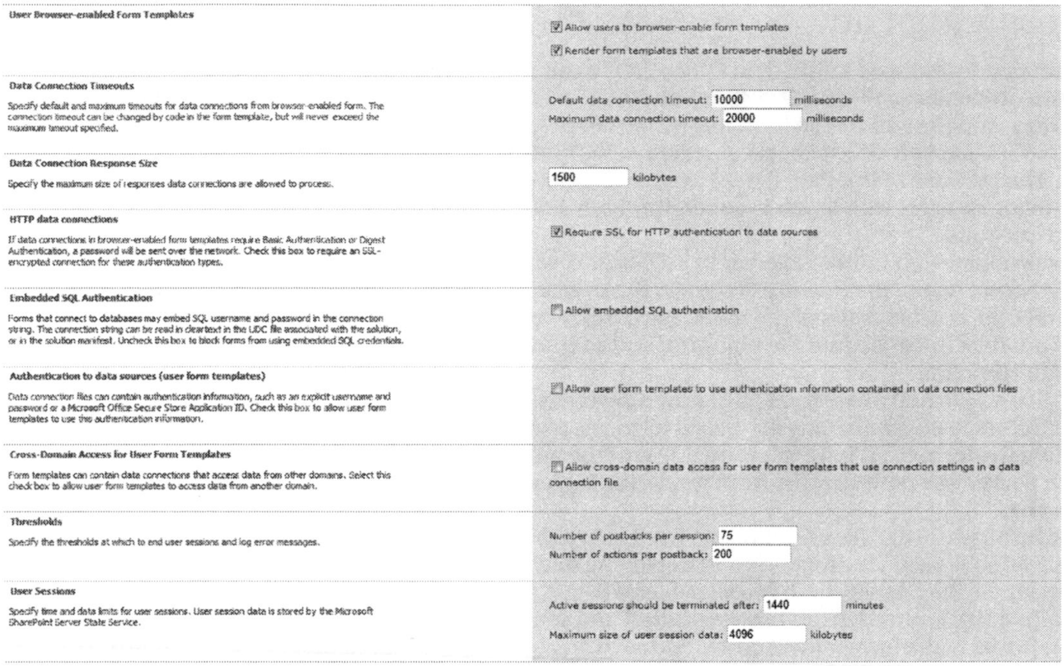

Figure 9-17. Configuring InfoPath Forms Services

Most of the settings on this page are self-explanatory. The User Browser-enabled Form Templates are specifically of interest because unchecking these options prevents browser-based forms from rendering in the browser.

4. Go back to the General Application Settings page, and review the various links under the InfoPath Forms Services heading:

- **Manage form templates:** Navigates the administrator to the master form templates list. By default, this list contains forms for use in various workflows across the farm.

- **Configure InfoPath Forms Services:** As described above, this link takes the administrator to a page to configure the general settings for InfoPath Forms Services.

- **Upload form template:** Provides a page where the administrator can upload an administrator-approved form to the master list.

- **Manage data connection files:** InfoPath forms typically use data connection files to define how to integrate data into the form (such as for drop-down list values) and where to submit posted data. This link provides the administrator with a place to upload and manage data connection files.

- **Configure InfoPath Forms Services Web Service Proxy:** Allows the administrator to enable a web service proxy for forms.

Deploying a Form via Central Admin

Forms deployed to Central Admin by administrators are available for use by other users in designated site collections. The following steps detail how to upload an InfoPath template (XSN file) to Central Admin.

1. Open Central Admin.

2. Click the General Application Settings heading.

3. Under the InfoPath Forms Services heading, click the Upload Form Template link.

4. Browse to the location of the XSN on disk.

5. You may click the Verify button to confirm that the form has no errors (I recommend it).

6. Click the Upload button, and then look to the status page, which should read success.

7. From the Manage form templates page, hover over the name of the form template you just uploaded.

8. Click the Activate to a Site Collection link.

9. Choose a site collection to activate the form; after completing this step, SharePoint makes the form available as a content type in the Content Type Gallery, for users to add to new and existing lists/libraries.

Rendering a Form Using the InfoPath Form Web Part

In the previous version of SharePoint, MOSS 2007, either forms were rendered in a new browser window executed by SharePoint, or site designers could host InfoPath forms in a Forms Server User Control. Neither option was particularly compelling. Microsoft now provides an InfoPath web part in SharePoint 2010.

The InfoPath web part allows any page contributor to host an existing InfoPath form on pages that support web parts, such as wiki pages and pages with web part zones. After inserting the web part on the page, you should see something like Figure 9-18. Click the link to show the tool part and follow the steps below to configure the web part to an existing InfoPath form.

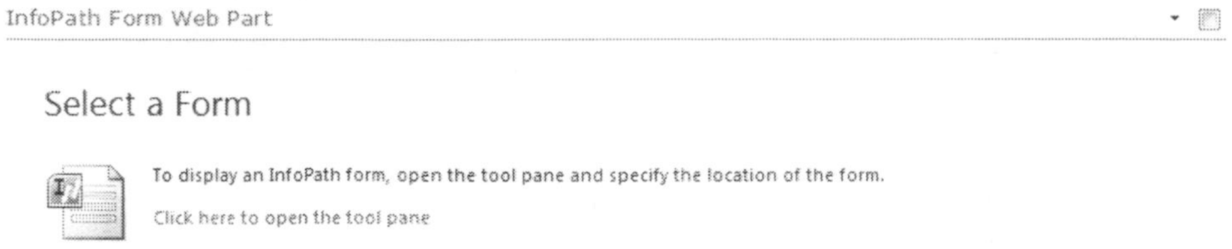

InfoPath Form Web Part ▾ ▢

Select a Form

To display an InfoPath form, open the tool pane and specify the location of the form.

Click here to open the tool pane

Figure 9-18. The InfoPath Web Part

1. The List or Library drop-down control contains all lists and libraries using InfoPath Form content types. Select the desired list to render the form.

2. Select the appropriate InfoPath Form Content type in the next drop-down control.

3. The checkbox Show InfoPath Ribbon or Toolbar instructs the web part to display the InfoPath Ribbon in the web part rendering. Unchecking this option will cause the web part to render only the form (which is often desirable for end users).

4. The checkbox Send Data to Connected Web Parts When Page Loads instructs the web part to activate any web part connections during page load.

5. The remaining controls pertain to rendering, such as the default view to render and what happens to the form after submission.

6. Click the OK button at the bottom of the tool pane to save your changes.

Customizing the Document Information Panel and List Forms

Earlier in this chapter, I introduced the Document Information Panel, which displays the metadata of a document from within the Office application. The DIP associates with a particular SharePoint content type for the open document. Using InfoPath and SharePoint 2010, administrators may customize the look of the DIP, following the steps below:

1. Open InfoPath Designer 2010.

2. Click the File tab to access the Backstage area.

3. Under the Advanced Form Templates heading, click the Document Information Panel form type.

4. Click the Design Form button on the right.

5. A wizard dialog appears (see Figure 9-19). Enter the URL of the SharePoint 2010 document library, and then click the Next button.

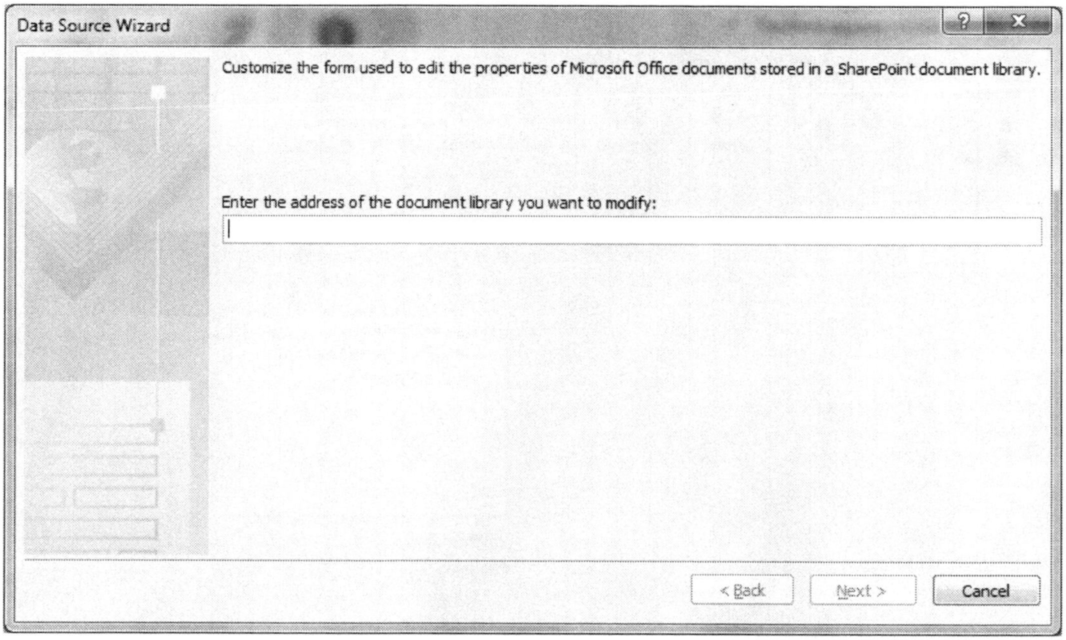

Figure 9-19. *Data Source Wizard for editing the DIP from InfoPath Designer 2010*

6. Select the Content Type to edit the DIP, and click the Next button.

7. The wizard displays a message about publishing the content type for the InfoPath form to work; click the Finish button.

InfoPath Designer 2010 now shows you a form to edit, complete with the DIP fields (see Figure 9-20).

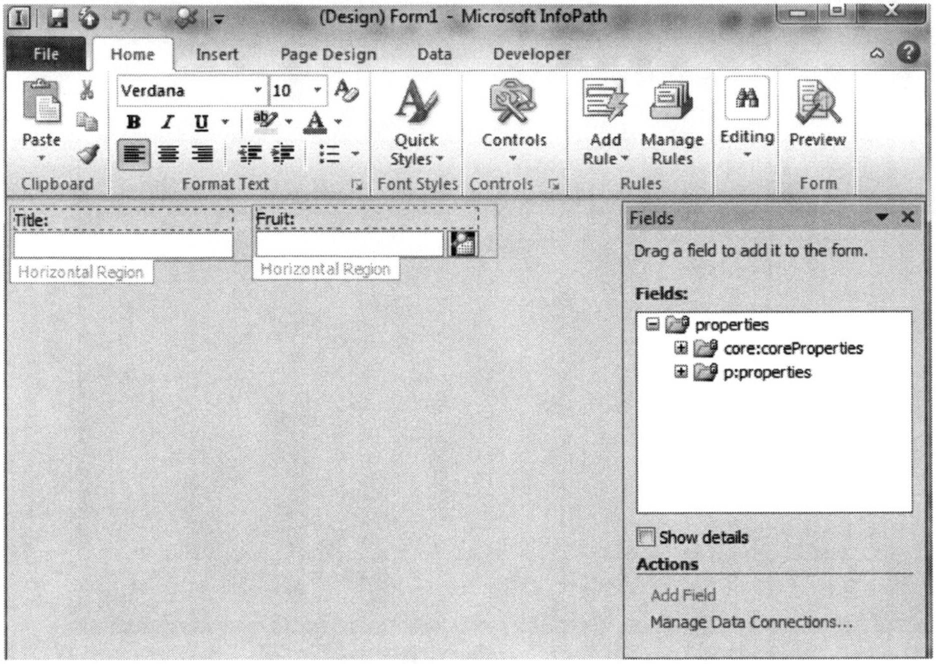

Figure 9-20. DIP in InfoPath Designer 2010

8. Experiment with editing the form; for example, change some colors, fonts, and so on.

9. To publish your changes to SharePoint, click the File tab, and then the Quick Publish button.

InfoPath Designer 2010 also allows administrators to edit List Form pages, such as the Edit form, or the New Item form. The following steps demonstrate.

10. Navigate to the SharePoint 2010 List or Library.

11. Click the List tab in the Ribbon, and then click the Customize Form Icon in the Ribbon.

12. InfoPath Designer 2010 opens, showing the Edit form with the active fields.

13. Customize the form. You may change the presentation any way you like, even adding or removing fields.

14. To publish your changes to SharePoint, click the File tab, and then the Quick Publish button.

15. Once published, your changes apply to the Edit (EditForm.aspx), New Item (NewForm.aspx), and Display (DispForm.aspx) forms.

16. Navigate to the list in SharePoint 2010 and add a new item. You should see the new InfoPath form loaded.

How do you revert to the SharePoint stock list forms?

17. Using Internet Explorer, navigate to the default view of the list.

18. Click the List tab on the Ribbon, and then click the List Settings icon.

19. Click the Form Settings link under General Settings.

20. Revert back to the SharePoint List forms, and click OK.

Microsoft Visio

The previous chapter demonstrated configuration and use of Visio Services. Visio Services exists as a managed service application and associated SharePoint 2010 service. Users may leverage Visio Services to provide a visual representation of tasks in a task list; the Ribbon includes an option to connect to Visio for task lists.

Chapter 8 also demonstrated using the Visio Web Part, which allows users to render Visio diagrams, whether directly connected to Visio Services, or simply static, within a SharePoint 2010 page.

For details on Visio integration, as part of Office 2010 integration, flip back to the previous chapter.

Microsoft Outlook

Microsoft Outlook is probably the most used Office Application in the suite. Microsoft Word and Excel are certainly popular with business users, but they look at their email in Outlook most often. It seems that Outlook is central to the world of the business user.

As much as it is popular, Microsoft is working to break users from the practice of storing all their business information in emails contained in Outlook. Storing multiple copies of documents in Outlook adds burden on the email server (typically Microsoft Exchange), and users who maintain personal folders effectively retain important data on their personal computer—not good for data integrity. So, how does Microsoft release user cohesiveness with Outlook and encourage these users to leverage SharePoint 2010 as a centralized collaborative repository for their data? The short answer is by making Outlook communicate with SharePoint, so users do not have to leave the comfort of their favorite email client.

Lists and Libraries

Users may connect many types of lists or document libraries to Outlook. These lists and libraries then appear in the hierarchy of folders that users of Outlook are familiar. Furthermore, depending on the list, type shall depict how Outlook displays the folder and the types of item contained. The following steps demonstrate how to connect a shared calendar in SharePoint with Outlook.

1. Open SharePoint 2010 and navigate to the share calendar default view.

2. Click the Calendar tab on the Ribbon, and then click the Connect to Outlook icon in the Connect & Export section of the Ribbon.

3. Outlook launches and displays a dialog asking you to confirm connecting the list to Outlook.

4. You may click the Advanced button to see additional options, such as to edit the name of the folder in Outlook.

5. Click the Yes button; Outlook displays the new calendar in the calendar area of the folder hierarchy.

6. If you have events in your SharePoint calendar, you should see them in Outlook (after the next Send & Receive); you can also make direct changes to the calendar in Outlook and see the changes reflected in SharePoint.

Outlook allows users to connect the following lists to Outlook in a similar process to the steps above: Document Libraries, Calendars, Tasks, Contacts, Picture Libraries, Document Sets (Individual Owned), Discussion Boards, and Project Tasks.

Outlook stores all connected list data in an offline PST file, called `SharePoint Lists.pst`. Readers should note that SharePoint 2010 downloads ALL content to this PST file, so if you have a large document library connected to Outlook, the combination of documents and metadata may take up considerable space on the client machine (not the e-mail server). Fortunately, administrators and list owners may prevent download of list content with the following steps:

7. Navigate to the list in SharePoint 2010.

8. Click the List or Library tab in the Ribbon.

9. Click the List or Library Settings in the Ribbon.

10. Click the Advanced Settings link.

11. Change the setting for Offline Client Availability to No. SharePoint then disables the Connect to Outlook icon on the Ribbon. Users with previous downloaded content still retain the offline copy in Outlook, but can no longer sync with SharePoint.

Outlook Social Connector

Back in Chapter 5, I covered the Outlook Social Connector, which displays profile data about a user in Outlook, sourced from SharePoint profiles. Using this connector and SharePoint 2010, users have complete control of their profile in SharePoint, and the information displayed to other email users in the organization, not just the information stored in the organization's Active Directory.

SharePoint Workspace—the New Groove

Microsoft introduced the Groove application in Office 2007, as an offline collaborative tool. The purpose of Groove was to share calendars, task lists, and file folders with other Groove users across the Internet. The Groove client leveraged Microsoft's Groove servers in the cloud, or organizations could deploy their own Groove server.

Collaborative tool, task lists, file share, and so on—the Groove application sounds very much like SharePoint! This was the problem; Groove closely mirrored the collaboration functionality of SharePoint. The SharePoint and Groove worlds were not isolated. Groove users could synchronize document libraries with SharePoint and then make these libraries available to their Groove peers.

With the release of SharePoint 2010 and Office 2010, Microsoft rebranded the Groove application, now called SharePoint Workspace.

SharePoint Workspace now gears more to offline access of SharePoint content and is not limited to document libraries. Users of SharePoint Workspace may synchronize almost any list content with the application so users may read and make changes to list data and documents, when not connected to the company SharePoint server. The following steps demonstrate connecting a SharePoint task list with SharePoint Workspace.

1. Open SharePoint 2010 (you must use Internet Explorer).

2. Navigate to the site containing your task list.

3. Click the Site Action menu.

4. Select the Sync to SharePoint Workspace menu item.

5. SharePoint Workspace launches and displays a dialog like that in Figure 9-21.

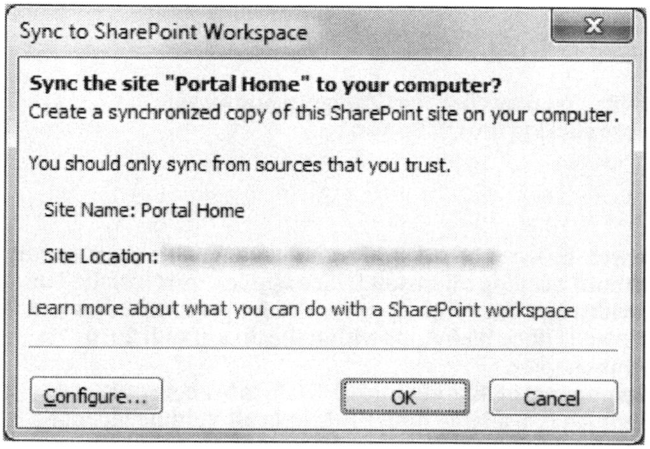

Figure 9-21. *The Sync to SharePoint Workspace dialog*

6. Click the Configure button.

7. SharePoint Workspace shows all the lists and libraries that it will sync with SharePoint; you may select each and decide whether to sync all or no content, and a specific view.

An alternative method to synchronize a SharePoint site with SharePoint Workspace is as follows:

8. Open SharePoint Workspace.

■ **Note** If you have not configured SharePoint Workspace with an account, the application will prompt you to do so before establishing sync profiles.

9. Click the New button in the main launch window.

10. Select SharePoint Workspace in the menu (Figure 9-22). Notice that you can still create legacy Groove workspaces with this tool.

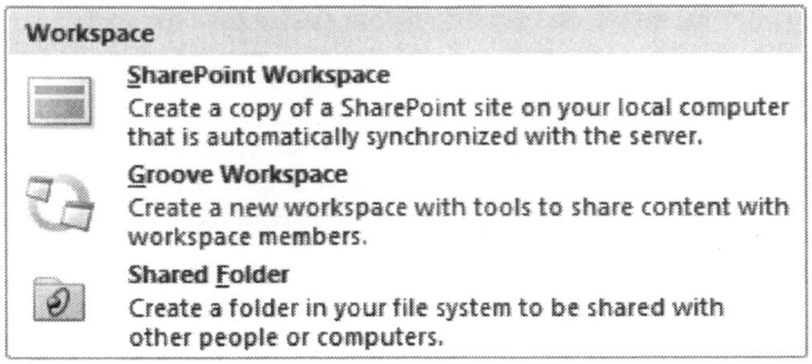

Workspace

SharePoint Workspace
Create a copy of a SharePoint site on your local computer that is automatically synchronized with the server.

Groove Workspace
Create a new workspace with tools to share content with workspace members.

Shared Folder
Create a folder in your file system to be shared with other people or computers.

Figure 9-22. Type of Workspace

> 11. Provide the URL of the SharePoint site. You may click the Configure button to choose the lists to synchronize, before clicking the OK button.

Office Web Applications

Office Web Applications (Office Web Apps) are web-browser based applications that enable users to edit Word, Excel, PowerPoint, and OneNote files without needing Microsoft Office applications installed on client machines. The Windows Live service provides an Office Web Apps service for personal users and consumers, and enterprise organizations may install Office Web Apps within the SharePoint 2010 infrastructure, which is what I shall discuss in this chapter.

Unlike most of the features and service components of SharePoint 2010, Office Web Apps is installed using a separate installation package, which is available from the Microsoft Volume License Center. To make life a little more complicated, Office Web Apps requires different steps to install, depending on the following scenarios in Table 9-3.

Administrators may install Office Web Apps with both SharePoint 2010 Foundation and Server.

Table 9-3. Pre-installation of Office Web Apps Scenarios

Starting Scenario	Description of Steps
Existing stand-alone SharePoint 2010 server	In this scenario, SharePoint 2010 is already installed as a stand-alone server (different from a single server farm), and the administrator has already run the SharePoint Products Configuration Wizard.
	The steps involve installing Office Web Apps and then re-running the wizard, before installing the services and service applications via Central Admin (or PowerShell).
New stand-alone SharePoint 2010 server	In this scenario, the administrator has not executed the SharePoint Products Configuration Wizard.
	The steps involve installing Office Web Apps and then running the wizard, which installs the service and service applications to run Office Web Apps.

Starting Scenario	Description of Steps
Existing SharePoint 2010 server farm	In this scenario, the administrator has already installed SharePoint 2010 as a server farm, and the administrator has already run the SharePoint Products Configuration Wizard.
	The steps involve installing Office Web Apps on each server in the farm and re-running the configuration wizard.
New SharePoint 2010 server farm	In this scenario, the administrator has not yet joined the servers to an existing farm or new farm, and not yet run the SharePoint Products Configuration Wizard.
	The steps involve installing Office Web Apps on each server in the farm and running the configuration wizard.

Installing Office Web Apps on an Existing Stand-Alone SharePoint 2010 Server

In this scenario, you have SharePoint 2010 installed in stand-alone mode, and thus the SharePoint Products Configuration Wizard already executed. Execute the following steps as a local administrator on the stand-alone SharePoint 2010 server.

1. Run the setup.exe application in the Office Web Apps installation folder.

2. Provide your product key and then click the Continue button.

3. Specify the installation location (or leave the default), and then click the Install button.

4. At the end of the installation, make sure the checkbox for Run the SharePoint Products Configuration Wizard Now is checked.

5. Click the Close button and the wizard starts.

6. If you forgot to check the check box to run the wizard, you may run the wizard from Start   All Programs   Microsoft SharePoint 2010 Products.

7. On the Welcome to SharePoint page, click the Next button.

8. The wizard will ask you about restarting services, click the Yes button.

9. When the wizard ends with a successful message, click the Finish button.

At this point, you installed everything and you now must start the necessary services and install the service applications for Office Web Apps to work.

10. Open Central Admin.

11. Click the Manage Services On Server link under the System Settings heading.

12. Start the following services:

- Excel Calculation Services

- PowerPoint Service

- Word Viewing Service

13. Navigate back to the home page of Central Admin.

14. Click the Manage Service Applications link, under the Application Management heading.

15. Click the New icon on the Ribbon and select the PowerPoint Service Application.

16. Provide a name, description, and application pool, and then click the OK button.

17. Click the New icon on the Ribbon and select the Word Viewing Service Application.

18. Provide a name, description, and application pool, and then click the OK button.

19. Click the New icon on the Ribbon and select the Excel Services Application.

20. Provide a name, description, and application pool, and then click OK.

At this point, you may activate the feature in your site collection to enable Office Web Apps for documents in your site hierarchy.

21. Navigate to your root SharePoint 2010 site collection.

22. Click the Site Actions menu.

23. Select the Site Settings menu item.

24. Click the Site collection Features link, under the Site Collection Administration heading.

25. Scroll to the Office Web Apps feature and click the Activate button.

Installing Office Web Apps on a New Stand-alone SharePoint 2010 Server

In this scenario, you have not configured the stand-alone server via the SharePoint Products Configuration Wizard. The following steps detail installing Office Web Apps in this scenario as an administrator.

1. Run the setup.exe application in the Office Web Apps installation folder.

2. Provide your product key and then click the Continue button.

3. Specify the installation location (or leave the default), and then click the Install button.

4. At the end of the installation, make sure the checkbox for Run the SharePoint Products Configuration Wizard Now is checked.

5. Click the Close button and the wizard starts.

6. If you forgot to check the check box to run the wizard, you may run the wizard from Start   All Programs   Microsoft SharePoint 2010 Products.

7. On the Welcome to SharePoint page, click the Next button.

8. The wizard will ask you about restarting services; click the Yes button.

9. When the wizard ends with a successful message, click the Finish button. Your browser opens to the site collection template selection page.

10. Click the preferred site template and customize the site using the Solutions Gallery section.

11. Click the OK button.

12. Set up the groups for your new site collection and then click OK to complete the installation.

Installing Office Web Apps into an Existing SharePoint 2010 Server Farm

A SharePoint 2010 server farm typically consists of multiple servers, but at the very least assumes separate installation of SQL Server (which can be on the same server as SharePoint 2010, but that is not recommended). This type of setup is different from the stand-alone setup where the SharePoint 2010 installer installs its own instance of SQL Server Express and preconfigures services and service applications. Similar to the main SharePoint 2010 install, Office Web Apps requires different steps to install in an existing server farm, where the administrator has already executed the SharePoint Products Configuration Wizard.

1. Run the setup.exe application in the Office Web Apps installation folder.

2. Provide your product key and then click Continue.

3. Specify the installation location (or leave the default), and then click Install.

4. At the end of the installation, make sure the checkbox for Run the SharePoint Products Configuration Wizard Now is checked.

5. Click the Close button and the wizard starts.

6. Repeat the above steps for all SharePoint servers in the farm (not the SQL Server if a separate server).

7. If you forgot to check the check box to run the wizard, you may run the wizard from Start   All Programs   Microsoft SharePoint 2010 Products.

8. On the Welcome to SharePoint page, click the Next button.

9. The wizard will ask you about restarting services; click Yes.

10. When the wizard ends with a successful message, click the Finish button.

11. On the Configure your SharePoint farm page, click No, I Will Configure Everything Myself to cancel.

▪ **Note** Do not run the Farm Configuration wizard.

At this point, you have installed everything and you now must start the necessary services and install the service applications for Office Web Apps to work.

12. Navigate to the home page of Central Admin.

13. Click the Manage Services on Server link under the System Settings heading.

14. Start the following services:

- Excel Calculation Services

- PowerPoint Service

- Word Viewing Service

15. Navigate back to the home page of Central Admin.

16. Click the Manage Service Applications link, under the Application Management heading.

17. Click the New icon on the Ribbon and select the PowerPoint Service Application.

18. Provide a name, description, and application pool, and then click OK.

19. Click the New icon on the Ribbon and select the Word Viewing Service Application.

20. Provide a name, description, and application pool, and then click OK.

21. Click the New icon on the Ribbon and select the Excel Services Application.

22. Provide a name, description, and application pool, and then click OK.

At this point, you may activate the feature in your site collection to enable Office Web Apps for documents in your site hierarchy.

23. Navigate to your root SharePoint 2010 site collection.

24. Click the Site Actions menu.

25. Select the Site Settings menu item.

26. Click the Site Collection Features link, under the Site Collection Administration heading.

27. Scroll to the Office Web Apps feature and click the Activate button.

Installing Office Web Apps into a New SharePoint 2010 Server Farm

In this scenario, I assume that you have yet to install or configure SharePoint 2010 as a new farm. The following steps may appear misleading because we start with an Office Web Apps binary install, regardless of whether you ever installed any SharePoint 2010 binaries. Do not worry; this is correct.

■ **Note** Some of the steps in the installation and SharePoint Products Configuration Wizard mirror those discussed in Chapter 2.

---

1. Run the setup.exe application in the Office Web Apps installation folder.

2. Provide your product key and then click the Continue button.

3. Specify the installation location (or leave the default), and then click the Install button.

4. At the end of the installation, make sure the checkbox for Run the SharePoint Products Configuration Wizard Now is checked.

5. Click the Close button, and the wizard starts.

6. Repeat the above steps for all SharePoint servers in the farm (not the SQL Server if a separate server).

7. If you forgot to check the check box to run the wizard, you may run the wizard from Start   All Programs   Microsoft SharePoint 2010 Products.

8. On the Welcome to SharePoint page, click the Next button.

9. The wizard will ask you about restarting services; click Yes.

10. On the following pages, either create a new farm or connect to an existing farm by providing connection settings for your SQL server.

11. Provide a passphrase for the farm.

12. Provide details for configuring a default web application (typically NTLM authentication and an application on port 80).

13. On the summary page, if this is the first server in the farm, click the Next button. If not, and you want to host Central Admin on the current server, click Advanced Settings and then click Use This Machine to Host the Web Site.

■ **Note** Make sure you have installed Office Web Apps and executed the SharePoint Products Configuration Wizard on ALL servers in the farm, before running the farm wizard.

---

14. Open Central Admin.

15. Run the Farm Configuration wizard.

Summary

In this chapter, we covered most of the applications part of the Microsoft Office 2010 suite. I showed you how these applications integrate with SharePoint 2010. We covered the basics of exporting and importing data, the commonalities in the Backstage area, live coauthoring, and the Document Information Panel.

As we progressed through the chapter, we looked at each application in turn and I demonstrated some of the specific integration features with SharePoint 2010.

We took a quick tour of InfoPath 2010—the filler and designer applications. You saw how to customize SharePoint 2010 list forms and the Document Information Panel.

I demonstrated the PowerPoint Broadcast Service to run a live meeting presentation through SharePoint.

At the end of this chapter, we tackled the installation and configuration of Office Web Applications, so your users can view and edit Office documents without the Office applications installed on client machines.

The next and final chapter draws this book to a close; I'll discuss the health and monitoring of your SharePoint infrastructure and how to prepare for disaster recovery.

CHAPTER 10

Health, Monitoring, and Disaster Recovery

As more and more organizations deploy SharePoint within an enterprise, and user adoption of the SharePoint solutions snowballs with each deployment, disaster recovery becomes very important. SharePoint 2010 has the capability to host terabytes of important data, so backup of this data is likely to be high on the agenda for any IT group that maintains SharePoint in an organization.

SharePoint 2007 introduced capabilities to make backup and restoration easier than in the past, and SharePoint 2010 continues to provide good backup and restore functionality to maintain the integrity of important data. I devote a large chunk of this chapter to the administration of disaster recovery features in SharePoint 2010, but, as the title suggestions, this chapter also contains details on Health and Monitoring of a SharePoint 2010 infrastructure.

SharePoint 2007 provided extensive logging (as does SharePoint 2010), but lacked some key monitoring functionality that administrators required to ensure their SharePoint solution was operating at peak performance. Sure, there were the ULS logs and the Windows event log, but these features require a certain amount of proactive behavior from the SharePoint administrator. SharePoint 2010 includes sophisticated health and monitoring features to alert the administrator when SharePoint is feeling a little under the weather.

After reading this chapter, any SharePoint administrator will, I am confident, be able to provide their organization with the peace of mind that their data integrity is intact and that the organization can count on bounce-back of their SharePoint service in the event of downtime or disaster.

Planning for Disaster Recovery

It is never a happy day for the IT group when an online service goes down, and this includes SharePoint. As fantastic as SharePoint 2010 is, it is inevitable that at some point in the lifecycle, the deployed SharePoint solution will suffer from downtime. Of course, downtime may occur for any number of reasons—human error, underlying hardware failure, power outage, faulty customizations, and so on. Since we cannot avert failure, your role as a SharePoint administrator is to account for such downtime and restore service to the users of the platform in a timely manner. Planning for loss of service and recovering is what I refer as to as planning for disaster recovery.

Minimizing downtime and averting loss in a disaster involves proactive process and planning. Those unfortunate readers who have experienced loss of data are likely all too familiar with data backup, which is one aspect of disaster recovery—I discuss managing content and data integrity shortly in this chapter. Another important aspect of disaster recovery includes techniques to minimize service downtime.

Minimizing downtime of a service factors both the *total time* to recover the service and the *point in time* from which recovery resumes. In short, if recovery consists of restoring data in a SharePoint site collection because of database corruption, then the time to restore the database from backup and the time when the last backup took place are both important factors for the success of restoration of the SharePoint site collection. A speedy restore is one thing, but if the data is already three months old then, depending on the frequency of change of the live data, the restoration is not necessarily successful.

Data/content recovery is one piece of a good disaster recovery plan—restoration of system hardware, the underlying operating system, system software, and configuration are all part of the plan. Since this book is about SharePoint 2010 administration, the topics concerning hardware and operating system recovery are outside its scope, except to say that virtualized platforms and snapshots now play a major part in alleviating many of the ills associated with hardware failure and/or operating system failure. At a conceptual (and practical) level, consider the following techniques to minimize downtime and provide warm recovery of service.

Load-Balanced Service

Load balancing involves either a hardware or software load balancer, running on a server, which intercepts all incoming web traffic on a specific IP address and redirects it to one of at least two web servers to service the request. The load balancer directs traffic either to the server with the least load (intelligent load balancing), or in turn, based on which server served the previous request (round robin).

Load balancing SharePoint consists of pointing a configured load balancer to multiple front-end SharePoint servers in the farm, which serve pages. SharePoint 2010 handles as many front-end web and application servers as the infrastructure can provide, thus scaling out to handle more traffic is simply a case of adding a new web server to the farm and registering the IP with the load balancer.

As well as providing for distributed load, most load balancers can detect if one of the servers in the pool is not responding, and redirect all traffic to the other responding servers. Large enterprise organizations that have the capability to host different servers in multiple geographic locations may redirect traffic to passive SharePoint servers, or completely mirrored SharePoint 2010 farms, to achieve redundancy and rapid recovery if a primary site hosting the main SharePoint infrastructure fails.

SQL Server Failover Clustering

SQL Server clustering consists of multiple SQL Server nodes, managed by a root cluster that provides redundancy at the SQL Server application level.

A cluster typically consists of an active node, a passive node, and a root instance—which redirects traffic to the passive node. The cluster maintains both nodes so that any database write operations update both the active and passive nodes, but the active node is handling most of the incoming requests in a typical load scenario. In the event that the active node fails, then the cluster switches over to use the passive node (running on different hardware).

The specifics of Microsoft SQL Server 2008 clustering are outside the scope of this book, except to say that clustering abstracts redundancy away from SharePoint and provides data integrity without SharePoint ever needing to switch database server. This is the beauty of it. SharePoint talks to a SQL cluster in the same way it talks to a single SQL server and never gets involved when the cluster fails over to a passive node.

■ **Note** You can read more about setting up clustering on SQL Server 2008 R2 at the following location: `http://msdn.microsoft.com/en-us/library/ms189134.aspx`.

I recommend the use of SQL clustering in any large organization or enterprise where SharePoint 2010 data is critical and exceeds 100GB, and the organization must limit the downtime in the event of failure. Traditionally, large-scale organizations using SharePoint 2010 with SQL clustering would host the actual data on a Storage Area Network, attached to the cluster, to provide an extra level of data redundancy and hot-swap capability with inexpensive disk storage.

SQL Server Database Mirroring

SQL Server mirroring also provides data redundancy at the SQL server, but unlike clustering, where the cluster is the data repository in entirety, mirroring consists of a warm-backup SQL server, separate from the main live server.

Clustering involves multiple storage nodes, connected by network links to a root SQL instance. Mirroring consists of two completely independent SQL servers with either *synchronous* or *asynchronous* copy, managed by each SQL Server instance. Synchronous mode provides hot standby because SQL Server ensures no data discrepancy between the principal and the mirror, whereas asynchronous provides warm backup and operates in a more passive copy mode.

■ **Note** You can read more about SQL Server 2008 mirroring at the following link: `http://msdn.microsoft.com/en-us/library/ms189852.aspx`

Administrators may provide high availability for SharePoint 2010 when using SQL Server mirroring in synchronous mode and using the database failover capabilities built into the SharePoint platform. SharePoint requires a SQL Server witness to manage the failover, in the event that the principal fails. The details surrounding SQL Server mirroring fall outside the scope of this book, but I'll show how to configure SharePoint 2010 for it, assuming you have SQL Server 2008 mirroring established in your infrastructure.

The following steps consist of PowerShell commands. To get started with PowerShell, from the Start menu, choose All Programs, click Microsoft SharePoint 2010 Products, and then click SharePoint 2010 Management Shell to launch the console.

1. Enter the following command into the PowerShell console to configure mirroring for the SharePoint 2010 configuration database:
   ```
   $database = Get-SPDatabase | where {$_.Name -match "SharePoint_Config"}
   $database.AddFailoverServiceInstance("mirror server name")
   $databse.Update()
   ```

2. Enter the following command into the PowerShell console to configure mirroring for your content database:
   ```
   $database = Get-SPDatabase | where {$_.Name -match "WSS_Content"}
   ```

```
$database.AddFailoverServiceInstance("mirror server name")
$databse.Update()
```

■ **Note** Both of the above commands assume your configuration database has the name `SharePoint_Config` and your content database is called `WSS_Content`. Change the names in the script to match your database names.

If you prefer to configure database mirroring via Central Administration, follow the steps below:

3. Open Central Admin.

4. Click the Application Management heading link.

5. Click the Manage Content Databases link.

6. Choose the relevant web application from the drop-down list.

7. Select the relevant content database.

8. On the settings page for the selected database, populate the Failover Database Server field with the mirrored server.

9. Click the OK button.

Maintaining Content Integrity

When we discuss disaster recovery, we are really talking about minimizing loss of user data and access to that user data. Loss of actual data (documents, files, web page content, data in a database or line-of-business system, and so on) is a disaster and we strive to avoid it in any trustworthy data management system, but loss of access to data because of downtime of the management system is almost as bad. In today's connected world, users rely on the uptime of data management systems—like SharePoint—and trust that these systems maintain the integrity of their content. Fortunately, SharePoint 2010 provides a number of approaches to maintaining content/data integrity.

SharePoint 2010 stores all content of your site in a content database. SharePoint 2010 content databases may contain one or many site collections, associated with a web application. One site collection *may not* span multiple content databases, which is important to note because backing up your content databases ensures complete recovery of your site collection. I discuss backup and restore of content and configuration databases a little later in this chapter.

Database backup is good in a disaster scenario… but what if a user loses a single document from their document library and wants to recover the document? A complete database restore is an overkill, not to mention considerable work in restoring the database to a separate location to retrieve the file. As administrators, we know users tend to lose files all the time. Fortunately, SharePoint 2010 includes features to retain content and data integrity without the need for complete database restore after small losses.

The Recycle Bin

Since SharePoint 2007 (WSS 3), the Recycle Bin has provided a mechanism for users to retrieve deleted lists and list items—this includes documents and document libraries. Users can find the Recycle Bin at the bottom of the left navigation (see Figure 10-1). In addition to lists and libraries, SharePoint 2010 (with Service Pack 1) allows administrators to recover deleted sites also (see the following URL for details: `http://technet.microsoft.com/en-us/library/hh272539.aspx`).

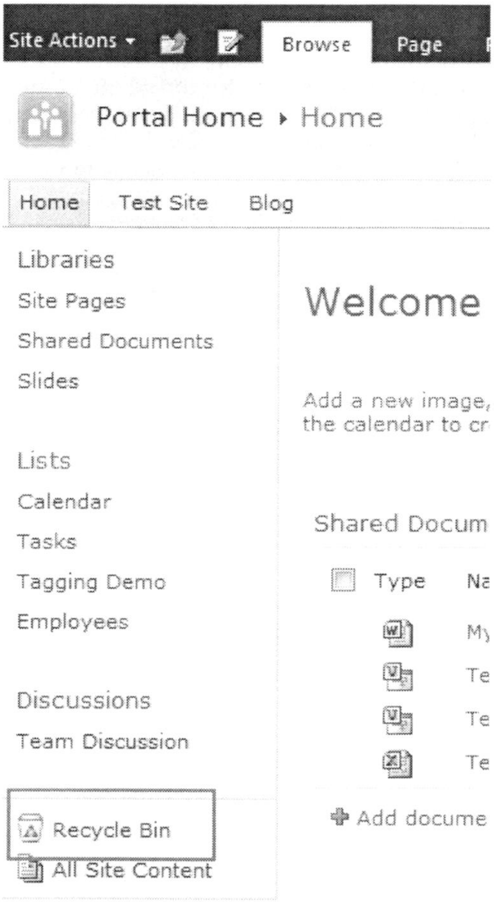

Figure 10-1. Location of the Recycle Bin

The Recycle Bin works in two stages, as described in Table 10-1, and is scoped at the web application level. Different web applications may have different configurations for their Recycle Bin.

Table 10-1. Recycle Bin Stages

Stage	Location	Details
Stage 1	Site	The stage 1 Recycle Bin is available to users with Contribute, Design, or Full Control permissions. Items and lists deleted at the site level reside in the stage 1 Recycle Bin until a time (defined by the administrator in Central Admin—typically 30 days) when the content moves to the stage 2 Recycle Bin. Content in the stage 1 Recycle Bin counts toward user storage

Stage	Location	Details
		quota.
Stage 2	Site Collection	The stage 2 Recycle Bin lives at the site collection, populated from stage 1 Recycle Bin content by a timer service. Only a site collection administrator may restore content from a stage 2 Recycle Bin, and content resides in this Recycle Bin for a time or until the Recycle Bin reaches a size, both specified by an administrator in Central Admin, before the oldest items are deleted. In addition to lists and list items, populated from the stage 1 Recycle Bin, the stage 2 Recycle Bin also contains deleted sites.
		The size of the stage 2 Recycle Bin is a percentage of the quota allocated to the entire site collection. Items in the stage 2 Recycle Bin do not count toward user storage quota, but they do eat up space in the overall site collection quota.

The following steps demonstrate how administrators may configure the Recycle Bin from Central Admin, to allow different item expiration times.

1. Open Central Admin.

2. Click the Manage Web Applications link under the Application Management heading.

3. Select the web application.

4. Click the General Settings icon in the Ribbon.

5. In the dialog, scroll to the Recycle Bin section (see Figure 10-2).

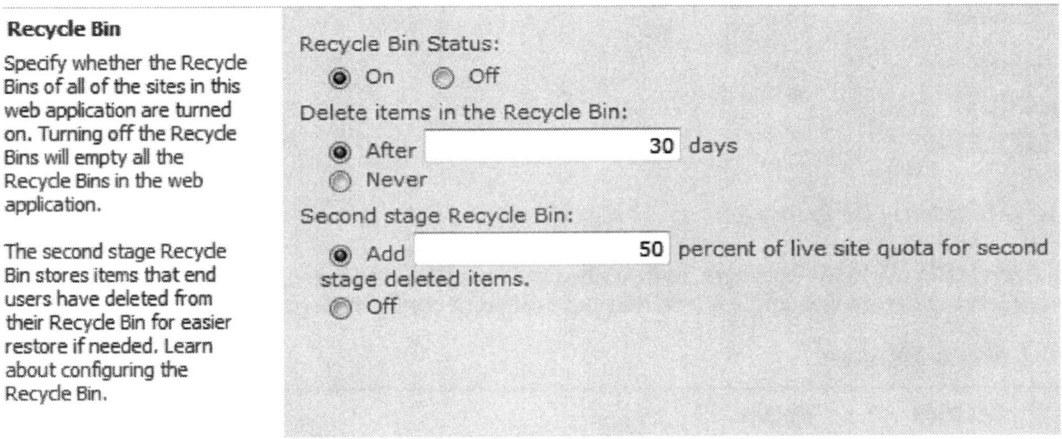

Recycle Bin

Specify whether the Recycle Bins of all of the sites in this web application are turned on. Turning off the Recycle Bins will empty all the Recycle Bins in the web application.

The second stage Recycle Bin stores items that end users have deleted from their Recycle Bin for easier restore if needed. Learn about configuring the Recycle Bin.

Recycle Bin Status:
⦿ On   ⊙ Off

Delete items in the Recycle Bin:
⦿ After [30] days
⊙ Never

Second stage Recycle Bin:
⦿ Add [50] percent of live site quota for second stage deleted items.
⊙ Off

Figure 10-2. Recycle Bin settings in General Web Application Settings

The following steps demonstrate working with the stage 1 and stage 2 Recycle Bins:

6. Navigate to a SharePoint site as a contributor.

7. Click the Recycle Bin icon at the bottom of the left navigation.

8. Figure 10-3 shows my stage 1 Recycle Bin for my root site.

■ **Note** The Root Site Collection Recycle Bin is not the stage 2 Recycle Bin; the root site also has a stage 1 Recycle Bin.

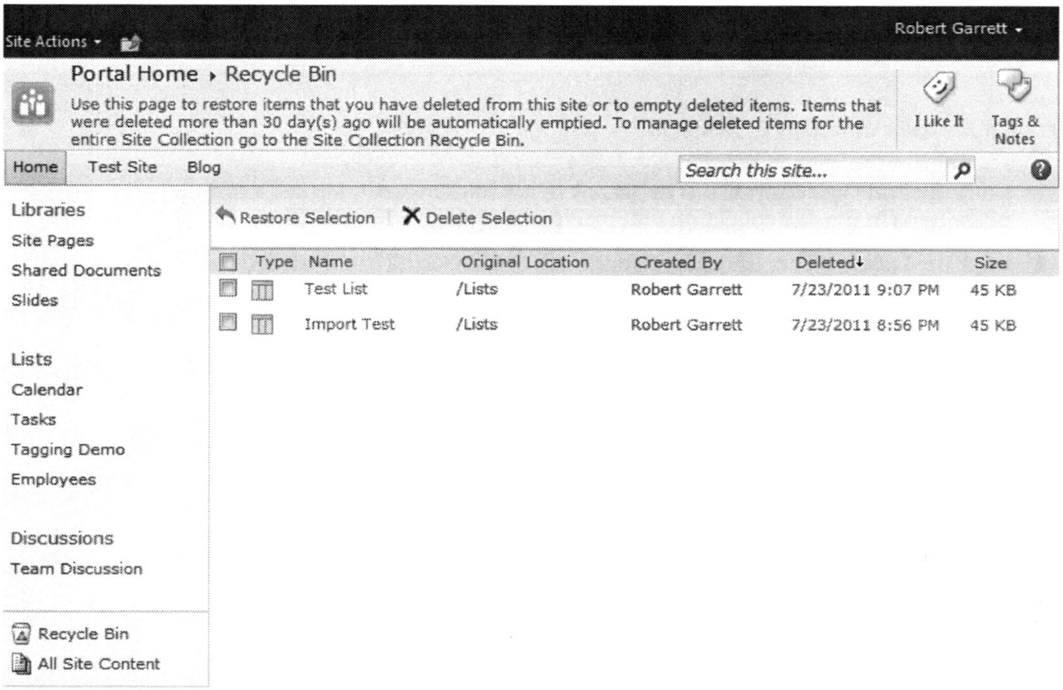

Figure 10-3. The stage 1 Recycle Bin

9. Check the boxes next to the items you wish to restore to original location before deletion, or to delete and send to the stage 2 Recycle Bin.

10. To access the stage 2 Recycle Bin, either click the link at the top of the page (as in Figure 10-3) or follow the next steps.

11. Navigate to the root site of the site collection.

12. Click the Site Action menu.

13. Click the Site Settings menu item.

14. Click the Recycle Bin link under the Site Collection Administration heading.

Figure 10-4 shows the site collection stage 2 Recycle Bin page.

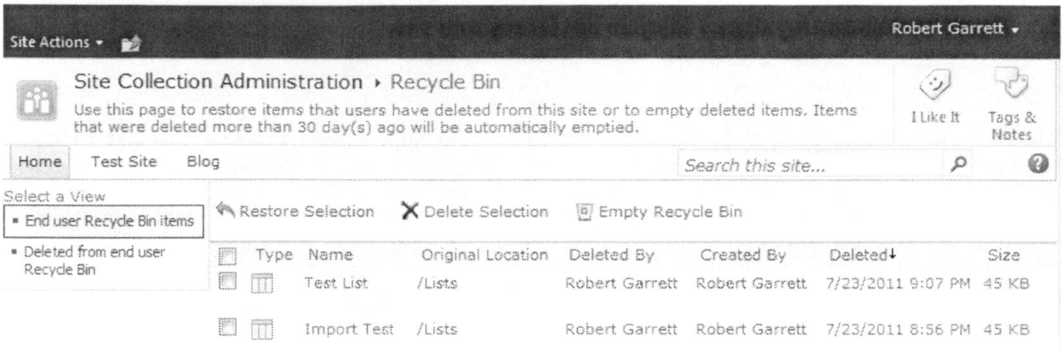

Figure 10-4. A site collection stage 2 Recycle Bin

15. Click the End User Recycle Bin Items link in the left navigation to see a roll-up of all items in the site collection that reside in site stage 1 Recycle Bins.

16. Click the Deleted from End User Recycle Bin link to see all items moved to the stage 2 Recycle Bin.

17. Check the check boxes next the items to restore or delete.

Versioning

Document and page versioning is another way in which users may self-maintain integrity of their content in SharePoint 2010. Library owners may enable versioning on a list or library so that when users with collaborative permissions upload changes, SharePoint keeps track of the version history. SharePoint library versioning is not new to SharePoint 2010; Microsoft introduced it with WSS 2.0, and it comes in two flavors:

- Major Version Numbers

- Major and Minor Version Numbers

Major and minor version numbers tie into the *publication status* of a document item. A major version in the format of xx.0 constitutes a published version, meaning that it is available to all users (including anonymous if the site allows anonymous user access). A minor version number, in the format of xx.1-9, constitutes an intermediate revision, and only the owner of the document, users with Approval permissions, and owners may see the latest changes.

The following steps detail how to enable versioning for a document library:

1. Navigate to the default view of the document library.

2. Click the Library tab in the Ribbon.

3. Click the Library Settings icon in the Ribbon.

4. Click the Versioning settings link.

5. Under Document Version History, select the desired versioning type, and the maximum number of draft and major versions to keep.

■ **Note** Lists also allow versioning, but do not provide minor (draft) versioning.

Backup and Restore

Backup and restoration of user data and system configuration is an intricate part of disaster recovery planning. After all, the user data is most precious and typically tantamount to the running of the organization business. SharePoint 2010 includes a number of backup and restoration methods, from complete farm backup/restore to granular backup/restore, such as site import and export or site collection backup. In this section, we shall visit each method and discuss the specific benefits and shortcomings of each, enabling you as the SharePoint administrator to make effective decisions in your disaster recovery plan.

As a general rule of thumb, I recommend that you employ various backup methods to ensure that you are able to recover your SharePoint farm in the event of a disaster. The following list summarizes, from a high level, what you should back up:

- All content databases

- All configuration and service application databases

- The SharePoint 2010 Hive on each web server (`c:\program files\common files\Microsoft shared\web server extensions\14\`)

- All virtual application directories on each web server (`c:\Inetpub\wwwroot\wss\VirtualDirectories`)

- Any custom databases or additional files that do not live in the hive or virtual application directories on each web server

- Site collection backups for faster restore, in the event of isolated data corruption or data loss in a particular site collection

When it comes to backup, more is better. Ideally, if you're running your farm on virtual hardware, you should snapshot all servers frequently. If space for backup is not as plentiful, then backup of all databases and custom "changes" to the hive and virtual application directories should allow you to recover your farm after a new installation.

With the high-level stuff out of the way, I shall now detail the various backup methods available in SharePoint 2010.

Site Collection Backups

Site collection backups are compelling in that they enable administrators to save a complete site collection to a file on disk. Administrators may backup a site collection using the STSADM command, PowerShell, or Central Admin—I shall demonstrate each below.

■ **Note** Site collection backup puts stress on SharePoint and consumes resources to complete the process. Microsoft does not recommend backing up site collections of more than 15GB, because of the drain on the live site collection, hosting web application, and the time to complete the backup. Site collection backup works well when moving data from one farm to another, or in conjunction with another backup scheme to ensure data integrity.

Site Collection Backup and Restore Using PowerShell

The following steps demonstrate backing up a site collection to a disk file, using PowerShell:

1. From the Start menu, choose All Programs, click Microsoft SharePoint 2010 Products, and then click SharePoint 2010 Management Shell to launch the console.

2. Type the following text into the console, replacing the appropriate placeholders:
   ```
   Backup-SPSite <site collection URL> -Path <backup file> [-Force] [-
   NoSiteLock] [-UseSQLSnapshot] [-Verbose]
   ```

Include the [Force] parameter to overwrite an existing backup file.

I recommend not using the [NoSiteLock] option, as this prevents SharePoint from putting the site collection in read-only state, meaning that users can write to the site collection during backup and potentially corrupt the database.

Use the [UseSQLSnapshot] option if you have SQL Server Enterprise edition, for more consistent backup.

The [Verbose] option provides more verbose output.

The following command demonstrates restoring a site collection from a backup file, using PowerShell:

- Type the following text into the console, replacing the appropriate placeholders:
  ```
  Restore-SPSite <site collection URL> -Path <backup file> [-DatabaseServer
  <database server name>] [-DatabaseName <database name>] [-HostHeader <host
  header>] [-Force] [-GradualDelete] [-Verbose]
  ```

Include the [Force] parameter to overwrite an existing backup file. Use the [-DatabaseServer] option if the server is not part of your farm. Include the [-GradualDelete] option to minimize locks on the database and provides for better restore performance for backups over 1GB when replacing an existing site collection, which SharePoint marks as deleted and the timer service deletes the legacy site collection later. Use the [-HostHeader] option if restoring a site collection to a web application that requires a unique host header.

Site Collection Backup and Restore using STSADM

Use the following STSADM command to back up a site collection to a disk file, replacing the appropriate placeholders:

```
STSADM -o backup -url <site collection url> -filename <filename>
```

Similar to the PowerShell command for backing up a site collection, you may provide the –overwrite option to overwrite an existing backup file, -nositelock to prevent site collection lock, and -usesqlsnapshot to use SQL Server Enterprise snapshot.

Use the following STSADM command to restore a site collection from backup file replacing the appropriate placeholders:

```
STSADM –o restore –url <site collection url> -filename <filename>
```

Similar to the PowerShell command for restoring a site collection, you may provide the –overwrite option to overwrite an existing site collection, -hostheaderwebapplicationurl to provide a host header URL, and -gradualdelete to provide better performance in overwriting an existing site collection (marks the overwritten site collection as deleted and the timer service deletes it later).

Site Collection Backup and Restore using Central Admin

The following steps demonstrate backing up a site collection to a disk file, using Central Admin:

1. Open Central Admin.

2. Click the Perform a Site Collection Backup link, under the Backup and Restore heading.

3. Click the drop-down control to change the site collection, and in the resulting dialog box, you may change the web application containing the site collection.

4. Provide the UNC path of the filename to save the backup.

5. Click the Start Backup button.

Readiness

✔ No site collection backup is in progress.
✔ Timer service is running.

Site Collection	
Select a site collection.	Site Collection: **http://robdev** ▾

File location:	
Specify the destination for the backup package.	Filename: ▯ ☐ Overwrite existing file Example: \\backup\SharePoint\Site1.bak

Start Backup	Cancel

Figure 10-5. The site collection backup page in Central Admin

Export and Import

SharePoint 2010 now supports granular export and import of sites, lists, and libraries. Earlier in this book we visited Content Deployment to send content changes from one farm to another (staging to production for example), which relies on site, list, and library export and import to operate. In this section, I shall demonstrate exporting and importing using the three tools of choice—PowerShell, STSADM, and Central Admin.

Export and Import Using PowerShell

The following steps demonstrate using PowerShell commands from the PS console to export a site to a file:

1. From the Start menu, choose All Programs, click Microsoft SharePoint 2010 Products, and then click SharePoint 2010 Management Shell to launch the console.

2. Type in the following text into the console, replacing the appropriate placeholders :
   `Export-SPWeb <site/list/library URL> -Path <filename>`

3. To export a specific list or library, provide the full URL to the list or library, otherwise PowerShell will export the site if the URL is to the main site location.

4. Include the [-Force] option to overwrite the file.

5. Include the [-HaltonError] or [-HaltOnWarning] options to stop the export process in the event of an error or warning.

6. Specify the [-IncludeUserSecurity] option if you need to ensure that all permissions applied to exported sites, lists, libraries, and contained items, include in the export file.

7. Include the [-IncludeVersions] option to instruct PowerShell to include version information of items in the export file.

8. Include the [-NoFileCompression] option to turn off file compression, this makes for a faster export but larger files on disk.

9. The [-NoLogFile] option prevents PowerShell from creating a log of the export (not recommended generally).

10. The [-UseSQLSnapshot] option is the familiar SQL snapshot option for deployments running on SQL Server Enterprise.

■ **Note** PowerShell provides help for all commands—you may get help on the export command by typing Get-help Export-SPWeb into the PowerShell console.

In partner to the export command, the following steps demonstrate importing an export file to a SharePoint site, list, or library:

11. From the Start menu, choose All Programs, click Microsoft SharePoint 2010 Products, and then click SharePoint 2010 Management Shell to launch the console.

12. Type the following text into the console, replacing the appropriate placeholders:
    `Import-SPWeb <site/list/library URL> -Path <filename>`

To import a specific list or library, provide the full URL to the list or library, otherwise PowerShell will import the site if the URL is to the main site location.

For brevity, most of the options specified in the export steps above exist for the import command. Use the Get-help feature of PowerShell to see all options.

Exporting of lists and libraries is new to SharePoint 2010. In SharePoint 2007, administrators could export and import sites only, using STSADM. SharePoint 2010 also supports STSADM export/import, but adds the capability of list and library export by providing the full URL to the list or library.

Export and Import Using STSADM

The following steps demonstrate export of a site, list, or library, using the STSADM command from a regular Windows command prompt:

1. Type the following text into the console, replacing the appropriate placeholders:
    STSADM -o export -url <site/list/library url> -filename <filename>

To export a specific list or library, provide the full URL to the list or library. Otherwise, PowerShell will export the site if the URL is to the main site location.

2. Include the –overwrite option to overwrite the file.

3. Include the –haltonfatalerror or -haltonwarning options to stop the export process in the event of an error or warning.

4. Specifying the -includeusersecurity option will ensure that all permissions applied to exported sites, lists, libraries, and contained items, include in the export file.

5. The -versions option instructs PowerShell to include version information of items in the export file.

6. Include the -nofilecompression option to turn off file compression; this makes for a faster export but larger files on disk.

7. The -nologfile option prevents PowerShell from creating a log of the export (not recommended generally).

8. The -usesqlsnapshot option is the familiar SQL snapshot option for deployments running on SQL Server Enterprise.

The following steps demonstrate using STSADM to import a site, list, or library. Look back through the command options above for the export, as some also apply to the import command:

9. Type the following text into the console, replacing the appropriate placeholders:
    STSADM -o import -url <site/list/library url> -filename <filename>

10. To import a specific list or library, provide the full URL to the list or library; otherwise PowerShell will import the site if the URL is to the main site location.

Export Using Central Admin

In this section, I demonstrate how to use Central Admin to export a site, list, or library. You may have noticed that this section does not cover import via the Central Admin web browser interface—this is because Central Admin does not provide a mechanism for site, list, or library import from a file. To import, use either STSADM or PowerShell options, discussed above.

1. Open Central Admin.

2. Click on the Backup and Restore heading link.

3. Click the Export a Site or List link under the Granular Backup heading.

4. On the resulting page, shown in Figure 10-6, select the site collection and then the site and/or list.

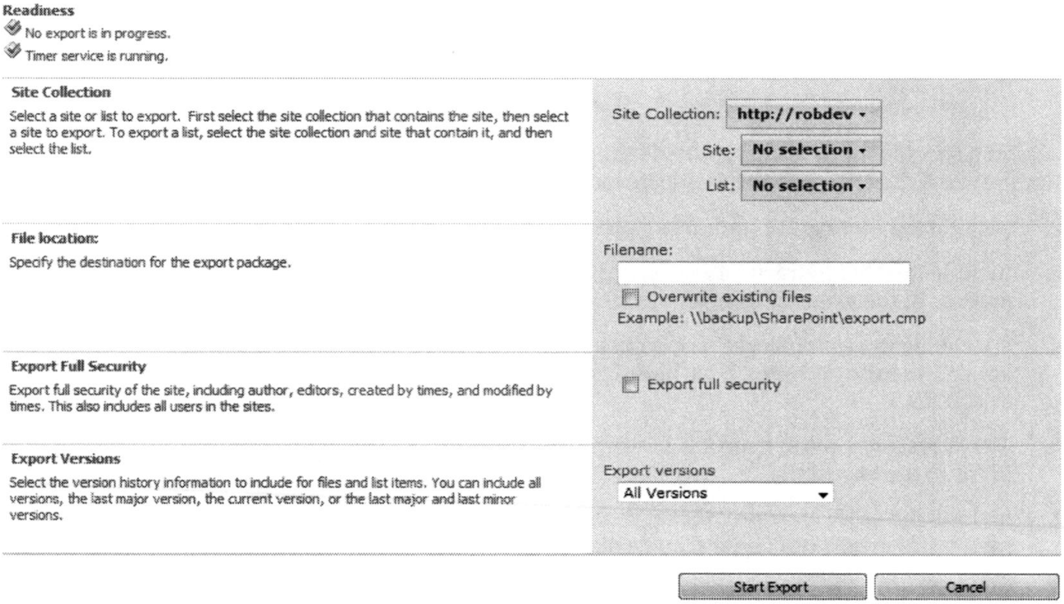

Readiness
- No export is in progress.
- Timer service is running.

Site Collection

Select a site or list to export. First select the site collection that contains the site, then select a site to export. To export a list, select the site collection and site that contain it, and then select the list.

Site Collection: **http://robdev ▾**

Site: **No selection ▾**

List: **No selection ▾**

File location:

Specify the destination for the export package.

Filename:

☐ Overwrite existing files
Example: \\backup\SharePoint\export.cmp

Export Full Security

Export full security of the site, including author, editors, created by times, and modified by times. This also includes all users in the sites.

☐ Export full security

Export Versions

Select the version history information to include for files and list items. You can include all versions, the last major version, the current version, or the last major and last minor versions.

Export versions
All Versions ▾

[Start Export]   [Cancel]

Figure 10-6. Exporting a site, list, or library from Central Admin

5. Provide the file location and toggle options for security and versions.

6. Click the Start Export button to begin the export.

Unattached Content Database Data Recovery

IT staff and database admins like to back up SQL databases—and there is nothing wrong with that! SQL Server provides options to administrators to run nightly backups, and many good backup applications include a SQL agent to back up live SQL database data to backup storage. What is not to like? The problem is that full SQL Server database backups only provide all-or-nothing restore of data. Restoring a single piece of data, such as a document, requires standing up content backup in a new SharePoint web application and site collection, to access the required data.

Rewind the clock a couple of years to the days of SharePoint 2007. In the event that an administrator needed to restore selected data (such as a site, list, or library) from an offline database, the process went something like the following:

1. Restore the SQL database backup from cold storage to a disk location, seen by SQL Server.

2. Attach the offline database data file and log file to SQL Server, using a different name to the current live SQL server, now becoming the backup database.

3. Associate the backup database with a fresh web application in SharePoint 2007, or another SharePoint 2007 farm.

4. Export the selected content from the backup, using STSADM (the minimum granularity was a sub-site).

5. Import the exported content to the current live site collection.

6. Restore the site, list, or library to the correct place in the live site collection, using SharePoint content tools, such as the Content Management UI.

The steps above seem like a lot of work to me. Further complications arose for the administrator in that SharePoint 2007 required any feature customizations to be installed to the backup web application before the administrator could access the backup site collection. If using a separate farm to host backup content data, the administrator would have to ensure that the version of the production farm was equal to or exceeded that of the backup farm for the data import to work. Yuk!

You no longer need to worry. SharePoint 2010 now allows you—the administrator—to drill into a SQL content database without ever having to attach it to the farm, as the following steps demonstrate:

7. Open Central Admin.

8. Click the Backup and Restore heading link.

9. Click the Recover Data from an Unattached Content Database link.

10. Provide the SQL Server name and database name for the warm unattached database backup (you still need to host the offline database in SQL Server somewhere).

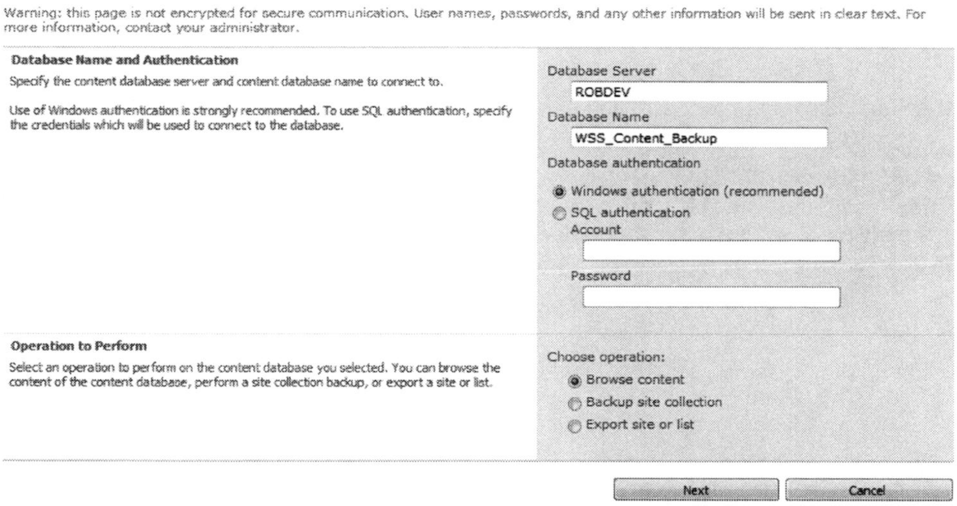

Warning: this page is not encrypted for secure communication. User names, passwords, and any other information will be sent in clear text. For more information, contact your administrator.

Database Name and Authentication

Specify the content database server and content database name to connect to.

Use of Windows authentication is strongly recommended. To use SQL authentication, specify the credentials which will be used to connect to the database.

Database Server
ROBDEV

Database Name
WSS_Content_Backup

Database authentication

● Windows authentication (recommended)
○ SQL authentication
   Account

   Password

Operation to Perform

Select an operation to perform on the content database you selected. You can browse the content of the content database, perform a site collection backup, or export a site or list.

Choose operation:
● Browse content
○ Backup site collection
○ Export site or list

[Next]   [Cancel]

Figure 10-7. The settings page for unattached content database recovery in Central Admin

11. In the Operation to Perform section you have three choices:

• Browse content in the backup database

• Backup a site collection contained in the database

• Export a site or list from the database

12. Select the Browse Content option.

13. Click the Next button.

14. On the next page (Figure 10-8), you may browse a site collection, site, and list, and then either back up the site collection or export the selected site and list.

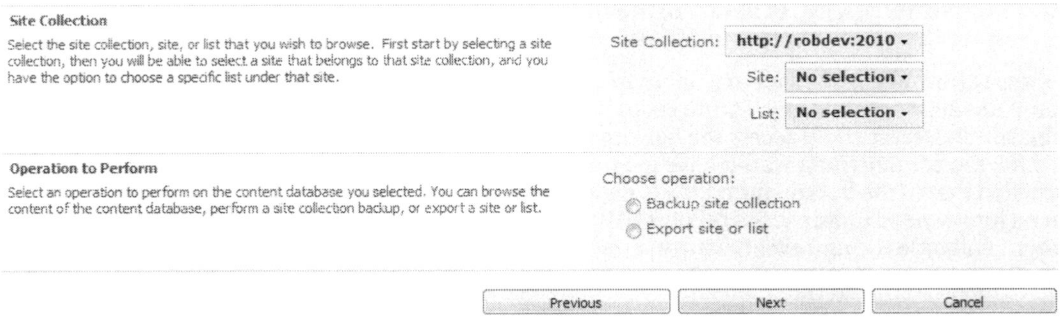

Figure 10-8. *Browse an unattached content database*

15. Try the site collection backup option and click the Next button.

SharePoint navigates you to a page to provide the site collection backup details, similar the page for site collection backup of an attached content database, discussed earlier in this chapter.

Had you selected the option to export a site or a list, or gone directly to the site collection backup or export operation on the main page in Figure 10-7, you would see the appropriate page for site collection backup or export.

16. Click the Start Backup button.

So far we have covered the granular backup methods. Next we visit complete farm backup and restore capabilities for SharePoint 2010. Before we leave granular backup, navigate back to the Backup and Restore page in Central Admin and click the Check Granular Backup Job Status link. Figure 10-9 shows the job status page for all granular backups, which provides for easy review of the health of your backup operations.

Readiness

✔ No site collection backup is in progress.

✔ No export is in progress.

✔ Timer service is running.

⟳ Refresh

Site Collection Backup	
Current Job	
Status	No operation in progress.
Previous Job	
Status	No previous job.
Content Export	
Current Job	
Status	No operation in progress.
Previous Job	
Status	No previous job.

Figure 10-9. *Granular backup status*

Farm Backup and Restore

Like the previous version, SharePoint 2010 provides complete SharePoint farm backup, using Central Admin. SharePoint 2010 also allows for backup and restore of the farm using PowerShell, and I will present steps for both procedures in this section of the chapter.

Up to now, we have discussed backup of content. Of course, content is vitally important because it is the user data of a system that give the system its value, and contributes to the running of the business for which the organization employs the system. But now that we are discussing farm backup, we have to consider more than just content—for example, system configuration settings. When faced with a total disaster and system loss, the IT team and administrators want to get a new system online as quickly as possible. Unfortunately, SharePoint, like most other enterprise systems today, has a considerable number of configuration options, and no administrator wants to reconfigure a virgin SharePoint 2010 installation, from the ground up, under the pressure of disaster recovery. Fortunately, the features in SharePoint 2010 that provide for complete farm backup allow for configuration backup. Here I'll discuss configuration backup and restore as part of farm backup.

The following sections first walk the reader through backup via the Central Admin browser interface and then cover PowerShell backup and restore commands.

Farm Backup Settings

Before we begin our first SharePoint 2010 farm backup, we should first visit the settings page, as follows:

1. Open Central Admin.

2.   Click on the Backup and Restore heading link.

3.   Click the Configure Backup Settings link.

4.   SharePoint displays a page for you to configure the number of threads for backup and restore, and a directory location (UNC path) to store farm backup files.

5.   The default of three threads is fine for most purposes.

Threads, in computer terms, much like the threads in clothing, consist of granular processing in the overall application process lifecycle. The CPU in the server slices time given to threads in a process to give the illusion of multithreading or multiple things happening at once.

Modern CPUs consist of multiple cores, which can process separate threads of a process at the same time (true multithreading). Backup and restore operations work well with multithreading because each thread dedicated to a CPU core may run independent backup and restore operations, thus providing for a more efficient backup and restore, which by its very nature is a timely process.

Performing a Backup

With the overall farm backup settings configured, we are now ready to perform our first backup. Follow the steps below:

1.   Navigate to the Backup and Restore page in Central Admin.

2.   Click the Perform a Backup link. SharePoint displays a page like that in Figure 10-10.

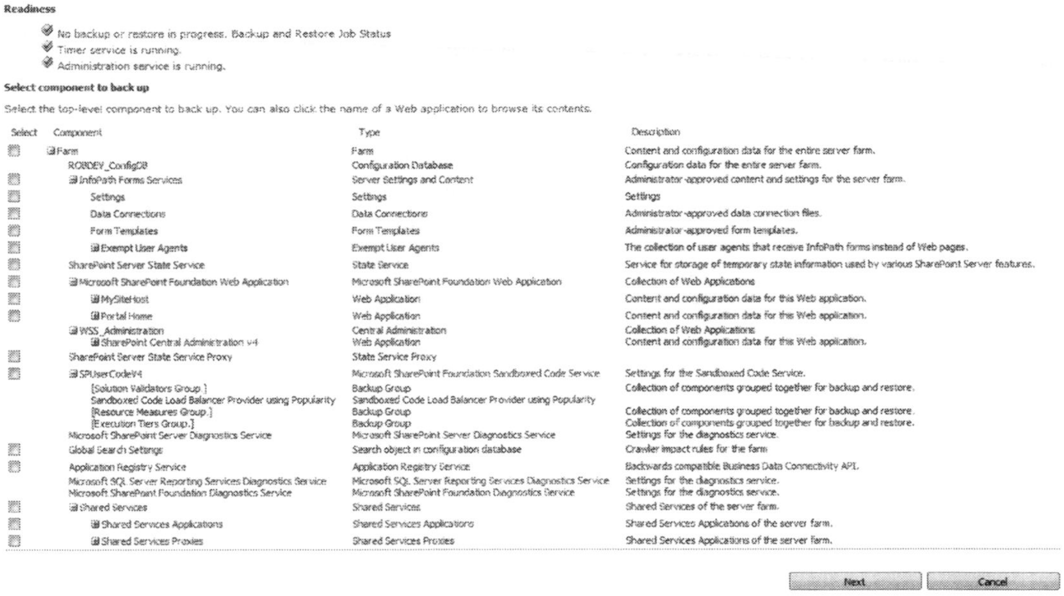

Figure 10-10. The farm backup page in Central Admin

This page is where it is all happening! Looking at Figure 10-10, which shows a summary of my farm, you can see several selection options to include in the farm backup.

Checking the checkbox at the top Farm level will enable all the options below it, which includes backup of the content databases, web application settings, and service application configuration.

At this point you may choose what to backup a la carte style, but for demonstration purposes I shall assume backup of the entire farm. This will also give you an idea of how long the process for complete farm backup usually takes (which changes by order of magnitude based on the content in your farm and services installed).

■ **Note** When backing up content, backup files typically consume 1.5 times as much space as the original content databases.

---

3. Check the checkbox next to the farm level, and then click the Next button.

Figure 10-11 shows the next page, where we specify the backup type.

Figure 10-11. Page 2 in the backup farm configuration process

If you followed the steps in the previous sub section to configure the backup location, you should see the same location specified in the location area of the page, as in Figure 10-11.

SharePoint provides you with a helpful summary of the running services, required for a farm backup, which include the timer service and administration service. The Backup Component section reminds you what you selected in the previous screen.

4. Select the backup type as either Full or Differential. A full backup is exactly that—SharePoint backs up *everything*. Differential backups run much smaller and faster, but they only back up changes since the last full backup. Consider the restore process when choosing the backup types. Full backup restores are easier but take longer than differential, which require multiple restores of the various differential backups to get the system current after a disaster.

■ **Note** As a good practice, I recommend a weekly full backup and daily differential backups.

---

5. For demonstration purposes, and since this is our first backup, choose Full.

The next section of the backup page allows you to specify backup of both content and configuration, or just configuration. The latter option comes in handy if you already have a content redundancy or backup process in place, and now just want to save the farm configuration.

6. Click the option to back up both content and configuration.

7. Click the Start Backup button to begin the process.

SharePoint 2010 shows a page like that in Figure 10-12, which displays the status of the backup.

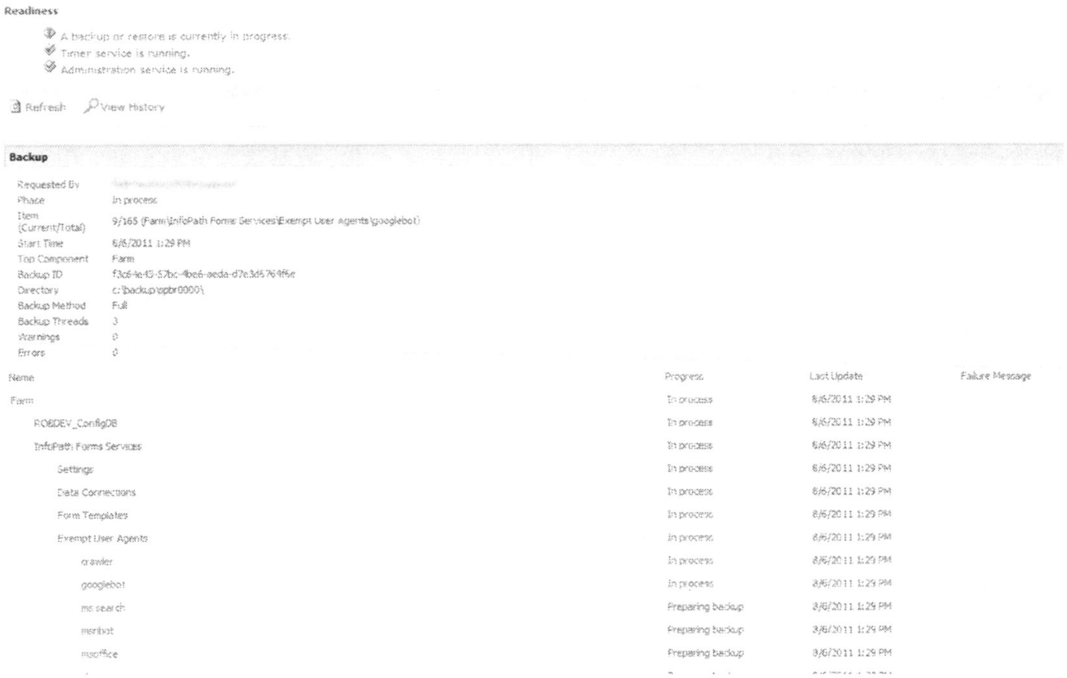

Figure 10-12. Farm backup status

8. Navigate back to the Central Admin Backup and Restore page.

9. Click the View backup and Restore History link to see a history of past backups.

If the backup is still running, then SharePoint 2010 will inform you with a link to the status page at the top of the history page—Backup and Restore Job Status.

10. You may also get to the Backup and Restore Status page by clicking the Check Backup and Restore Job Status link in the Backup and Restore page.

Performing a Restore

Performing a SharePoint 2010 farm restore is much the inverse of the backup process. Assuming you have performed a successful farm backup, the following steps demonstrate the farm restore process:

1. Navigate to the Backup and Restore page in Central Admin.

2. Click the Restore from a Backup link, and SharePoint 2010 displays a page like Figure 10-13.

Figure 10-13. Restoring the farm from backup

3. Choose the backup instance from the history list, and then click the Next button.

SharePoint 2010 shows a page like that in Figure 10-14.

Readiness

✔ No backup or restore in progress. Backup and Restore Job Status
✔ Timer service is running.
✔ Administration service is running.

Select component to restore

Select the top-level component to restore.

Select	Component	Type	Backup Failure Message
☐	⊟ Farm	Farm	
	ROBDEV_ConfigDB	Configuration Database	
☐	⊟ InfoPath Forms Services	Server Settings and Content	
☐	Settings	Settings	
☐	Data Connections	Data Connections	
☐	Form Templates	Form Templates	
☐	⊟ Exempt User Agents	Exempt User Agents	
☐	SharePoint Server State Service	State Service	
☐	⊟ Microsoft SharePoint Foundation Web Application	Microsoft SharePoint Foundation Web Application	
☐	⊞ MySiteHost	Web Application	
☐	⊞ Portal Home	Web Application	
	⊟ WSS_Administration	Central Administration	
	⊞ SharePoint Central Administration v4	Web Application	
☐	SharePoint Server State Service Proxy	State Service Proxy	
☐	⊟ SPUserCodeV4	Microsoft SharePoint Foundation Sandboxed Code Service	
	[Solution Validators Group.]	Backup Group	
	Sandboxed Code Load Balancer Provider using Popularity	Sandboxed Code Load Balancer Provider using Popularity	
	[Resource Measures Group.]	Backup Group	
	[Execution Tiers Group.]	Backup Group	
	Microsoft SharePoint Server Diagnostics Service	Microsoft SharePoint Server Diagnostics Service	
☐	Global Search Settings	Search object in configuration database	
☐	Application Registry Service	Application Registry Service	
	Microsoft SQL Server Reporting Services Diagnostics Service	Microsoft SQL Server Reporting Services Diagnostics Service	
	Microsoft SharePoint Foundation Diagnostics Service	Microsoft SharePoint Foundation Diagnostics Service	
☐	⊟ Shared Services	Shared Services	
☐	⊞ Shared Services Applications	Shared Services Applications	
☐	⊞ Shared Services Proxies	Shared Services Proxies	

[Previous]   [Next]   [Cancel]

Figure 10-14. Farm Restore Selection

Similar to the backup process, this selection screen allows you to choose what configuration and content in the farm to restore.

4. Make your selection, and then click the Next button.

The next page (too large to illustrate here) shows various options for the selected service and content configuration.

5. Choose whether you wish to overwrite configuration or create new. The option to create new services from backup is useful when restoring a new farm from scratch after disaster; use Overwrite when replacing the existing configuration.

6. Click the Start Restore button to begin the restore process.

Using PowerShell

As one might expect, SharePoint 2010 allows administrators to perform farm backup with PowerShell.

■ **Note** Before embarking on this route of backup/restore, ensure that the user running the script is a member of the `SharePoint_Shell_Access` role in the main SharePoint configuration database, and is a member of the Windows security group `WSS_ADMIN_WPG`.

Follow the steps below to back up the farm using PowerShell:

7. From the Start menu, choose All Programs, click Microsoft SharePoint 2010 Products, and then click SharePoint 2010 Management Shell to launch the console.

8. Type the following text into the console, replacing the appropriate placeholders::
   ```
   Backup-SPFarm –Directory <Backup Folder> -BackupMethod {Full |
   Differential} [-Verbose]
   ```

9. Add the [-Force] parameter to force overwrite of existing backup files.

10. Add the [-ConfigurationOnly] option to backup configuration without content.

Follow the steps below to restore a farm from backup using PowerShell:

11. From the Start menu, choose All Programs, click Microsoft SharePoint 2010 Products, and then click SharePoint 2010 Management Shell to launch the console.

12. Type the following text into the console, replacing the appropriate placeholders:
   ```
   Restore-SPFarm –Directory <Backup Folder> -RestoreMethod {New |
   Overwrite} [-Verbose]
   ```

13. Add the [-Force] parameter to force overwrite of existing backup files.

14. Add the [-ConfigurationOnly] option to backup configuration without content.

Health and Monitoring

The health of your new SharePoint 2010 deployment is very important. Your organization, you, and your administration team have likely spent considerable time installing, configuring, and deploying SharePoint 2010 to accommodate the needs of the enterprise. In my time as a SharePoint Architect, I have seen a number of organizations stop here, but the fact of the matter is that SharePoint 2010 requires a certain amount of care and feeding, just like any enterprise computer system. This is not to say that SharePoint 2010 left alone will fall over in time, but as more users pump data into the system, eating up storage space, and the system grows a larger user base, administrators should expect to monitor SharePoint and the underlying server infrastructure for stress areas and efficiency optimization.

Organizations understand that it is costly to stand up large-scale enterprise systems, and they rely on them as an integral part of their daily business. Spending more money ensuring that such systems remain healthy and sustain significant uptime is just as important as the upfront investment in the creation of the system. Consider how much money an organization might lose if its core information system falls over and suffers downtime.

Earlier in this chapter, we looked at disaster recovery. I demonstrated several planning techniques to recover in the event that your SharePoint 2010 infrastructure fails. Disaster recovery is akin to planning for what to do when a hurricane hits your town, but it would sure be nice to factor in some notice before the storm hits—this analogy is what health and monitoring is all about.

In the previous versions of SharePoint, administrators tended to work in reactive mode—typically, users of the system would report performance issues or loss of access to their data in SharePoint, and the IT department would then jump on the case to rectify the issue. SharePoint 2010 now provides health and monitoring features to give the IT group a heads-up of potential issues in the platform, long before users ever see an issue. In the remainder of this chapter, I shall describe these new features and how to configure them to give you advanced warning of problems brewing in the platform, so that you may remedy issues and users may never know there was a problem in the first place.

Logging

Logging is an important part of health monitoring because it is via various log files that SharePoint 2010 may alert administrators to issues in the system.

The Unified Logging Service (ULS), which also existed in SharePoint 2007, provides administrators with an extensive dump of information, warning, and errors occurring in the platform. When something goes wrong, the user typically sees either a custom-developed "oops" message in their browser, or a default SharePoint error message. It is the job of SharePoint administrators to find out what went wrong, and the ULS logs will likely give an indication to the problem—especially if it is recurring.

■ **Note** By default, the ULS logs live on each SharePoint 2010 server in the Logs folder of the hive, typically
`c:\program files\common files\Microsoft shared\web server extensions\14\logs`.

Figure 10-15 shows an Explorer view of the ULS log folder on my SharePoint 2010 development server. The log folder consists of a number of files, both log and usage files (all text files), that have a filename in the format of year, month, day, and time. If you crack-open any of the log files you can see lots of detail, reported by the various functional areas of the SharePoint platform—notice that the Timer Service reports lots of information events.

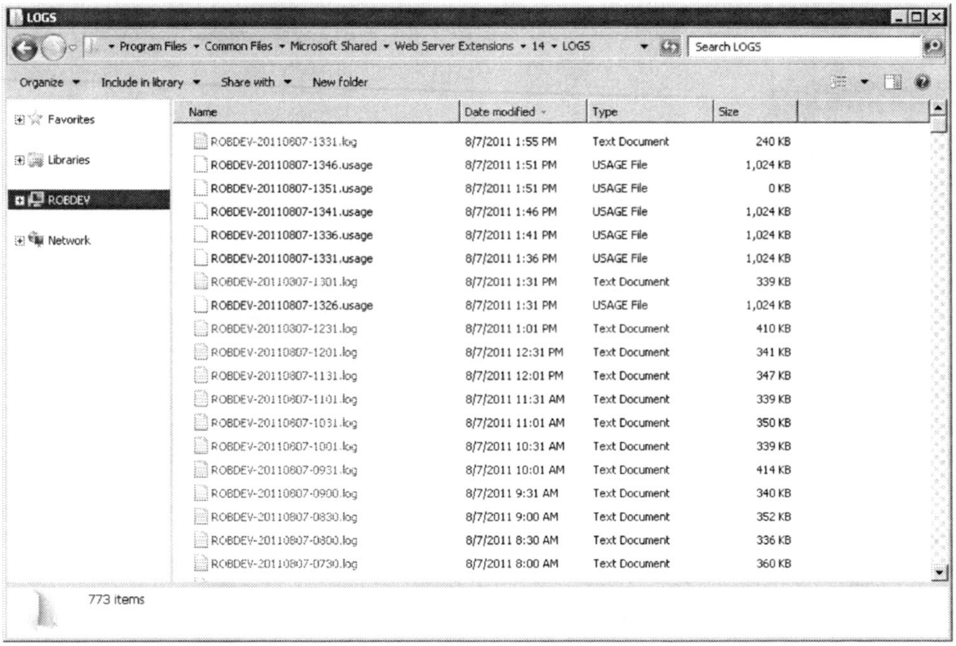

Figure 10-15: A log folder in SharePoint 2010

SharePoint 2010 allows you to fine-tune the ULS log files to contain information most important to you. The Trace Log Service, which controls output of the ULS log files, also operates in a variety of verbosity modes, ranging from error reporting to very detailed information for every action in the platform. As you might expect, Central Admin is the place to configure the ULS settings, as demonstrated in the following steps:

1. Open Central Admin.

2. Click on the Monitoring link.

3. Click the Configure Diagnostic Logging link, which then shows a page like Figure 10-16.

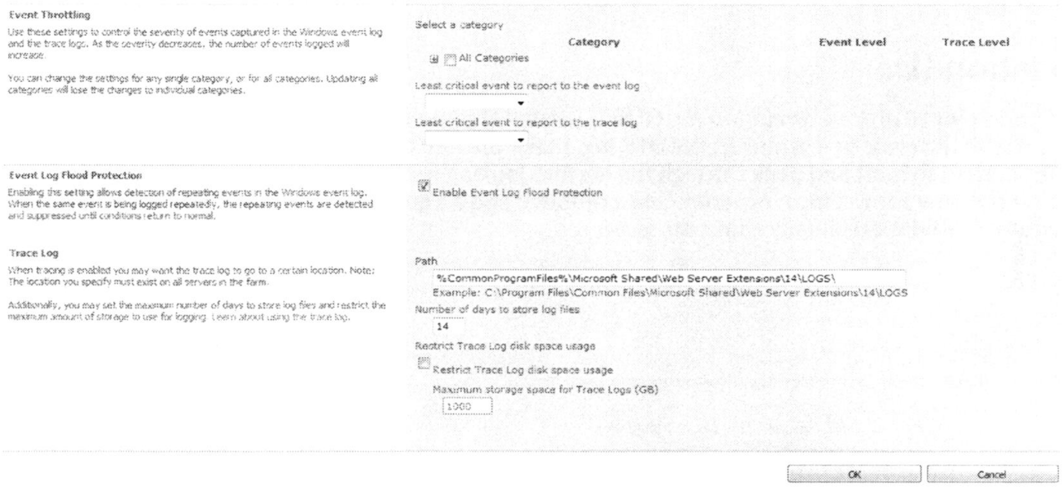

Figure 10-16. ULS logs settings

4. Expand the Categories node and specify the types of events you wish SharePoint to log in the ULS logs.

5. When an error occurs in the platform, SharePoint reports events to both the ULS and Windows Event Log; you may control the severity (verbosity level) of events logged to both in the Throttling section of the page.

■ **Note** This page does not show you the current configuration for throttling; it defaults to empty drop-down controls, and no categories selected.

---

6. Flood protection consists of preventing SharePoint logging the same repeated event to the Windows event log when a consistent problem arises. For example, if a timer service job runs every 5 minutes and fails, you really do not

want hundreds of event log errors of the same message because an administrator did not get to the issue for a few hours.

7. Finally, the Trace Log section defines the location of ULS log files, the number of days of history to store, and the maximum size of log files.

■ **Note** When changing settings for diagnostic logging, I recommend you restart the SharePoint 2010 Tracing service in Windows Services. Also, stop this service if you need to delete any of the ULS log files.

Correlation IDs

New to SharePoint 2010 are *Correlation IDs* GUIDs (Global Unique Identifiers) that map an event in SharePoint with the error or warning in the ULS log. In the previous versions of SharePoint, the administrator had to hunt and peck through the log files looking for the event that caused the error. Correlation IDs now allow a user, experiencing a problem and an error page, to send the ID to the administrator to find more details about the issue.

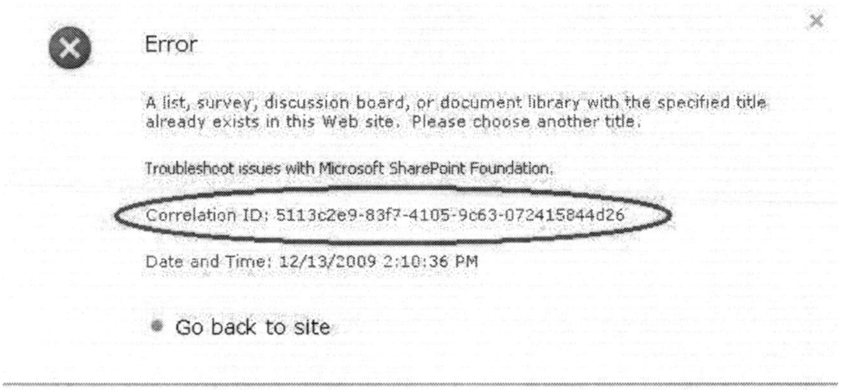

Figure 10-17. Correlation ID in a SharePoint 2010 error page

As well as using a text-editor-find action to find errors in the logs files, SharePoint 2010 includes a very nice PowerShell command to simplify finding the messages with a given correlation ID:

```
Get-SPLogEvent | ?{$_.Correlation -eq "<ID>"}
```

The Logging Database

The new Logging Database in SharePoint 2010 provides developers with a central data store to capture all events occurring in the platform. Microsoft introduced the logging database both to provide a transactional database of all events for easy query and to herd developers away from executing custom queries directly against content and configuration databases in the farm.

The logging database provides a central location to query all events occurring in the farm, whereas ULS logs only report information per the verbosity settings (see previous sections of this chapter) and spread across servers in the farm. The following steps demonstrate how to configure the logging database for your farm:

1. Open Central Admin.

2. Click the Monitoring heading link.

3. Click the Configure Usage and Health Data Collection link.

Figure 10-18 shows a page like that for configuring the health data collection events.

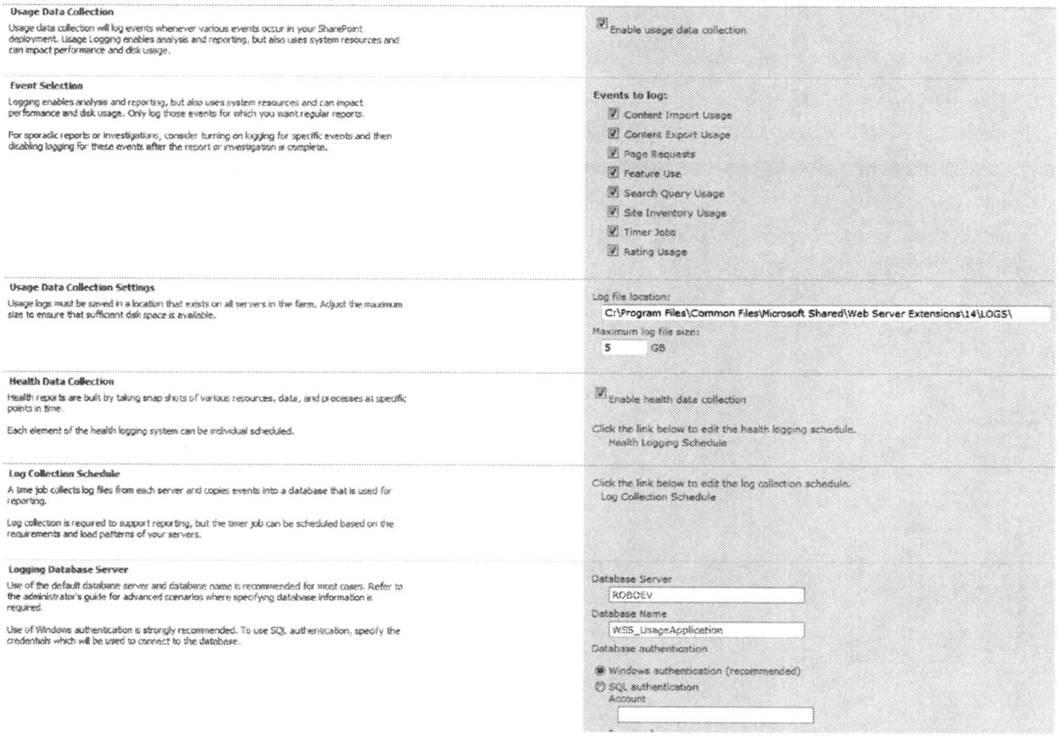

Figure 10-18. Configure health data collection

4. Ensure that the topmost check box is checked to enable usage data collection.

5. Select the events you wish SharePoint 2010 to capture; by default the page shows you all events.

6. In the Usage Data Collection Settings section, notice the location defaults to the same folder as ULS logs, looking into this folder you should see usage files as well as the familiar log files.

7. Ensure that the checkbox is checked for the Health Data Collection setting to monitor SharePoint 2010 farm health, which is in addition to usage.

8. Click the Health Logging Schedule link if you wish to change the schedule that the health logging timer services run (several of them).

9. SharePoint 2010 populates the logging database using the various usage files on each SharePoint server. A timer service collects data from these files and populates the database configured in the Logging Database Server section; click the link to configure the schedule of the log collection timer service.

Allow the usage collection to run for a day or two and interact with your farm to generate usage events. Next, I shall show you the logging database, which in my farm is the WSS_UsageApplication database.

10. Open SQL Server Management Studio.

11. Navigate to the logging database (in my case WSS_UsageApplication).

12. If you expand the Tables node, you should see a large number of partitioned tables, which is not too helpful; expand the Views node instead.

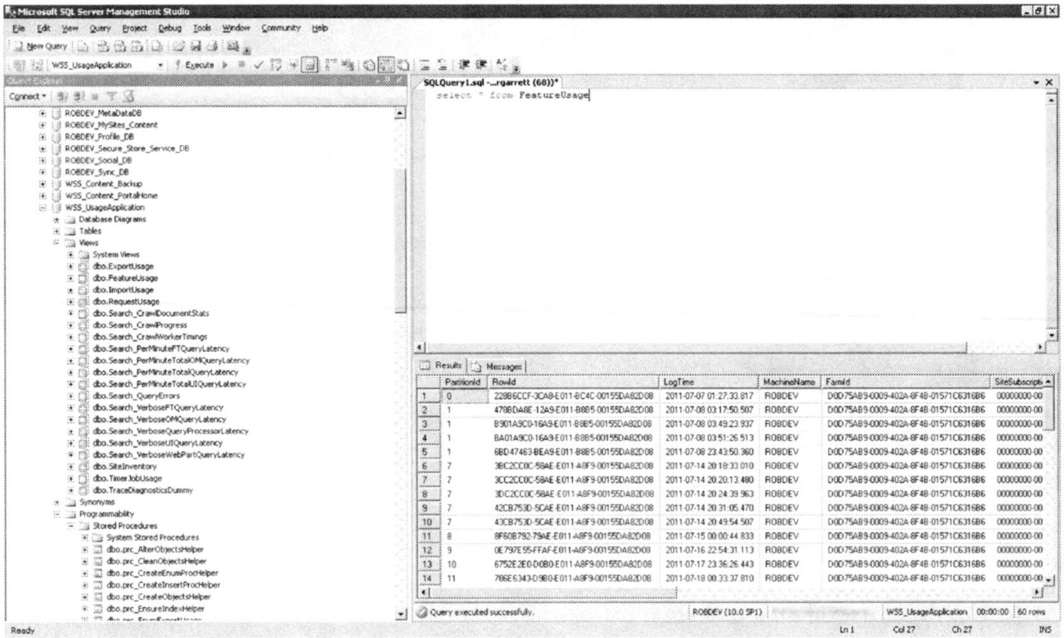

Figure 10-19. SQL Server Management Studio and the logging database

13. You may execute SQL queries against the views; in Figure 10-19 I ran a select T-SQL statement over the dbo.FeatureUsage view.

The logging database also contains a number of stored procedures that return tabular usage data. As you can see, the logging database provides a nice collection of usage event data that developers may query in custom controls, without having to dip into the main farm content and configuration databases. The premise here is that Microsoft optimizes the configuration and content databases for SharePoint 2010 and does not guarantee consistency in the schema between versions. The logging database is isolated from the other farm databases and offers consistency, allowing developers the confidence that their queries remain working with future upgrades of the platform.

SharePoint 2010 caters to developers, but at the same time, it does not leave administrators out in the cold—SharePoint 2010 provides several administrative, usage, and health reports, which rely on the logging database.

14. Click the Monitoring heading link from the Central Admin home page.

15. Click the View Administrative Reports link to review a document library of administrative reports—the reports are simple ASPX pages, which developers may download and edit.

16. Click the View Health Reports link to see health reports.

17. Click the View Web Analytics Reports link to view analytic usage reports.

Note The reports require a working State Service Application, and the Web Analytics Reports require the Web Analytics Service Application running.

Date Range 7/8/2011 - 8/6/2011 (UTC-05:00) Eastern Time (US and Canada) Change Settings					
Summary					
Traffic	Category	Metrics	Value (Current)	Value (Previous)	Trend
Number of Page Views	Traffic				
Number of Daily Unique Visitors		Total Number of Page Views	0	0	-
Number of Referrers		Average Number of Page Views per Day	0	0	-
Top Pages		Total Number of Daily Unique Visitors	0	0	-
Top Visitors		Average Number of Unique Visitors per Day	0	0	-
Top Referrers		Total Number of Referrers	0	0	-
Top Destinations		Average Number of Referrers per Day	0	0	-
Top Browsers	Search				
		Total Number of Search Queries	0	0	-
Search		Average Number of Search Queries per Day	0	0	-
Number of Queries	Inventory				
		Number of Site Collections	-	-	-
Inventory					
Number of Site Collections					
Customized Reports					

Figure 10-20. The Web Analytics report page

The Health Analyzer

The previous few sections of this chapter were concerned with reviewing the health of SharePoint 2010 proactively. When I first mentioned health and monitoring in this chapter, I said that SharePoint has the capability to monitor and report itself and give administrators a heads-up when potential problems in the platform are brewing. This is the job of the Health Analyzer.

1. Open Central Admin.

2. Click the Monitoring heading link.

3. See the links under the Health Analyzer heading.

Because the job of the Health Analyzer and reporting issues is important, you may notice that the HA displays a banner on the home page of the Central Administration home page when it detects problems.

Figure 10-21. Health Analyzer alerts the administrator of problems via the home page of Central Administration.

4. Click the View These Issues link, which navigates you to the same page as the Review Problems and Solutions link under the Monitoring heading.

If the Health Analyzer has picked up issues to address in your farm, the Review Problems and Solutions page should list those issues. See Figure 10-22 for an example from my development farm.

	Title	Failing Servers	Failing Services	Modified
	Category : Security (4)			
	Web Applications using Claims authentication require an update.	ROBDEV	SPTimerService (SPTimerV4)	8/7/2011 12:00 AM
	The server farm account should not be used for other services.		SPTimerService (SPTimerV4)	8/7/2011 12:00 AM
	Accounts used by application pools or service identities are in the local machine Administrators group.	ROBDEV	SPTimerService (SPTimerV4)	8/7/2011 12:00 AM
	The Unattended Service Account Application ID is not specified or has an invalid value.		VisioGraphicsService	8/7/2011 12:00 AM
	Category : Performance (1)			
	Databases exist on servers running SharePoint Foundation.	ROBDEV	SPTimerService (SPTimerV4)	8/7/2011 12:00 AM
	Category : Configuration (6)			
	Missing server side dependencies.		SPTimerService (SPTimerV4)	8/7/2011 12:00 AM
	Outbound e-mail has not been configured.		SPTimerService (SPTimerV4)	8/7/2011 12:00 AM
	Verify that the Activity Feed Timer Job is enabled.		UserProfileService	8/7/2011 12:00 AM
	Verify each User Profile Service Application has an associated Search Service Connection.		UserProfileService	8/7/2011 12:00 AM
	Built-in accounts are used as application pool or service identities.		SPTimerService (SPTimerV4)	8/7/2011 12:00 AM
	InfoPath Forms Services forms cannot be filled out in a Web browser because no State Service connection is configured.	ROBDEV	SPTimerService (SPTimerV4)	8/7/2011 12:00 AM
	Category : Availability (2)			
	Drives are at risk of running out of free space.	ROBDEV	SPTimerService (SPTimerV4)	8/7/2011 4:00 PM
	Database has large amounts of unused space.		SPTimerService (SPTimerV4)	8/7/2011 12:00 AM

✱ Add new item

***Figure 10-22.** A list of problems and solutions identified by the Health Analyzer*

5. Click any of the issues, and SharePoint 2010 will open a dialog with more specifics about the issue.

6. In some cases, SharePoint 2010 can help you fix issues, with the Repair Automatically icon in the dialog Ribbon.

7. If SharePoint 2010 cannot automatically fix an issue, fix the issue manually; then come back to the issue and click the Reanalyze Now icon to request that the Health Analyzer determine if the issue is remedied.

The Health Analyzer uses a series of rules to determine if a particular area of the SharePoint 2010 platform needs attention:

8. Navigate back to the Monitoring page in Central Admin.

9. Click the Review Rule Definitions link.

SharePoint 2010 shows a page like that in Figure 10-23, which consists of a standard list of rules.

☐ Title	Schedule	Enabled	Repair Automatically
⊿ Category : **Security** (4)			
Accounts used by application pools or service identities are in the local machine Administrators group.	Daily	Yes	No
Web Applications using Claims authentication require an update.	Daily	Yes	No
The server farm account should not be used for other services.	Weekly	Yes	No
The Unattended Service Account Application ID is not specified or has an invalid value.	Daily	Yes	No
⊿ Category : **Performance** (17)			
Application pools recycle when memory limits are exceeded.	Weekly	Yes	No
Databases used by SharePoint have fragmented indices.	Daily	Yes	Yes
Databases exist on servers running SharePoint Foundation.	Weekly	Yes	No
The paging file size should exceed the amount of physical RAM in the system.	Weekly	Yes	No
Databases used by SharePoint have outdated index statistics.	Daily	Yes	Yes
The timer service failed to recycle.	Weekly	Yes	No
Search - One or more property databases have fragmented indices.	Weekly	Yes	Yes
Search - One or more crawl databases may have fragmented indices.	On Demand	Yes	Yes
The Visio Graphics Service has a maximum cache age setting that will adversely impact performance.	Daily	Yes	No
The Visio Graphics Service has a maximum Web Drawing size setting that will adversely impact performance.	Daily	Yes	No
The Visio Graphics Service has a maximum recalc duration setting that will adversely impact user perceived performance.	Daily	Yes	No
The Visio Graphics Service has a minimum cache age setting that will adversely impact performance.	Daily	Yes	No
The Visio Graphics Service has a minimum cache age setting that may cause a security issue.	Daily	Yes	No
Web Analytics: Monitors the health of the Report Consolidator component. ⧉ New	Daily	Yes	No
Web Analytics: Monitors the health of the Logging Extractor component. ⧉ New	Daily	Yes	No
Web Analytics: Monitors the health of the Data Analyzer Light component. ⧉ New	Daily	Yes	No
Web Analytics: Monitors the health of the User Behavior Analyzer component. ⧉ New	Daily	Yes	No
⊿ Category : **Configuration** (30)			
Alternate access URLs have not been configured.	Daily	Yes	No
The Application Discovery and Load Balancer Service is not running in this farm.	Hourly	Yes	No

Figure 10-23. Rule defintions for the Health Analyzer

10. Click the name of any list item in the appropriate category to view the dialog for the rule list item.

11. You may click the Edit icon to edit the rule list item—you may change the name, scope, schedule, and whether SharePoint can configure the issue automatically.

Since Health Analyzer rules consist of list items, Microsoft and third parties may add additional rules later.

Timer Jobs

Time Jobs work at the heart of a SharePoint 2010 farm. Each SharePoint server (web-front-end or application server) hosts a SharePoint 2010 Timer service, which is a Windows service. This service is responsible for running SharePoint jobs—designated units of functionality to execute a designated time and perhaps recurring.

SharePoint 2010 relies on a vast number of timer service jobs to maintain operation of the farm. The following steps demonstrate how to view the available timer job definitions in the farm:

1. Open Central Admin.

2. Click the Monitoring heading link.

3. Click the Review Job Definitions link, under the Timer Jobs heading.

SharePoint displays a page like that in Figure 10-24.

Service: Microsoft SharePoint Foundation Timer ▾   View: Service ▾

Title	Web Application	Schedule Type
Application Addresses Refresh Job		Minutes
CEIP Data Collection		Daily
Delete Job History		Weekly
Diagnostic Data Provider: Event Log		Disabled
Diagnostic Data Provider: Performance Counters - Database Servers		Disabled
Diagnostic Data Provider: Performance Counters - Web Front Ends		Disabled
Diagnostic Data Provider: SQL Blocking Queries		Disabled
Diagnostic Data Provider: SQL DMV		Disabled
Diagnostic Data Provider: SQL Memory DMV		Disabled
Diagnostic Data Provider: Trace Log		Disabled
Health Analysis Job (Daily, Microsoft SharePoint Foundation Timer, All Servers)		Daily
Health Analysis Job (Daily, Microsoft SharePoint Foundation Timer, Any Server)		Daily
Health Analysis Job (Hourly, Microsoft SharePoint Foundation Timer, All Servers)		Hourly
Health Analysis Job (Hourly, Microsoft SharePoint Foundation Timer, Any Server)		Hourly
Health Analysis Job (Monthly, Microsoft SharePoint Foundation Timer, Any Server)		Monthly
Health Analysis Job (Weekly, Microsoft SharePoint Foundation Timer, All Servers)		Weekly
Health Analysis Job (Weekly, Microsoft SharePoint Foundation Timer, Any Server)		Weekly
InfoPath Forms Services Maintenance		Daily
Password Management		Daily
Product Version Job		Daily
State Service Delete Expired Sessions		Hourly
Timer Service Recycle		Daily
UPS Service Application - Social Rating Synchronization Job		Hourly
UPS Service Application - User Profile to SharePoint Full Synchronization		Hourly
UPS Service Application - User Profile to SharePoint Quick Synchronization		Minutes

Figure 10-24. *Timer job definitions*

Timer job definitions exist either as common to the SharePoint 2010 Foundation Timer service or associated with other SharePoint 2010 services, such as the Access or Excel services.

4. Click the Service drop-down box in the top right to change the service. You may also list timer services by web application, by changing the far-right drop-down from Service to Web Application.

5. Click the name of any of the timer job definitions to see the details of the job.

Administrators may change the schedule of most jobs. They may also disable and enable jobs. SharePoint 2010 only allows creation of new jobs via code and feature deployment, so seek a developer if you need a special job created.

Some of the functional features of SharePoint 2010 create timer jobs to perform their tasks; for example, Content Deployment creates a new timer job to deploy content to another farm.

6. Navigate back to the Monitoring page of Central Admin.

7. Click the Check Job Status link, and SharePoint 2010 shows you a page of upcoming scheduled jobs, running jobs, and a history of jobs executed, with their completion status.

Web Application: http://robdev/ ▾   View: Web Application ▾

Scheduled

Job Title	Server	Web Application	Next Start Time
Scheduled Approval	ROBDEV	Portal Home	8/7/2011 4:35 PM
Variations Propagate Site Job Definition	ROBDEV	Portal Home	8/7/2011 4:35 PM
Variations Create Site Job Definition	ROBDEV	Portal Home	8/7/2011 4:35 PM
Solution Resource Usage Log Processing	ROBDEV	Portal Home	8/7/2011 4:35 PM
Immediate Alerts	ROBDEV	Portal Home	8/7/2011 4:35 PM
Scheduled Unpublish	ROBDEV	Portal Home	8/7/2011 4:35 PM
Document Conversions	ROBDEV	Portal Home	8/7/2011 4:36 PM
Variations Propagate Page Job Definition	ROBDEV	Portal Home	8/7/2011 4:42 PM
Workflow Failover	ROBDEV	Portal Home	8/7/2011 4:45 PM
Solution Resource Usage Update	ROBDEV	Portal Home	8/7/2011 4:45 PM

1-10 ▸

Running

Job Title	Server	Progress	Status	Started

History

Job Title	Server	Web Application	Duration (hh:mm:ss)	Status	Completed
Document Conversions	ROBDEV	Portal Home	0:00:00	Succeeded	8/7/2011 4:35 PM
Scheduled Unpublish	ROBDEV	Portal Home	0:00:00	Succeeded	8/7/2011 4:34 PM
Scheduled Approval	ROBDEV	Portal Home	0:00:00	Succeeded	8/7/2011 4:34 PM
Document Conversions	ROBDEV	Portal Home	0:00:00	Succeeded	8/7/2011 4:34 PM
Scheduled Unpublish	ROBDEV	Portal Home	0:00:00	Succeeded	8/7/2011 4:33 PM
Scheduled Approval	ROBDEV	Portal Home	0:00:00	Succeeded	8/7/2011 4:33 PM
Document Conversions	ROBDEV	Portal Home	0:00:00	Succeeded	8/7/2011 4:33 PM
Scheduled Unpublish	ROBDEV	Portal Home	0:00:00	Succeeded	8/7/2011 4:32 PM
Scheduled Approval	ROBDEV	Portal Home	0:00:00	Succeeded	8/7/2011 4:32 PM

Figure 10-25. Timer Job Status

The Developer Dashboard

As much as this book is about administration and not development, I need to say a few words about the SharePoint 2010 Developer Dashboard. This new feature in SharePoint 2010 provides performance and tracing information within SharePoint rendered pages, so that developers (and administrators) may diagnose slow-rendering pages. Figure 10-26 is an example of the Developer Dashboard output.

Developer Dashboard

- Request (GET:http://o14:80/Pages/default.aspx) (1331.15 ms, 13.18 MB)
  - BeginRequestHandler (0.23 ms)
  - PostAuthenticateRequestHandler (0.07 ms)
  - PostResolveRequestCacheHandler (46.64 ms)
    - GetWebPartPageContent (25.60 ms)
      - GetFileAndMetaInfo (24.23 ms)
  - GetWebPartPageContent (26.94 ms)
    - GetFileAndMetaInfo (26.17 ms)
  - GetWebPartPageContent#1 (24.46 ms)
    - GetFileAndMetaInfo (24.18 ms)
  - PostMapRequestHandler (0.01 ms)
  - Add WebParts (2.95 ms)
    - Press Releases (0.90 ms)
    - Sandbox Web Part (0.14 ms)
    - Developer Dashboard WebPart (0.11 ms)
    - Bad Web Part (0.26 ms)
    - Content Editor (0.32 ms)
  - EnsureListItemsData (26.13 ms)
  - EnsureListItemsData#1 (25.61 ms)
  - SPPageStateControl:OnLoad (0.16 ms)
  - SPPageStateControl:OnPreRender (0.25 ms)
  - Render Ribbon. (8.02 ms)
  - Render WebPart Zone TopZone (24.20 ms)
    - Render WebPart Developer Dashboard WebPart (0.60 ms)
    - Render WebPart Bad Web Part (0.16 ms)
    - Render WebPart Sandbox Web Part (0.13 ms)
    - Render WebPart Content Editor (0.15 ms)
    - Render WebPart Press Releases (22.82 ms)
      - Xslt Transform (22.45 ms)

Web Server

SPRequest Objects	3
Execution Time	1331.61 ms
Current User	STEVE\speschka
Page Checkout Level	Checkout
Current SharePoint Operations 1	
Working Set Delta	13.18 MB
Log Correlation Id	07cc6d07-9c7c-4e5e-ab27-216ccf610fa8

Database Queries

dbo.proc_getObjectsByBaseClass	6.76 ms
dbo.proc_getObjectsByBaseClass	5.06 ms
dbo.proc_getObjectsByBaseClass	5.14 ms
proc_FetchDocForHttpGet	23.18 ms
proc_FetchDocForHttpGet	21.52 ms
proc_FetchDocForHttpGet	20.58 ms
dbo.proc_getObjectsByBaseClass	6.73 ms
dbo.proc_getObjectsByBaseClass	4.73 ms
dbo.profile_GetUserProfileData	6.10 ms
proc_GetListMetaDataAndEventReceivers	10.08 ms
SELECT t11.*, t13.[MetaInfo],	11.06 ms
proc_GetDocsMetaInfo	8.11 ms
SELECT t14.[ntext2],	32.11 ms
proc_GetDocsMetaInfo	8.58 ms
proc_SecGetPrincipalByLogin	5.12 ms
SELECT t14.[ntext2],	18.18 ms
proc_GetListItemWorkflows	7.26 ms
dbo.proc_getDependentObjectsByBaseClass	20.79 ms
proc_ListContentTypesInWebRecursive	13.73 ms
proc_FetchDocForHttpGet	9.06 ms
proc_FetchDocForHttpGet	8.82 ms
proc_FetchDocForHttpGet	9.36 ms
proc_FetchDocForHttpGet	10.68 ms
proc_FetchDocForHttpGet	9.63 ms
proc_FetchDocForHttpGet	8.80 ms
proc_FetchDocForHttpGet	8.90 ms

Figure 10-26. Output from the Developer Dashboard

The following STSADM command demonstrates enabling the Developer Dashboard:

```
STSADM-o setproperty –pn developer-dashboard -pv ondemand on
```

The following command disables it:

```
STSADM-o setproperty –pn developer-dashboard -pv ondemand off
```

Summary

In this chapter, we discussed planning for disaster, and you read about how to recover in the event of service downtime. Good planning of your infrastructure enables you to take advantage of warm-standby scenarios, and I covered how SharePoint 2010 may leverage SQL clustering, SQL mirroring, and failover.

SharePoint 2010 provides users of the platform with a degree of control over content integrity, via document versioning, and the Recycle Bin to recover deleted lists and list items.

No disaster recovery plan is without a mention of backup and restore of content and configuration. I walked the reader through backup and restore of both content and SharePoint configuration, using Central Admin, PowerShell, and STSADM tools.

Toward the end of this chapter, we explored the new Health Analyzer, usage, and health monitoring capabilities of SharePoint 2010 to alert administrators of potential problems in their SharePoint 2010 farm. As a nice treat for developers, I introduced you to the Developer Dashboard, so that you may troubleshoot slow-rendering pages in SharePoint 2010.

This chapter concludes *Pro SharePoint 2010 Administration*. I hope I have provided you with good coverage of the SharePoint 2010 product, how to administer any deployment—from basic to complicated enterprise deployment, and a good sense of the capabilities of the platform. I have enjoyed writing this book, and I hope you—the reader—have enjoyed reading my insights.

Index

CPSIA information can be obtained at www.ICGtesting.com
Printed in the USA
LVOW020232251111

256391LV00010B/9/P